DATE DUE

MAY 06 2004			

Eager to Learn

Educating Our Preschoolers

Committee on Early Childhood Pedagogy

Barbara T. Bowman, M. Suzanne Donovan,
and M. Susan Burns, *Editors*

Commission on Behavioral and
Social Sciences and Education

National Research Council

NATIONAL ACADEMY PRESS
Washington, DC

NATIONAL ACADEMY PRESS • 2101 Constitution Avenue, N.W. • Washington, D.C. 20418

NOTICE: The project that is the subject of this report was approved by the Governing Board of the National Research Council, whose members are drawn from the councils of the National Academy of Sciences, the National Academy of Engineering, and the Institute of Medicine. The members of the committee responsible for the report were chosen for their special competences and with regard for appropriate balance.

The study was supported by Grant No. R307U970002 between the National Academy of Sciences and the U.S. Department of Education, the Spencer Foundation, and the Foundation for Child Development. Any opinions, findings, conclusions, or recommendations expressed in this publication are those of the author(s) and do not necessarily reflect the view of the organizations or agencies that provided support for this project.

Library of Congress Cataloging-in-Publication Data

National Research Council (U.S.). Committee on Early Childhood Pedagogy.
Eager to learn : educating our preschoolers / Committee on Early
Childhood Pedagogy, Commission on Behavioral and Social Sciences and
Education, National Research Council ; Barbara T. Bowman, M. Suzanne
Donovan, and M. Susan Burns, editors.
     p. cm.
Includes bibliographical references and index.
     ISBN 0-309-06836-3
     1. Education, Preschool—United States. 2. Learning—Social
aspects—United States. I. Bowman, Barbara T. II. Donovan, Suzanne.
III. Burns, M. Susan (Marie Susan) IV. Title.
     LB1140.23 .N38 2000
     372.21'0973—dc21
                                        00-011192

Additional copies of this report are available from National Academy Press, 2101 Constitution Avenue, N.W., Lockbox 285, Washington, D.C. 20055; (800) 624-6242 or (202) 334-3313 (in the Washington metropolitan area); Internet, http://www.nap.edu

Printed in the United States of America

Suggested citation: National Research Council (2001) *Eager to Learn: Educating Our Preschoolers.* Committee on Early Childhood Pedagogy. Barbara T. Bowman, M. Suzanne Donovan, and M. Susan Burns, editors. Commission on Behavioral and Social Sciences and Education. Washington, DC: National Academy Press.

THE NATIONAL ACADEMIES

National Academy of Sciences
National Academy of Engineering
Institute of Medicine
National Research Council

The **National Academy of Sciences** is a private, nonprofit, self-perpetuating society of distinguished scholars engaged in scientific and engineering research, dedicated to the furtherance of science and technology and to their use for the general welfare. Upon the authority of the charter granted to it by the Congress in 1863, the Academy has a mandate that requires it to advise the federal government on scientific and technical matters. Dr. Bruce M. Alberts is president of the National Academy of Sciences.

The **National Academy of Engineering** was established in 1964, under the charter of the National Academy of Sciences, as a parallel organization of outstanding engineers. It is autonomous in its administration and in the selection of its members, sharing with the National Academy of Sciences the responsibility for advising the federal government. The National Academy of Engineering also sponsors engineering programs aimed at meeting national needs, encourages education and research, and recognizes the superior achievements of engineers. Dr. William A. Wulf is president of the National Academy of Engineering.

The **Institute of Medicine** was established in 1970 by the National Academy of Sciences to secure the services of eminent members of appropriate professions in the examination of policy matters pertaining to the health of the public. The Institute acts under the responsibility given to the National Academy of Sciences by its congressional charter to be an adviser to the federal government and, upon its own initiative, to identify issues of medical care, research, and education. Dr. Kenneth I. Shine is president of the Institute of Medicine.

The **National Research Council** was organized by the National Academy of Sciences in 1916 to associate the broad community of science and technology with the Academy's purposes of furthering knowledge and advising the federal government. Functioning in accordance with general policies determined by the Academy, the Council has become the principal operating agency of both the National Academy of Sciences and the National Academy of Engineering in providing services to the government, the public, and the scientific and engineering communities. The Council is administered jointly by both Academies and the Institute of Medicine. Dr. Bruce M. Alberts and Dr. William A. Wulf are chairman and vice chairman, respectively, of the National Research Council.

ALEXANDRA K. WIGDOR, *Deputy Director*, Commission on
  Behavioral and Social Sciences and Education
M. SUSAN BURNS, *Study Director*
M. SUZANNE DONOVAN, *Senior Project Officer*
MARIE SUIZZO, *Research Associate*

Preface

THE LAST HALF OF THE 20TH CENTURY witnessed an outpouring of research on cognition and learning, child development, and the social and cultural context of learning. One clear message to emerge from this explosion of knowledge is the prodigious enthusiasm and competence for learning shown by young children. *Eager to Learn: Educating Our Preschoolers* is the most recent publication from a series of National Research Council (NRC) studies sponsored by the Department of Education for the purpose of making scientific research accessible and salient to educators, policy makers, and parents. (Others include *Preventing Reading Difficulties in Young Children* [1998]; *Starting Out Right: A Guide to Promoting Children's Reading Success* [1999]; *How People Learn: Mind, Brain, Experience, School—Expanded Edition* [2000].) It represents the first attempt at a comprehensive, cross-disciplinary synthesis of the theory, research, and evaluation literature relevant to early childhood education.

Eager to Learn: Educating Our Preschoolers is the product of a 3-year study during which 17 experts, appointed by the NRC as members of the Committee on Early Childhood Pedagogy, reviewed studies from many fields in the behavioral and social sciences that used many different research methods, both quantitative and qualitative, and both observational and experimental. We restricted our attention to those aspects of the research literature that have clear implications for what and how young children are taught. (A second National Research Council/Institute of Medicine study, *From Neurons to Neighborhoods: The Science of Early Child Development* [2000], looks more generally at the health and well-being of young children.) Nevertheless, the attempt to develop an integrated picture of early learning and how the education of young children outside the home should proceed has been an enormous task. Fortunately, we were able to call on the expertise and assistance of many other people in the course of our work.

This project has been supported with patience and generosity by the Office of Education Research and Improvement (OERI) of the U.S. Department of Education. In particular, we thank Kent McGuire, assistant secretary for OERI; Naomi Karp, director of the Early Childhood Institute, whose passion to improve the life chances of all young children inspired the study; Gail Houle, of the Office of Special Education Programs; and Carol Rasco, director, America Reads Challenge, who made possible the presentation of the conclusions and recommendations of *Eager to Learn* to 600 state education and human services officials who participated in Secretary Riley's Early Childhood Summit.

We also thank the Spencer Foundation, for its support of the project and for making it possible to hold a workshop on global perspectives on early childhood education, and the Early Childhood Foundation, for its support.

Individually and collectively, members of the committee had discussions with experts on many of the issues and topics in learning, development, and early care and education. We offer a special note of thanks to Mark Wolery, Vanderbilt University, who was helpful in sharpening the discussion of educating children with disabilities even as he juggled moving vans and house closings. John Bransford, chair of the NRC Committee on Developments in the Science of Learning, generously shared the insights of that committee and Lucia French, University of Rochester, provided valuable assistance with the description of mathematics and science programs for preschool children.

We also commissioned work on a number of topics of special interest as the study progressed. Our particular thanks go to Ellen Frede, The College of New Jersey, for her background paper on model programs and the evaluation data supporting them; to Carol Ripple, Yale University, who developed an information base on early childhood state standards; and to Douglas H. Clements, State University of New York, Buffalo, who prepared a background paper on the practical use of technology in early childhood programs.

To broaden its understanding of early childhood care and education, the committee commissioned a number of papers which were presented at a workshop entitled, "Global Perspectives on Early Childhood Education," held at the National Academy of Sciences on April 6-7, 1999. Our special thanks go to Jerome Bruner, whose keynote address conveyed the wisdom of a lifetime's work on the learning of young children; Shiela B. Kamerman, "Early Childhood Education and Care: Preschool Policies and Programs in the OECD Countries;" Rebecca S. New, "Italian Early Childhood Education: Variations on a Cultural Theme;" Cigdem Kagitcibasi, "Early Learning and Human Development: The Turkish Early Enrichment Program;" Susan D. Holloway, "Beyond the 'Average Native': Cultural Models of Early Childhood Education in Japan." Our thanks as well to discussant Robert G. Myers.

This report has been reviewed in draft form by individuals chosen for their diverse perspectives and technical expertise, in accordance with procedures approved by the NRC's Report Review Committee. The purpose of this independent review is to provide candid and critical comments that will assist the institution in making the published report as sound as possible and to ensure that the report meets institutional standards for objectivity, evidence, and responsiveness to the study charge. The review comments and draft manuscript remain confidential to protect the integrity of the deliberative process.

We wish to thank the following individuals for their participation in the review of this report: Sue Bredekamp, Council for Professional Recognition in Early Childhood, Washington, DC; Roy G. D'Andrade, Department of Anthropology, University of California, San Diego; Rheta DeVries, Regents' Center for Early Developmental Education, University of Northern Iowa; Jacqueline Jones, Educational Testing Service, Princeton, New Jersey; Susan Kontos, Department of Child Development and Family Studies, Purdue University; Eleanor Maccoby, Department of Psychology, Stanford University (emeritus); Rebecca New, Department of Education, University of New Hampshire; Lawrence J. Schweinhart, High/Scope Educational Research Foundation, Ypsilanti, Michigan; Catherine Snow, Graduate School of Education, Harvard University; and Bernard Spodek, College of Education, University of Illinois.

Although the individuals listed above have provided constructive comments and suggestions, it must be emphasized that responsibility for the final content of this report rests entirely with the authoring committee and the institution.

Finally, there are several members of the NRC staff who made significant contributions to our work. Susan Burns, now a faculty member at George Mason University, served as study director during much of the life of the committee. Marie Suizzo, as research associate, was instrumental in organizing the workshop on global perspectives. Christine McShane, editor, worked with us on several drafts of the report and significantly improved the text. Shirley Thatcher and Carey Munteen spent many weeks tracking down errant references and otherwise filling in the blanks. A special thanks to Suzanne Donovan, a senior member of the research staff, who took time from her other duties to help with the final revisions to the manuscript.

> Barbara Bowman, *Chair*
> Committee on Early Childhood Pedagogy
> Alexandra K. Wigdor, *Deputy Director*
> Commission on Behavioral and Social Sciences
>   and Education

Contents

Tables, Boxes, and Figures

TABLES

BOXES

FIGURES

Eager to Learn

Executive Summary

CHILDREN COME INTO THE WORLD eager to learn. The first five years of life are a time of enormous growth of linguistic, conceptual, social, emotional, and motor competence. Right from birth a healthy child is an active participant in that growth, exploring the environment, learning to communicate, and, in relatively short order, beginning to construct ideas and theories about how things work in the surrounding world. The pace of learning, however, will depend on whether and to what extent the child's inclinations to learn encounter and engage supporting environments. There can be no question that the environment in which a child grows up has a powerful impact on how the child develops and what the child learns.

Eager to Learn: Educating Our Preschoolers is about the education of children ages 2 to 5. It focuses on programs provided outside the home, such as preschool, Head Start, and child care centers. As the twenty-first century begins, there can be little doubt that something approaching voluntary universal early childhood education, a feature of other wealthy industrialized nations, is also on the horizon here. Three major trends have focused public attention on children's education and care in the preschool years:

1. the unprecedented labor force participation of women with

young children, which is creating a pressing demand for child care;

2. an emerging consensus among professionals and, to an ever greater extent, among parents that young children should be provided with educational experiences; and

3. the accumulation of convincing evidence from research that young children are more capable learners than current practices reflect, and that good educational experiences in the preschool years can have a positive impact on school learning.

The growing consensus regarding the importance of early education stands in stark contrast to the disparate system of care and education available to children in the United States in the preschool years. America's programs for preschoolers vary widely in quality, content, organization, sponsorship, source of funding, relationship to the public schools, and government regulation.

Historically, there have been two separate and at times conflicting traditions in the United States that can be encapsulated in the terms *child care* and *preschool*. A central premise of this report, one that grows directly from the research literature, is that *care and education cannot be thought of as separate entities in dealing with young children*. Adequate care involves providing quality cognitive stimulation, rich language environments, and the facilitation of social, emotional, and motor development. Likewise, adequate education for young children can occur only in the context of good physical care and of warm affective relationships. Indeed, research suggests that secure attachment improves social and intellectual competence and the ability to exploit learning opportunities. Neither loving children nor teaching them is, in and of itself, sufficient for optimal development; thinking and feeling work in tandem.

Learning, moreover, is not a matter of simply assimilating a store of facts and skills. Children construct knowledge actively, integrating new concepts and ideas into their existing understandings. Educators have an opportunity and an obligation to facilitate this propensity to learn and to develop a receptivity to learning that will prepare children for active engagement in the learning enterprise throughout their lives. This report argues, therefore, that promoting young children's growth calls for early childhood settings (half day or full day, public or private, child care or preschool) that support the development of the full range of capacities that will serve as a foundation for school learning. As the child is assimilated into the culture of education in a setting outside the home, early childhood programs must be sensitive and responsive to the cultural contexts that define the child's world outside the school or center, and they must build on the strengths and supports that those contexts provide.

CONTEXT OF THE REPORT AND COMMITTEE CHARGE

As Americans grapple with decisions about early childhood education that many European countries have already made, we can draw on certain advantages. We have a strong research community investigating early childhood learning and development and producing evidence on which to base the design, implementation, and evaluation of programs. And we have a tradition of experimentation and observation in preschools that gives us access to a wealth of experience in early childhood education.

The Committee on Early Childhood Pedagogy was established by the National Research Council in 1997 to study a broad range of behavioral and social science research on early learning and development and to explore the implications of that research for the education and care of young children ages 2 to 5. More specifically, the committee was asked to undertake the following:

• Review and synthesize theory, research, and applications in the social, behavioral, and biological sciences that contribute to our understanding of early childhood pedagogy.

• Review the literature and synthesize the research on early childhood pedagogy.

• Review research concerning special populations, such as children living in poverty, children with limited English proficiency, or children with disabilities, and highlight early childhood education practices that enhance the development of these children.

• Produce a coherent distillation of the knowledge base and develop its implications for practice in early childhood education programs, the training of teachers and child care professionals, and future research directions.

   • Draw out the major policy implications of the research findings.

   The study was carried out at the request of the U.S. Department of Education's Office of Educational Research and Improvement (Early Childhood Institute) and the Office of Special Education Programs, the Spencer Foundation, and the Foundation for Child Development. An important motivation for sponsors of the study is to help public discussion of these issues move away from ideology and toward evidence, so that educators, parents, and policy makers will be able to make better decisions about programs for the education and care of young children.

   In accordance with the charge to the committee, this report focuses primarily on research and practice of relevance to programs for young children that take place outside the home, especially center-based programs. Yet it is important to underscore the point that children's learning and development are strongly influenced by myriad family factors, including parental interaction styles and family aspirations and expectations for achievement. It is also important to note that many of the committee's findings, especially those on children's learning and development, are likely to apply to in-home settings and to parents who care for their own children, and they should also be of interest to family literacy and two-generation programs.

NEW UNDERSTANDINGS OF EARLY CHILDHOOD DEVELOPMENT AND PEDAGOGY

   Current conceptions of early childhood development and pedagogy are built on a century of research and experience. Many of the theoretical perspectives that have held sway during that period have been incorporated in some form into early childhood practice. These include the "behaviorist" view of the role of positive reinforcement in behavior and learning, as well as the focus on children's affective-social development—an influence of Freudian theory. A more recent (1970s) influence on preschool practice comes from Piagetian theory, which emphasizes stages of development that are systemically defined. From Piaget's perspective, the emerging capacities of the preschool (or "preoperational") period involve the development of symbolic abilities: language, imitation, symbolic play, and drawing. While much learning is involved, it takes place in the here and now and focuses largely on the perceptible.

More recent research has led many to reinterpret the stage theorists' views; there is strong evidence that children, when they have accumulated substantial knowledge, have the ability to abstract well beyond what is ordinarily observed. Indeed, the striking feature of modern research is that it describes unexpected competencies in young children, key features of which appear to be universal. These data focus attention on the child's exposure to learning opportunities, calling into question simplistic conceptualizations of developmentally appropriate practice that do not recognize the newly understood competencies of very young children, and they highlight the importance of individual differences in children, their past experiences, and their present contexts.

Recent research on cognitive development also emphasizes the role a supportive context can play in strengthening and supporting learning in a particular domain. Indeed, techniques that provide a window into the developing brain allow us to see that stimulation from the environment changes the very physiology of the brain, interlocking nature and nurture. Research from a variety of theoretical perspectives suggests that a defining feature of a supportive environment is a responsible and responsive adult. Parents, teachers, and caregivers promote development when they create learning experiences that build on and extend the child's competence—experiences that are challenging, but within reach. To do so, these adults must be sensitive to individual and developmental characteristics of the child.

VARIATION AMONG CHILDREN

Developmental trends occur in a similar fashion for all children. This does not, however, imply uniformity. On the contrary, individual differences due to genetic and experiential variations and differing cultural and social contexts have strong influences on development. The notion of *lockstepped* development in children is not useful; the potential of human development interacts with diversity among individuals, available resources, and the goals and preferred interaction patterns of communities in a way that links the biological and the social in the construction of diverse developmental pathways.

Children present themselves to preschool teachers or caregivers with many differences in their cognitive, social, physical, and motor skills. These differences are associated with both "functional" characteristics—such as temperament, learning style, and motivation—and "status" characteristics—including gender, race, ethnicity, and social class. Data on children as they enter kindergarten suggest that there are significant differences in many aspects of development by the time children reach the schoolhouse door. Resources (like books and audio recordings) and activities (book reading, story telling, verbal interaction) to which children of higher socioeconomic status (SES) are typically exposed are strong correlates of many aspects of cognitive development, and SES is correlated with social and some forms of physical development as well.

QUALITY IN EDUCATION AND CARE

The issue of quality in early childhood education and care has many dimensions, including political and social dimensions, not all of which lend themselves to research and analysis. Research can, however, inform views of best practice by providing information about the consequences of program features and of curriculum and pedagogy for young children's learning, development, and well-being. A number of distinct, but overlapping, research literatures provide relevant insights. Several decades of research have been conducted on the effects of a wide range of preschool programs on children's learning and development. This research includes experimental comparisons of carefully specified alternative approaches; experimental and quasi-experimental studies of the effects of "model" programs, Head Start, and public preschool programs on children in poverty; studies relying on "natural variation" among child care programs to examine the effects of program features and quality on the learning and development of children from a broad cross-section of society; studies of programs for English-language learners; and descriptions of exemplary programs in other countries. These literatures provide insight into important components of the quality of preschool programs, one of which is support for cognitive development. Other literatures (including research in cognitive science) focus less on the study of preschool programs and more on the study of children's development and their learning in specific cognitive domains, such as reading, mathematics, and science. These literatures also have implications for curriculum content and pedagogy.

FEATURES OF QUALITY PROGRAMS

There are a number of broadly supported findings regarding components of quality preschool programs:

• *Cognitive, social-emotional (mental health), and physical development are complementary, mutually supportive areas of growth all requiring active attention in the preschool years.* Social skills and phy-sical dexterity influence cognitive development, just as cognition plays a role in children's social understanding and motor competence. All are therefore related to early learning and later academic achievement and are necessary domains of early childhood pedagogy.

• *Responsive interpersonal relationships with teachers nurture young children's dispositions to learn and their emerging abilities.* Social competence and school achievement are influenced by the quality of early teacher-child relationships, and by teachers' attentiveness to how the child approaches learning.

• *Both class size and adult-child ratios are correlated with greater program effects.* Low adult-child ratios are associated with more extensive teacher-child interaction, more individualization, and less restrictive and controlling teacher behavior. Smaller group size has been associated with more child initiations, and more opportunities for teachers to work on extending language, mediating children's social interactions, and encouraging and supporting exploration and problem solving.

• *While no single curriculum or pedagogical approach can be identified as best, children who attend well-planned, high-*

quality early childhood programs in which curriculum aims are specified and integrated across domains tend to learn more and are better prepared to master the complex demands of formal schooling. Particular findings of relevance in this regard include the following:

1. Children who have a broad base of experience in domain-specific knowledge (for example, in mathematics or an area of science) move more rapidly in acquiring more complex skills.

2. More extensive language development—such as a rich vocabulary and listening comprehension—is related to early literacy learning.

3. Children are better prepared for school when early childhood programs expose them to a variety of classroom structures, thought processes, and discourse patterns. This does not mean adopting the methods and curriculum of the elementary school; rather it is a matter of providing children with a mix of whole class, small group, and individual interactions with teachers, the experience of discourse patterns associated with school, and such mental strategies as categorizing, memorizing, reasoning, and metacognition.

• *Young children who are living in circumstances that place them at greater risk of school failure—including poverty, low level of maternal education, maternal depression, and other factors that can limit their access to opportunities and resources that enhance learning and development—are much more likely to succeed in school if they attend well-planned, high-quality early childhood programs.* Many children, especially those in low-income households, are served in child care programs of such low quality that learning and development are not enhanced and may even be jeopardized.

The importance of teacher responsiveness to children's differences, knowledge of children's learning processes and capabilities, and the multiple developmental goals that a quality preschool program must address simultaneously all point to the centrality of teacher education and preparation.

- *The professional development of teachers is related to the quality of early childhood programs, and program quality predicts developmental outcomes for children.* Formal early childhood education and training have been linked consistently to positive caregiver behaviors. The strongest relationship is found between the number of years of education and training and the appropriateness of a teacher's classroom behavior.

- *Programs found to be highly effective in the United States and exemplary programs abroad actively engage teachers and provide high-quality supervision.* Teachers are trained and encouraged to reflect on their practice and on the responsiveness of their children to classroom activities, and to revise and plan their teaching accordingly.

CURRICULUM AND PEDAGOGY

Much of the research on young children's learning investigates cognitive development in language, mathematics, and science. Because these appear to be "privileged domains," that is, domains in which children have a natural proclivity to learn, experiment, and explore, they allow for nurturing and extending the boundaries of the learning in which children are already actively engaged. Developing and extending children's interests is particularly important in the preschool years, when attention and self-regulation are nascent abilities.

What should be learned in the preschool curriculum? In addressing this question, the committee focused largely on reading, mathematics, and science because a rich research base has provided insights in these domains suggesting that more can be learned in the preschool years than was previously understood. This does not imply, however, that many of the music, arts and crafts, and physical activities that are common in quality preschool programs are of less importance. Indeed, the committee supports the notion that it is the *whole* child that must be developed. Moreover, these activities—important in their own right—can provide opportunities for developing language, reasoning, and social skills that support learning in more academic areas.

An extensive body of research suggests the types of activity that promote emergent literacy skills. These include story reading and "dialogic reading," providing materials for scribbling and "writing" in pretend play, participating in classroom conversation, and identifying letters and words. In mathematics and science, research indicates that children are capable of thinking that is both complex and abstract. Curricula that work with children's emergent understandings and provide the concepts, knowledge, and opportunities to extend those understandings, have been used effectively in the preschool years. When these activities operate in the child's "zone of proximal development," where learning is within reach but takes the child just beyond his or her existing ability, these curricula have been reported to be both enjoyable and educational.

While the committee does not endorse any particular curriculum, the cognitive science literature suggests principles of learning that should be incorporated into any curriculum:

- Teaching and learning will be most effective if they engage and build on children's existing understandings.
- Key concepts involved in each domain of preschool learning (e.g., representational systems in early literacy, the concept of quantity in mathematics, causation in the physical world) must go hand in hand with information and skill acquisition (e.g., identifying numbers and letters and acquiring information about the natural world).
- Metacognitive skill development allows children to learn to solve problems more effectively. Curricula that encourage children to reflect, predict, question, and hypothesize (examples: How many will there be after two numbers are added? What happens next in the story? Will it sink or float?) set them on course for effective, engaged learning.

How should teaching be done in preschool? Research indicates that many teaching strategies *can* work. Good teachers acknowledge and encourage children's efforts, model and demonstrate, create challenges and support children in extending their capabilities, and provide specific directions or instruction. All of these teaching strategies can be used in the context of play and structured activities. Effective teachers also organize the class-room environment and plan ways to pursue educational goals for each child as opportunities arise in child-initiated activities and in activities planned and initiated by the teacher.

This panoply of strategies provides a tool kit from which the teacher can select the right tool for the right task at the right time. Children need opportunities to initiate activities and follow their interests, but teachers are not passive during these initiated and directed activities. Similarly, children should be actively engaged and responsive during teacher-initiated and directed activities. Good teachers help support the child's learning in both types of activities. They also recognize that children learn from each other and from interactions with the physical environment. Since pre-school programs serve so many ends simultaneously, multiple pedagogical approaches should be expected.

ASSESSMENT IN EARLY CHILDHOOD EDUCATION

If the trend of increasing enrollments in early childhood education programs continues in this country, the use of assessments and tests as instruments of education policy and practice is also likely to increase. There is great potential in the use of assessment to support learning. The importance of building new learning on prior knowledge, the episodic course of development in any given child, and the enormous variability among children in background and development all mean that assessment and instruction are inseparable parts of effective pedagogy. What preschool teachers do to guide and promote learning needs to be based on what each child brings to the interaction, cognitively, culturally, and developmentally. Careful assessment is even more critical to effective strategies for working with children with disabilities and special needs.

The growing sense of public responsibility for the quality of early childhood programs means that there are also external pressures to use tests and assessments for program evaluation and monitoring and for school accountability. Such high-stakes uses of assessment data for purposes external to the classroom increase the requirement for measurement validity and heighten the need for caution in interpreting results.

All assessments, and particularly assessments for accountability, must be used carefully and appropriately if they are to resolve, and not create, educational problems. Assessment of young children poses greater challenges than people generally realize. The first five years of life are a time of incredible growth and learning, but the course of development is uneven and sporadic. The status of a child's development as of any given day can change very rapidly. Consequently, assessment results—in particular, standardized test scores that reflect a given point in time—can easily misrepresent children's learning.

Few early childhood teachers or administrators are trained to understand traditional standardized tests and measurements. As a consequence, misuse is rampant, as experience with readiness tests demonstrates. Likewise, early childhood personnel are seldom offered real preparation in the development and use of alternative assessments.

Assessment itself is in a state of flux. There is widespread dissatisfaction with traditional norm-referenced standardized tests, which are based on early 20th century psychological theory. There are a number of promising new approaches to assessment, among them variations on the clinical interview and performance assessment, but the field must be described as emergent. Much more research and development are needed for a productive fusion of assessment and instruction to occur and if the potential benefits of assessment for accountability are to be fully realized.

RECOMMENDATIONS

What is now known about the potential of the early years, and of the promise of high-quality preschool programs to help realize that potential for all children, stands in stark contrast to practice in many—perhaps most—early childhood settings. In the committee's view, bringing what is known to bear on what is done in early childhood education will require efforts in four areas: (1) professional development of teachers; (2) development of teaching materials that reflect research-based understandings of children's learning; (3) development of public policies that support—through standards and appropriate assessment, regulations, and funding—the provision of quality preschool experiences; and (4) efforts to make more recent understandings of development in the preschool years common public knowledge. The committee proposes recommendations in each of these areas.

Professional Development

At the heart of the effort to promote quality early childhood programs, from the committee's perspective, is a substantial investment in the education and training of those who work with young children.

> **Recommendation 1: Each group of children in an early childhood education and care program should be assigned a teacher who has a bachelor's degree with specialized education related to early childhood (e.g., developmental psychology, early childhood education, early childhood special education). Achieving this goal will require a significant public investment in the professional development of current and new teachers.**

Sadly, there is a great disjunction between what is optimal pedagogically for children's learning and development and the level of preparation that currently typifies early childhood educators. Progress toward a high-quality teaching force will require substantial public and private support and incentive systems, including innovative educational programs, scholarship and loan programs, and compensation commensurate with the expectations of college graduates.

> **Recommendation 2: Education programs for teachers should provide them with a stronger and more specific foundational knowledge of the development of children's social and affective behavior, thinking, and language.**

Few programs currently do. This foundation should be linked to teachers' knowledge of mathematics, science, linguistics, literature, etc., as well as to instructional practices for young children.

> **Recommendation 3: Teacher education programs should require mastery of information on the pedagogy of teaching preschool-aged children, including:**

• Knowledge of teaching and learning and child development and how to integrate them into practice.

• Information about how to provide rich conceptual experiences that promote growth in specific content areas, as well as particular areas of development, such as language (vocabulary) and cognition (reasoning).

• Knowledge of effective teaching strategies, including organizing the environment and routines so as to promote activities that build social-emotional relationships in the classroom.

• Knowledge of subject-matter content appropriate for preschool children and knowledge of professional standards in specific content areas.

• Knowledge of assessment procedures (observation/performance records, work sampling, interview methods) that can be used to inform instruction.

• Knowledge of the variability among children, in terms of teaching methods and strategies that may be required, including teaching children who do not speak English, children from various economic and regional contexts, and children with identified disabilities.

• Ability to work with teams of professionals.

• Appreciation of the parents' role and knowledge of methods of collaboration with parents and families.

• Appreciation of the need for appropriate strategies for accountability.

Recommendation 4: A critical component of preservice preparation should be a supervised, relevant student teaching or internship experience in which new teachers receive ongoing guidance and feedback from a qualified supervisor.

There are a number of models (e.g., National Council for Accreditation of Teacher Education) that suggest the value of this sort of supervised student teaching experience.

Recommendation 5: All early childhood education and child care programs should have access to a qualified supervisor of early childhood education.

Teachers should be provided with opportunities to reflect on practice with qualified supervisors.

Recommendation 6: Federal and state departments of education, human services, and other agencies interested in young children and their families should initiate programs of research and development aimed at learning more about effective preparation of early childhood teachers.

Recommendation 7: The committee recommends the development of demonstration schools for professional development.

The U.S. Department of Education should collaborate with universities in developing the demonstration schools and in using them as sites for ongoing research:

• on the efficacy of various models, including pairing demonstration schools as partners with community programs, and pairing researchers and in-service teachers with exemplary community-based programs;

• to identify conditions under which the gains of mentoring, placement of preservice teachers in demonstration schools, and supervised student teaching can be sustained once teachers move into community-based programs.

Educational Materials

Recommendation 8: The committee recommends that the U.S. Department of Education, the U.S. Department of Health and Human Services, and their equivalents at the state level fund efforts to develop, design, field test, and evaluate curricula that incorporate what is known about learning and thinking in the early years, with companion assessment tools and teacher guides.

Each curriculum should emphasize what is known from research about children's thinking and learning in the area it addresses. Activities should be included that enable children with different learning styles and strengths to learn.

Each curriculum should include a companion guide for teachers that explains the teaching goals, alerts the teacher to common misconceptions, and suggests ways in which the curriculum can be used flexibly for students at different developmental levels. In the teacher's guide, the description of methods of assessment should be linked to instructional planning so that the information acquired in the process of assessment can be used as a basis for making pedagogical decisions at the level of both the group and the individual child.

Recommendation 9: The committee recommends that the U.S. Department of Education and the U.S. Department of Health and Human Services support the use of effective technology, including videodiscs for preschool teachers and Internet communication groups.

The process of early childhood education is one in which interaction between the adult/teacher and the child/student is the most critical feature. Opportunities to see curriculum and pedagogy in action are likely to promote understanding of complexity and nuance not easily communicated in the written word. Internet communication groups could provide information on curricula, results of field tests, and opportunities for teachers using a common curriculum to discuss experiences, query each other, and share ideas.

Policy

States can play a significant role in promoting program quality with respect to both teacher preparation and curriculum and pedagogy.

Recommendation 10: All states should develop *program* standards for early childhood programs and monitor their implementation.

These standards should recognize the variability in the development of young children and adapt kindergarten and primary programs, as well as preschool programs, to this diversity. This means, for instance, that kindergartens must be readied for children. In some schools, this will require smaller class sizes and professional development for teachers and administrators regarding appropriate teaching practice, so that teachers can meet the needs of individual children, rather than teaching to the "average" child. The standards should outline essential components and should include, but not be limited to, the following categories:

- School-home relationships,
- Class size and teacher-student ratios,
- Specification of pedagogical goals, content, and methods,
- Assessment for instructional improvement,
- Educational requirements for early childhood educators, and
- Monitoring quality/external accountability.

Recommendation 11: Because research has identified content that is appropriate and important for inclusion in early childhood programs, *content* standards should be developed and evaluated regularly to ascertain whether they adhere to current scientific understanding of children's learning.

The content standards should ensure that children have access to rich and varied opportunities to learn in areas that are now omitted from many curricula—such as phonological awareness, number concepts, methods of scientific investigation, cultural knowledge, and language.

Recommendation 12: A single career ladder for early childhood teachers, with differentiated pay levels, should be specified by each state.

This career ladder should include, at a minimum, teaching assistants (with child development associate certification), teachers (with bachelor's degrees), and supervisors.

Recommendation 13: The committee recommends that the federal government fund well-planned, high-quality center-based preschool programs for all children at high risk of school failure.

Such programs can prevent school failure and significantly

enhance learning and development in ways that benefit the entire society.

The Public

Recommendation 14: Organizations and government bodies concerned with the education of young children should actively promote public understanding of early childhood education and care.

Beliefs that are at odds with scientific understanding—that maturation automatically accounts for learning, for example, or that children can learn concrete skills only through drill and practice—must be challenged. Systematic and widespread public education should be undertaken to increase public awareness of the importance of providing stimulating educational experiences in the lives of all young children. The message that the quality of children's relationships with adult teachers and child care providers is critical in preparation for elementary school should be featured prominently in communication efforts. Parents and other caregivers, as well as the public, should be the targets of such efforts.

Recommendation 15: Early childhood programs and centers should build alliances with parents to cultivate complementary and mutually reinforcing environments for young children at home and at the center.

FUTURE RESEARCH NEEDS

Research on child development and education can and has influenced the development of early childhood curriculum and pedagogy. But the influences are mutual. By evaluating outcomes of early childhood programs we have come to understand more about children's development and capacities. The committee believes that continued research efforts along both these lines can expand understanding of early childhood education and care, and the ability to influence them for the better.

Research on Early Childhood Learning and Development

Although it is apparent that early experiences affect later ones, there are a number of important developmental questions to be studied regarding how, when, and which early experiences support development and learning.

Recommendation 16: The committee recommends a broad empirical research program to better understand:

• The range of inputs that can contribute to supporting environments that nurture young children's eagerness to learn;

• Development of children's capacities in the variety of cognitive and socioemotional areas of importance in the preschool years, and the contexts that enhance that development;

• The components of adult-child relationships that enhance the child's development during the preschool years, and experiences affecting that development for good or for ill;

• Variation in brain development, and its implications for sensory processing, attention, and regulation, are particularly relevant;

• The implications of developmental disabilities for learning and development and effective approaches for working with children who have disabilities;

• With regard to children whose home language is not English, the age and level of native language mastery that is desirable before a second language is introduced and the trajectory of second language development.

Research on Programs, Curricula, and Assessment

Recommendation 17: The next generation of research must examine more rigorously the characteristics of programs that produce beneficial outcomes for all children. In addition, research is needed on how programs can provide more helpful structures, curricula, and methods for children at high risk of educational difficulties, including children from low-income homes and communities, children whose home language is not English, and children with developmental and learning disabilities.

Research on programs for any population of children should examine such program variations as age groupings, adult-child ratios, curricula, class size, and program duration. These questions can best be answered through longitudinal studies employing random assignment. In developing and assessing curricula, new research must also continue to consider the interplay between an individual child's characteristics, the immediate contexts of the home and classroom, and the larger contexts of the formal school environment.

Recommendation 18: A broad program of research and development should be undertaken to advance the state of the art of assessment in three areas: (1) classroom-based assessment to support learning (including studies of the impact of methods of instructional assessment on pedagogical technique and children's learning); (2) assessment for diagnostic purposes; and (3) assessment of program quality for accountability and other reasons of public policy.

Research on Ways to Create Universal High Quality

Recommendation 19: Research to fully develop and evaluate alternatives for organizing, regulating, supporting, and financing early childhood programs should be conducted to provide an empirical base for the decisions being made.
The current early childhood system is fragmented, lacks uniform standards, and provides uneven access to all children. Numerous policy choices have been proposed. This research would inform public policy decision making.

CONCLUSION

At a time when the importance of education to individual fulfillment and economic success has focused attention on the need to better prepare children for academic achievement, the research literature suggests ways to make gains toward that end. Parents are relying on child care and preschool programs in ever larger numbers. We know that the quality of the programs in which they leave their children matters. If there is a single critical component to quality, it rests in the relationship between the child and the teacher/caregiver, and in the ability of the adult to be responsive to the child. But responsiveness extends in many directions: to the child's cognitive, social, emotional, and physical characteristics and development.

Much research still needs to be done. But from the committee's perspective, the case for a substantial investment in a high-quality system of child care and preschool on the basis of what is already known is persuasive. Moreover, the considerable lead by other developed countries in the provision of quality preschool programs suggests that it can, indeed, be done on a large scale.

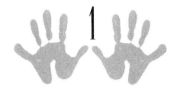

Introduction

AMERICA'S YOUNG CHILDREN STAND on the brink of a new era for preschool learning, occasioned by three converging trends: (1) an unprecedented number of working mothers, creating a strong and increasing demand for child care; (2) a consensus among professionals and (increasingly) parents that the care of young children should provide them with educational experiences; and (3) growing evidence from child development research that young children are capable learners and that educational experience during the preschool years can have a positive impact on school learning. Thus, a convergence of practical, moral, and scientific considerations leads to heightened interest in the education of young children and new opportunities for the improvement of their learning and the enhancement of their lives.

There is currently no single preschool system in the United States. The public school system (kindergarten through 12th grade) is decentralized—i.e. organized by state and school district rather than by the federal government—but state school systems are similar in overall structure and the types of services offered and are tax supported. American preschools, however, vary widely in organization, sponsorship, sources of funding, relationship to the public schools, government regulation, content, and quality. If preschools are to realize the hopes of parents and educators, more attention is needed to their content, quality, and performance. In this rapidly growing sector of education, there are many choices to be made concerning goals, pedagogies, programs, and means of ensuring quality.

America has come late to mass preschool education compared with other wealthy industrialized countries. Some Western European countries have long had nearly universal enrollment of young children in preschools, with high standards of teacher training and impressive curricula. What was until the mid-19th century a matter of private charity, became in the course of the 20th century a public responsibility. In most of Europe, public financing is at this point the dominant mode of support and these early childhood programs are increasingly viewed as a public obligation (Kamerman, 1999). In some countries, preschool service is free regardless of parents' employment status or income; in others, the programs combine government funding and income-related parent fees. France, for example, provides free preschool programs for all children ages 2-6. Germany and Italy make preschool available to all 3- to 6-year-olds and social welfare child care to the children under age 3, with something less than 20 percent of costs borne by parents (see Table 1-1).

But as the United States embarks on a voyage previously taken by others, certain advantages are evident: we have a strong research community investigating early childhood learning and development and producing evidence on which to base the design, implementation, and evaluation of programs. We have a tradition of experimentation and observation in preschools that gives us access to a wealth of experience *before* preschool attendance becomes a universal feature of American childhood. Thus we can begin the latter part of the voyage with better maps and navigational instruments than might be expected at this point in our history; we are better able to know where we're going and how to measure our progress. This report is intended to help prepare for the journey by reviewing what is known about early childhood development and preschool programs and suggesting how to proceed in educating young children in the 21st century.

At present, more than 60 percent of American mothers with children under age 6 are in the labor force (U.S. Department of the Treasury, 1998; U.S. Bureau of Labor Statistics, 1999). There are approximately 3.8 million children in each age cohort with which this report is concerned: ages 2, 3, 4, and 5—figures that are projected to be relatively stable for the next decade and then rise toward 4 million (U.S. Bureau of the Census, 1996). Figure 1-1 shows how steeply the enrollments of American 3- and 4-year-olds in early childhood education programs have increased over the last 35 years. In 1965, only a small minority of children (under 20 percent) was enrolled, but by 1990 the majority of 4-year-olds and one-third of 3-year-olds were. The 1997 figures (collected on a somewhat different basis) show some 65 percent of 4-year-olds and almost 40 percent of 3-year-olds enrolled in early childhood education. These figures strongly suggest that preschool enrollments are large, growing, and here to stay.

As the number of children cared for outside the home has grown, so has the conviction that education should be included in their care. Our society's concern with the quality and effectiveness of schooling—so prominent in public discussion over the last 15 years—has naturally spread to the care of young children. There has been in the past a sharp distinction between child care, i.e., full-day programs of care for children whose parents are working, and *preschool*, i.e., half-day programs focused on children's social and academic learning, but this is changing. Child care professionals increasingly define their mission in educational terms, with growing support from parents and educators. This does *not* mean that child care should be devoted to academic training for children under 5 any more than preschool. The developing consensus is that out-of-home care for young children should attend to their education, including school readiness, *as well as* providing protection and a facilitating environment for secure emotional development and sound relationships with other children and adults. A central theme of this report is that preschools, child care, and other early childhood settings must combine loving care with learning, as implied by the terms "educare" and "early childhood care and education." We recommend it as a fundamental premise of public policy on early childhood.

Scientific knowledge of early childhood development, and of children's learning and behavior in preschool and child care settings, has increased enormously over the past 30 years. The research findings summarized in this report show that 2- to 5-year-old children are more capable learners than had been imagined

TABLE 1-1 Early Childhood Education and Care Policy Dimensions in
Selected OECD Countries

Country	Locus of Policy Making	Administrative Auspice	Age Group Served (years)
Austria	State and local	Welfare	3-6 0-3
Belgium	State	Education Welfare (Center and FDC)	$2\frac{1}{2}$-6 under 3
Denmark	National and local	Education Welfare	5-7 6 mos.-6 yrs.
Finland	National and local	Education Welfare	6 1-7
France	National (primarily) and local	Education Health and welfare	2-6 3 mos.-3 yrs.
Germany	State	Education Welfare	3-6 under 3
Italy	National Local	Education Health and welfare	3-6 under 3
Sweden	National and local (primarily)	Education	0-6
United Kingdom	National and local	Education Welfare	3-4 0-4

SOURCE: Kamerman (1999: Table 2).

Eligibility Criteria	Funding Sources	Subsidy Strategies
Working parents	State and local government and parent fees	Supply
Universal Working parents, with special needs, poor	Government—free Government, employer, parent fees (income-related)	Supply Supply and demand
Universal Working parents	Government Government (local); parent fees (income-related—maximum 20-30% of costs)	Supply
Universal Universal for working parents	National and local government Parent fees income-related at 10% of costs	Supply and demand
Universal	Government—free to parents	Supply
Working parents, with special needs	Mixed local government, family allowance, and parent fees (income-related, maximum 25% of costs)	Supply and demand
Universal With special needs, poor, working parents	State and local government plus parent fees (income-related, maximum 16-20 % of costs)	Supply
Universal Working parents	National government—free Local government and parent fees, income-related, average 12% of costs, maximum 20%	Supply
Universal, working parents, with special needs	National and local government, parent fees (income-related, about 13% of costs)	Supply
	Government— free	Supply and demand
With special needs, poor	Free or income related fees	

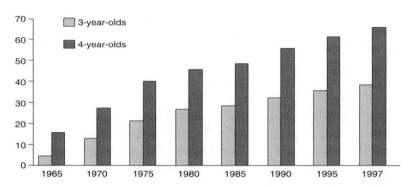

FIGURE 1-1 Percentage of 3- and 4-year-olds enrolled in early childhood education (both private and public): October 1965 to October 1997. NOTE: Data for 1995 and 1997 were collected using new procedures and may not be comparable to figures prior to 1994. SOURCE: National Center for Education Statistics (1998).

and that their acquisition of linguistic, mathematical, and other skills relevant to school readiness is influenced (and can be improved) by their educational and developmental experiences during those years. Such findings are helping to point the way, creating a scientifically informed basis for the construction and evaluation of educational settings and programs of instruction. Thus, the knowledge base for improvement of early childhood pedagogy has grown along with parents' needs for more child care and the commitment to education. Research is providing both increased understanding of pedagogy and important tools for improving early childhood care and education. The opening chapters of this report present a distillation of some of the most salient issues and findings.

As America progresses toward more and better preschools, questions concerning children from low-income and educationally disadvantaged families and those with physical and mental disabilities deserve special attention. A strong finding from research is that early intervention can help prevent or mitigate the development of learning difficulties. Preschool programs can be an important vehicle for enhancing the school readiness of both groups of children. This report describes, as far as the current state of the evaluation literature permits, the specific conditions required for optimizing their learning environments during early childhood.

Looking to the future, there can be little doubt that the United States is on its way to universal, voluntary, preschool attendance, not as the result of government mandate or expert recommendation, but as a consequence of parental demand and a myriad of private, state, and federal initiatives that are continuing to extend early education throughout the country. We are already more than half of the way there. Research suggests that there are few disadvantages and many potential advantages to taking more seriously the capacity of young children to profit from early education.

Bruner has described pedagogy as "an extension of culture [without which] we would simply fail to pass on the culture at large, to enable human beings to use effectively the vast resources that any and every culture has to offer to those within its ambit" (Bruner, 1999:12). As the upbringing of America's children, and therefore the transmission of its culture, relies more and more on out-of-home providers of early education and care, there is a growing public interest in ensuring that this happens well and safely. Indeed, this report recommends the adoption of program standards and professional requirements. Still it is important to note at the outset that establishing standards of quality for early education in a country as large, diverse, and rapidly changing as the United States is a challenge. There is the danger that attempts to set common standards, or even to formulate what children need, may reflect the preferences of a particular group rather than the good of American children as a whole.

Promoting quality in early education need not mean insisting on uniformity. There is general agreement that the care of young children should facilitate their intellectual, emotional, and social development in ways that support their subsequent learning and social participation, in school and other settings. Beyond this, the elements of pedagogical quality with which this report is primarily concerned can be embedded in programs that are responsive to various cultural conceptions of early childhood and several alternative models of preschool education.

ABOUT THIS REPORT

Committee Charge

The Committee on Early Childhood Pedagogy was established by the National Research Council in 1997 at the request of the U.S. Department of Education's Office of Educational Research and Improvement (Early Childhood Institute) and the Office of Special Education Programs. (Supplementary support was provided by the Spencer Foundation and the Foundation for Child Development.) This cross-disciplinary team of scientists and practitioners was asked to survey a broad range of behavioral and social science research on early learning and development and to explore the implications of that research for the education and care of young children ages 2 to 5. A central purpose of the study is to help move the public discussion of these issues away from ideology and toward evidence, so that educators, parents, and policy makers will be able to make better decisions about programs for the education and care of young children. More specifically, the committee was asked to undertake the following:

• Review and synthesize theory, research, and applications in the social, behavioral, and biological sciences that contribute to the understanding of early childhood pedagogy.

• Review the literature and synthesize the research on early childhood pedagogy.

• Review research concerning special populations, such as children living in poverty, children with limited English proficiency, and children with disabilities, and highlight early childhood education practices that enhance the development of these children.

• Produce a coherent distillation of the knowledge base and develop its implications for future research directions, practice in early childhood education programs, and the training of teachers and child care professionals.

• Draw out the major policy implications of the research findings.

In trying to build bridges between research and practice, perhaps the greatest challenge is to find ways to translate scholarly findings into a form that practitioners and others can use to review and revise policies, programs, and practices. The lack of clarity in the field of early childhood pedagogy makes this especially difficult. Many disciplines have something to say about early learning and development; there are many lenses through which one can examine issues in the education and care of young children. In the course of our work, the committee has tried to frame the issues in a way that will be useful to teachers, asking such questions as:

1. What kinds of settings enhance children's learning in preparation for schooling? How have these settings fulfilled their educational objectives?
2. What kinds of educational programs—content and methods—have been found to promote learning and school success?
3. What has been found to limit the effectiveness of these programs?
4. What does responsiveness mean in the context of early childhood education—what do such teacher/child interactions look like?
5. What recommendations based on expert knowledge can be brought to bear to improve the status quo?

Scope of the Report

It is important to note at the outset that this is the first attempt at a comprehensive, cross-disciplinary examination of the accumulated theory, research, and evaluation literature relevant to early childhood education. The task was huge and the research both varied and of variable quality. This is not a book that offers definitive answers for all time; it does offer strong advice on applications that comport with the present state of knowledge.

The report is oriented toward research and practice in out-of-home group programs for young children. Its recommendations extend to all children, including those who are at high risk for having academic difficulties and those with identifiable disabilities. The findings are focused especially on center-based programs, since the goals and structure of these settings are the most controversial. However, there is no reason to believe that the research presented on early development and learning is less relevant to parents and caregivers at home or in parent education and support programs. It is our hope that the findings will be applied in these settings as well.

Knowledge about early childhood care and education derives from work conducted in several disciplines, in laboratory settings as well as in homes, classrooms, and child care centers, and from a range of methodological perspectives. Ethnographers, sociologists, historians, psychologists, educators, and neurobiologists, among others, study early childhood care and education. The committee has found knowledge and insight in all these perspectives and has tried to weave from them a coherent picture.

Committee Perspective

Care *and* Education

Based on research and on the expert judgment of its members, the committee takes as given that good pedagogy includes meeting children's basic needs and providing emotional guidance and support, as well as motivating, instructing, and supporting their learning. There are a number of words and phrases designed to convey this idea, such as "educare" and "the whole child." Under whatever rubric, the important point is that *adequate care* involves cognitive and perceptual stimulation and growth, just as *adequate education* for young children must occur in a safe and emotionally rich environment. Too often, education has been taken to mean a narrow focus on learning as a compiling of knowledge and skills. This is not our intent. The overriding goal of this report is to address how early childhood settings can support the full range of capacities children will need as a foundation for school and life

The importance of children's relationships with caregivers (parents, teachers, child care professionals) is another core principle that grows out of our work. The report carefully examines research on the interactions of children and their teacher/caregivers to determine how they influence children's learning trajectories (Bloom, 1964; Howes, 1997; Pianta, 1992). Although this study is about early childhood education in out-of-home settings, its emphasis on the critical role of adult responsiveness in support of the child's intellectual and emotional development is as germane to parents as to teachers. And such family factors as parental aspirations and expectations for achievement, parental strategies for controlling child behavior, maternal teaching style, linguistic orientation, beliefs about the causes of child success and failure in school, children's home environment, and family stress and poverty (Powell, 1997) all affect the child in preschool.

In line with Bruner's proposition that pedagogy is an extension of culture, the committee also recognizes that families, communities, and the nation want children to grow up to be productive citizens. This requires good health, social responsibility, and psychological well-being, as well as knowledge and skills. As a consequence, we have been particularly alert to research that identifies the qualities that contribute to these goals. "Quality" as it is used in this report connotes pedagogy that cultivates the process of development and learning and is not just custodial care.

Definitional Issues

Because a number of the key terms used in this report may have varied meanings, we present below the definitions used by the committee in its work.

We use *development* broadly to encompass cognitive, emotional, social, and physical growth. Conceptually, development means the process of becoming "more complex or intricate; to cause gradually to acquire specific roles, functions, or forms, to grow by degrees into a more advanced or mature state" (*American Heritage Dictionary*, 1992). What is critical about developmental theory is that it focuses on dynamic change over time (Miller, 1989).

Pedagogy is also conceived broadly, as cultivating the process of development within a given culture and society. At its simplest, it may be defined as "any conscious activity by one person designed to enhance the learning in another" (Watkins and Mortimore, 1999:3). Pedagogy has three basic components: (1) the content of what is being taught, (2) the methodology or the way in which teaching is done and (3) the repertoire of cognitive and affective skills required for successful functioning in the society that it promotes.

The *content* of teaching may be designed to encourage learning processes (memory, attention, observation) and cognitive skills (reasoning, comparing and contrasting, classification), as well as the acquisition of specific information, such as the names of the letters of the alphabet (Wiggins and McTighe, 1998).

Methods are the arranged interactions of people and materials planned and used by teachers and caregivers. They include the teacher role, teaching styles, and instructional techniques (Siraj-Blatchford, 1998); the key informing principle for early childhood pedagogy is responsiveness.

Cognitive socialization is the role that teachers/caretakers in early childhood settings play, through their expectations, their teaching strategies, their curricular emphases, to promote the repertoire of cognitive and affective characteristics and skills that the young child needs to move down the path from natal culture to school culture to the culture of the larger society.

Standards of Evidence

The methods used by social and behavioral scientists to gain knowledge in the field of education are very diverse. Here we describe very briefly the scientific standards used in conducting this review; a fuller statement appears in the Appendix.

Scientists engage in observation, description, classification, hypothesis testing, and theory building. Individual scientists are likely to focus on certain of these activities, such as observation and description, and not on others, such as theory building and hypothesis testing, depending on their own interests and the phenomena they are studying. Similarly, some domains of research involve a predominance of some forms of scientific activity to the relative exclusion of others. For instance, research on demographic trends in child care tends to be largely descriptive, whereas research on the effects of variation in curriculum tends to involve hypothesis testing.

In writing this report, we considered many types of studies, including ethnographic, descriptive, correlational, quasi-experimental, and experimental forms of research. Within each body of evidence produced by these methodologies, we examined studies that flowed from strong theories, as well as those that were more inductively driven. The studies we examined were conducted for many different purposes, with a wide variety of designs and analytic strategies. Our use of these studies is based on our evaluation of their validity and generalizability and the convergence among different studies and methods.

The research base is variable. On one hand, the documentation of impressive learning abilities in young children by many methods and investigators represents a strong source of data in support of our conclusions on the need for early childhood educators to engage children in cognitively rich tasks. On the other hand, our desire to draw conclusions about the efficacy of particular pedagogical methods was frequently frustrated by the paucity of the evidence, due in part to ethical and practical limitations on research designs that can be applied in early childhood settings. In the appendix, we discuss some of these difficulties and provide some methods for addressing them.

OVERVIEW OF THE REPORT

The first two chapters following this introduction focus on the young child. Chapter 2 presents research and theory on the general processes of early development, emphasizing the ability of the environment to substantially affect developmental outcomes. It examines research on the interdependence of cognitive, emotional, and social development and explores the literature on the importance of infants' and children's early relationships with adults. Chapter 3 examines the numerous factors that express themselves as variation in development. These functional and status characteristics are discussed within the framework of the dimensions of variation that require particular attention from preschool teachers.

The next four chapters focus on early childhood education in out-of-home settings. Chapter 4 addresses the issue of quality in the context of five bodies of research, dealing respectively with: (a) programs designed to enhance the learning of economically disadvantaged children, (b) studies that provide empirical information about the effects of typical variations in program quality on the general population of students, (c) studies of programs for English-language learners, (d) exemplary international programs, and (e) studies of interventions for children with disabilities.

Chapter 5 explores curriculum and pedagogy, the what and the how of early childhood education. The analysis integrates recent findings about children's early learning capabilities (presented in Chapter 2) with research data on the general principles and approaches to early childhood care and education. Chapter 6 deals with assessment, particularly assessment to support learning. A number of assessment approaches are reviewed that hold potential as tools for preschool teachers to use to ascertain the nature of thinking and extent of knowledge for each child. Because of the vulnerability of assessment—and especially standardized tests—to misuse and misinterpretation when used with young children, the discussion emphasizes the need for caution.

Chapters 7 and 8 address the supports needed as the United States moves toward universal preschool attendance. Chapter 7 looks at the preparation of early childhood teachers and caregivers, emphasizing the need for professionalization of the field, including more and better training, to enable them to engage their charges effectively. Chapter 8 analyzes the need for program and practice standards to promote quality in early childhood education.

Our conclusions and recommendations are presented in Chapter 9.

What Does the Science of Learning Contribute to Early Childhood Pedagogy?

A S RECENTLY AS 50 YEARS AGO, it was widely believed that the major tasks for children during the preschool years were those of socialization: separating from home, learning how to interact with peers and unfamiliar adults, and experiencing new materials in a novel environment. Today we recognize the first five years as a time of enormous growth of linguistic, conceptual, and social competence. Right from birth, healthy infants use their limited response abilities to explore—and even control—their environments. They gather information about faces, about sounds and language, about objects and events (Morton and Johnson, 1991; Spelke, 1990; Kuhl et al., 1992; Mehler et al., 1986; Gopnik and Meltzoff, 1992).

How do we know that infants are active participants in their learning when their abilities and competence are so clearly limited? Careful observation reveals that infants indicate attentiveness through gestures such as shifting their gaze, turning their head slightly, actively kicking their legs or waving their arms, and engaging in nonnutritive sucking. These indicators of selective attention have allowed researchers to study the capacity of babies to participate actively in learning about the world around them.

A study of 4-month-old infants, for example, found that they engaged in vigorous nonnutritive sucking when first introduced to the phoneme "ba." With repeated exposure, the infants lose interest (the sucking wanes). But when presented with the new phoneme "pa," sucking again becomes vigorous, signaling recognition of the change (Eimas et al., 1971). Similar research has indicated attentiveness in the form of shifting gaze in infants as young as 5 months in response to changes in number (Canfield and Smith, 1996). And bodily actions such as kicking and arm waving have, in controlled experiments, indicated the object recognition capacity of infants (Rovee-Collier, 1989).

As they have crafted procedures suited for toddlers and preschool-age children, researchers have documented early cases of abstract reasoning and self-motivated efforts to learn (National Research Council, 1999; Goswami, 1995). In a study by Karmiloff-Smith and Inhelder (1974-1975), preschool children were offered repeated opportunities (over several sessions) to balance each one of a set of blocks on top of another block. Some of the blocks had concealed weights and therefore did not balance at their geometric centers. Initially children succeeded at balancing each block, no matter what kind it was, by using a combination of trial and error and brute force. When a trick block fell, a child moved it around while pushing down on it until balance was achieved. After repeated opportunities to play with the blocks, children started to behave as if they were systematically applying a "blocks balance at their midpoint" hypothesis. As a result, they now started to make errors with the trick blocks. These they placed aside, saying things like "don't work."

Of special interest is the fact that there came a time when children changed their strategy again, in a seeming effort to find an all-inclusive solution. *On their own* they came to realize that they would have to use a third block as a counterweight for blocks that they could feel would not balance at their geometric center. Therefore, they were once again able to balance all the blocks. It is important to highlight the fact that these children gave up the trial-and-error solution that worked in favor of a more systematic one. Had they not done so, they would not have generated the negative data that eventually encouraged them to find a yet more advanced solution.

This view of the child as having ideas or theories about how things work, and as actively engaged in the construction of knowledge stands in stark contrast to earlier views of development. Advances in cognitive abilities do not simply unfold with age; nor is the child a passive receptacle for the knowledge delivered by others. Rather, current understandings suggest that cognitive development takes place in the context of the child's interactions with others and with the environment—interactions in which the child is a very active participant. The implications for learning opportunities and for early childhood pedagogy are substantial. The child's current understandings must be engaged and built on; knowledge cannot simply be provided for the child. When learning is the product of the child's guided construction rather than the teacher's transmission and the child's absorption, what is learned becomes very individualized. And teaching becomes a two-way relationship in which the teacher's understanding of the child is at least as important as the child's understanding the teacher.

Current conceptions of early childhood development and pedagogy are built on a century of research. A review of central ideas from that research literature can inform the understanding of current pedagogical ideas and beliefs.

THEORIES OF COGNITIVE DEVELOPMENT

Philosophers such as Renee Descartes, John Locke, Immanuel Kant, and Karl Marx have heavily influenced developmental psychology (for a history of these influences, see Cairns, 1983). The powerful influences of these different philosophical traditions, combined with the complex nature of human development, help explain the diversity of theories germane to early childhood pedagogy.

Over the course of this century, preschool pedagogy in the United States has tended to focus on one or two grand theories for a period, then move on to another theoretical perspective, and so on. For example, at mid-century there were many who embraced the ideas of "behavioral objectives" and positive reinforcement. Others focused on the idea that young children's affective-social systems should be the focus of attention, a clear influence of Freud.

By the 1970s, Piagetian stage theory helped educators structure exploratory learning opportunities, especially as regards one involving the ability to use symbols and reason about quantities, classifications, and the perspective of others. From Piaget's point of view, the main accomplishments of the preschool (or "pre-operational") period involve the development of symbolic abilities, language, imitation, symbolic play, and drawing. There is no doubt that there is a great deal of learning in these symbolic abilities. Still, for Piaget, the young child's thoughts take place in the here and now and on the perceptual level. Preschool children therefore do not have the conceptual structures that enable hierarchical classification skills or sophisticated quantitative reasoning.

This side of Piaget's theory of preschool thought is shared by two other prominent child development thinkers, Jerome Bruner and Lev Vygotsky. Despite their differences, all converge on the premise that preschool children's conceptual abilities are perception-bound. The influence on preschool pedagogy of this confluence was straightforward. It was appropriate to provide children with concrete materials to explore and categorize. However, it was developmentally inappropriate to include learning opportunities about abstract categories, measurement, and advanced arithmetic, for doing so was asking children to deal with tasks for which they lacked the conceptual capabilities.

This assumption continues to be prevalent in the world of practice, especially as regards some interpretations of the notions of "readiness" and what is "developmentally appropriate." However, the very definitions of these terms are being redefined as new research on the abilities and potential competencies of young children emerges. It has now been shown, for example, that whether or not young children use abstract classification schemes is very dependent on what they know about the materials to be sorted.

Beyond Piaget

The kinds of data that stage theorists of cognitive development obtained are reliable across a wide range of conditions and domains. However, those data coexist with evidence that, when they have accumulated substantial knowledge, children can perform in a particular domain at a level of development beyond what is expected given the child's age and development in other domains.

When children know a great deal about something—so much so that we can say they have achieved a principled organization of it—they *can* deploy hierarchical classification structures. A compelling example comes from studies by Gobbo and Chi (1986) of preschool dinosaur experts. These children were able to sort dinosaurs on the basis of multiple criteria (whether they were land-living or not, meat-eating or not, and so on), demonstrating classification ability that was beyond expectation. Since children who know much less about dinosaurs generate data that resemble the results from the traditional classification tasks, it appears that the key variable here is knowledge, not the presence or absence of classification abilities per se (see Carey, 1985).

The effect of knowledge on competence is demonstrated in two cognitive tasks that young children often fail: a perspective-taking task and a conservation of number task. On the perspective-taking task, young children are found to lack the ability to take a perspective other than their own. However, as shown by Borke (1975), if the task is presented in a familiar context, in this case as characters from "Sesame Street," they are more likely to be able to take a perspective other than their own. On the conservation of number task, young children will mistake a longer line of items as having "more" even though a longer line has the same number of items with bigger spaces between them. This is the case even when the two lines of items are initially the same length and it is pointed out that they have the same number of items. However, Donaldson (1978) found that if a "Puppet—Naughty Teddy" messed up two lines with equal numbers, making one line longer, children were less likely to indicate that the longer line had more.

The tension between the view of cognitive development as taking place systemically in response to endogenous, often biological change, and the view that it occurs in specific domains in response to exogenous influences has fueled much research that is still ongoing. Researchers from different theoretical perspectives frame their questions differently, and their inquiry often uses different research techniques (Case, 1991). Compelling findings from both lines of inquiry call for a more integrated understanding of cognitive development in which both exogenous and endogenous factors are at play, and in which some systemic limits are recognized which, while providing a ceiling on development, allow for wide variation below that ceiling in response to exogenous influences. Indeed, numerous theories do incorporate the idea of structured cognitive development, but allow for cognitive structures to be assembled independently rather than systemically, with environmental context and culture playing a central role in the development of the individual's cognitive landscape (Case, 1985; Fischer, 1980; Halford, 1982; Halford and Leitch, 1988; Pascual-Leone, 1988a, 1988b).

Cognition in Context

Closely tied to the understanding of the influence of knowledge acquisition on cognitive development is the research on "cognition in context." Although Piaget made it clear that the development of cognitive structure depends on the opportunity for children to interact with supporting environments, he did not focus on how to characterize relevant inputs for epigenesis. The late 1980s witnessed an explosion of work on the social and cultural contexts of cognitive development (e.g., Bronfenbrenner and Ceci, 1994; Rogoff, 1990; Sternberg, 1985; Fischer and Knight, 1990). For example, drawing on a train metaphor, Bronfenbrenner and Ceci proposed that "the basic psychological and biological processes are the 'engines' that drive intellectual development and context provides the fuel and steering wheel to determine how far and in what direction it goes" (1994:404).

Social-cultural contexts affect cognitive processing in multiple ways, and different lines of research focus on different aspects of context. Sociocultural theory emphasizes that cognitive activity and development occur in social situations. Children engage in problem-solving activities in collaboration with an adult who structures and models ways to solve the problem. This is referred to as coconstruction. Vygotsky (1978) and Rogoff (1990) best articulate the theory by which children's problem solving is conducted under the guidance and supervision of adults, who structure the interaction to guide children through tasks that are just beyond their capacities. The window of opportunity for the adult to enter into the child's experience and enable him to move toward developing higher mental processes is called the zone of proximal development (ZPD). "The lower level of the ZPD is defined by the child's independent performance and its upper level is defined by the most a child can do with assistance" (Bodrova, 1997:20). As long as the child's knowledge remains where improvement is still possible with adult assistance, the child is said to be within the ZPD. With adult help, the child may advance toward independent and autonomous thinking.

One important strategy that the adult employs is called scaffolding, in which questions or discussion are used to help the child advance incrementally to a higher level of thinking. In a way, this is analogous to Piaget's notion of the child moving from stage to stage. The difference is that in Vygotsky's approach the movement upward is possible with appropriate guidance; it is not as dependent on the unfolding of an endogenous developmental process. Vygotsky thus gives instruction a more central role in development than does Piaget.

Another critical concept in the Vygotskyan perspective is that of mental tools. For a child to acquire these tools en route to higher-order mental function like abstract reasoning, the child has to be helped by knowing individuals, teachers, or parents. This can occur in school or at home. Mental tools come in various forms including the development of strategies to remember and to solve problems (such as trial-and-error and counting-on strategies), developing analogies, or reviewing related information or ideas. Their common characteristic is that they help the child restructure his thinking. Gelman, in discussing the teaching of arithmetic to young children, emphasizes the importance of recognizing that even the young child develops some knowledge and concepts of mathematics that can be built on (Gelman, 2000). The use of questions and demonstrations can help draw out existing knowledge and build on it, contributing to a restructuring of the child's understanding.

The last 30 years have witnessed a considerable growth in evidence of strategic and metacognitive competence at an early age, especially when children are asked about topics or problems they understand (Brown and DeLoache, 1978; DeLoache et al., 1998). Children can think about their own thinking and the thinking and intentions of others. Recent research on "theories of mind" suggest that not only can children intentionally learn, but they can develop theories of what it means to learn and to understand that affect how they function in situations that require effortful learning (Bereiter and Scardamalia, 1989). The more they understand what the learning process requires—that it is not simply a matter of knowing or not knowing, of performing well or of failing to perform—the more directed they will be toward the learning goal (Dweck, 1989; Dweck and Elliott, 1983; Dweck and Leggett, 1988). Researchers have documented cases of preschool children using strategies to remember (Wellman et al., 1975; DeLoache et al., 1985), to count (Siegler, 1988) and to solve problems (National Research Council, 1999).

An older and large body of research, less explicitly linked to sociocultural theory but also focusing on the role of the adult, suggests an optimal adult-child interaction for children's cognitive and language development. It is one that fosters reciprocity in which adults make overtures to children that are in tune with their current attentional focus, building on the children's activities, prior knowledge, and skill level (Akhtar et al., 1991; Belsky et al., 1980; Bloom et al., 1976; Bornstein and Tamis-LeMonda, 1989; Bruner and Olson, 1977; Gralinski and Kopp, 1993; Kuczynski, 1984; Landry et al., 1997; Rocissano and Yatchmink, 1984; Parpal and Maccoby, 1985; Schaffer and Crook, 1980; Tomasello and Farrar, 1986a, 1986b). This reciprocal and responsive adult-child interaction is related to better cognitive and language outcomes (Bornstein and Tamis-LeMonda, 1989; Crockenberg and Litman, 1990; Maccoby and Martin, 1983; Power and Chapieski, 1986; Olson et al., 1984; Tomasello and Farrar, 1986a, 1986b; Weiss et al., 1992). This literature is based primarily on maternal behavior. Its relevance to early education and care is expanded in Chapter 5 and also in Chapter 7, when we discuss professional development.

In a similar vein, Kurt Fischer and his colleagues argue that competence is "an emergent characteristic of a person-in-context, not a person alone" (Fischer et al., 1993). They conducted many research studies on children between 3 and 18 years of age to measure the influence of contextual support on competence. Children were asked to carry out tasks (such as producing mean and nice stories, sorting blocks into boxes) in contexts ranging from no support (spontaneous performance) to high support (in the form of direct modeling of the performance task).

Performances were then rated on a developmental scale. A consistent, substantial difference in performance was found between the "functional level" in the low support context, and the "optimal level" in the high support context. In one such study conducted with 7-year-olds, the children were asked to produce stories about mean and nice, and their spontaneous responses were scored at or below stage 3 on the developmental scale, whereas their independently executed response after modeling was at or below stage 6, suggesting a potentially powerful influence of context (Fischer et al., 1993). Fischer refers to the gap as the child's "developmental range," a concept that differs somewhat from Vygotsky's zone of proximal development. The adult does not actually help the child do the more difficult aspects of the task. Rather, the child observes through exposure or modeling more developmentally sophisticated approaches to a task, which changes his or her own performance.

Much research has also emphasized the role of cultural context on cognition. Culture is seen as providing the content—the objects and ideas—of thinking. For example, in a study of schooled and unschooled children from an agricultural community outside the United States and schoolchildren from the United States, Lantz (1979) found that a simple change from thinking about an unfamiliar set of objects to a familiar set of objects dramatically affected children's performance. Both the rural unschooled and schooled children outperformed children from the United States when the task involved seeds and grains. However, children from the United States did much better than the other children when the same task was presented using a set of colored disks. Thus, although the children were asked to do the same thing with the seeds and grains as with the colored disks, the content of the task affected their performance.

Cultural context also determines the tools people use to support thinking. Brazilian children who work as street vendors mentally complete mathematical computations in their normal business transactions every day. However, when these children were given paper-and-pencil versions of the same problems, their performance declined significantly. Schliemann et al. (1998) suggested that oral mathematics and written mathematics relied on different symbolic representations of the information, which in turn lent themselves to different strategies for solving the problems. The children had become experts in solving problems according to one strategy, but not the other. Similarly, Scribner (1984, 1985) posited that the tools and features of everyday contexts become part of people's thought processes. In her studies of problem solving in work contexts, she observed the ways in which individuals developed problem-solving strategies that capitalized on features of their work environments.

Functional familiarity also affects thinking. An expert-novice study of recall for the configuration of chess pieces by Chase and Simon (1973) demonstrated the role of functional familiarity in a memory task. When the chess pieces were arrayed in meaningful chess patterns, i.e., in terms of the game's structure, expert chess players well outperformed the novices in their ability to remember where the pieces were on the board when it was no longer in view. However, when the chess pieces were placed in random positions on the board, the experts did not do any better than the novices—even though the task was ostensibly the same task. Chi (1978) replicated these results comparing expert child chess players with novice adult chess players. Just as an array of chess pieces can represent a strategy or pattern that is recognizable to those familiar with the game of chess but unrecognizable to chess novices, objects and ideas will take on different meaning to individuals that reflect the function or importance of those ideas in an individual's culture. And in doing so, culture influences their thought processes.

Implications

The more global limitations on developmental stages suggested by Piagetian and neo-Piagetian theorists, confirmed in many empirical studies, give meaning to the notion of "developmentally appropriate" preschool programs. There do appear to be limits on the capacities of children in a developmental period that represent a ceiling beyond which very few can go. At the same time, however, there is much research to suggest that children are capable of learning a great deal when they are in environments that support their development. The responsiveness of children's development to exogenous opportunities to learn, and to interactions that support their learning, suggests the potentially important role that preschool programs can play in providing a context and a set of relationships that can promote development.

What are the characteristics of context in which a child's development is well supported? There is a growing body of research that suggests that cognitive stimulation—exposure to ideas, information, and stories—is one element of a picture in which the social and emotional context of learning is prominently featured. Piaget wrote of the link between the emotional and the cognitive quite eloquently: "There is a constant parallel between the affective and intellectual life throughout childhood and adolescence. This statement will seem surprising only if one attempts to dichotomize the life of the mind into emotions and thoughts. But nothing could be more false or superficial. In reality, the element to which we must constantly turn in the analysis of mental life is 'behavior'. . . . All behavior presupposes instruments and a technique: movements and intelligence. But all behavior also implies motives and final values (goals): the sentiments. Thus affectivity and intelligence are indissociable and constitute the two complementary aspects of all human behavior" (Piaget, 1967:15).

Emotion and behavior are, like cognition, located not just in the individual, but in the individual in context. Emotional security allows for more effective exploitation of learning opportunities. Moreover, learning requires self-regulation. Therefore behavioral issues, and the social and emotional environment of preschool classrooms that affect behavior, are crucial to effective learning.

SOCIAL AND EMOTIONAL CONTEXT:
THE IMPORTANCE OF RELATIONSHIPS

As is the case with cognitive development, the social and emotional development and behavior of children has been the subject of a plethora of theories in the past century. In earlier years the theories generally attributed children's behavior to their parents' childrearing, though the specifics of the explanations varied. However, there has been an evolution in complexity in the models used by developmental researchers since the 1940s (e.g., Sameroff, 1994). A relatively consistent position can be seen across most contemporary approaches and models in accepting the bidirectionality (mutuality) of influences between a child and parents, teachers, siblings, or peers, and for an expanded understanding of the role of the environment.

Tronick (1989) clearly indicates the centrality of the role of emotional communication from the earliest moments in a child's development. The effectiveness of emotional communication between infants and caregivers contributes to a child's eventual well-being. Tronick argues that infants' emotional communication is more organized than heretofore considered, that an infant appreciates how caretakers respond to him, which allows for a mutual regulation of their interactions. When the interactions are positive, when the two are synchronized and mutually supporting, development is enhanced. And negative communication yields negative consequences.

Tronick offers a prototypical example where the infant is reaching for an object but cannot retrieve it, so the infant indicates distress. After two tries the adult moves the object closer and the child retrieves the object and smiles. It is at these types of intersections where the adult responds positively to the child's intention from which healthy emotional development will eventuate. Therefore, rather than consider cognition and emotion as distinct domains, the implication of Tronick's study and others like it is that cognition and emotion are part of the whole.

More recent models that assign importance to interactions between the child and adults other than the mother are applicable to the behavior of children in preschool settings. The transactional model of Sameroff and Chandler (Sameroff, 1975), for example, is equally appropriate for families and classrooms because it takes into account whatever environment the child is in. In applying this model the child's behavior is viewed in the context of the classroom, including physical arrangement, the curriculum materials, the schedule or ordering of events, the classroom rules, and ongoing processes, as well as the teacher and peers. The child brings his or her own characteristics, clearly influenced by relationships in the home environment, as well as the family's culture, values, and beliefs.

Children and Adults

There is evidence that the transactional processes manifested by children and their parents in the home are seen in child-child and child-teacher relationships in school settings. Relevant work on these occurrences has been conducted by Patterson and his colleagues on the origins of antisocial behavior in childhood (Patterson, 1986).

John Bowlby's attachment theory (1969) has been expanded in the past decade (Howes 1999; Pianta, 1994) to encompass the notion of attachment networks. This contrasts with its earlier emphasis on the primacy of the child-mother attachment. In these more recent formulations, teachers in early childhood education programs are considered attachment figures because they provide physical and emotional care, and they are consistent and predictable in children's lives. From the children's perspective, these adults provide comfort, a secure base, and serve to organize the children's behaviors in the setting.

Research that examines behavior in contexts outside the home has produced a large body of evidence on the validity of assessing relationships between children and teachers, identifying and examining antecedents of different qualities of the relationships, and examining the concurrent and long-term correlates of relationship qualities and children's social competence. The findings of these studies suggest that the quality of a child-teacher attachment can be reliably and validly assessed, that similar processes are implicated in the formation of attachments of different qualities with alternative caregivers and with the child's mother, and that attachment security with the alternative caregiver predicts social competence in the long and the short term. Children with more positive teacher-child relationships appear more able to exploit the learning opportunities available in classrooms (Howes and Smith, 1995), construct positive peer relationships (Howes et al., 1994), and adjust to the demands of formal schooling (Birch and Ladd, 1997; Pianta and Steinberg, 1992; Lynch and Cicchetti, 1992). An important caveat to this research is that the way in which secure attachment relationships are demonstrated may differ across cultural groups (e.g., Harwood, 1992).

The quality of children's early relationships with their teachers in child care is emerging as an important predictor of children's social relations with peers (Howes et al., 1994; Howes and Tonyan, in press), their behavior problems (Howes et al., 1998), and school achievement as older children (Howes et al., in press). Perhaps most important for the work of this committee, if children feel emotionally secure with the teacher, they can use her as a secure base and a resource for exploring the learning opportunities of the classroom (Birch and Ladd, 1997; Howes et al., in press; Howes and Smith, 1995; Lynch and Cicchetti, 1992; Pianta and Steinberg, 1992).

More recent theoretical work from this perspective has included the social-emotional climate of the classroom as well as the individual relationship between the child and the teacher (Boyce et al., and the MacArthur Network on Psychopathology and Development, 1998). According to this perspective, the individual child-teacher relationship and teacher perceptions of individual children's behavior problems are constructed in the context of classroom climates. The classroom social-emotional climate is defined as consisting of the level of aggression and other behavior problems in the group of children, the nature of the child-teacher relationships, and the frequency and complexity of play with peers. Using this notion of classroom climate, classrooms can be described on a continuum from positive, prosocial environments characterized by close adult-child relationships, intricate pretend play scenarios, and little disruptive behavior to angry, hostile environments characterized by conflictual child-teacher-relationships, angry disruptive children, and little constructive peer play or collaborative learning.

An alternative approach to early childhood pedagogy, also derived from attachment theory, emphasizes the socialization function of the adult. If a teacher constructs positive and secure attachment relationships with children, in part by responding positively and consistently to children's appropriate behavior, so that there is a predominance of what Kochanska (1997) calls mutually reciprocal relationships, then classroom management becomes an issue of constructing, maintaining, and sustaining harmonious relationships rather than managing and avoiding potential conflict. There is very little empirical data on this topic, however.[1]

Early researchers examining links in infants between attachment security and self-regulation found that infants who were classified as secure were more compliant and showed less frustration and aggression as toddlers (Matas et al., 1978; Londerville and Main, 1981). More recently, Kochanska (1997) has used Maccoby's (1984) construct of a mutually reciprocal relationship to examine the processes linking secure attachment and self-regulation. If toddlers trust their caregiver, then they are more willing and eager to be socialized. Furthermore, the experience of a mutually reciprocal relationship means that both partners, the toddler and the adult, feel invested in and responsible for each other's welfare; each feels concern for and acts responsively to the other's needs, and, at the same time, each comes to expect the other to be responsive to one's needs and to be concerned about one's welfare (Kochanska, 1997:94).

This kind of relationship is very different from the adversarial relationship sometimes implied in the socialization literature. In terms of behavioral interaction, a mutual responsive relationship means that there is a diminished need for adult use of power or coercion strategies. Instead, because the child is eager to cooperate with the adult, socialization strategies do not need to be harsh or restrictive. The existence of a mutually reciprocal relationship means that children's socialization can extend beyond task compliance toward building a foundation for rules of conduct and morality.

There are implications in these associations between attachment security and self-regulation for classroom management in early childhood programs. If teachers can construct secure attachments with the children in their care, then they may have less need for discipline strategies, such as time out or behavior conse-

---

[1] All the literature available was conducted with regard to infant-mother attachment. Since child-teacher attachments appear to function similarly to infant-mother attachments (Howes, 1999), a similar pattern of results could be assumed for child-teacher attachment relationships.

quences that are outside a cooperative relationship. To develop that sort of trust between caregiver and child, it is necessary to provide positive consequences, a point that has been stressed by the behavioral approaches, as has the need for setting expectations and giving clear directions. This literature does bring with it a wealth of empirical support that bolsters the notion that teachers who have a relatively sophisticated grasp of the attachment and behavioral literature, can promote the kind of attachment that helps children develop self-regulation.

In sum, one of the most consistent findings in the early childhood literature is that an emotionally warm and positive approach in learning situations leads to constructive behavior in children. The teacher's tone of voice and the use of positive consequences to encourage desired behavior, just to mention two examples, are key to teacher strategies advocated by virtually all preschool programs.

Importance of Peers

Attention to peer relations dates back to the 1930s and 1940s when researchers studied children's friendship patterns; interest reemerged again in the 1970s, with major contributions occurring during the past two decades (e.g., Hartup, 1983). Children's peer relations are seen as more complex than was initially conceptualized, with areas such as social group status, mutual friendships, and peer networks seen as separate aspects of peer relations (Bierman and Welsh, 1997). Aspects of children's development such as communication skills, helping behavior, play, and conflict resolution, are important dimensions of peer relations (Greenfield and Suzuki, 1998). Parent-child interactions and family experiences influence peer relations (e.g., Parke and Ladd, 1992) as well as the child's culture and beliefs (Greenfield and Suzuki, 1998; Bierman and Welsh, 1997). Another major variable influencing peer relations is a child's social competence, that is, the child's ability to elicit positive responses from others (Dodge, 1985).

One of the most compelling findings related to peer relations is that positive peer relations have a significant role in supporting a child's social and emotional development (Parker et al., 1995). A number of studies have documented relationships between poor peer relationships and children's later school difficulties and mental health problems (e.g., Parker et al., 1995). From a longitudinal study of kindergarten children (Wasik et al., 1993; Wasik, 1997), results showed that children's peer status, as rated by their peers within the first three months of kindergarten, was highly predictive of their social and academic performance in third grade. Other researchers have documented the predictive value of children's social status in the elementary grades for later school success and mental health adjustment in adolescence (Lynch and Cicchetti, 1997).

Collectively these findings and those of many other researchers during the past two decades make it clear that children's social interactions and peer relations are critical considerations when young children come together in education and care settings. Teachers and other staff need to be careful observers and knowledgeable of ways to facilitate positive peer relations.

DEVELOPMENT OF THE BRAIN

The proliferation of research on the brain that has accompanied advances in brain imaging technology has provided a physiological description of the mind's organ that in some respects complements the understanding that is emerging from research in developmental and cognitive psychology. The brain undergoes enormous changes as a child grows and acquires skill in dealing with the environment. We first consider some findings in neurobiology related to the role of experience in shaping brain circuits. Then we examine findings based on neuroimaging of the anatomy and circuitry involved in high-level skills.

It is important at the beginning of this discussion to caution against thinking that brain research is directly applicable to instruction and pedagogy. There are many popular accounts and heavily promoted learning programs that make that leap, but so far, there is no evidence of the effectiveness of particular educational programs, methods, or techniques on brain development (see National Research Council, 1999: Chapter 5; Bruer, 1997).

Genetics and Environment

Recent research in developmental biology has already altered the basis of the traditional nature-nurture debate. One is born with a given set of genes; however, the expression of those genes in the characteristics of the individual is not fixed; gene expression depends on the environment. Thus, the interaction between nature and nurture operates at every level, including the molecular one. A view of genetic expression as quintessentially dependent on environmental interactions allows for acceptance of genetic influences on the part of the behavioral sciences without the need to forfeit the important role played by the social environment. Indeed, there is every reason to expect some social environments to influence biological variables.

While much of the nervous system develops prior to birth, for primates and particularly humans a long period of postnatal development is needed to complete the basic formation of the brain. Two basic biological principles dominate current understanding of how nervous systems are put together. The first, neuronal specificity, posits that neuronal connections are specified with great precision during their development (Sperry et al., 2000). This principle has been used to support the *selectionist* view, according to which the role of experience is limited to selecting from a rich innate repertoire of connections. This view stresses the overproduction of synapses in early life and their pruning in development. Findings of the capabilities of infants in processing features of language, numbers, and objects that were discussed at the start of this chapter provide some support for the selectionist viewpoint by showing that basic building blocks of cognition are present at or near birth. The second principle posits that correlated firing of cells leads to increased connections between them (Hebb, 1983). This principle ensures that cells that fire together will be strongly represented in connections. It has been used to support the *constructivist* view (e.g., Quartz and Sejnowski, 1997), in which development is seen as progressive increase in the representational properties of the cortex. The environment shapes the specific organization of sensory systems tuned to visual, auditory, or other aspects of stimuli. In support of this view is evidence that children deprived of sensory input (e.g., deaf from birth) show specific alterations in the organization of other senses (Neville, 1995). This view stresses how learning organizes brain circuits. But whether through pruning or through circuit organization, both views converge on the importance of experience in shaping the physiology of the brain.

Neuroimaging

It is now possible to observe changes in the brain in normal subjects as they perform tasks involving thought and emotion (Posner and Raichle, 1994; Thatcher et al., 1996). The development of methods of imaging the human brain increases our ability to observe and study how it changes with experience.

When neurons are active, they change their own local blood supply. This makes it possible to track areas of the brain active during cognitive processes by methods designed to study changes in blood flow. The two most prominent methods for doing this are positron emission tomography (PET) and functional magnetic brain imaging (fMRI). These two methods are fully complementary and have usually provided converging evidence when applied to cognitive studies (Posner and Raichle, 1994, 1998).

A major achievement of brain imaging studies has been consistent localization of brain areas that perform particular functions or mental operations, including precise localization of the processing of motion, color, shape, and other object features in the human visual cortex. For high-level cognitive tasks, the almost universal finding has been the activation of networks of small numbers of often widely separated brain areas. Subjects of early pedagogy, such as listening, remembering, searching visual arrays, processing music, learning sequences of spatial locations, and reading, have been among the tasks studied by neuroimaging. In the case of reading, these have reflected known features of the task, such as synthesis of letters into word chunks, input and output phonology, semantic association, grammatical markers, etc. Meta-analysis based on combining data across studies and laboratories has proven an important vehicle for summarizing the almost overwhelming number of results obtained from studies conducted in the past 10 years (for reviews see Posner and Raichle, 1994, 1998).

For example, a recent meta-analysis (Bush et al., 1998, 1999) has shown that many tasks involving the selection of cognitive and emotional information activate separate but adjacent areas of the anterior cingulate gyrus along the midline of the frontal lobe. The area activated by emotional input has strong connections to the amygdala and other emotional brain centers. In some situations, the cognitive and emotional brain areas appear to be mutually inhibitory (Drevets and Raichle, 1998). Studies of the growth and development of this area in childhood (Casey et al., 1997a, 1997b) suggest a role in self-monitoring and the regulation of behavior. While much needs to be learned about the organization, relation, and function of these areas, the discovery of adjacent cognitive and emotional brain areas in the cingulate provides general support for the importance of appropriate emotion and cognitive input during development.

Plasticity

Plasticity refers to the ability of the brain to modify over time in response to change. The change might be major—as when a section of the brain is damaged in an accident—or minor—as when the brain changes in response to daily experience. The use of neuroimaging methods has provided some interesting vignettes, however. A few minutes of practice at generating associations for a particular word, for example, has been shown to shift activity from one brain pathway to another (Raichle et al., 1994). This work has begun to allow us to consider different physiological mechanisms for many of the types of changes that are likely to be involved in child learning and education.

Recent research indicates some of the ways in which a person's own activity, or learning from external events, might work to change brain circuitry on a temporary or permanent basis. The findings of the most relevant research are highlighted below.

• *Attention* allows rapid amplification of blood flow in local brain areas performing computations in high-level skills (Corbetta et al., 1993). By giving priority to some computations, attention can serve to reprogram the circuits by which tasks are executed.

In high-level skills (like reading), several years appear to be required to develop attentional systems that perform the required regulatory functions (Posner and Rothbart, 1998). While the orienting of attention appears to develop in the first year of life (Johnson, 1998; Johnson et al., 1991), ages 3 to 5 appear to be very important in the achievement of the kind of attentional control needed for high-level skills (Posner and Rothbart, 1998).

- *Priming* is produced by the presentation of a sensory event (e.g., a visual or auditory word) that changes the pathway so that new stimuli that share some or all of that pathway will be processed more efficiently. Apparently this is done by the prime tuning neurons involved in the processing of the sensory, phonological, and semantic codes of the word, so that fewer neurons are required by the subsequent target (Ungerleider et al., 1998).

- Research on *practice* by Raichle et al. (1994) has shown that the anatomical area for generating the use of a word changes when the same word list has been practiced for a few minutes. When generation has become automated with practice, it uses the same circuit as skilled readers use to read words aloud. When dealing with a new word, several cortical areas become involved that drop out with practice. However, automating the learning of entirely new words requires much longer practice.

- In a recent study of *learning* 40 lexical items in a new artificial language, it took 20 to 50 hours of practice before the same superiority in reaction time was shown for the items that is usually found for reading the native language (McCandliss et al., 1997).

- The brain area that represents English orthography (*rule learning*) within the visual system (visual word form) appears to require some years to develop and, once developed, may be strongly resistant to change (McCandliss et al., 1997).

The plasticity of the brain is not a characteristic that is confined to the early years of life. Nevertheless, the rapid growth of the brain in the early years provides an opportunity for the environment to play an enormous role in development. The findings from research on the brain suggest that helping children to pay attention, as well as the particular tasks to which their attention is drawn, will influence circuit development in the brain. And by providing opportunity for repetition (of routines, stories, and activities that promote social and cognitive skill development) and practice of valued skills, the brain becomes more efficient in those areas, freeing attention for higher-order thinking.

SUMMARY

Early childhood is a period of tremendous cognitive, social, and emotional growth. While there do appear to be systemic stages of development that place a ceiling on what a child can do or learn, beneath that ceiling there is significant variation among children, and across domains in a given child. The window into the developing brain allows us to see that stimulation from the environment changes the very physiology of the brain, with implications for cognitive, social, and emotional growth.

The ability of the environment to substantially alter developmental outcomes in the early years suggests the potential for preschool programs to have a powerful impact on child development. But a large research base supports the notion that if that impact is to be positive, preschool programs must attend to cognitive, social, and emotional development simultaneously. We addressed the importance of children's early relationships with adults, emphasizing that emotionally secure relationships are crucial in early education and care settings and are predictive of children's social relations with peers, their manifestation of behavior problems, and school achievement when they are older.

The thrust of the research reviewed above suggests that development is not simply an unfolding of innate capacity, but varies with context. It is a dance in which nature—what the child brings into the world—and nurture—the relationships and other aspects of the child's context—are partnered. Because nature and nurture are unique for every child, we observe remarkable variation among children even at very early ages. The research reviewed above suggests that responsiveness of those in the nurturing role to the developmental level and characteristics of the child is key to supporting further development. We therefore turn our attention in the next chapter to some of the central aspects of variation among preschool-age children to which an attentive adult might respond.

The Importance of
Individual and
Cultural Variations

WHILE DEVELOPMENT OCCURS IN A similar fashion for all children, developmental differences are the inevitable result of individual genetic and experiential variations and differing cultural and social contexts. In the past several decades, social scientists who study children have paid greater attention to this diversity in development. The potential of human development interacts with diversity among individuals, available resources, and the goals and preferred interaction patterns of communities in a way that links the biological and the social in the construction of diverse developmental pathways.

Among the many differences with which children present themselves to preschool teachers, we highlight three dimensions of variation that require particular attention on the part of a responsive preschool teacher:

1. The child's level of development in the cognitive skills and knowledge of relevance to the preschool classroom,
2. The child's social skills and behavior in a classroom context and the familiar norms of interaction with peers and adults, and
3. The child's level of physical and motor development.

These differences are associated with functional characteristics—such as temperament, learning style, and motivation—and from status characteristics—including gender, race, ethnicity, and social class (Gordon and Shipman, 1979).

VARIATION IN COGNITIVE SKILLS AND KNOWLEDGE

Children come to preschool with a set of cognitive skills and proficiencies that include language and literacy, reasoning, and general knowledge (Kagan et al., 1995). Although virtually all preschool children by age 3 or so have mastered the basic grammar and phonology and a reasonably large vocabulary for everyday learning and play, there are nevertheless large individual differences in areas that are related to achievement in formal learning settings. They vary widely in their language acquisition and use, their language comprehension, their understanding of number and causation, and their knowledge about the world around them. We review findings in the area of language and literacy, where much research has been done, and in mathematics, where a smaller but growing body of research is available.

Language Development

A major source of variation among children is their rate of language development, a difference that begins in the early months of life. Roe (1974) found that, among 28 infants, the earlier a high rate of babbling occurred, the earlier every subsequent index of language maturity was likely to occur. Some researchers have found a pattern of gender difference in language learning, with girls more advanced in vocabulary learning than boys (Huttenlocher et al., 1991).

Although research has shown the developmental sequence of language learning to be much the same for all children, great variation in the rate of language learning occurs across as well as within languages. Each language has its own areas of complexity and irregularity, leading to slow acquisition, and its own areas of relative ease. Slobin (1985) tested children ages 2 to 4 who were learning one of four languages: English, Italian, Serbo-Croatian, or Turkish. Before age 2, the children learning Turkish were using productively the 16 case inflections required on nouns plus much of the verb morphology, whereas the "absence of a regular and predictable system contributes to the prolonged and confused course of inflectional acquisition in English" (Slobin, 1985:151). In Turkish, inflectional morphemes are stressed, obligatory, regular, and distinct. Children do not have to deal with homonyms, as in " She ate eight cookies," with irregularities such as "cows, mice, sheep," with contrasts such as "ring/rang, bring/brought," or "eat/ate, beat/beat, treat/treated," or with acceptable options such as "None of these go/goes." Regardless of the sentence structure heard, the objective case ending enabled the children learning Turkish to identify the receiver of an action correctly 80 percent of the time. The children learning English, who had to rely on sentence structure (as in "The ball hit the boy" versus "The ball hit by the boy"), were 3 1/2 years old before reaching that level of accuracy.

Among children learning English, the range in age at particular stages and in the amount and kinds of language they acquire is very wide. Among the 42 children Hart and Risley (1999) observed longitudinally, the average age of saying the first word was 11 months; the range, however, was 8 to 14 months. The average age at which half of what the children said contained recognizable words was 19 months, with a range of 15 to 30 months. At age 2, the variation was enormous: children produced an average of 338 comprehensible utterances an hour, with a range from 42 to 672; they used 134 different words per hour on average, with a range from 18 to 286. The range in vocabulary size parents reported for their 2-year-olds was 50 to 550 words in another study of several hundred children (Fenson et al., 1994).

The range of language abilities confronting preschool teachers is wider the younger the children in the classroom. Significantly delayed language occurs in a relatively large number of 2-year-olds, with a progressively smaller proportion of children affected across the preschool years (Whitehurst and Fischel, 1994). For example, in one study, between 9 and 17 percent of 2-year-olds (varying with socioeconomic status) met a criterion for expressive delay of fewer than 30 words and no word combinations at 24 months (Rescorla, 1989). By 36 months, estimated prevalence of specific and secondary delay dropped to between 3 and 8 percent (Silva, 1980; Stevenson and Richman, 1976). The longitudinal study by Silva (1980) indicates that the prevalence of secondary and specific forms of developmental language delay dropped by another 60 percent between ages 3 and 5. This would indicate a prevalence of between 1 and 3 percent at age 5.

Approaches to Language Learning

Children differ in how they approach the task of learning language. Bates et al., (1988) describe a continuum ranging from children who approach language holistically, acquiring whole sentences in chunks ("Leave me alone," "I want some more"), to children who take an analytical approach, learning one word at a time. Children who approach language analytically are described as having a referential bias (Nelson, 1973); they acquire large initial vocabularies of object labels (or of verbs if they are learning Korean or Chinese, languages in which verbs occur in salient positions at the beginnings and ends of sentences, where nouns occur in English (see Choi and Bowerman, 1991; Tardiff, 1996). Children with a holistic approach are described as less interested in objects than in social interaction, such that they acquire larger initial vocabularies of expressions and action words (Nelson, 1973).

Children also differ in the extent to which they are risk-takers (Peters, 1983). Some children appear to prefer to listen: there may be a prolonged "silent period" followed by starting to talk at a skill level comparable to that of children who have been practicing speaking for months (Saville-Troike, 1988). Other children begin exploring the effects of words heedless of accuracy and inflection. Nelson (1973) found talkativeness positively associated with all aspects of learning to talk when children were 2 years old. Talkativeness has been found positively associated with larger expressive vocabularies and faster vocabulary growth rates at age 3 (Hart and Risley, 1999), and with use of more sophisticated syntax at age 4 and 5 (Landon and Sommers, 1979). Talkativeness is important, because the language children display influences communicative interactions with caregivers (Hart and Risley, 1999; Oller et al., 1995).

Sources of Language Differences

Culture. Children learn language in the process of becoming members of a culture (Schieffelin and Ochs, 1986; Tomasello, 1992), and cultural practices are likely to be the chief determinant both of the amount and kinds of language children learn and of the environmental support provided for language learning (Schieffelin and Ochs, 1983). American families differ greatly in how much talking customarily goes on (Hart and Risley, 1995), and cultures differ in how much talking is acceptable on the part of little children (Schieffelin and Eisenberg, 1984). Heath (1989) and Schieffelin and Eisenberg (1984) describe cultures in which children are expected to learn from listening to the adult conversations going on around them, speaking only when asked to do so, so that the children's contributions will be relevant, well formed, and both sharing the conversational topic and contributing new information.

There is ample evidence that cultural influences in terms of language affect children's thinking, problem solving, and interpersonal interactions. For example, studies have shown that Japanese children excel in mathematics compared with U.S. children. One of the reasons for this may reside in the transparent nature of the base 10 counting system in the Japanese language. Similar differences might be found in classification because of different criteria and labels available. For example, Navaho-speaking children have more difficulty than English-speaking children classifying by color, but excel in classifying by shape, reflecting the presence of shape-dependent morphemes in their language.

Ochs (1986) notes the increasing number of cross-cultural studies showing that societies differ in language-socializing procedures, resulting in variation in language development associated with cultural context. "Prompting a child what to say appears widespread, but procedures described as facilitating language acquisition in studies of interactions between American middle-class parents and their children—fine-tuning, simplified, stressed speech, asking leading questions, expanding children's utterances—are not characteristic in non-Western cultures" (Ochs, 1986:6). Studies by Pye (1986) and Schieffelin and Ochs (1983) also suggest that the environmental support provided by American middle-class parents reflects the demands of a technological society in which a cultural priority is preparing children for academic achievement and managerial and professional occupations (Hart and Risley, 1995).

However, Fernald and Morikawa (1993) compared the interactions of 30 middle-class American parents to those of 30 monolingual wives of affiliates of Japanese companies visiting in America. All the parents, given identical sets of toys and videotaped in 10 to 15 minutes of toy play during home visits, were found to fine-tune their speech to the skill levels of their children. The American parents talked with their 6-, 12-, and 19-month-old children primarily about objects (naming them), and the Japanese parents talked primarily about social relations (polite verbal routines accompanying the exchange of objects, encouraging positive actions on toys: "pat it gently"). The major influence on the language children learn is the culture's socialization practices, which aim to establish and maintain the "language learning games" of the culture (Tomasello, 1992).

Socioeconomic Status. A significant association between children's performance on cognitive tasks and parent income and years of education is well documented (see Gottfried, 1984; Neisser et al., 1996; Stipek and Ryan, 1997), both within and across cultural groups. Parents with the advantages of education are reported to interact with their infants in ways relevant to mainstream schooling. They prompt their infants to respond to books and pictures, ask questions that promote organizing knowledge into names and categories (Schieffelin and Ochs, 1983), and arrange for children to have materials, uninterrupted time, and adult support for exploratory play that challenges them to initiate actions and combine and modify them in order to achieve a goal (Bruner, 1974). Duncan et al. (1994) demonstrated that the effect of poverty is partially mediated by the home environment. One-third of the variance in age 5 IQ scores that was associated with income was eliminated when measures of the home learning environment, family social support, maternal depression, and active behavioral coping were included in the model. The extent to which poverty is related to quality of the home environment depends on the degree of poverty: Garrett et al. (1994) found that as the income-to-needs ratio increased, the quality of the home environment increased. Moreover, the severity of the impact of socioeconomic status (SES) on the child's development appears to be highly responsive to the number of risk factors that characterize the home environment; poverty alone would predict an impact far smaller than poverty in the context of a single-parent home with low parental education and maternal depression (Sameroff, 1989).

Implications

The preschool period is a time when the environment in which children develop can contribute to large differences in language and literacy skills. Before children can actually read, they generally acquire some sense of the purposes and mechanics of the reading enterprise. For some children, opportunities to learn about reading are many, and for others, they are few (McCormick and Mason, 1986). Those who can identify letters and are familiar with the concept and purpose of print are considered "reading ready" (National Research Council, 1998). Reading readiness at school entry is highly correlated with reading ability in the primary grades (Hammill and McNutt, 1980; Scarborough, 1998).

The National Center for Education Statistics recently published the results of a survey of America's kindergarten class of 1998-99 (National Center for Education Statistics, 2000). The survey recorded the number of first-time-to-kindergarten children with literacy skills that are prerequisites to learning to read: knowing that print reads left to right, knowing where to go when a line of print ends, and knowing where the story ends. The results: 37 percent of first-time kindergartners could do all three of these skills, but 18 percent could do none of the three (Table 3-1). As they enter kindergarten, 66 percent of children recognize their letters, 29 percent recognize beginning sounds in words, and 17 percent recognize ending sounds (Table 3-2).

Several factors, including gender and age, affect test results. Girls perform better than boys in the test, and the age of the student at first entry matters. The latter variable in particular suggests that normal developmental processes are at work in the development of literacy skills. But environmental factors are clearly

TABLE 3-1 Percentage Distribution of First-Time Kindergartners by Print Familiarity Scores, by Child and Family Characteristics: Fall 1998

Characteristic	0 Skills	1 Skill	2 Skills	3 Skills
Total	18	21	24	37
Child's Sex				
Male	20	20	23	37
Female	17	21	25	38
Child's Age at Entry				
Born Jan.-Aug. 1992	11	17	22	50
Born Sep.-Dec. 1992	13	18	24	45
Born Jan.-Apr. 1993	17	20	24	38
Born May-Aug. 1993	22	22	24	32
Born Sep.-Dec. 1993	27	25	22	26
Mother's Education				
Less than high school	32	28	24	17
High school diploma or equivalent	23	23	24	30
Some college, including vocational/technical	17	20	24	39
Bachelor's degree or higher	8	14	23	56
Family Type				
Single mother	26	24	24	25
Single father	22	25	24	29
Two parent	16	19	24	41
Welfare Receipt				
Utilized AFDC	32	27	22	19
Never utilized AFDC	17	19	24	40
Primary Language Spoken in Home				
Non-English	26	22	24	28
English	18	20	24	38
Child's Race/Ethnicity				
White, non-Hispanic	14	18	24	45
Black, non-Hispanic	29	26	24	21
Asian	15	19	22	43
Hispanic	24	23	26	27
Hawaiian Native/Pacific Islander	30	27	19	23
American Indian/Alaska Native	38	27	18	17
More than one race, non-Hispanic	18	23	24	35

TABLE 3-1 *Continued*

Characteristic	0 Skills	1 Skill	2 Skills	3 Skills
Child's Race/Ethnicity by Maternal Education				
High school diploma/equivalent or more				
White, non-Hispanic	12	17	24	47
Black, non-Hispanic	27	25	25	23
Asian	14	17	22	46
Hispanic	22	22	25	31
Less than high school diploma or equivalent				
White, non-Hispanic	26	26	25	22
Black, non-Hispanic	40	30	20	11
Asian	22	36	23	19
Hispanic	32	26	27	15

NOTES: Estimates based on first-time kindergartners who were assessed in English (approximately 19 percent of Asian children and approximately 30 percent of Hispanic children were not assessed). Percentages may not sum to 100 due to rounding.
SOURCE: National Center for Education Statistics (2000:Table 5).

relevant as well: when the survey data are arrayed according to family characteristics, maternal education, poverty (as measured by welfare receipt), family type, and race/ethnicity are all shown to be correlated with literacy skills.

Through what mechanisms do demographic characteristics operate? Research and survey data suggest that families from lower-SES groups provide a similar array of language experiences as families in higher-SES groups, but the quantity of verbal interaction, and thus the vocabulary of the child, is much more limited (Hart and Risley, 1995). Moreover, language-rich environments are typically associated with activities like book reading, which by itself has a relatively modest predictive value (National Research Council, 1998). The NCES data indicate that mother's education level is positively correlated with the number of books and music recordings in the home, that single-parent families and those receiving welfare have fewer books and recordings, and that these parents read and tell stories less often to their children (Tables 3-3 and 3-4). The relationship is not as strong for song singing or arts and crafts projects, however (Table 3-5).

As we indicated in the previous chapter, recent theories have

TABLE 3-2 Percentage of First-Time Kindergartners Passing Each Reading Proficiency Level, by Child and Family Characteristics: Fall 1998

Characteristic	Letter Recognition	Beginning Sounds	Ending Sounds	Sight Words	Words in Context
Total	66	29	17	2	1
Child's Sex					
Male	62	26	15	3	1
Female	70	32	19	2	1
Child's Age at Entry					
Born Jan.-Aug. 1992	76	38	24	5	2
Born Sep.-Dec. 1992	73	36	22	4	2
Born Jan.-Apr. 1993	67	31	17	2	1
Born May-Aug. 1993	60	23	13	1	1
Born Sep.-Dec. 1993	56	20	11	1	1
Mother's Education					
Less than high school	38	9	4	*	*
High school diploma or equivalent	57	20	11	1	*
Some college, including vocational/technical	69	30	17	2	1
Bachelor's degree or higher	86	50	32	6	2
Family Type					
Single mother	53	18	10	1	*
Single father	58	21	11	2	1
Two parent	70	33	19	3	1
Welfare Receipt					
Utilized AFDC	41	11	5	1	*
Never utilized AFDC	69	31	18	4	1
Primary Language Spoken in Home					
Non-English	49	20	12	3	2
English	67	30	17	2	1
Child's race/ethnicity					
White, non-Hispanic	73	34	20	3	1
Black, non-Hispanic	55	19	10	1	*
Asian	79	43	29	9	5

TABLE 3-2 *Continued*

Characteristic	Letter Recognition	Beginning Sounds	Ending Sounds	Sight Words	Words in Context
Hispanic	49	19	10	1	1
Hawaiian Native/ Pacific Islander	55	24	14	2	1
American Indian/ Alaska Native	34	11	6	*	*
More than one race, non-Hispanic	61	27	16	4	2
Child's Race/Ethnicity by Maternal Education					
High school diploma/equivalent or more					
White, non-Hispanic	75	36	21	3	1
Black, non-Hispanic	59	22	12	1	1
Asian	82	47	32	10	5
Hispanic	55	23	13	1	1
Less than high school diploma or equivalent					
White, non-Hispanic	47	12	6	*	*
Black, non-Hispanic	37	7	3	*	*
Asian	60	20	9	1	1
Hispanic	29	6	3	*	*

NOTES: Estimates based on first-time kindergartners who were assessed in English (approximately 19 percent of Asian children and approximately 30 percent of Hispanic children were not assessed). Percentages may not sum to 100 due to rounding.
*less than 0.5 percent.
SOURCE: National Center for Education Statistics (2000:Table 6).

emphasized the influence of relationships and interactions with caregivers other than parents on children's development. Research on children during the school years that measures SES as a *group* risk factor (measured at the school level) suggests that it has a large, significant impact on reading ability, mediating the effect of SES as an *individual* risk factor (Bryk and Raudenbush, 1992). Children who come from low-SES families but are in schools with students from higher-SES families are at less risk than those in low-SES schools. A plausible interpretation of these data is that schools with large populations of low-SES students are more likely to be substandard schools (National Research

TABLE 3-3 Percentage Distribution of First-Time Kindergartners by Numbers of Books and Children's Records, Audiotapes, or CDs in the Home, by Child and Family Characteristics: Fall 1998

Characteristic	Number of Children's Books in Child's Home			
	<26	26-50	51-100	101 +
Total	26	28	29	17
Child's Sex				
Male	27	28	28	16
Female	25	28	29	17
Child's Age at Entry				
Born Jan.-Aug. 1992	18	25	33	24
Born Sep.-Dec. 1992	25	28	29	18
Born Jan.-Apr. 1993	26	28	29	17
Born May-Aug. 1993	27	29	28	17
Born Sep.-Dec. 1993	30	28	27	15
Mother's Education				
Less than high school	62	24	10	4
High school diploma or equivalent	31	32	26	11
Some college, including vocational/technical	17	31	33	19
Bachelor's degree or higher	7	22	40	31
Family Type				
Single mother	40	30	21	10
Single father	37	30	22	10
Two parent	21	28	32	19
Welfare Receipt				
Utilized AFDC	52	27	14	7
Never utilized AFDC	23	28	31	18
Primary Language Spoken in Home				
Non-English	65	25	7	3
English	20	29	32	19

Number of Children's Records, Audio Tapes, or CDs in Child's Home				
None	1-5	6-10	11-20	21 +
13	24	22	21	20
14	25	22	20	19
12	24	21	23	21
11	18	24	21	26
13	24	21	22	21
12	24	22	21	20
13	24	22	21	19
14	26	21	21	18
35	33	15	9	8
15	29	22	19	16
8	24	25	23	22
3	12	22	31	32
19	29	20	17	15
18	27	18	20	18
11	23	22	23	22
26	32	17	14	11
11	23	22	22	21
25	38	16	12	9
11	22	22	23	22

continued on next page

TABLE 3-3 *Continued*

| Characteristic | Number of Children's Books in Child's Home | | | |
	< 26	26-50	51-100	101 +
Child's Race/Ethnicity				
White, non-Hispanic	9	28	38	25
Black, non-Hispanic	50	31	15	4
Asian	46	26	20	8
Hispanic	52	27	16	6
Hawaiian Native/Pacific Islander	34	41	16	9
American Indian/Alaska Native	51	22	16	11
More than one race, non-Hispanic	20	36	28	16
Child's Race/Ethnicity by Maternal Education				
High school diploma/equivalent or more				
White, non-Hispanic	7	27	39	26
Black, non-Hispanic	46	32	17	5
Asian	39	29	22	10
Hispanic	38	32	21	9
Less than high school diploma or equivalent				
White, non-Hispanic	30	38	22	10
Black, non-Hispanic	69	23	6	2
Asian	72	16	12	*
Hispanic	77	17	5	1

NOTE: Estimates based on first-time kindergartners who were assessed in English.
Percentages may not sum to 100 due to rounding.
*less than 0.5 percent.

Council, 1998). To the extent that the same dynamic is at work in preschool programs, we would expect that the potential for preschool to provide opportunities for children from low-SES groups to acquire skills they might not otherwise acquire will be realized only if those programs provide the quality of learning experience to which children in higher-SES groups are exposed. As Chapter 4 reports, high-quality model programs for low-SES children have been demonstrated to have very positive outcomes.

There are other factors affecting children's language learning. In particular, poor outcomes vary directly with the generality of delay and the length of time the impairments persist. Thus a 5-

| Number of Children's Records, Audio Tapes, or CDs in Child's Home | | | | |
None	1-5	6-10	11-20	21 +
7	19	23	26	25
22	29	21	15	13
14	22	20	22	21
22	36	18	13	11
15	29	20	17	20
29	30	13	14	14
11	26	21	21	21
5	18	24	27	26
17	30	22	16	14
9	21	21	25	25
13	34	22	17	14
25	27	20	14	13
39	27	16	10	8
41	29	14	10	7
38	40	12	6	4

SOURCE: National Center for Education Statistics (2000:Table 19).

year-old with impaired nonverbal IQ as well as impairments in all domains of language would have the highest risk of poor outcomes in school, whereas a 2-year-old with an exclusively phonological impairment would have a much lower risk (Whitehurst and Fischel, 1994).

Mathematics Skills

Research on the responsiveness of infants to change in number has suggested that humans are "predisposed" to learn simple

TABLE 3-4 Percentage Distribution of First-Time Kindergartners by the Number of Times Each Week Family Members Read Books and Tell Stories to Them, by Child and Family Characteristics: Fall 1998

Characteristic	Reading			
	Not at All	1-2	3-6	Every Day
Total	1	19	35	45
Child's Sex				
Male	1	21	35	43
Female	1	17	35	47
Child's Age at Entry				
Born Jan.-Aug. 1992	1	16	40	44
Born Sep.-Dec. 1992	1	19	37	42
Born Jan.-Apr. 1993	1	19	35	45
Born May-Aug. 1993	1	19	35	45
Born Sep.-Dec. 1993	1	18	31	49
Mother's Education				
Less than high school	4	34	27	36
High school diploma or equivalent	1	24	36	39
Some college, including vocational/technical	*	15	40	45
Bachelor's degree or higher	*	7	34	59
Family Type				
Single mother	2	27	32	39
Single father	*	22	35	40
Two parent	1	16	36	47
Welfare Receipt				
Utilized AFDC	3	32	28	38
Never utilized AFDC	1	17	36	46
Primary Language Spoken in Home				
Non-English	4	28	30	38
English	1	17	36	46
Child's Race/Ethnicity				
White, non-Hispanic	1	13	37	49
Black, non-Hispanic	2	31	33	35
Asian	1	23	29	47

Tell Stories			
Not at All	1-2	3-6	Every Day
8	36	30	25
9	36	30	25
7	37	31	26
8	32	34	25
8	38	31	24
8	37	30	26
8	37	31	25
8	33	30	29
10	42	25	23
9	39	29	23
7	35	32	26
5	31	35	29
9	38	28	25
12	34	28	26
7	36	31	26
8	39	26	26
8	36	31	25
10	37	27	26
7	36	31	25
7	35	33	25
10	40	26	24
7	37	28	28

continued on next page

TABLE 3-4 *Continued*

Characteristic	Reading			
	Not at All	1-2	3-6	Every Day
Hispanic	3	27	31	39
Hawaiian Native/Pacific Islander	*	19	35	45
American Indian/Alaska Native	3	33	25	40
More than one race, non-Hispanic	*	15	42	43
Child's Race/Ethnicity by Maternal Education				
High school diploma/equivalent or more				
White, non-Hispanic	*	12	38	50
Black, non-Hispanic	1	29	35	35
Asian	1	21	29	49
Hispanic	2	22	34	42
Less than high school diploma or equivalent				
White, non-Hispanic	3	25	30	43
Black, non-Hispanic	4	41	23	32
Asian	4	35	26	34
Hispanic	5	36	26	33

NOTES: Estimates based on first-time kindergartners. Percentages may not sum to 100 due to rounding.
*less than 0.5 percent.

mathematics, just as they are predisposed to learn language (Gelman and Gallistel, 1978; National Research Council, 1999). As with language, however, there is variability in the rate at which an understanding of early mathematical knowledge and concepts is acquired. These early concepts and skills include the recognition of shape and size and eventually pattern, the ability to count verbally (first forward and later backward), the recognition of numerals, and the ability to identify quantity from a very general level (more and less) to a specific level requiring the mastery of one-to-one correspondence (e.g., knowing which group has four and which has five). Case et al. (1999) argue that in acquiring early mathematical concepts, young children create a mental number line and come to understand that movement forward and backward along the cardinal numbers on that line represents a

Tell Stories			
Not at All	1-2	3-6	Every Day
9	39	27	25
3	29	36	33
6	41	22	30
8	29	36	28
7	34	34	25
9	39	28	24
5	36	28	30
8	37	28	27
8	38	25	28
13	45	21	21
16	39	28	17
11	43	24	22

SOURCE: National Center for Education Statistics (2000:Table 20).

reliable change in quantity. Facility with the mental number line, their research suggests, is required to master first grade addition and subtraction.

A survey by the National Center for Education Statistics (2000) of America's first-time-to-school kindergartners found that, at entry, the large majority (94 percent) were able to read numerals, recognize shapes, and count to 10. A smaller percent (58 percent) could count beyond 10, sequence patterns, and use nonstandard units of length to compare objects. On level 3 tasks—sequencing numbers, reading two-digit numerals, identifying ordinal position of an object, and solving a simple word problem—20 percent passed (Table 3-6).

Differences in mastery of early mathematical concepts is, like language mastery, related to socioeconomic status (Case and Griffin, 1990; Case et al., 1999; National Center for Education Statis-

TABLE 3-5 Percentage Distribution of First-Time Kindergartners by the
Number of Times Each Week Family Members Sing Songs and Do Arts and
Crafts with Them, by Child and Family Characteristics: Fall 1998

| | Sing Songs | | | |
Characteristic	Not at All	1-2	3-6	Every Day
Total	5	23	27	45
Child's Sex				
Male	7	27	27	40
Female	4	19	27	50
Child's Age at Entry				
Born Jan.-Aug. 1992	5	26	27	42
Born Sep.-Dec. 1992	6	24	26	44
Born Jan.-Apr. 1993	6	23	27	45
Born May-Aug. 1993	5	22	27	46
Born Sep.-Dec. 1993	5	21	27	47
Mother's Education				
Less than high school	12	27	19	43
High school diploma or equivalent	6	24	25	46
Some college, including vocational/technical	4	21	29	47
Bachelor's degree or higher	3	21	32	44
Family Type				
Single mother	6	21	22	51
Single father	12	28	25	36
Two parent	5	23	28	44
Welfare Receipt				
Utilized AFDC	7	22	21	49
Never utilized AFDC	5	23	28	44
Primary Language Spoken in Home				
Non-English	11	28	23	38
English	4	22	27	46

Arts and Crafts			
Not at All	1-2	3-6	Every Day
7	40	32	20
8	42	32	18
7	38	33	23
6	44	32	18
8	41	31	19
7	40	32	21
8	39	33	21
7	37	33	23
14	41	22	23
9	41	30	20
5	39	35	20
3	38	39	20
10	40	29	21
9	43	22	26
6	40	34	20
11	40	26	24
7	40	33	20
15	38	25	23
6	40	34	20

continued on next page

TABLE 3-5 *Continued*

Characteristic	Sing Songs			
	Not at All	1-2	3-6	Every Day
Child's Race/Ethnicity				
White, non-Hispanic	4	23	29	44
Black, non-Hispanic	4	20	21	54
Asian	14	30	22	35
Hispanic	9	25	24	41
Hawaiian Native/Pacific Islander	4	20	37	39
American Indian/Alaska Native	10	25	18	47
More than one race, non-Hispanic	4	21	26	49
Child's Race/Ethnicity by Maternal Education				
High school diploma/equivalent or more				
White, non-Hispanic	4	22	30	44
Black, non-Hispanic	3	20	22	55
Asian	9	29	24	37
Hispanic	6	22	27	45
Less than high school diploma or equivalent				
White, non-Hispanic	7	25	17	51
Black, non-Hispanic	7	22	19	52
Asian	37	28	13	22
Hispanic	15	30	19	35

NOTE: Estimates based on first-time kindergartners. Percentages may not sum to 100 due to rounding.

tics, 2000). Mother's education, family type, welfare receipt, race/ ethnicity, and primary language are all related to test scores (see Table 3.6). Child's age at kindergarten entry has a positive effect as well, but, unlike language, gender has no systematic effect.

The difference in performance on mathematics tasks across SES groups is one of degree, not kind. Children from low-income families show understanding of the same basic kinds of mathematical concepts and strategies as do children from middle-class families (Ginsburg and Russell, 1981). Indeed, there is evidence of considerable generality of such concepts in many cultures around the world (Ginsburg et al., 1997) and also evidence of con-

Arts and Crafts			
Not at All	1 –2	3-6	Every Day
5	40	36	19
11	39	26	23
8	35	28	29
13	41	26	20
8	39	36	17
9	48	27	24
5	39	34	22
4	40	37	19
10	41	27	22
7	34	31	29
11	39	30	21
9	42	27	23
13	35	21	31
13	41	16	30
18	43	20	19

SOURCE: National Center for Education Statistics (2000:Table 21).

siderable mathematical skill developed by young children who do not attend school (Saxe, 1991).

Griffin et al. found that children from lower-SES categories acquired the level of skill of those in higher-SES categories, but with a delay (Griffin et al., 1996). In a number knowledge test, low-income 5- to 6-year-olds performed much like middle-income 3- to 4-year-olds. The delay, however, can have long-term consequences when a first grade mathematics curriculum assumes that children have mastered the concepts that most, but not all, have acquired. The failure to learn because the prerequisite concepts are not in place may mistakenly be attributed to innate ability, with long-run consequences for expectations and performance.

TABLE 3-6 Percentage of First-Time Kindergartners Passing Each
Mathematics Proficiency Level, by Child and Family Characteristics:
Fall 1998

Characteristic	Number and Shape	Relative Size	Ordinal Sequence	Add/ Subtract	Multiply/ Divide
Total	94	58	20	4	*
Child's Sex					
Male	93	57	21	5	1
Female	95	59	20	4	*
Child's Age at Entry					
Born Jan.-Aug. 1992	97	74	37	10	2
Born Sep.-Dec. 1992	96	67	29	7	1
Born Jan.-Apr. 1993	95	60	21	4	*
Born May-Aug. 1993	92	51	14	2	*
Born Sep.-Dec. 1993	89	42	10	2	*
Mother's Education					
Less than high school	84	32	6	1	*
High school diploma or equivalent	92	50	13	2	*
Some college, including vocational/technical	96	61	20	4	*
Bachelor's degree or higher	99	79	37	9	1
Family Type					
Single mother	90	44	11	2	*
Single father	91	51	16	3	*
Two parent	95	63	23	5	*
Welfare Receipt					
Utilized AFDC	85	33	6	1	*
Never utilized AFDC	95	61	22	5	1
Primary Language Spoken in Home					
Non-English	89	45	13	3	*
English	94	59	21	4	*
Child's Race/Ethnicity					
White, non-Hispanic	96	66	26	5	*
Black, non-Hispanic	90	42	9	1	*

TABLE 3-6 *Continued*

Characteristic	Number and Shape	Relative Size	Ordinal Sequence	Add/ Subtract	Multiply/ Divide
Child's Race/Ethnicity					
Asian	98	70	31	9	1
Hispanic	90	44	12	2	*
Hawaiian Native/ Pacific Islander	91	48	11	2	*
American Indian/ Alaska Native	80	34	8	1	*
More than one race, non-Hispanic	94	54	17	4	*
Child's Race/Ethnicity by Maternal Education					
Maternal education:					
High school diploma/equivalent or more					
White, non-Hispanic	97	68	27	6	*
Black, non-Hispanic	91	45	10	1	*
Asian	97	73	34	10	2
Hispanic	93	49	14	2	*
Maternal education:					
Less than high school diploma or equivalent					
White, non-Hispanic	87	40	9	1	*
Black, non-Hispanic	83	27	4	*	*
Asian	94	58	16	4	1
Hispanic	82	27	5	1	*

NOTES: Estimates based on first-time kindergartners who were assessed in English (approximately 19 percent of Asian children and approximately 30 percent of Hispanic children were not assessed). Percentages may not sum to 100 due to rounding.
* less than 0.5 percent.
SOURCE: National Center for Education Statistics (2000:Table 24).

The responsiveness of preschool teachers to the developmental level of a child in the domain of mathematics, helping to put in place the concepts that are prerequisite to success in first grade arithmetic, can provide the foundation for performance in the school years.

Differences in Approaches Toward Learning

Students differ not only in the experiences that support learning, but also in what they draw from those experiences. The acquisition of skills and knowledge is closely tied to children's approaches to learning.

In the not-so-distant past, differences in what children learned from an experience were widely attributed to innate ability. Today, children (and adults) are viewed as having a set of intellectual strengths and weaknesses that allow them to make better use of some types of learning experiences than others, and of having different capacities to attend and persist that facilitate or hinder effective learning.

Those with linguistic, logical/mathematical, spatial strengths will learn about a topic most effectively with presentations that build on that capacity (Krechevsky and Seidel, 1998). A preschool class looking at wheels, for example, might reach some children most effectively through narrative—stories in which the use of a wheel changes experience and possibility—and others through the opportunity to construct with wheels. Those who are "intelligent" at constructing may not be those who are best at articulating ideas about why some wheel combinations work better than others. Access to learning opportunities that provide multiple points of entry is of particular importance in early childhood education, for young children have not yet had the instruction that would enable them to use less naturally favored approaches.

The NCES survey collected parent ratings on children's task persistence, eagerness to learn, and creativity, and teacher ratings on persistence, eagerness to learn, and attentiveness. Each scale was dichotomous, distinguishing never/sometimes from often/very often. Both parents and teachers found that a little more than a quarter of the children had limited persistence at tasks, with girls and older children rated as persisting more often than boys and younger children (Tables 3-7 and 3-8).

Parents perceive their children as being more eager to learn than do teachers, and while parents see a small difference by gender and age, teachers see a larger one. Teachers see quite substantial differences in attention by gender and age, as well. Only 58 percent of boys were rated as being able to attend often, compared with 74 percent of girls, and only 50 percent of the youngest age cohort was rated high in attention, compared with 70 percent of the oldest cohort.

In all areas, both teachers and parents rate children substantially higher in all attributes as the level of the mother's education rises. Similarly, children from two-parent families are rated higher on all attributes than children from single-parent families, with a positive correlation between attribute ratings and never having received welfare. White and Asian children, and to a smaller extent children whose primary language at home is English, are rated higher on persistence by both parents and teachers. As noted, there is considerable divergence between teachers and parents in "eagerness to learn" ratings for all races, however. And teachers rate minority children other than Asians as less attentive than white and Asian children. (Whether this means that Asian and white children learn to be more attentive at home or that teachers are less able to communicate expectations well to some minority children is, of course, open to question, as is the accuracy of perceptions of difference.)

VARIATION IN SOCIAL AND EMOTIONAL DEVELOPMENT

The ability of children to take advantage of learning opportunities in a preschool classroom is greatly influenced by their ability to establish a secure tie to the teacher, and to successfully negotiate relationships with peers (see Chapter 2). But children vary with respect to the social and emotional development that facilitates positive relationship formation. Moreover, the ease with which they adapt to the expectations of the classroom will vary with their temperament, regulatory capacity, and cultural familiarity with the modes of interaction that are encouraged.

Social Skills

Socialization of children is, in and of itself, a goal of early childhood education (Meisels et al., 1996). But successful social relationships provide benefits for cognitive development as well, since social skills are related to later academic achievement (Swartz and Walker, 1984).

TABLE 3-7 Percentage Distribution of First-Time Kindergartners by the Frequency with Which Parents Say They Persist at a Task, Are Eager to Learn New Things, and Are Creative in Work or Play, by Child and Family Characteristics: Fall 1998

	Persist	
Characteristic	Never/ Sometimes	Often/ Very Often
Total	27	73
Child's Sex		
Male	31	69
Female	23	77
Child's Age at Entry		
Born Jan.-Aug. 1992	24	76
Born Sep.-Dec. 1992	26	74
Born Jan.-Apr. 1993	27	73
Born May-Aug. 1993	28	72
Born Sep.-Dec. 1993	31	69
Mother's Education		
Less than high school	35	65
High school diploma or equivalent	30	70
Some college, including vocational/technical	26	74
Bachelor's degree or higher	19	81
Family Type		
Single mother	32	68
Single father	30	70
Two parent	25	75
Welfare Receipt		
Utilized AFDC	35	65
Never utilized AFDC	26	74
Primary Language Spoken in Home		
Non-English	29	71
English	27	73

Eager to Learn		Creative	
Never/ Sometimes	Often/Very Often	Never/ Sometimes	Often/Very Often
8	92	15	85
9	91	17	83
7	93	13	87
8	92	14	86
7	93	14	86
8	92	15	85
8	92	16	84
10	90	20	80
15	85	27	73
9	91	17	83
6	94	12	88
5	95	11	89
10	90	18	82
9	91	15	85
7	93	14	86
11	89	20	80
8	92	15	85
13	87	23	77
8	92	15	85

continued on next page

TABLE 3.7 *Continued*

	Persist	
Characteristic	Never/ Sometimes	Often/ Very Often
Child's Race/Ethnicity		
White, non-Hispanic	25	75
Black, non-Hispanic	32	68
Asian	24	76
Hispanic	29	71
Hawaiian Native/Pacific Islander	38	62
American Indian/Alaska Native	30	70
More than one race, non-Hispanic	31	69
Child's Race/Ethnicity by Maternal Education		
High school diploma/equivalent or more		
White, non-Hispanic	24	76
Black, non-Hispanic	30	70
Asian	21	79
Hispanic	28	72
Less than high school diploma or equivalent		
White, non-Hispanic	34	66
Black, non-Hispanic	41	59
Asian	32	68
Hispanic	33	67

NOTE: Estimates based on first-time kindergartners. Percentages may not sum to 100 due to rounding.

The NCES survey of children as they enter kindergarten collected parent and teacher ratings of the children's prosocial and problem behaviors. Parents were asked to rate children on the frequency with which they easily join others in play, make and keep friends, and comfort or help others. Teachers rated children on the frequency with which they accept peers' ideas for group activities, form and maintain friendships, and comfort or help other children (National Center for Education Statistics, 2000).

According to parents, the large majority of children (over 80 percent) engage in prosocial behavior often or very often (Table 3-9). Teachers rate a somewhat smaller majority—about three quarters—as accepting peer ideas and forming friendships often,

Eager to Learn		Creative	
Never/ Sometimes	Often/Very Often	Never/ Sometimes	Often/Very Often
7	93	11	89
10	90	20	80
12	88	24	76
10	90	21	79
19	81	29	71
10	90	23	77
8	92	13	87
6	94	11	89
8	92	19	81
8	92	20	80
7	93	17	83
10	90	21	79
17	83	27	73
27	73	37	63
15	85	30	70

SOURCE: National Center for Education Statistics, (2000:Table 19).

but only a slim majority (51 percent) as comforting others (Table 3-10).

Both parents and teachers see substantial gender differences, with girls engaging in comforting behaviors more often. Children from families with characteristics that were risk factors for math and language development—single mothers with low education levels who have received or are receiving welfare—also show somewhat less prosocial behavior.

Children were rated on a dichotomous scale for exhibiting problem behaviors—arguing with others, fighting with others, and angering easily—by both teachers (Table 3-11) and parents

TABLE 3-8 Percentage Distribution of First-Time Kindergartners by the Frequency with Which Teachers Say They Persist at a Task, Are Eager to Learn New Things, and Pay Attention Well, by Child and Family Characteristics: Fall 1998

	Persist	
Characteristic	Never/ Sometimes	Often/Very Often
Total	29	71
Child's Sex		
Male	35	65
Female	22	78
Child's Age at Entry		
Born Jan.-Aug. 1992	21	79
Born Sep.-Dec. 1992	22	78
Born Jan.-Apr. 1993	27	73
Born May-Aug. 1993	34	66
Born Sep.-Dec. 1993	37	63
Mother's Education		
Less than high school	39	61
High school diploma or equivalent	30	70
Some college, including		
vocational/technical	27	73
Bachelor's degree or higher	21	79
Family Type		
Single mother	37	63
Single father	39	61
Two parent	26	74
Welfare Receipt		
Utilized AFDC	41	59
Never utilized AFDC	27	73
Primary Language Spoken in Home		
Non-English	31	69
English	28	72

Eager to Learn		Attention	
Never/ Sometimes	Often/Very Often	Never/ Sometimes	Often/Very Often
25	75	34	66
29	71	42	58
22	78	26	74
21	79	30	70
20	80	27	73
23	77	32	68
30	70	39	61
34	66	43	57
38	62	45	55
28	72	36	64
22	78	32	68
17	83	25	75
33	67	44	56
33	67	45	55
23	77	31	69
38	62	47	53
24	76	32	68
32	68	37	63
25	75	34	66

continued on next page

TABLE 3-8 *Continued*

Characteristic	Persist Never/ Sometimes	Often/Very Often
Child's Race/Ethnicity		
White, non-Hispanic	25	75
Black, non-Hispanic	38	62
Asian	19	81
Hispanic	33	67
Hawaiian Native/Pacific Islander	36	64
American Indian/Alaska Native	36	64
More than one race, non-Hispanic	27	73
Child's Race/Ethnicity by Maternal Education		
High school diploma/equivalent or more		
White, non-Hispanic	23	77
Black, non-Hispanic	36	64
Asian	18	82
Hispanic	31	69
Less than high school diploma or equivalent		
White, non-Hispanic	39	61
Black, non-Hispanic	50	50
Asian	18	82
Hispanic	35	65

NOTE: Estimates based on first-time kindergartners. Percentages may not sum to 100 due to rounding.

(Table 3-12).   These numbers are, in a sense, the flip side of the prosocial behaviors.   The large majority of children are reported by both parents and teachers as infrequently engaging in fighting and angering easily, although teachers report fewer problem behaviors than parents.   Teachers and parents also diverge on observations of gender differences; teachers report substantial differences between the genders, with boys engaging in problem behaviors far more frequently than girls.   Parents report a difference that is considerably smaller in magnitude.

Race/ethnicity is correlated with reports of problem behaviors, but parents and teachers once again diverge in their observa-

Eager to Learn		Attention	
Never/ Sometimes	Often/Very Often	Never/ Sometimes	Often/Very Often
22	78	30	70
34	66	45	55
20	80	29	71
30	70	38	62
32	68	41	59
28	72	48	52
28	72	33	67
20	80	28	72
31	69	42	58
18	82	28	72
27	73	36	64
35	65	44	56
47	53	58	42
23	77	32	68
36	64	41	59

SOURCE: National Center for Education Statistics, (2000:Table 18).

tions. Teachers report a higher incidence of problem behaviors among black children than do parents, with Asian children reported by both groups to engage less in arguing and fighting. Both parents and teachers report more problem behaviors when a child is in a single-parent family than in a two-parent family.

Temperament

Some of the variation in social and emotional development observed among children can be attributed to differences in temperament. Temperament is defined as a pattern of arousal and

TABLE 3-9 Percentage Distribution of First-Time Kindergartners by the Frequency with Which Parents Say They Engage in Prosocial Behavior, by Child and Family Characteristics: Fall 1998

	Join Others	
Characteristic	Never/ Sometimes	Often/Very Often
Total	14	86
Child's Sex		
Male	14	86
Female	15	85
Child's Age at Entry		
Born Jan.-Aug. 1992	14	86
Born Sep.-Dec. 1992	13	87
Born Jan.-Apr. 1993	14	86
Born May-Aug. 1993	14	86
Born Sep.-Dec. 1993	18	82
Mother's Education		
Less than high school	21	79
High school diploma or equivalent	15	85
Some college, including		
vocational/technical	13	87
Bachelor's degree or higher	12	88
Family Type		
Single mother	16	84
Single father	12	88
Two parent	14	86
Welfare Receipt		
Utilized AFDC	17	83
Never utilized AFDC	14	86
Primary Language Spoken in Home		
Non-English	23	77
English	13	87
Child's Race/Ethnicity		
White, non-Hispanic	10	90
Black, non-Hispanic	16	84
Asian	22	78

Make Friends		Comfort Others	
Never/ Sometimes	Often/Very Often	Never/ Sometimes	Often/Very Often
11	89	18	82
13	87	22	78
10	90	14	86
11	89	18	82
11	89	18	82
11	89	18	82
12	88	18	82
14	86	20	80
20	80	29	71
12	88	18	82
9	91	15	85
9	91	15	85
13	87	19	81
11	89	19	81
11	89	18	82
15	85	21	79
11	89	17	83
21	79	30	70
10	90	17	83
9	91	15	85
13	87	19	81
18	82	28	72

continued on next page

TABLE 3-9 *Continued*

Characteristic	Join Others	
	Never/ Sometimes	Often/Very Often
Child's Race/Ethnicity (continued)		
Hispanic	20	80
Hawaiian Native/Pacific Islander	40	60
American Indian/Alaska Native	15	85
More than one race, non-Hispanic	14	86
Child's Race/Ethnicity by Maternal Education		
High school diploma/equivalent or more		
White, non-Hispanic	10	90
Black, non-Hispanic	15	85
Asian	21	79
Hispanic	18	82
Less than high school diploma or equivalent		
White, non-Hispanic	13	87
Black, non-Hispanic	21	79
Asian	27	73
Hispanic	25	75

NOTE: Estimates based on first-time kindergartners. Percentages may not sum to 100 due to rounding.

emotionality that is characteristic of an individual. It is one of the most easily and reliably measurable aspects of children's personalities because several of its components are measured by using laboratory instruments to record physical changes, such as heart rate increase. It can therefore be assessed at infancy, and it has been shown to endure over time (Caspi et al., 1995; Guerin and Gottfried, 1994; Plomin et al., 1993; Kagan, 1994), although the degree of stability in temperament varies (Cole, 1996).

Temperament among toddlers and young children in some studies is measured by asking parents or teachers to observe the children in prescribed or natural situations and then to rate their behaviors on a questionnaire that assesses the various dimensions of temperament. In one of the earliest studies of this type,

Make Friends		Comfort Others	
Never/ Sometimes	Often/Very Often	Never/ Sometimes	Often/Very Often
17	83	24	76
28	72	24	76
13	87	16	84
10	90	14	86
8	92	15	85
12	88	18	82
17	83	25	75
14	86	18	82
15	85	20	80
19	81	25	75
25	75	41	59
22	78	36	64

SOURCE: National Center for Education Statistics (2000:Table 8).

Alexander Thomas and Stella Chess (1984) identified nine dimensions of children's temperament: activity level, rhythmicity, approach-withdrawal, adaptability, threshold of responsiveness, intensity of reaction to new stimuli, quality of mood, distractibility, and attention span or persistence. They, and others, have suggested that a key dimension of temperament is the ease with which a child adapts to new circumstances (Kagan, 1989, 1994). At one extreme is the inhibited child, who exhibits fear and effortful control (difficulty maintaining equilibrium when confronted with challenging situations) when exposed to novelty (Kochanska, 1991, 1995), and at the other extreme is the uninhibited child, who responds to novelty with fearless confidence and interest. Often, the inhibited child has a higher level of percep-

TABLE 3-10 Percentage Distribution of First-Time Kindergartners by the
Frequency with Which Teachers Say They Engage in Prosocial Behavior, by
Child and Family Characteristics: Fall 1998

	Accept Peer Ideas	
Characteristic	Never/ Sometimes	Often/Very Often
Total	26	74
Child's Sex		
Male	29	71
Female	23	77
Child's Age at Entry		
Born Jan.-Aug. 1992	27	73
Born Sep.-Dec. 1992	25	75
Born Jan.-Apr. 1993	25	75
Born May-Aug. 1993	27	73
Born Sep.-Dec. 1993	31	69
Mother's Education		
Less than high school	31	69
High school diploma or equivalent	27	73
Some college, including vocational/technical	25	75
Bachelor's degree or higher	24	76
Family Type		
Single mother	31	69
Single father	33	67
Two parent	24	76
Welfare Receipt		
Utilized AFDC	33	67
Never utilized AFDC	25	75
Primary Language Spoken in Home		
Non-English	29	71
English	26	74

Form Friendships		Comfort Others	
Never/ Sometimes	Often/Very Often	Never/ Sometimes	Often/Very Often
23	77	49	51
27	73	57	43
20	80	40	60
25	75	46	54
20	80	46	54
22	78	48	52
26	74	51	49
26	74	54	46
30	70	58	42
25	75	50	50
22	78	47	53
19	81	43	57
29	71	54	46
33	67	59	41
21	79	47	53
33	69	57	43
22	78	47	53
28	72	56	44
23	77	48	52

continued on next page

TABLE 3-10 *Continued*

Characteristic	Accept Peer Ideas	
	Never/ Sometimes	Often/Very Often
Child's Race/Ethnicity		
White, non-Hispanic	24	76
Black, non-Hispanic	32	68
Asian	25	75
Hispanic	27	73
Hawaiian Native/Pacific Islander	26	74
American Indian/Alaska Native	30	70
More than one race, non-Hispanic	29	71
Child's Race/Ethnicity by Maternal Education		
High school diploma/equivalent or more		
White, non-Hispanic	23	77
Black, non-Hispanic	32	68
Asian	25	75
Hispanic	25	75
Less than high school diploma or equivalent		
White, non-Hispanic	29	71
Black, non-Hispanic	33	67
Asian	24	76
Hispanic	31	69

NOTE: Estimates based on first-time kindergartners. Percentages may not sum to 100 due to rounding.

tual sensitivity (Ahadi et al., 1993), and is thus more reactive in an environment that is loud, busy, or unpredictable. Once fearful inhibition is established, individual differences in the relative strength of approach versus avoidance appear to be relatively enduring aspects of temperament in novel or intense situations (Rothbart and Jones, 1998). Effortful control, in contrast, emerges among toddlers and undergoes strong development at ages 2 to 4 but continues to develop in later childhood and adolescence.

More fearful preschool-age children are more likely to be high in signs of moral internalization, especially when their caregivers have used gentle discipline techniques (Kochanska, 1991, 1995). Internalized control is also facilitated in children high in effortful control (Kochanska et al., 1996). Effortful control has been shown to be related to the development of the ability to select from com-

Form Friendships		Comfort Others	
Never/ Sometimes	Often/Very Often	Never/ Sometimes	Often/Very Often
20	80	45	55
29	71	56	44
27	73	50	50
26	74	55	45
31	69	58	42
32	68	55	45
27	73	47	53
19	81	44	56
27	73	54	46
26	74	50	50
24	76	53	47
31	69	53	47
35	65	66	34
25	75	51	49
27	73	58	42

SOURCE: National Center for Education Statistics (2000:Table 9).

peting dimensions (Posner and Rothbart, 1998). This ability in turn has been related in neuroimaging studies to the area of the midfrontal cortex. One example of this link is a "Stroop task," in which one element of a set of conflicting stimuli must be identified (e.g., identifying ink color as green when the word written in green ink is "red"). Performance in this task activates areas along the frontal midline. The skill involved in this task develops strongly between ages 2 and 4, and it correlated with effortful control as a temperament dimension (Posner and Rothbart, 1998).

One of the most important conclusions from recent research about temperament differences in children has been that the actual temperament category or personality style has less importance than the "goodness of fit" or appropriateness of that category or style with the child's larger community (Rothbart et al.,

TABLE 3-11 Percentage Distribution of First-Time Kindergartners by the Frequency with Which Teachers Say They Exhibit Antisocial Behavior, by Child and Family Characteristics: Fall 1998

	Argue with Others	
Characteristic	Never/ Sometimes	Often/Very Often
Total	89	11
Child's Sex		
Male	87	13
Female	92	8
Child's Age at Entry		
Born Jan.-Aug. 1992	89	11
Born Sep.-Dec. 1992	89	11
Born Jan.-Apr. 1993	89	11
Born May-Aug. 1993	88	12
Born Sep.-Dec. 1993	89	11
Mother's Education		
Less than high school	87	13
High school diploma or equivalent	88	12
Some college, including vocational/technical	90	10
Bachelor's degree or higher	91	9
Family Type		
Single mother	85	15
Single father	82	18
Two parent	90	10
Welfare Receipt		
Utilized AFDC	84	16
Never utilized AFDC	90	10
Primary Language Spoken in Home		
Non-English	91	9
English	89	11

Fight with Others		Easily Get Angry	
Never/ Sometimes	Often/Very Often	Never/ Sometimes	Often/Very Often
90	10	89	11
89	11	86	14
92	8	91	9
91	9	89	11
91	9	90	10
91	9	89	11
89	11	88	12
88	12	86	14
86	14	87	13
90	10	88	12
91	9	89	11
93	7	90	10
87	13	86	14
82	18	85	15
91	9	90	10
85	15	85	15
91	9	89	11
89	11	88	12
90	10	89	11

continued on next page

TABLE 3-11 *Continued*

Characteristic	Argue with Others	
	Never/ Sometimes	Often/Very Often
Child's Race/Ethnicity		
White, non-Hispanic	90	10
Black, non-Hispanic	83	17
Asian	94	6
Hispanic	90	10
Hawaiian Native/Pacific Islander	86	14
American Indian/Alaska Native	86	14
More than one race, non-Hispanic	90	10
Child's Race/Ethnicity by Maternal Education		
High school diploma/equivalent or more		
White, non-Hispanic	91	9
Black, non-Hispanic	84	16
Asian	94	6
Hispanic	90	10
Less than high school diploma or equivalent		
White, non-Hispanic	87	13
Black, non-Hispanic	80	20
Asian	97	3
Hispanic	89	11

NOTE: Estimates based on first-time kindergartners. Percentages may not sum to 100 due to rounding.

2000). In other words, individual differences in temperament and personality cannot be examined in the absence of the context in which individual children are being socialized. A child with an inhibited or slow-to-warm temperament may actually be more similar to his or her peers if that child is living in a Japanese community, and in such a context, an uninhibited child may actually suffer greater negative consequences.

The interaction between temperamental characteristics and environmental demands has important implications for early childhood education and care. Inhibition in a preschool child may be considered a sign of poor social competence, just as uninhibited behavior at the opposite extreme may be viewed as an inap-

Fight with Others		Easily Get Angry	
Never/ Sometimes	Often/Very Often	Never/ Sometimes	Often/Very Often
92	8	90	10
86	14	85	15
93	7	91	9
89	11	88	12
89	11	88	12
85	15	87	13
90	10	88	12
92	8	90	10
87	13	85	15
92	8	90	10
90	10	89	11
88	12	87	13
83	17	85	15
97	3	95	5
86	14	86	14

SOURCE: National Center for Education Statistics (2000:Table 11).

propriate lack of self-control. A responsive teacher will recognize that children with different temperaments are challenged by different preschool demands and settings. The inhibited child may need help from a teacher to feel secure and to become comfortable with routine in order to make use of learning opportunities. The uninhibited child may need the most help when she or he is being asked to engage in activity that is more quiet, focused, and routine. The key is to recognize that social competence is itself a measure of adaptability within a particular social group, and that there are numerous appropriate ways of demonstrating social competence that are in some cases in direct opposition to one another.

TABLE 3-12 Percentage Distribution of First-Time Kindergartners by the Frequency with Which Parents Say They Exhibit Antisocial Behavior, by Child and Family Characteristics: Fall 1998

| | Argue with Others | |
Characteristic	Never/ Sometimes	Often/Very Often
Total	67	33
Child's Sex		
Male	67	33
Female	68	32
Child's Age at Entry		
Born Jan.-Aug. 1992	68	32
Born Sep.-Dec. 1992	68	32
Born Jan.-Apr. 1993	68	32
Born May-Aug. 1993	67	33
Born Sep.-Dec. 1993	69	31
Mother's Education		
Less than high school	64	36
High school diploma or equivalent	65	35
Some college, including		
vocational/technical	69	31
Bachelor's degree or higher	72	28
Family Type		
Single mother	65	35
Single father	68	32
Two parent	69	31
Welfare Receipt		
Utilized AFDC	64	36
Never utilized AFDC	68	32
Primary Language Spoken in Home		
Non-English	73	27
English	67	33

Fight with Others		Easily Get Angry	
Never/ Sometimes	Often/Very Often	Never/ Sometimes	Often/Very Often
85	15	83	17
84	16	81	19
86	14	85	15
87	13	84	16
86	14	84	16
86	14	84	16
84	16	82	18
85	15	81	19
79	21	71	29
83	17	82	18
87	13	86	14
90	10	88	12
82	18	78	22
90	10	84	16
86	14	85	15
79	21	74	26
86	14	84	16
85	15	79	21
85	15	84	16

continued on next page

TABLE 3-12 *Continued*

| | Argue with Others | |
Characteristic	Never/ Sometimes	Often/Very Often
Child's Race/Ethnicity		
White, non-Hispanic	67	33
Black, non-Hispanic	67	33
Asian	78	22
Hispanic	70	30
Hawaiian Native/Pacific Islander	71	29
American Indian/Alaska Native	66	34
More than one race, non-Hispanic	65	35
Child's Race/Ethnicity by Maternal Education		
High school diploma/equivalent or more		
White, non-Hispanic	68	32
Black, non-Hispanic	69	31
Asian	77	23
Hispanic	70	30
Less than high school diploma or equivalent		
White, non-Hispanic	53	47
Black, non-Hispanic	58	42
Asian	85	15
Hispanic	72	28

NOTE: Estimates based on first-time kindergartners. Percentages may not sum to 100 due to rounding.

But while temperament may profoundly influence the functioning of a child in a preschool context, it does not predict the acquisition of knowledge, skills, or beliefs. "Put simply, the contents of the mind are determined primarily by exposure; the initial emotional reactions to new knowledge are influenced by temperamental processes" (Kagan, 1994:77).

Motivation

Much of the history of motivation among young children has emphasized traditional concerns about developing positive feel-

Fight with Others		Easily Get Angry	
Never/ Sometimes	Often/Very Often	Never/ Sometimes	Often/Very Often
86	14	85	15
84	16	81	19
90	10	84	16
84	16	79	21
80	20	84	16
82	18	81	19
86	14	80	20
87	13	87	13
86	14	84	16
89	11	84	16
84	16	82	18
73	27	71	29
75	25	67	33
96	4	79	21
83	17	73	27

SOURCE: National Center for Education Statistics (2000:Table 10).

ings toward the self, emotional control in social settings, and positive support from significant adults, such as teachers, parents, and significant others. Much of the research on children's emotional well-being has been incorporated into the motivational context. With the change in emphasis from a primarily socialization model of preschool pedagogy to a more cognitive one (discussed in Chapter 2), new research directions have appeared; one of the most promising is the development of interest.

Renninger (1992:370) reports studies dealing with interest and development, in which she demonstrates that young children do manifest particular interest in some objects but not others. Her studies reveal that preschool children's interests influence the quality of their play and social interaction. She writes that for children between the ages of 3 and 4, "there seems to be an increased coordination of children's friendship around objects of interest . . . suggesting that children are increasingly attentive to both the other and the object of exchange over time" (p. 370).

It is clear from the work of Renninger and others that children's interest and follow-through are related to their problem-solving ability and knowledge, especially in free play contexts. There is also general agreement that interest can be viewed as a disposition that is relevant not only for young children but also for adults, although their motivation differs. The young child is an active, outreaching individual whose interest is related to exploration and acquisition of knowledge of the surrounding environment. These interests are subsequently internalized and are related to the child's developing intrinsic motivation.

This process is well described in Deci's theory of self-determination, which holds that interest is a powerful motivator and has effects on subsequent learning and school achievement (Deci and Ryan, 1994)). The work of Renninger, then, demonstrates the significance of interest in social and cognitive functioning in preschool children, especially through play. Deci's self-determination theory indicates the significance of interest in the development of intrinsic motivation and internalization of interest associated with particular activities. Each of these writers offers a comprehensive view of interest as a significant motivator for ongoing knowledge acquisition.

Culture and Ethnicity

The influence of culture on social and emotional development has long been apparent to anthropologists, but it has now become a widely accepted notion in the field of developmental psychology. Beginning with the classic studies of Margaret Mead and John and Beatrice Whiting of young children and families in the Pacific Islands, Africa, India, and South America as well as in the United States, there is a solid knowledge base on variations around the world in children's social developmental pathways. We know, for example, that social competence is a culturally determined construct and that the countries of Japan and India tend to promote more collectivist or group-oriented values, whereas European and North American countries value the achievement of independence and autonomy (García-Coll and Magnuson, 2000). Similarly, we have learned that despite the universality of basic human emotions, the manifestation of these emotions differs a great deal across cultures, as do the events, circumstances, and conditions under which these emotions are expressed (Small, 1998). In addition, the emotion of guilt or shame has been found to have more prominence among Chinese people than among North Americans, for example, suggesting that even the influence of this emotion on children growing up in China shapes their social development differently.

More and more research is now being conducted on the various cultural groups that make up the population of the United States. Developmental psychologists are paying more careful attention to the influence of cultural background on the development of children's social and emotional capacities.

Cultural context creates the social settings in which people act and shapes their expectations within these settings. For example, Heath (1983) described a community in the Piedmont Carolinas in which children were rarely asked to answer questions from adults. Children did not take the role of an information giver. Heath suggested that when these children went to school, they were confused when they were constantly asked to respond to questions from their teachers—particularly when the children knew that the teachers already knew the answers to the questions. The children did not know what to do. The school context did not give them the necessary cues to know that this odd form of dialogue was a way for teachers to assess children's knowledge.

Cultural context specifies what constitutes an acceptable answer. It establishes the criteria for what is accepted as a "good" answer or as "good thinking." The classic example of Kpelle farmers in Liberia was observed by Cole and his colleagues (Cole et al., 1971). They presented the men with a set of 20 items, 5 each from four categories. The men were asked to sort the items into groups of objects that go together. Instead of putting objects into the four taxonomic categories, the Kpelle farmers would, for example, put the potato with the pot, reasoning that someone would need the pot to cook the potato. The farmers repeatedly told the researchers that this is the way a wise man would put things together. Finally, when the psychologists asked the farmers how a fool would put things together, the taxonomic categories appeared. The Kpelle farmers had the ability to do taxonomic classifications, but a taxonomic classification was not a sensible response according to their standards.

Finally, cultural context influences what parents expect of early childhood education. Lucia French's work with Korean preschoolers, for example, notes a curricular commitment to enhancing children's attentional skills rather than any particular domain of content or knowledge (French and Song, 1998).

Cultural differences between children's natal culture and the culture of the school have been posited by educational theorists (Erickson, 1993; Tharp, 1989; Trueba, 1988; Vogt et al., 1987) to explain some of the variation in the ability of American schools to educate children. The following sections discuss four ways in which children may experience discontinuity between their family culture and the school culture.

Social Organization

Large-group instruction, in which all of the children in the class listen to the teacher's comments and instructions, has been a typical pattern in classrooms in the United States. Children are expected to work quietly and independently on their assignments. Individual achievement is emphasized. Cultures within the United States vary in the degree to which children are socialized in their families to be accustomed to the social structure of mainstream classrooms.

The prototypical nuclear American family may be linked historically to a society focused on independence and individual accomplishment (deToqueville, 1945). Children in middle-class nuclear families may spend much of their time in dyadic interactions with an adult in contexts conducive to instructional and cognitive games and exploratory play (Schieffelin and Ochs, 1983). They are likely to have more varied experiences with a greater variety of people (Chisholm, 1981) on trips to distant relatives, in music lessons or sports practice (Huntsinger et al., 1998). The children may enter school well practiced in coping with new environments, readily accepting unfamiliar adults as sources of knowledge and help.

The social organization of the family and community in which non-middle-class, non-European-American children are raised may lend themselves to different experiences and expectations. Chisholm (1981) found fear of strangers continuing well past age 2 among children in American Indian extended families living in sheep-herding camps on the Navajo reservation. She noted that some children "might never meet an actual stranger until they went away to school at age 5" (Chisholm, 1981:11). In the extended families of Hispanic cultures, adults are described as especially nurturing and protective (Durrett et al., 1975; Zuniga, 1992). The children meet fewer people but have close relationships with more people. Like Navajo children, the children are described as shy and often as having difficulty adapting to school (Field and Widmayer, 1981).

Tharp (1989) described the extended families in which many Hawaiian children are regularly cared for by siblings, and bands of children organize for themselves activities in which learning is collaborative, mediated through peer assistance. On entering school, the children sought interaction with other children rather than attending to teacher instruction (Gallimore et al., 1974). Modifications in the social organization of the classroom, which allowed for peer-assisted learning and for children to shape their activities, in addition to adaptations in instructional practices designed to be more compatible with Native Hawaiian culture, resulted in marked academic improvement in primary grade children's performance (Vogt et al., 1987). These researchers advocated for selective accommodation of the classroom to children's natal culture. In the Hawaiian study, the classroom environment was only minimally similar to children's home contexts. "The only compelling similarities are the absence of direct adult regulation or scaffolding of performances, and the opportunity for children to engage in shared activities, organized more or less as the children prefer" (Weisner et al., 1988:344). Selective accommodation of the classroom environment to cultural preferences may be sufficient to enable children to make the transition from learning in their family and neighborhood contexts to learning in school.

Sociolinguistics

Differences in the social rules of conversation between children's natal culture and mainstream school culture may inhibit some children's participation in classroom learning activities. Tharp (1989) described the effects of differences in wait time, the time between the end of one person's communication and the beginning of the respondent's reply. Native Hawaiian children show their interest in a conversation by engaging in overlapping speech; that is, they begin to talk before the speaker has finished. When teachers discourage this behavior, children's participation in learning activities decreases. In contrast to the Native Hawaiian culture, some American Indian peoples utilize a longer wait time. For example, Pueblo Indian children have been observed to wait longer before they respond to a question. When teachers are accustomed to a shorter wait time, these children do not participate as frequently in discussion.

Differences in rules for speaking, listening, and turn-taking in conversations may also make it more difficult for Choctaw children to participate in classroom activities. Greenbaum (1985) observed that Choctaw children made more unsuccessful attempts to gain the floor, gazed more at peers while the teacher was talking to the class, engaged in more choral responses (where two or more students respond simultaneously or in a quick sequence), spoke individually less often, and provided shorter utterances when responding individually than other children did. Greenbaum suggested that the Choctaw children were members of a community in which sharing, cooperation, and primacy of group needs over individual needs were highly valued, and as such they did not want to participate on an individual basis in classroom conversation (shorter and fewer utterances when speaking individually) and were attempting to identify with the group (choral responses and peer-directed gazing).

Interaction Styles

Cultural differences in mothers' interaction styles may influence how children approach learning in school. Fajardo and Freedman (1981) coded videotapes of white, black, and Navajo mothers interacting with their 3- to 5-month-old infants. More often than the other mothers, the white mothers prompted and instructed their infants; they were more intrusive, and their infants spent more time looking away. This style may prepare children both to enjoy bouts of high-density attention and to develop strategies for coping with overstimulation and waiting for an adult to be available for interaction (Richman et al., 1988). The black mothers were just as stimulating as the white mothers, but less demanding of their infant's attention. The black mothers seemed "to put on a performance for the infant, and invite him [or her] to join" (Fajardo and Freedman, 1981:144). This style may prepare children for street talk (Smitherman, 1977) and the drama of group competitions in classrooms (Tharp, 1989). The Navajo infants looked at their mothers longer and more steadily than either the black or white infants. Their mothers seldom spoke to them and least often tried to get the infants' attention when the infants were looking elsewhere. This style may prepare children for the self-sufficiency needed in a culture in which 6-year-olds begin to herd sheep far from home, alone (Tharp, 1989).

Tharp (1989) also described cultural differences in styles of learning. One is the verbal and analytic, in which phenomena are systematically taken apart, each piece named and its relation to all the other pieces described, before putting the pieces back together in a higher-order concept. This style predominates in mainstream schooling and employment; it may be seen contributing to the instructional and cognitive games parents play with their children. The second style is the visual and holistic, one in which phenomena are observed, committed to memory, and acted on only when competence can be displayed. In American Indian cultures, children are not asked to describe the objects or events in a story, but are expected to listen quietly and abstract and elaborate an inner representation of what may be an outwardly simple narrative (Tharp, 1989).

As mentioned earlier in connection with language learning, Saville-Troike (1988) describes a "silent period" of one to three months in which six of nine 3- to 8-year-old monolingual Asian children enrolled in an English-only classroom regularly interacted nonverbally, but spoke to their native-language peers only. One child when interviewed in his native language during this period explained that he knew the teachers and other children were not going to learn Chinese, so he was learning English and was going to speak that. Another child said of her teachers that "there was this English and it was too hard, so she stopped talking to them" (Saville-Troike, 1988:575). When the six children began speaking English, their utterances were as complex and well formed as those of the children who had spend an equivalent time in the new language setting but who had not experienced a silent period.

Children in some black rural (Ward, 1971) and urban (Heath, 1989) poor families are expected to learn language by listening to adults and to speak only when spoken to, so that what they say is appropriate and informative, thus they are more likely to be silent and verbally non-competitive around adults. Learning through observation may predominate in communities in which possessions, especially toys, are few and competition is devalued. One of the most important challenges for teachers may be teaching children whose learning styles do not lead them to respond when they are expected to display what they know verbally.

There is some additional work by Gauvain specific to mother-child interaction that has interesting implications. Gauvain studied variations in mothers' instructional behavior (demonstrations, suggestions, prompts, calm directives, explicit instruction) and found not only relations between individual variations in these behaviors and children's problem-solving behaviors, but also that mothers vary their instructional strategies according to their perceptions of the child. For example, in one longitudinal study, children perceived as difficult were given fewer opportunities to discover strategies on their own, received more disapproving comments and physical redirecting of their actions by their mothers, and worked with mothers who tended to take charge of the more challenging tasks, thereby giving children less opportunity to practice these aspects of the task (Gauvain and Fagot, 1995).

Children who were less involved in performing tasks during mother-child interaction performed less well individually at the follow-up.

Early childhood education is, among other things, a process of gradual transition from cultural and family patterns to the expectations of a new social context. It is critical that the child's background and experience be understood and respected, that the school be responsive to the child, and that the child be introduced to school culture and practices step by step.

VARIATIONS IN PHYSICAL AND MOTOR DEVELOPMENT

Children vary substantially in many aspects of their physical development. Here we focus on those aspects that are most directly related to early childhood pedagogy: fine motor skills, gross motor skills, and disabling conditions.

Fine motor skills influence success in many of the activities in a preschool program. Lack of fine motor skills can make it difficult to hold a pencil, limiting early efforts at printing letters and drawing. Fine motor skills also influence eye movement and can predict reading, mathematics, and general school achievement (Tramontana et al., 1988).

The NCES survey of children as they enter kindergarten measured fine motor skills (with ECLS-K direct measures) involved in constructing forms with wooden blocks, copying simple figures, and drawing a person. It also assessed gross motor skills, exemplified by balancing and hopping on each foot, skipping, and walking backward on a line. The scores for gross and fine motor skills were divided into approximate thirds, referred to as lower, middle, and higher. The middle group includes those children performing at age-expected level, and the lower group at one or more standard deviations below the average.

The results suggest that girls score somewhat higher than boys on both fine and gross motor skills, but age at entry makes a far bigger difference. These findings are consistent with those obtained from the standardization of the Early Screening Inventory—Revised, from which the NCES direct motor measures were derived (Meisels et al., 1993, 1997). Mother's education is highly correlated with fine motor skills: 42 percent of children in families in which the mother had less than a high school education were rated as having low fine motor skills, and 22 percent were rated as high. In families in which the mother was a college graduate, 18 percent scored low on the fine motor scale, and 46 percent scored high (Table 3-13). There is also substantial variation by race/ethnic category for both fine and gross motor skills. In the fine motor skills tests, Asian children scored highest (49 percent in the high category) and black children scored lowest (41 percent in the low category). For gross motor skills, black children scored highest, with 46 percent in the higher portion of the distribution, followed by 38 percent of Asian children and 37 percent of white and Hispanic children (Table 3-14).

TABLE 3-13 First-Time Kindergartners' Mean Fine Motor Skills Score and Percentage Distribution of Scores, by Child and Family Characteristics: Fall 1998

Characteristic	Mean Score	Score Distribution (percent)		
		Lower	Middle	Higher
Total	6	29	36	35
Child's Sex				
Male	6	31	37	33
Female	6	26	36	38
Child's Age at Entry				
Born Jan.-Aug. 1992	6	20	36	44
Born Sep.-Dec. 1992	6	20	36	44
Born Jan.-Apr. 1993	6	25	37	38
Born May-Aug. 1993	5	34	37	29
Born Sep.-Dec. 1993	5	45	33	22
Mother's Education				
Less than high school	5	42	35	22
High school diploma or equivalent	5	33	36	31
Some college, including vocational/technical	6	25	37	39
Bachelor's degree or higher	6	18	36	46

TABLE 3-13 Continued

Characteristic	Mean Score	Score Distribution (percent)		
		Lower	Middle	Higher
Family Type				
Single mother	5	37	35	28
Single father	6	31	41	28
Two parent	6	26	37	37
Welfare Receipt				
Utilized AFDC	5	44	33	23
Never utilized AFDC	6	26	37	37
Primary Language Spoken in Home				
Non-English	6	31	35	34
English	6	28	36	36
Child's Race/Ethnicity				
White, non-Hispanic	6	24	37	39
Black, non-Hispanic	5	41	33	26
Asian	7	15	36	49
Hispanic	6	31	36	33
Hawaiian Native/Pacific Islander	6	27	32	41
American Indian/Alaska Native	6	31	39	30
More than one race, non-Hispanic	6	28	41	31
Child's Race/Ethnicity by Maternal Education				
High school diploma/equivalent or more				
White, non-Hispanic	6	23	37	40
Black, non-Hispanic	5	39	33	28
Asian	7	14	36	50
Hispanic	6	27	35	38
Less than high school diploma or equivalent				
White, non-Hispanic	5	44	34	22
Black, non-Hispanic	4	51	34	16
Asian	6	18	33	49
Hispanic	5	39	37	24

NOTE: Estimates based on first-time kindergartners. Percentages may not sum to 100 due to rounding. Scale 0–9.
SOURCE: National Center for Education Statistics (2000:Table 13).

TABLE 3-14 First-Time Kindergartners' Mean Gross Motor Skills Score and Percentage Distribution of Scores, by Child and Family Characteristics: Fall 1998

Characteristic	Mean Score	Score Distribution (percent)		
		Lower	Middle	Higher
Total	6	26	35	39
Child's Sex				
Male	6	31	36	33
Female	7	22	34	44
Child's Age at Entry				
Born Jan.- Aug. 1992	7	21	32	47
Born Sep.-Dec. 1992	7	21	33	46
Born Jan.-Apr. 1993	6	24	35	41
Born May-Aug. 1993	6	31	36	33
Born Sep.-Dec. 1993	6	37	35	28
Mother's Education				
Less than high school	6	30	35	35
High school diploma or equivalent	6	28	35	37
Some college, including vocational/technical	6	25	35	40
Bachelor's degree or higher	5	24	34	42
Family Type				
Single mother	6	26	33	41
Single father	6	33	33	34
Two parent	6	27	35	38
Welfare Receipt				
Utilized AFDC	6	29	32	38
Never utilized AFDC	6	26	35	39
Primary Language Spoken in Home				
Non-English	6	30	34	36
English	6	26	35	39
Child's Race/Ethnicity				
White, non-Hispanic	6	28	35	37
Black, non-Hispanic	7	21	33	46

TABLE 3-14 *Continued*

Characteristic	Mean Score	Score Distribution (percent)		
		Lower	Middle	Higher
Child's Race/Ethnicity				
Asian	6	26	36	38
Hispanic	6	28	35	37
Hawaiian Native/Pacific Islander	6	26	40	34
American Indian/Alaska Native	6	31	29	40
More than one race, non-Hispanic	6	24	38	38
Child's Race/Ethnicity by Maternal Education				
High school diploma/equivalent or more				
White, non-Hispanic	6	27	35	38
Black, non-Hispanic	7	21	33	46
Asian	6	26	35	39
Hispanic	6	28	35	37
Less than high school diploma or equivalent				
White, non-Hispanic	6	36	34	30
Black, non-Hispanic	7	22	35	43
Asian	6	33	34	33
Hispanic	6	29	36	35

NOTE: Estimates based on first-time kindergartners. Percentages may not sum to 100 due to rounding. Scale 0–8.
SOURCE: National Center for Education Statistics (2000:Table 14)

CHILDREN WITH DISABILITIES

At one end of the distribution of physical and motor abilities are those children with disabling conditions. These conditions range from those that are low in incidence but high in impact— such as cerebral palsy, Down syndrome, muscular dystrophy, and autism—to less disabling, but higher-incidence disorders—such as learning disabilities and attention deficit and hyperactivity disorder. The number of identifiable conditions is far too great for concise summary (see Batshaw, 1997).

Children with disabilities vary as much as all children do in temperament, personality, and family culture (Meisels and Shonkoff, 2000). Studies have shown, however, that chiefly on the basis of language and conversational skills, children with disabilities are incorrectly (or inaccurately) perceived as being of lower social status (Hemphill and Siperstein, 1990) and are treated as such by their peers in preschool classrooms, both those who do and who do not have disabilities (Guralnick, 1990). In preschool, children with disabilities tend to have more extensive interactions with adults than with other children, which is the reverse of their age mates without disabilities (Herink and Lee, 1985). The children are likely to initiate less often to other children, and their initiations are more likely to be ignored (Rice et al., 1991; Vandell and George, 1981). The more severe the disability, the less the amount of interaction with peers (Guralnick and Paul-Brown, 1986).

Since 1992 states have been required to make a free appropriate public education available to all children with disabilities ages 3 through 5 in order to be eligible for funding under the Preschool Grants Program of the Individuals with Disabilities Education Act (P.L. 10 1-476, 1990). The number of students in that category who are being served increased steadily over the subsequent five years, with 4.6 percent of children in this age group being served in 1996-1997 (U.S. Department of Education, 1999). A little over half of these students (51.6 percent) were served in regular preschool classrooms.

The NCES survey collected data on children at kindergarten entry who have developmental difficulties as reported by parents in the areas of activity level, attention, coordination, and articulation (Table 3-15). These difficulties are not necessarily indicators of a disability or diagnosis; parents were simply asked to rate their children in comparison to other children of the same age, and risk of developmental difficulty was indicated if the child was considered "a lot more" active, paid attention "less well or much less well," or if coordination and word pronunciation was "slightly less or much less" than other children of that age (National Center for Education Statistics, 2000).

While only 4 percent of children were considered to be less coordinated than their peers, 11 percent were rated as being less articulate. Parents rated 13 percent of children as attending less well or much less well than their peers, and 18 percent as being a lot more active. Boys were more often identified than girls, and

TABLE 3-15 Percentage of First-Time Kindergartners Whose Parents Reported Developmental Difficulty in Terms of Activity Level, Attention, Coordination, and Pronunciation of Words: Fall 1998

Characteristic	Activity level	Attention	Coordination	Articulation
Total	18	13	4	11
Child's Sex				
Male	20	18	5	14
Female	16	9	3	7
Child's Age at Entry				
Born Jan.-Aug. 1992	20	18	8	18
Born Sep.-Dec. 1992	19	13	4	10
Born Jan.-Apr. 1993	18	12	3	10
Born May-Aug. 1993	18	15	4	11
Born Sep.-Dec. 1993	17	14	4	11
Mother's Education				
Less than high school	24	17	4	14
High school diploma or equivalent	19	14	4	12
Some college, including vocational/technical	18	14	4	10
Bachelor's degree or higher	14	10	5	8

continued on next page

TABLE 3-15 *Continued*

Characteristic	Activity level	Attention	Coordination	Articulation
Family Type				
Single mother	25	16	4	11
Single father	22	15	4	10
Two parent	16	12	4	10
Welfare Receipt				
Utilized AFDC	26	19	4	15
Never utilized AFDC	17	13	4	10
Primary Language Spoken in Home				
Non-English	17	9	2	10
English	19	14	4	11
Child's Race/Ethnicity				
White, non-Hispanic	16	13	5	11
Black, non-Hispanic	30	17	3	11
Asian	16	9	3	12
Hispanic	17	11	3	10
Hawaiian Native/Pacific Islander	15	12	5	12
American Indian/Alaska Native	25	15	5	10
More than one race, non-Hispanic	20	17	2	12

Child's Race/Ethnicity by Maternal Education

High school diploma/equivalent or more				
White, non-Hispanic	15	13	5	10
Black, non-Hispanic	28	15	3	9
Asian	17	9	3	11
Hispanic	17	12	3	10
Less than high school diploma or equivalent				
White, non-Hispanic	28	23	5	17
Black, non-Hispanic	36	25	5	19
Asian	12	7	3	16
Hispanic	16	10	3	9

NOTE: Estimates based on first-time kindergartners. Developmental difficulties are defined as: activity level a lot more active than children the same age and attention, articulation and coordination are less well or much less well than children the same age.

SOURCE: National Center for Education Statistics (2000:Table 16).

in the areas of attention and articulation they were identified at twice the rate. Mother's education has a substantial impact on activity level, attention, and articulation ratings, as does single-parent status and welfare receipt. English speakers were identified with all characteristics more often than non-English speakers. Reported attention and activity level vary substantially by race, with black, American Indian, and mixed race children identified considerably more often than other race or ethnic groups. There were small differences in coordination and articulation by race, with black, Hispanic, Asian, and mixed race children identified less often with coordination problems than other races.

SUMMARY

While development occurs in a similar fashion for all children, developmental differences are the inevitable result of individual genetic and experiential variations and differing cultural and social contexts. In the past several decades, variability has been taken more seriously by social scientists who study children. From that research base we are learning ever more about the magnitude and sources of variation among children.

Chapter 2 suggested that development is fostered when a child is engaged in activities (both cognitive and social) that are at an appropriate level of difficulty: challenging, but within the reach of the child's competence. We suggested further that development is very much dependent on context, and that an adult who is responsive to the child's level of social, emotional, and cognitive development is a key feature of a supportive context. The research reviewed in this chapter suggests the variability of competencies in children by the end of the preschool years. In both cognitive and social skills, and in the physical and motor development that support those skills, young children vary enormously.

Biology's contribution to temperament, learning style, and motor facility clearly influences children's developmental pathways. To effectively foster growth in children with very different temperaments, learning styles, activity levels, and abilities to attend will require different types of interaction and opportunities to learn.

We know, moreover, that the resources (books, audio recordings, and the like) and activities (book reading, story telling, verbal interaction) to which children in higher-SES categories are exposed are strong correlates of cognitive development, and that SES is correlated with social and some forms of physical development as well. By the time children reach kindergarten, these differences are already noteworthy. If preschool programs are to help all children develop their potential in early years, those from less enriched environments will need opportunities to acquire the skills of those in more enriched environments, as well as to develop to the maximum the unique skill sets they bring to the formal school setting.

Children with disabilities vary as much as all children do in temperament, learning style, and family culture. In preschool, children with disabilities tend to have more extensive interactions with adults than with other children, which is the reverse of their age mates without disabilities. Children with disabilities are likely to initiate less often to other children and their initiations are more likely to be ignored. An adult who is responsive to the developmental needs of the child with disabilities will help facilitate relationships with other children. The inclusion of children with disabilities in child care settings is required by law, but beyond meeting the legal mandate, the addition of children with disabilities can add to the diversity, and thus the richness, of all children's experience.

Regarding cultural background, there is a solid knowledge base on variations around the world in children's social developmental pathways, such as those needed for collectivist values and those for societies that value independence and autonomy. In the United States, research is now being conducted on the various cultural groups that make up the population, for certain developmental psychologists are paying more careful attention to the influence of cultural background on the development of children's social and emotional capacities. Research on cultural background and schooling identify many factors as important. Among these are the effects of the knowledge base, social organization (value placed on working quietly, acceptance of help from unfamiliar adults, etc), and social rules of conversation (child initiating, "wait" time, etc).

Preschool Program Quality

THE DEFINITION OF QUALITY IN EARLY childhood education and care has many dimensions, including political and social dimensions, not all of which lend themselves to research and analysis (Bruner, 1985). Views of how and what children should learn at an early age are guided by cultural values that may be so transparent as to be invisible to most of us. Research can, nevertheless, inform the definition of best practice by providing information about the consequences of pedagogy for young children's learning, development, and well-being. This chapter summarizes research findings from five separate, but somewhat overlapping, literatures:

1. Studies of preschool programs designed to enhance the learning and development of economically disadvantaged children, including studies of model programs. These programs provide information about effective practices and the potential magnitude of preschool program effects on learning and development for this population.

2. Studies of the relationship between preschool program quality, or components of quality, and children's learning and development. These results are drawn both from research on model programs for disadvantaged children and from research on "naturally occurring" variations that compare children's experiences

and outcomes in community programs with different features. This research provides information about the effects of typical variations in program quality on the general population of children (including, but not limited to, economically disadvantaged children).

3. Studies of programs for English-language learners. This relatively small literature is similar to the first two, but it focuses specifically on the effects of variation in the approach to second-language acquisition on competence both in the primary language and in English.

4. Descriptions of exemplary international programs. This literature suggests features that contribute to program quality, but provides relatively little empirical verification.

5. Studies of clinical and program interventions for children with disabilities and the relationship of salient child and family characteristics to intervention methods. This research confirms the value of educational, therapeutic, and social services for infants and young children with disabilities.

PROGRAMS FOR
ECONOMICALLY DISADVANTAGED CHILDREN

Beginning in the early 1960s, preschool programs were developed to provide educational experiences to young children growing up in poverty. These programs sought to improve learning and development for these children in response to growing awareness of social inequalities and changing beliefs about the role of the environment in development. The context for these new efforts was vividly described by Caldwell and Richmond (1968:341):

> During the late 1950's and early 1960's a sure path to ostracism in the field of early childhood education was to emphasize attendance at nursery school as an influence on intellectual development. Debunking the Iowa studies [conducted at the Iowa Child Welfare Research Station of the State University of Iowa by Skeels, Wellman, and colleagues], which demonstrated intellectual gains associated with nursery school attendance, became a popular sport . . . and the implication that such an experience could have lasting cognitive effects was subject to ridicule.

Changing views led to a more positive reconsideration of the Iowa research (Skeels and Dye, 1939; Wellman, 1940; Skodak and Skeels, 1949; Skeels, 1966) and other studies (Spitz, 1945; Spitz and Wolfe, 1946). Theoretical support came from scholars who built on the work of Hebb (1949) and, later, Piaget. New work by Kirk (1958), Hunt (1961, 1964), and Bruner (1962) provided more support for a renewed emphasis on environmental intervention in the early years. Perhaps no one pushed the environmentalist view further than Bloom (1964), who argued that development was most sensitive to the influences of environment during periods of rapid growth and that half of adult intelligence was developed by age 5.

The preschool programs developed for disadvantaged children in the 1960s and 1970s not only built on this new work but also incorporated views of theory and practice from a wide variety of traditions in psychology and education. Despite the programs' emphasis on their potential cognitive benefits, most sought to enhance the development and well-being of the whole child (Day and Parker, 1977). Especially in the early years, they had to address concerns that preschool programs might negatively affect social and emotional development by separating children from their mothers (Caldwell and Smith, 1968). Researchers developed "model" programs specifically to investigate the potential for preschool education to influence the learning and development of economically disadvantaged children. Much of what is known about the nature and magnitude of preschool education's influences derives from rigorous studies of these model programs. Such studies also provide considerable information about the characteristics of highly effective programs.

Over the past four decades, many studies have been conducted of the immediate and short-term (one or two years) effects of programs on the learning and development of children from low-income families. Both quantitative research syntheses (that pool estimates across studies and apply statistical tests) and traditional best-evidence reviews have found that such programs produced meaningful gains in cognitive, social, and emotional development during the preschool years (White and Casto, 1985; McKey et al., 1985; Ramey et al., 1985). Although the studies of Head Start and public preschool programs have tended to employ weaker methodologies, these studies indicate that public programs have been able to produce the same types of immediate and short-term effects (Barnett, 1995, 1998). Also, public preschool programs have successfully provided broader services to improve children's nutrition and access to medical and dental services (Fosburg et al., 1984; Hale et al., 1990; Barnett and Brown, 2000).

The average size of the immediate effect of these preschool programs on cognitive development and achievement was about one-half of a standard deviation; effects in other domains tended to be slightly smaller (Barnett, 1998). Cross-study comparisons and a few planned within-study comparisons indicate that the magnitude of initial effects varies with the intensity and duration of the program (Ramey et al., 1985; Barnett and Camilli, in press; Wasik et al., 1990; St. Pierre et al., 1998). The programs with the largest initial effects on learning and development tended to be those that provided the greatest quantity of services (operating for more hours per year and continuing for more years) with high staff-to-child ratios (e.g., 1 to 3 for infants, 1 to 6 at ages 3 and 4) and highly qualified staff (Barnett and Camilli, in press; Frede, 1998).

There is some disagreement about the extent to which the effects of preschool education programs persist (Barnett, 1998; McKey et al., 1985; Woodhead, 1988; Haskins, 1989; Locurto, 1991; Spitz, 1986). In many studies—of both model programs developed by researchers and less intensive public programs—some of the estimated effects decline over time and are negligible several years after children leave the programs (see reviews by Barnett, 1998; White and Casto, 1985; McKey et al., 1985; Ramey et al., 1985). Some scholars have argued that fade-out occurs because of weaknesses in the schools that disadvantaged children attend after leaving the preschool programs (Lee and Loeb, 1995). Others (Herrnstein and Murray, 1994) have concluded that public programs like Head Start do not improve cognitive functioning, although more intensive and more costly preschool programs may do so. Close examination of the results from these studies suggests that there are long-term positive effects on children's learning and subsequent school success, although the effects on IQ decline over time (Barnett, 1998; Barnett and Camilli, in press).

A substantial body of empirical evidence indicates these preschool programs have prevented grade repetition and special education placements for disadvantaged children over the long term. A review of over 30 longitudinal studies by Barnett (1998) concluded that preschool programs serving disadvantaged children also produced long-term gains in achievement as measured by standardized tests. In drawing this conclusion, Barnett relied heavily on the findings of controlled experiments with sound longitudinal follow-ups that lost few study participants over time. The few studies that have examined high school graduation rates found sizable effects on these as well (Barnett, 1998).

In contrast to the findings for other outcomes, initial effects on IQ tests clearly disappear over time in the vast majority of studies. Why this occurs and how important it is are much less clear. There is considerable controversy about how well IQ measures intelligence in the way it is commonly understood by the general public (Sternberg and Detterman, 1986; Neisser et al., 1995). The lack of long-term gains in IQ, at the same time that such gains are produced in subject-matter-specific knowledge and skills and school success, raises similar questions. However, two of the most intensive programs, which began full-day, year-round educational child care in the first year of life and continued to age 5, produced very large initial IQ effects and some IQ advantage that persisted years after leaving the program (Garber, 1988; Campbell and Ramey, 1993). Even in these studies, the size of the effect on IQ declines over the years, while the improvements in achievement and school success do not (Barnett, 1998). It is also interesting that a similar program, with a primary focus on parents and relatively greater emphasis on social-emotional development, did not sustain effects on IQ even up to the end of the program (Lally et al., 1987).

The programs that researchers developed specifically to investigate the influence of preschool education on economically disadvantaged children are a useful source of information about positive influences on development. These programs have been found to be highly effective in producing immediate benefits for children and to produce longer-term effects in at least a dozen rigorous longitudinal studies. Some of the studies with the strongest outcomes were highly controlled random assignment experiments. Moreover, these programs seem to produce larger effects than ordinary public programs that have been less well funded and thus more constrained with respect to quality. These programs provide models for best practice. In developing these models, researchers drew on the wide range of theoretical and practical traditions that have influenced early childhood education in the United States, going back to Froebel and Seguin and including McMillan, Montessori, Dewey, Smith Hill, Gesell, Thorndike, Freud, and Piaget (Condry, 1983; Spodek, 1991).

Frede (1998) investigated commonalties and differences among the model programs with evidence of long-term effectiveness. The models she examined had been subject to outcome studies at least through elementary school, provided center-based preschool experiences for low-income children, and included in their reports written descriptions of their curriculum and classroom practices (see Table 4-1). Based on close analyses of these descriptions, the following factors were found to be present in most programs:

• Curriculum content and learning processes that cultivate school-related skills and knowledge, with a heavy focus on language development,
• Qualified teaching staff who use reflective teaching practices aided by highly qualified supervisors,
• Low teacher-child ratio and small class sizes,
• Intense and coherent programming, and
• Collaborative relationships with parents.

Detailed descriptions of the curricula used across the longitudinal studies exist for some programs (Bereiter and Engelmann, 1966; Garber, 1988; Karnes et al., 1972; Lally and Honig, 1977; Miller and Dyer, 1975; Palmer and Siegel, 1977; Ramey et al., 1982; Weikart, 1972; Weikart et al., 1967, 1978). Data based on actual classroom observation of the teacher practices are rare, although Weikart et al. (1978) provide an important exception. On the basis of the descriptions, Frede (1998) derived several generalizations about the process and content of the curricula employed by the model programs.

While classroom interactions are different from those at home

TABLE 4-1 Longitudinal Studies

Researcher	Age Group	Ratio	Group size	Duration
Abecedarian Project (Campbell and Ramey, 1994)	Infants, preschool	1:3 1:6	14 12	5 years
Brookline Early Education Project (Hauser-Cram et al., 1991)	Infants, preschool	1:1 1:6	18	5 years
Early Childhood Education Project (Sigel et al., 1973; Cataldo, 1978)	2-3 years	1:7	22	3 years
Early Training Project (Gray et al., 1982)	Preschool	1:5	20	2 or 3 years
Family Development Research Program (Honig and Lally, 1982)	Infants, preschool	1:4	8	5 years
Harlem Training Project (Palmer, 1983)	Preschool	1:1	NA	1-2 years
Infant Health and Development Program (Ramey et al., 1992; Infant Health and Development Program Consortium, 1990)	1-2 years 2-3 years	1:3 1:4	6 8	3 years
Milwaukee Project (Garber, 1988)	2 years 3 years preschool	1:2 1:3 1:7	?	6 years
Perry Preschool Project (Schweinhart and Weikart, 1993)	Preschool	1:5	20-25	2 years
Project CARE (Wasik et al., 1990)	Infants, preschool	1:3 1:6	14 12	5 years

SOURCES: Data from Frede (1998) and Lazar et al. (1977).

Intensity	Curriculum	Teacher Qualifications	Activities for Parents
Full-day	Interactive	Experienced paraprofessionals to certified teachers	Group meetings, home visits
Part- or full-day	Interactive	Certified teachers	Home visits, guided observation in classroom
Half-day	Interactive	Certified teachers and 2 paraprofessionals	None
Part-day 10 weeks summer	Structured interactive	Certified teacher	Weekly home visits during academic year
Full-day	Interactive but less structured	Paraprofessional— Home visitors/ professional teachers	Weekly home visits— informal class visits and daily notes home
2 week	2 tutoring approaches: concept training or discovery	Tutors change every 6 weeks—high school to Ph.D. candidate	None
Full-day	Interactive	Bachelor's degree with Early Childhood Education specialty	Home visits
Full-day	Cognitive curriculum	Paraprofessional/ certified teacher at 4 years	Job training, social services, home visits
Half-day	Interactive	Certified teachers	Weekly home visits
Full-day	Interactive	Experienced paraprofessionals to certified teachers	Group meetings, home visits

for all children, they were most dissimilar from the home settings of low-income and minority children (Heath, 1983). At least some of the time, teachers used a discourse pattern that engages children in an initiation-reply-evaluation sequence (Mehan, 1979). As an example, the teacher might ask, "Which of these do you think will float in water?" The child replies, "The cork." The teacher says, "Let's see if you are right." Preschool children also were introduced to such strategies for remembering as rehearsal and categorization (Cole et al., 1971; Wagner, 1978).

Although the models differed philosophically with respect to methods, program content was similar across programs because to some extent they all drew on traditional kindergarten and nursery school practices in the United States (Frede, 1998). Typical classroom activities and materials involved shapes, colors, sizes, numbers, animals, transportation, prepositions, seasons, and holidays. Programs shared a strong emphasis on language. Teachers provided a model of standard English and a context that provided opportunities and incentives for children to learn to speak so that they could be understood, to learn to understand others, and to express symbolic concepts through speech.

Of course, these model programs also differed in the focus of the teachers and the program developers. For example, some focused most intensely on cognitive development, while others focused more on social and emotional development (Day and Parker, 1977; Lazar et al., 1977). Despite their differences, the commonalties reported above appear to be sufficient to ensure that all of them produced significant gains in cognitive development. However, program differences may have produced some differences in cognitive effects and, to a greater extent, in social and emotional development. Research comparing these programs and others developed based on these models has accumulated over the years and provides significant insights into the importance of differences among the models.

Questions have been raised about the extent to which the results from longitudinal studies of high-quality interventions for preschool children from low-income families can be generalized to widespread, poorly funded programs (Barnett and Camilli, in press; Chubrich and Kelley, 1994; Haskins, 1989; Woodhead, 1988). The critics suggest that the public programs are not replicating the quality and intensity of the preschool programs in the original efficacy studies, and thus the same effects cannot be expected. Others believe that one preschool intervention is much the same as the next, and the positive benefits of the experimental programs studied in longitudinal research will automatically devolve on community-based programs. The empirical evidence supports the former view, namely, that less well-funded public programs do not provide the same quality of education and result in smaller benefits for learning and development. Barnett and Camilli (in press) note that studies of Head Start and public school preschool programs found smaller long-term effects on school success than did studies of model programs. Seppanen and colleagues (1993) found that preschool classrooms for disadvantaged children (Title I) did not provide regular activities dealing with mathematics, language, and science and were lacking in small-group interaction and individual attention. The Cost and Quality Team (1995) found that the majority of child care programs provide mediocre to low-quality experiences. These studies remind us that the quality of specific services provided in preschool programs determines the benefits low-income children will derive from them.

PRESCHOOL PROGRAM QUALITY AND CHILDREN'S LEARNING AND DEVELOPMENT

Model Programs

As Frede (1998) makes clear, determining the effects of curricula or teaching methods on young children is a complex and difficult task. A number of problems result from the difficulties of measuring learning and development in young children. Standardized tests of cognitive ability in early childhood are of questionable validity (Kamii, 1990). Measures of social development are problematic, since they often fail to discriminate adequately among children (Datta, 1983). Different curricular approaches have different goals; thus different outcomes should be expected, and comparing the programs on the same outcome measures can bias findings in favor of one approach or another. The same type of bias can occur in trying to measure treatment implementation:

the appropriate observation techniques for one approach may fail to discern important practices or failures in implementation of another approach.

Significant limitations of many early education comparison studies make it difficult to draw strong conclusions about the relative effectiveness of different curricula. Rarely are experimental methods used, which makes generalization questionable. When random assignment is not used, it is extremely difficult to disentangle the effects of the educational model from family characteristics that lead parents to choose a program using a particular approach, child characteristics that lead to the choice of a particular program that is thought to best meet the needs of the child, neighborhood characteristics, and other program characteristics that may be associated with choice of model. Another complication is that children's development is influenced by many factors, children influence their own environments, and development occurs in multiple domains, which may be differentially affected by particular methods.

Since the expansion of early childhood education that began in the 1960s, several studies comparing the effects of various program models have been reported and reviewed. The comparison studies were designed to determine whether a program based on one theory of learning and development was more beneficial to children's learning and development than one based on another theory. Children who attended classrooms using one program model were compared with children in classrooms using other models (Karnes et al., 1983; Miller and Bizzell, 1983, 1984; Weikart et al., 1978). Other possibly important sources of influence on learning and development, such as teacher-child ratio, class size, teacher training, and child characteristics, were held constant.

Reflecting the dominant interests of the era, the comparison studies reviewed here contrasted three basic types of curricula, which Goffin (1994) describes as direct instruction, traditional, and cognitive. In *direct instruction,* the teacher presents information to the children in structured, drill-and-practice group lessons that are fast-paced, teach discrete skills in small steps, and involve frequent praise. *Traditional approaches* flow from a belief that children must direct their own learning and will learn when they are ready, as long as the teachers provide stimulating materials and support for the children's choices. Socialization is often the main goal of this curriculum. *Cognitive curriculum* adherents view learning as an active exchange between the child and her environment, one key element of which is the teacher. In this model, teachers initiate activities designed to foster children's reasoning and problem-solving abilities, and they interact with children during child-designed activities to add new ideas or enhance learning. The open classroom and interactive curricula are both considered nondidactic because teachers rarely instruct children in groups on discrete skills, although they do use direct instruction with individual children.

Table 4-2 presents characteristics of the major curriculum comparison studies. Looking at results across these studies does not reveal consistent differences in child outcomes among the various curricula. Some studies report apparent differences in outcomes for subgroups, but these are all post-hoc comparisons.

In studies comparing direct instruction and cognitive-interactive curricula (Cole et al., 1991, 1993), researchers found that the different approaches failed to produce consistently differential results on measures of general cognitive abilities (McCarthy Scales), language development (TELD, PPVT-R), or highly specific skills similar to those taught in the direct instruction approach. These findings suggested that the direct instruction approach is not so narrow that children fail to obtain general learning gains and that the cognitive approach is not so general that children fail to learn specific skills. The researchers found some evidence of treatment-by-aptitude interactions, with children who scored lowest on pretest measures gaining more in the cognitive curriculum. However, these interactions were sufficiently small to raise questions about their practical significance (Cole et al., 1993; Mills et al., 1995).

In an experimental comparison with long-term follow-up, Schweinhart et al. (1986) found no significant differences in cognitive (IQ and achievement) outcomes. However, they found that a direct instruction model in preschool did not have the same effects on socialization as child-centered approaches. Children who attended the direct instruction program had higher rates of delinquency and were less willing to help others and participate in civic activities. The direct instruction model also appeared to be

TABLE 4-2 Curriculum Comparison Studies Completed*

Researcher	Ratio	Group Size	Duration
Miller (4 curricula)	1:7	15	1 year
Dale and Cole (2 curricula)			2 years
Karnes (5 curricula)	1:5 1:8	15 16	8 months
Weikart (3 curricula)	1:8	15-16	2 years

*Studies completed by a researcher who was a developer of one of the models compared.
SOURCES: Data from Dale and Cole (1988), Karnes et al. (1977, 1983), Miller and Bizzell (1983, 1984), Miller and Dyer (1975), Weikart et al. (1978).

less effective at preventing emotional impairments, as measured by placements in special education for emotional impairment or disturbance when compared with a cognitively oriented model and a "traditional" nursery school that allow for substantial initiation of activities by the child. These results have been questioned on methodological grounds by, among others, the developers of the direct instruction curriculum (Bereiter, 1986; Gersten, 1986). Their major complaint is that model developers should not evaluate the effects of their own models. If evaluator bias was introduced, it does not appear to have been through faulty program implementation. Training in the direct instruction model was provided by that model's developers. All three approaches were observed by 12 national experts in the field of early childhood education and care, who concluded that the classrooms and the teachers' explanations of their teaching were faithful examples of the differing models (Weikart et al., 1978).

Intensity	Curriculum	Teacher Qualifications	Activities for Parents
Full-day	4 curricula comparison: varying from highly structured to traditional	Unclear for all, some teachers had master's degrees	Head Start parent involvement
Part-day	2 curricula comparison: direct instruction and cognitive curriculum		
Part-day	5 curricula comparison: varying from highly structured to traditional	Certified teachers in at least 3 programs	2 curricula held parent conferences and school visits by parents
Part-day	3 curricula comparison: direct instruction, interactive, traditional	Certified teachers	Biweekly home visits

The Planned Variation Head Start study (Rivlin and Timpane, 1975), in which multiple curricula were implemented in Head Start Programs throughout the country, produced inconclusive results about differential effects. Maccoby and Zellner (1970) reviewed 10 contrasting models used in Project Follow-Through, which followed preschool children from Head Start. These programs were referred to as experimental *intervention programs* and were designed or modified to continue the preschool models into the primary grades. Miller (1979) classified the competing program models as "regular" or "traditional," the latter based on "the prevailing wisdom at established child development institutes" (p. 196). The regular models were generally school-like in that they offered formal instruction in preacademic skills involving letter recognition and learning sounds and numbers (Miller, 1979). Roopnarine and Lohnson (1993) use the term *approach* rather than model to suggest main elements or directions of the program rather than ideal and detailed versions of how they should be implemented.

No significant differences in child cognitive outcomes were consistently found among the different models or between the model programs and typical Head Start. There was considerable variation within different classrooms using the same model as well as between classrooms using different models. However, the comparisons were fraught with possible confounds. Fidelity of implementation was highly variable; the same supervisors were used for model and regular Head Start classrooms, making treatment diffusion likely; and, as stated above, outcome measures appropriate for one curriculum are unlikely to be appropriate for another.

One of the difficulties in making cross-program comparisons is that programs can vary on many dimensions that are hard to control and may be related to program quality (Frede, 1998). Many characteristics influence a program's capacity to provide children with frequent optimal interactions with adults, other children, and the physical environment. If experimental studies were conducted on a large scale with large numbers of classrooms, variations in the other program characteristics could be expected to average out. But most curriculum comparison studies have been quite small.

The Family and Child Experiences Survey (FACES) provides some recent evidence regarding Head Start outcomes, though it is at best suggestive as the research design is weak for addressing questions of outcomes. The study employed no pretest or comparison group. Zill and colleagues (1998) found the median standard score on the Peabody Picture Vocabulary Test (PPVT-III) to be 89.5 for Head Start 4-year-olds in the spring prior to kindergarten entry. They suggest that this score is 4 to 8 points higher than would be expected for a typical low-income child of the same age. They also find that PPVT-III scores increase with program quality. This would be expected if the program was responsible for gains, but it would also be true if less disadvantaged children attended better Head Start programs. Unfortunately, there is no way to judge accurately how Head Start children in the study would have scored on the PPVT-III without intervention. Findings of very small effects on child development in randomized trials of the Comprehensive Child Development Program and Even Start (where Head Start provided much of the service) suggest that an estimated effect of 4 points might be an upper bound (St. Pierre et al., 1998). Estimates in this range are smaller than the estimates in randomized trials of more intensive interventions (Barnett and Boocock, 1998).

Research on Natural Variation

A second major source of information about "what works" is provided by research that takes advantage of naturally occurring variations among early childhood programs. Such studies draw inferences about what works by examining the correlation between program characteristics and program outcomes. Some studies relate program structure (e.g., class size, teacher qualifications) directly to child development and learning. Others relate program structure to program processes, i.e., teacher practices and children's activities in the classroom. Finally, some studies relate measures of program processes to child development and learning. Thus, program quality (what works) may be thought of at the levels of both structure and process, and structure is thought to affect child development and learning through its influence on process. A limitation of these studies is that program characteristics and child outcomes may vary together because both are influenced by another variable such as family background, and it can be difficult for statistical procedures to correctly adjust for the effects of these other influences.

One strand of this research investigates the effects on children of programs that follow professional guidelines for developmentally appropriate practices, called DAP (Bredekamp and Copple, 1997).

The research on developmentally appropriate practices, focusing on natural variations across many community settings and with different groups of children, indicates that developmentally appropriate practices, similar to those used in the child-centered curricula, do promote better child development outcomes than non-DAP practices in preschool and child care settings. One study (Charlesworth et al., 1993; Burts et al., 1990) found that the developmental appropriateness of the kindergarten classroom was particularly important for low SES children. Such children, placed in developmentally inappropriate kindergartens, experienced more stress (e.g., nail biting, fighting, tremors, feeling sick) and received lower grades in school than did their counterparts in developmentally appropriate programs. Another study (Holloway and Reichart-Erikson, 1988) found more positive interactions among children in child care classrooms rated as developmentally appropriate. In a more recent study of preschool programs for children from low-income families, those who attended developmentally appropriate programs as opposed to direct instruction classrooms were more successful academically as assessed by teacher grades of the extent to which they mastered basic skills in elementary school (Marcon, 1992, 1994). At least one study of preschool programs serving children from middle-class families (Hyson et al., 1990) found results similar to those for low-SES children. The middle-class children who attended developmentally appropriate programs did slightly better than those in highly academic ones on measures of academic skills and creativity. They also exhibited fewer anxious behaviors. In this study, Hyson and colleagues noted a relationship between parental beliefs and practices and the type of center their child attended.

FINDINGS ACROSS EARLY EDUCATION APPROACHES

In our review of program approaches, we found the following converging results across studies.

Teacher-Child Ratio and Class Size

Both class size and staff-child ratio critically influence program quality and children's learning and development. Class size in the model preschool programs that provide much of the research on positive outcomes for children tended to be low even compared with the recommendations of the National Association for the Education of Young Children. For example, the two best-known programs—the High/Scope Perry Preschool and the Abecedarian programs—had class sizes of 12 to 13 children with 2 teachers (Weikart et al., 1967; Ramey and Campbell, 1984). Small classes and better ratios enable teachers to provide more individual attention and nurturing interactions. They are associated with higher scores on global measures of quality and, more specifically, more extensive teacher-child interaction, more individualization, less restrictive and controlling teacher behavior, and children engaging in more social interaction, more extensive and complex language, and more complex play (McGurk et al., 1995; Layzer et al., 1993; Clarke-Stewart and Gruber, 1994; Howes, 1997; Kontos et al., 1997; Howes et al., 1992). Smith (1999) found that smaller group size was associated with more child initiations and more opportunities for teachers to work on extending language, mediating children's social interactions, and encouraging and supporting exploration and problem solving.

Given the effects of group size and ratio on classroom processes, effects on learning and child development should be expected to follow. Research widely confirms this result. Studies of large samples of programs that encompass the range of class sizes and ratios currently experienced by children in the United States consistently find that smaller preschool classes and higher teacher-child ratios are associated with greater cognitive gains as measured by IQ, achievement tests, and school success and better social outcomes, including classroom behavior, for children (Phillipsen et al., 1997; Dunn, 1993; Clarke-Stewart and Gruber, 1994; Howes, 1997; Howes et al., 1992; Kontos et al., 1997; Phillips et al., 1987, 1986). The National Day Care Study (Ruopp et al., 1979) determined that even when ratios were held constant, smaller classes were better for children.

Research on kindergarten and the early grades provides further evidence of the importance of class size for young children. Moreover, some of these studies are experiments or quasi-experiments in which class size was systematically varied so that they provide greater confidence that the results are not due to some coincidental factor (Achilles et al., 1995; Russell, 1985). In Australia, Russell (1985) found that reducing kindergarten class size led to more staff interaction with children and less teasing and annoying of others by children. In the United States, smaller class sizes were found to increase student achievement, and children from lower-income families and inner cities benefited most from smaller classes (Achilles et al., 1995; Ferguson, 1998; Krueger, 1997; Wenglinsky, 1997; Mosteller, 1995). Large-scale studies in

Tennessee, North Carolina, and Wisconsin have found that reducing class size to 15 in the early grades produced substantial long-term gains in student achievement (Achilles et al., 1995). The largest of these studies found that reducing class size from 22-26 to 13-17 children in kindergarten through grade 3 increased student achievement in reading, math, and science through middle school, decreased grade repetition, and increased high school graduation rates (Boyd-Zaharias and Pate-Bain, 2000; Krueger, 1999; Finn et al., 1999).

The distinction between ratio and class size is important, although it is difficult to disentangle class size and ratio in most studies. Undoubtedly, both are important, but the studies that are able to disentangle them (e.g., Mosteller, 1995; Boyd-Zaharias and Pate-Bain, 2000) indicate that improving the ratio without reducing class size does not yield the same effects. Randomized trials in kindergarten through grade 3 compared the effects of adding an aide to the classroom to reductions in class size that produced the same adult-child ratio and found that the added aide did not produce the substantial, persistent gains in achievement obtained from reducing class size (Mosteller, 1995). Thus, a class size of 22 with a teacher and two aides is not an adequate substitute for a class size of 15 with a teacher and one aide.

The existing research is not sufficient to suggest the optimal class size for children at each age. However, it does indicate that smaller class sizes and better ratios than are now commonly required would benefit children, especially children from low-income families. Ratios in the experimental literature rarely exceeded one teacher for every 7 children, which is better than prevailing practices in many education and care programs today (U.S. General Accounting Office, 1995). Only one state requires child care centers to maintain a ratio of one teacher for 7 or 8, 3- and 4-year old children, and regulations in other states range from 10 to 20 children per teacher. Class sizes in early care and education rarely are as small as 15 and frequently exceed 20 (Gormley, 1995). Moreover, unless they are in a Head Start program (where standards are relatively high), low-SES children, who would benefit most from small class sizes, tend to have the largest class sizes in early care and education as well as in kindergarten programs.

Program Intensity and Coherence

Although one would expect the most effective programs to be those with the most intense and long-lasting interventions, comparisons among the longitudinal research studies allow only general conclusions regarding the benefits of program intensity and duration (McKey et al., 1985; Ramey et al., 1985). As Tables 4-1 and 4-2 show, some effective programs offered only a half-day program during the school year, and others began intervention in infancy and continued through to elementary school; one of these continued intervention in the early grades for some of the children. Another study began in preschool but provided intervention into the elementary school. Two of the studies that began in infancy are the only longitudinal studies to find lasting IQ gains for the experimental group, with the exception of the Harlem Study (where design limitations raise questions about this finding). The Harlem Study offered one-to-one tutoring to boys in Harlem twice a week at age 2 or 3. In addition, the Perry Project that offered one or two years of preschool intervention has shown remarkable effects of the program into adulthood (Schweinhart et al., 1993). Given the number of ways in which intensity and continuity of service can vary, these must be viewed as more than a simple function of time in a program. Obviously, two 1-hour sessions per week one-on-one with a teacher is intensive in a different way than 6-10 hours every weekday in a classroom. Other programs have sought to increase intensity with lower ratios, home visiting components, and high levels of engagement.

Responses to Parents

The attitudes of early childhood practitioners toward parents also show both similarities and differences across early childhood programs. Early in the century, parents came to be considered crucial players, as the new social and health sciences informed them about the best ways to rear their children. William John Cooper, then U.S. Commissioner of Education commented, "No longer may we assume that it [parenting] is an inborn capacity. So to mother's heart must now be added mother's head" (Powell, 1991:93). In early childhood classrooms, parents were encouraged to observe or to work with children under the guidance of a professional teacher, thereby joining parents' involvement and children's education (Schlossman, 1986).

Attitudes toward parents varied according to social class. Unlike preschools and centers serving low-income children and those with special needs, middle-class nursery schools assumed that parents were interested in and capable of educating themselves. They were offered voluntary opportunities for learning and involvement in their children's education, and their participation was expected but not required. This contrasted with the view that poor parents need to be encouraged to change their childrearing practices. Child care programs, organized and administered by social service agencies, tended to view families as distressed and instructed poor and immigrant families on appropriate childrearing. The interest of early childhood programs in educating parents about child development was spurred by new research. In general, over the century, parent education moved from a focus on physical health (primarily sanitation and inoculations), to mental health at midcentury (relationships and emotional well-being), and to cognitive and social development (school success and social tractability) as the century ended (Bowman, 1997).

Many believe that helping parents improve their skills as caregivers is an effective method of improving children's life chances; however, according to St. Pierre et al. (1998), experience has shown that programs for parents alone do not influence children's development as strongly as do programs that involve children directly. Most of the longitudinal studies reviewed earlier in this chapter combined center-based experiences for children with extensive parent involvement components. Weekly or biweekly home visits by the child's teacher, parent group meetings, and parent involvement in the classroom were methods used by many of the programs. In most programs, the staff strove to establish a collaborative relationship with the parents in which knowledge about the child was shared from both the home and the classroom perspective. Frede (1998) suggests that this intimate and collegial relationship would further two goals. First, it would help parents in their interactions with the child. Second, it would help the teacher understand the child better and thereby facilitate more effective teaching in the classroom. Not only would this understanding of the child as an individual be beneficial, but the teacher would also have a better understanding of the contexts in which the child must function, of the parent's aims and hopes for the child, and of the values of the child's culture. Frede (1998) posits that this collaboration would result in the adults helping the children make sense of their worlds, rather than leaving it up to the child to integrate dissimilar contexts.

Few current early childhood programs continue to offer the kind of parent involvement characteristic of programs in the experimental studies. In most Head Start programs, if home visits are offered, they are infrequent, and the child's classroom staff (Brush et al., 1993; Zigler and Styfco, 1994) does not conduct them. Child care centers and other community programs are unlikely to involve most parents in activities other than occasional meetings or parent conferences (U.S. General Accounting Office, 1995). The extent to which program effects on children could be enhanced by improved parent involvement is unclear. Although the theoretical basis for efficacy is clear, many current efforts to work with parents do not appear to be effective (Boutte, 1992 ; White et al., 1992; Gomby et al., 1999). Given this apparent discrepancy, rigorous research aimed at identifying highly effective parent involvement strategies would be extremely valuable.

Staff Qualifications

Decades of research on teaching have found the teacher's intellectual abilities to be a strong predictor of how much a child learns from a teacher (Hanushek, 1971; Murnane and Phillips, 1981; Ferguson, 1998). In addition, teachers who attended "better" (more selective) colleges are associated with higher student achievement (Ballou and Podgursky, 1997; Ferguson, 1998). Findings of research on early childhood care and education are entirely consistent with the larger literature on teacher effectiveness.

Early childhood teachers' education and training have been linked to global measures of program quality, language and social exchanges between teachers and children, enhanced classroom literacy environments, more positive and less negative teacher affect, and better child behavior and development

(Barnett et al., 1999; Barnett et al., 1987; Clarke-Stewart and Gruber, 1994; Howes and Olenick, 1986; Whitebook et al, 1989; Howes et al., 1992; Ruopp et al., 1979). While any teacher education related to early childhood development or education is better than none, teachers with bachelor's (or higher) degrees in early childhood development appear to be most effective (Arnett, 1989; Tizard et al., 1976; Ruopp et al., 1979; Finkelstein, 1983; Whitebook et al., 1989; Dunn, 1993; Howes, 1997). Teacher compensation also is strongly related to program quality. Teacher compensation rates in early education and care are quite low compared with other fields; higher pay allows programs to attract and retain more highly qualified teachers (Whitebook et al., 1993). Employing qualified teachers who are satisfied with their compensation is associated with programs providing higher-quality early childhood experiences for children (Phillipsen et al., 1997; Scarr et al., 1994).

Why does a teacher of preschool-aged children need a college degree and specialized preparation in early childhood education? The research suggests that while young children are capable of learning a vast amount quickly and with enthusiasm, what and how much they learn are highly dependent on the adults with whom they interact. Adults provide the structure and support for children's learning through the activities they choose, the concepts they stress, and the frequency of their interactions with children. For example, the frequency of meaningful conversation with adults, along with the adults' uses of vocabulary and grammar, strongly influences a child's verbal knowledge. If early childhood teachers are to meet the needs of children individually and in groups and to design curricula and plan interactions that are meaningful they require a grounding in the content and methods of early childhood education and a sound knowledge of early learning and child development. They also need a rich, integrated subject matter mastery, if they are to artfully weave skill and content learning into activities. In most programs reporting increased social and educational achievement, the teachers are highly educated, specially trained to work with young children, well supervised, and actively involved in program planning and evaluation.

Teachers as Reflective Practitioners

Another important commonality across effective programs using specific models was that the teachers/caregivers were involved in conducting research and in model development (Frede, 1998). There is good reason to believe that this led them to be more effective teachers and was not simply an example of the Hawthorne effect, in which involvement in any innovation enhances outcomes. In most programs, the teachers were either highly educated or specially trained to work with young children or already had years of supervised experience. In addition, teachers were engaged in regular reflection on their teaching practices, with support from the research and curriculum specialists. As Neilson (1990) has suggested, teaching at its best is research: teachers generate questions, gather data, test hypotheses, and draw conclusions. In the studies reviewed by Frede (1998), this process was systematized and augmented by teachers' interactions with the research teams. As the following sample excerpts from program descriptions indicate, in the experimental programs, teachers and other staff met often to discuss the program and the development of individual children:

> The research staff offered consulting service on all aspects of the program. Weekly seminars were held for the entire preschool staff in order to discuss with authorities in various fields the topics pertinent to the operation of the program. . . . There was a constant effort to meet individual needs . . . to evaluate each child's understanding of an experience (Weikart et al., 1967:76, 24).

> During the year, staff held weekly case conferences, in which the progress, problems and strengths of a particular youngster were discussed in depth. . . . Plans were drawn up for possible ways to enhance the child's participation in the program. . . . Input from every staff member was valued when such a problem arose and over time many became more skillful in helping individual children (Lally et al., 1987:8-9).

> *Teachers are given inservice training and consultative help in assessing children's needs, setting objectives, planning and implementing activities that will stimulate particular kinds of communication and in evaluating their own interactions with children. . . . Consultants helped them to select objectives to work on in the classroom each week, and guided them in devising activities that would help children reach the objectives set (Ramey et al., 1982:163-165).*

> *An ongoing training program that included group meetings, on the job training, and annual seminars was implemented by the curriculum supervisor. . . . The second portion of the group meetings centered around the personal needs of the caregivers and sensitizing the caregivers to the needs of the children. . . . Discussions emphasized personal attitudes toward specific children, education, . . . specific behavior. . . . This enabled placement of each child with a caregiver who felt positively about him/her (Garber, 1988:42-43).*

This attention to teacher thinking, planning, and evaluating with outside support can be seen across very different curricular approaches and is an essential feature of some curriculum models (e.g., see the discussion below of Reggio Emilia). In discussing the traditional, child-centered curriculum employed in the High/Scope Curriculum Demonstration Project, Weikart quotes the classroom teachers: "The specific plans are formulated on a day-to-day basis, since the plans for one day depend on the successes or failures of the day before. Just as important as the planning is the evaluation immediately following each day" (Weikart, 1972:196). But this approach was not limited to the nondidactic programs. Joseph Glick commented, after observing all three of the classrooms in this study, "Common to all of the groups is the tremendous amount of preparation" (cited in Weikart et al., 1978:50). There is evidence in both the Curriculum Demonstration Project and the Karnes comparison study (Karnes, 1983) that even the teachers in the "programmed" approach spent time reflecting on their practice, meeting with curriculum experts, and making adjustments to make the program fit the children they were teaching. By contrast, caregivers who work in community child care programs and even many preschool teachers in public programs lack time for planning, reflection, and assessment, and few receive regular supervision by trained educational leaders (Fenichel, 1992; Jorde-Bloom, 1988).

The proponents of the teacher as a reflective practitioner hold the view that reflection leads to improved and more expert teaching (Richardson, 1994). In the model programs studies in the 1960s and 1970s, teachers were given time to reflect and evaluate. Time was structured for this to occur through interactions with other teachers and with outside experts. The outside experts came into the classroom to conduct observations, by which they enhanced their ability to facilitate the teachers' reflections. In addition, teachers had opportunities to discuss their reflections with children's parents on a regular and intimate basis.

Influences of Classroom Activities on Children's Learning and Development

A considerable number of studies have investigated the effects of the quality of early education and care environments on children's abilities. These studies examine teachers' behavior and their interactions and relationships with children, as well as child behavior and children's interactions with their peers and the physical environment of the classroom and playground. The most commonly used measure of quality is the Early Childhood Environmental Rating Scale—ECERS (see Box 4-1; Harms and Clifford, 1980). However, evidence of the relationship between classroom processes and child outcomes is not limited to any one approach to measuring process quality.

McCartney (1984) examined the quality of nine child care centers in Bermuda using the ECERS. The range of ECERS summary scores for these nine centers was moderately large (ranging from 66.5 to 191). McCartney found that the ECERS summary scores for the child care centers were moderately correlated ($r = 0.23$) with the children's receptive vocabulary scores (PPVT-R). In a related study, McCartney et al., (1985) compared 22 disadvantaged children in Bermuda attending a high-quality, government-run intervention program with 144 children attending other child care programs in Bermuda of varying quality on intellectual, lan-

---

BOX 4-1
The Early Childhood Environmental Rating Scale

The ECERS is a rating scale designed for preschool classes, which provides an assessment of aspects of the curriculum, the environment, teacher-child interactions, and teaching practices in the classroom (Bryant et al., 1989). Based on a three-hour observation in the classroom, each item on the ECERS is scored from 1 to 7. Descriptions are anchored at odd numbers (1 = inadequate, 3 = minimal, 5 = adequate, 7 = excellent). A summary score can be obtained by totaling scores on the 37 subscales.

---

guage, and social skills. Children were age 3 or older. Although the mothers of the children in the intervention group had lower IQ scores and were of lower occupational status than mothers of children in the comparison group, the intervention group children were rated by their caregivers as having better communicative skills than the children attending other child care programs. There were no differences between the two groups on ratings of maladjustment or dependency. When the children in the intervention group were compared with children of similar family background, these findings held and, in addition, the children in the intervention group had higher scores on both the Peabody Picture Vocabulary Test—Revised (PPVT-R) and the Preschool Language Assessment Instrument.

In contrast to the previous findings, Kontos and Fiene (1991) found near-zero correlations between ECERS scores for Pennsylvania child care centers and children's language ability (Slossom-IQ and a subscale of the Classroom, Behavior Inventory, and language scores Test of Early Language Development), a finding that may be attributable to the relatively restricted range of the ECERS scores for the centers in this sample (from 111 to 176), compared with the McCartney sample.

Simple correlations between ECERS scores and children's receptive vocabulary scores are potentially misleading because they do not account for the entering abilities of the preschool children. Entering abilities may covary with the quality of child care centers for the same reasons that better public schools are found in neighborhoods with more advantaged families (Coleman et al., 1966; Jencks, 1972). Thus the higher-quality child care centers as measured by the ECERS may have more advantaged children at their exit from child care because those children were more advantaged upon entry into child care.

ECERS is a global measure of quality that has many components. Researchers have attempted to reduce the causal ambiguity in ECERS analyses by controlling for family background and home environment and by using additional measures of quality (e.g., Kontos, 1991; Phillips et al, 1987; Goelman and Pence, 1988). A recent example is provided by a study in which Bryant et al. (1994) measured the quality of 32 Head Start classrooms in North Carolina. It also measured the cognitive ability of 145 children from these classes using the Kaufman ABC (K-ABC), a normed test that provides a mental processing composite standard score and an achievement standard score. The quality of the home environment was assessed using the Home Screening Questionnaire, completed during an interview with the parent. The Home Screening Questionnaire included questions about the language stimulation in the environment, schedule and organization at home, use of punishment by parents, and family activities. When home environment was controlled statistically, ECERS scores were still predictive of children's K-ABC mental processing composite and achievement subscales. These data provide further evidence that the preschool environment can have positive effects on children's abilities, although in this case the abilities measured were more generally cognitive, rather than strictly linguistic.

Schliecker et al. (1989) also accounted for home variables in their analyses. They examined the quality of 11 Montreal child care centers using the ECERS. The range of ECERS summary scores was moderately large (from 93 to 239). Schliecker and colleagues found relations between ECERS scores and children's receptive vocabulary scores (PPVT-R) (beta = 0.29) after the socioeconomic status of the family was controlled (R^2 increment = 0.07; $p < 0.01$).

That correlation has been observed between ECERS scores and children's development is consistent with the view that ECERS measures a general construct related to center quality.

Harms and Clifford (1980) report high content validity (78 percent agreement of importance among experts), and subscales provide some information about specific program components and activities (e.g., physical environment and resources, language and reasoning activities, teacher-child interactions). Yet it is possible for similar totals to mask important differences between programs and even for the subscales do not capture all of the differences among programs that one would expect to contribute to quality. Additional measures with greater specificity are required to investigate the relative importance of various aspects of quality for enhancing children's experiences and development. A number of other quality measures have been developed, some with a much more specific focus (e.g., Arnett, 1989; High/Scope Educational Research Foundation, 1998; Howes and Stewart, 1987; Stipek et al., 1992). Two examples of research with other measures are provided below.

Frede et al. (1993) investigated the effects of specific preschool teacher behaviors associated with developmentally appropriate practice on children's cognitive skills at entry to first grade (*Cognitive Skills Assessment Battery*, Boehm and Slater, 1981). An advantage of this study was that a pretest measure (DIAL-R, Mardell-Czudnowzki and Goldenberg, 1984) was employed to adjust for preexisting differences in children's abilities. Frede and colleagues not only found that the magnitude of child gains varied with their global assessment of program quality, but also that more positive child cognitive development was predicted by such specific teacher behaviors as modeling appropriate communication techniques, extending children's activities and problem solving by making suggestions, and using a variety of strategies to make children's recall time (reporting back to the group) interesting.

The National Institute of Child Health and Human Development's Study of Early Child Care (NICHD Early Child Care Research Network, 1996) is a 10-site longitudinal study of 1,364 children assessed at 6, 15, 24, and 36 months of age in five types of nonmaternal child care (center, child care homes, in-home sitters, grandparents, and fathers). Assessments included observations of the child's child care environment, of the child's home environment, and standardized measures of the child's cognitive and language development. In contrast to other instruments such as the ECERS, an observational instrument, the Observational Record of Caregiving Environments (ORCE), was developed to focus on caregivers' behaviors with a specific child in addition to observations of what was happening in a classroom as a whole.

Results from the NICHD study so far indicate that child and family characteristics are the most significant predictors of child cognitive and language outcomes. Child care variables, however, consistently make an additional small but statistically significant contribution. Quality of provider-child interaction (more positive caregiving and language stimulation) was related to better language scores when the children were 15, 24, and 36 months old. The number of hours of out-of-home care was unrelated to language outcomes.

PROGRAMS FOR ENGLISH-LANGUAGE LEARNERS

In the United States, at least one in seven people speak a language other than English in the home (U.S. Bureau of the Census, 1997). Head Start (SocioTechnical Research Applications, Inc., 1996) reports that 74 percent of its students speak English, 22 percent speak Spanish, and 4 percent speak one of 139 other languages. What is the most beneficial language environment for use in early childhood programs that include children who have home languages other than English?

Tabors (1997) asserts that early childhood education and care programs functioning currently can be divided in three major groups: first-language classrooms, bilingual classrooms, and English-language classrooms (described in Table 4-3). Below we present examples of these types of programs.

The Carpinteria Preschool Program is an example of a first-language classroom. The teachers and children are native speakers of Spanish, and Spanish is the language used in the program. An evaluation study of the Carpinteria Preschool Program shows positive effects of first-language (L1) use on second-language (L2) acquisition when the children are older (Campos and Rosemberg, 1995). Even though their preschool program was conducted entirely in Spanish, by first grade almost half of the Carpinteria children were fluent in English on the Bilingual Syntax Measure, com-

TABLE 4-3 Types of Preschool Education Settings for Children from Other than English-Speaking Homes in the United States

	First-Language Classroom	Bilingual Classroom	English-Language Classroom
Teachers	Native speakers of L1[a]	Bilingual in L1 and English or native speaker of L1 paired with native speaker of English	Native speakers of English
Children	Native speakers of L1	All native speakers of L1 or mixture of L1 and English speakers	Native speakers of L1 or native speakers of different L1s or either of above and English speakers
Classroom Organization	All interaction in L1	Interaction split between L1 and English	All interaction in English
Language Outcomes	Development of L1; no development of English	Maintenance or development of L1, while also developing English	Development of English; no maintenance or development of L1

SOURCE: Tabors (1997:4); used by permission.

[a]L1 = any specific native language that is not English.

pared with fewer than 10 percent of English-language learners from child care and other programs. Campos and Rosenberg concluded (p. 46):

> There was no evident delay in the rate of English acquisition by the Carpinteria Preschool students, and they demonstrated competency in applying their English language skills. When compared with the language-minority comparison preschool group, they acquired English language fluency faster, transitioned out of bilingual education classrooms sooner, and achieved in English language classrooms and on English language standardized tests better. First language development in their preschool program did

not interfere or delay their second language learning. Instead the results suggest that they were better prepared to understand and utilize opportunities in their learning environment.

Furthermore, the investigators reported that these students had apparently maintained their bilingual skills and that almost all were expected to graduate from high school.

Several studies have examined bilingual programs and English-language programs on overall language and cognitive development (see August and Hakuta, 1997). Recall from Table 4-3 that bilingual programs have teachers who are bilingual in L1 and English or are native speakers of L1 paired with a native speaker of English. Children in bilingual programs are all native speakers of L1 or a mixture of L1 and English speakers. Classroom interactions are split between L1 and English. Winsler et al. (1999) compared low-income, Spanish-speaking Mexican-American children in a bilingual (Spanish and English) preschool program with those staying at home. The 3- and 4-year-old children in the study were living at a poverty income level and had a demonstrated need for child care. The comparison group was equivalent in income level and neighborhood/school zone but did not attend formal child care. Children who attended the bilingual preschool had gains in Spanish-language development parallel to those of children who stayed home; they also had greater increases in English-language proficiency over time, replicating the findings of a similar study by Rodriguez et al. (1995). Paul and Jarvis (1992) compared English-language learners in bilingual and monolingual prekindergarten classrooms and found positive outcomes for the children in the bilingual classrooms on a criterion-referenced test, the Chicago Early Assessment and Remediation Laboratory.

An English-language classroom (Language Acquisition Project) has been described by Bunce (1995), Rice (1991), and Rice and Wilcox (1990, 1995). Recall from Table 4-3 that in English-language classrooms, the teacher is a native speaker of English and the children are native speakers of one or more L1s, possibly including English. All classroom interactions are in English.

The Language Acquisition Project served two groups of English speaking students (typically developing and those with specific language impairments) and students speaking languages other than English. The program focussed on verbal activities and the encouragement of verbal interaction among the children. All three groups of children made significant progress in learning English.

While all three approaches to teaching language-minority students have been shown to have positive effects on langugage development, the research does not allow for direct comparison of the three methods with each other. As with much of the research reviewed here, the design of the studies does not allow for a definitive conclusion.

EARLY CHILDHOOD PROGRAMS IN OTHER COUNTRIES

Taking a close look at early childhood programs abroad brings into relief what the United States has in common with other countries, what features are in some sense distinctively American, and what options are foreclosed and left open as we consider how best to educate young children in America. We are accustomed to thinking of the United States as being part of the industrialized world, as represented by the G-7 and the Organization for Economic Cooperation and Development (OECD), and we share with others in those wealthy groups low rates of infant and child mortality and high rates of school enrollment. In certain other respects, however, the United States resembles the poor countries of the world: a central government that takes little or limited *action* in the area of early childhood, and a lack of collective standards for the care and education of young children. What is distinctively American is the amount and quality of thinking, imagination, research, analysis, and debate about young children that goes on, as about families generally.

Programs first imagined and experimented with in the United States have become national policy elsewhere. In Europe there are countries in which publicly funded and regulated programs for preschool-aged children are the norm. These programs permit us to see what can happen when early education is taken on as a public responsibility.

In preparation for this report, the committee held a workshop, "Global Perspectives on Early Childhood Education." Early childhood education in Japan and Reggio Emilia, Italy, drew particular attention. Susan Holloway's description (1999)[1] of Japanese preschools emphasized their ideological and programmatic diversity, in contrast with the group-oriented preschools described in the literature. The directors and teachers of all ideologies and programs worked long hours and could be found in the schools in the evening, although the pupils were there only four hours a day. This can be interpreted in terms of the role perfectionism of Japanese workers, including housewives and mothers, as described in the anthropological literature on Japan. Workers identify with their jobs and strive to do well to an extent that looks extreme to a foreign observer. Similarly, in Reggio Emilia, Rebecca New (1999—see footnote 1) and Jerome Bruner (1999—see footnote 1), describe an extraordinary commitment and devotion to the children, quite apart from the content of the pedagogy.

These examples and others suggest that the overseas cases of early education taken to be exemplary are ones in which the teachers and others involved view their jobs as highly professional, whether inspired by a pedagogy that rests on philosophical and political premises, as in Reggio Emilia, or by an emotional identification with an educational role, as in Japan. This level of commitment and dedication, however inspired by ideology, does not occur in an economic and structural vacuum. As Boocock et al. (1999) say:

> Some indicators of quality considered essential by American evaluators are accorded less importance elsewhere. For example, the highly regarded preschools in the Italian town of Reggio Emilia . . ., as well as the French *ecole maternelle* and most Japanese nursery schools, routinely have class sizes and child-to-staff ratios far in excess of NAEYC standards. . . . What these high quality programs do have, however, is well-trained personnel. . . . [I]n nations with high proportions of well-trained teachers and caretakers, salaries tend to be relatively high and staff turnover relatively low (p. 9).

In other words, in the European and Japanese preschools where teachers are observed to be devoted to their pedagogical tasks, they are not only trained and certified but also have good

---

[1]See the agenda book for the workshop, *Global Perspectives on Early Childhood Education*, held April 6-7, 1999, at the National Academy of Sciences.

enough pay and security of employment to build socially respectable careers as early childhood educators. The authors imply that training and staff stability may to some extent offset the disadvantage (by American standards) of large child-to-staff ratios. These systems have chosen to invest in teachers' careers rather than keeping classroom ratios small. While this suggests that programs in the United States might benefit from increased investment in teaching staff, it does not follow that this should be financed by increasing class size and student-teacher ratio. The large ratios in Japanese classrooms have been acknowledged to produce a tendency toward chaos in the classroom (McGurk et al., 1995). Moreover, the estimated effects of the French program on the school success of disadvantaged children are quite small by American standards, much smaller than the estimated effects of both model and public school and Head Start programs in the United States (Boocock et al., 1999).

Sheila Kamerman (1999—see footnote 1) pointed out at the committee's workshop that there are great methodological difficulties in comparing early childhood education across countries, even though the countries being compared are the most developed and have the best record-keeping systems in other respects. Assessment is absent or rare in some countries with national systems of early education. Without a strong base in comparable empirical evidence, generalizations about the impact of policies on educational practices and child outcomes can only be crude and tentative. If we are to learn more from the wide range of variation in policies and practices among the OECD countries, more research leading to comparable data will be necessary.

In considering the role of culture in preschool pedagogy, a problem often raised is whether programs to improve children's abilities to learn in school tend to impose the acquisition of middle-class American culture, particularly its interpersonal values fostering individualism and competition as opposed to cooperation, on children whose parents' cultures favor more collective or cooperative values. This is an issue in the multiculturalism debate of American education, but it is relevant in many other places, virtually everywhere that agrarian peoples move to cities or to other countries more influenced by Western values.

In addressing the issue of multiculturalism, Cigdem

Kagitcibasi (1996, 1999—see footnote 1) suggests there are two independent dimensions involved: interpersonal distance (a separateness-relatedness continuum) and agency (an autonomy-heteronomy continuum). Psychology as we know it, reflecting its American cultural values, confounds the two in positing separateness and autonomy as a single universal direction for child development. But it is possible and desirable, she argues, to foster the autonomy needed to become competent in school (and in later life in a contemporary urban setting) without imposing separateness as a value on children whose parental culture favors interpersonal relatedness. She illustrated this with the preschool program she devised for poor children in Istanbul, Turkey, demonstrating a long-term improvement in assessed academic proficiency from a program modeled on the Home Instruction Program for Preschool Youngsters (HIPPY; Baker and Piotrowski, 1995) that adds the instruction of mothers to the teaching of preschool children in centers. (In evaluating the generalizability of this program, it is important to bear in mind that the Turkish mothers had an average of only 5.36 years of schooling and the fathers 5.81. Thus the more modest gains for the HIPPY in the United States may have to do with the much greater school experience of the populations in the American studies.)

Kagitcibasi's (1996, 1999—see footnote 1) claim that preschools can simultaneously promote a child's academic competence and culturally preferred relatedness brings us back to the Japanese literature, particularly the synthesis by Catherine Lewis (1996). The model she describes for preschools is that of Holloway's (1999—see footnote 1) "relational" centers, but it is also characteristic of Japanese pedagogy in many other settings throughout the lifespan, according to the ethnographic literature in English, and may be a foundational cultural schema for instruction. In this model, the assumption is that the first and most necessary step in instruction is to build a strong positive relationship between teacher and learner, with the teacher acting as an emotionally supportive coach, avoiding any expression of anger or confrontation that might threaten the relationship. Much time is spent in relationship-building, prior to the most important pedagogical content, in order to create a highly motivated learning relationship in which the pupil will eagerly engage the instructional tasks as they are set. Thus the Japanese preschools that do not teach academic skills are nonetheless rationalized in terms of a long-term pedagogical sequence that takes motivation as the initial prerequisite for school learning, and a nurturing relationship as the prerequisite for academic motivation. This is our fullest example to date of a culturally distinctive pedagogy that seems to work as well, in terms of academic performance, as those with which we are more familiar. It is not independent of Western influence, of course, and some Japanese experts attribute it in part to Froebel and Dewey, but its focus on the social and emotional rather than the cognitive aspects of learning gives it a distinctive quality (similar to the "traditional" American nursery school) that merits further investigative attention.

The workshop and the research literature point to several conclusions. First is that the comparative data on what works at the preschool level, even among the OECD countries, is inadequate and needs to be improved in order to take advantage of wide variation in policy and practice for purposes of research and practical knowledge. Second is the suggestion that the examples of good practice in other countries rest in part on observations of exceptionally dedicated preschool educators and are associated with their superior training and stability, which in turn reflects the investment in their careers. Third, there are lessons to be learned from abroad in how to provide preschoolers with skills for academic learning without indoctrinating them in a single American model of interpersonal behavior. Here again, the evidence is suggestive rather than definitive but, as it addresses a central issue in the multiculturism debate, it is worthy of more intensive and systematic research.

CHILDREN WITH IDENTIFIED DISABILITIES[2]

Children with different gifts, abilities, challenges, and resources from a variety of cultural backgrounds come together in early childhood settings. In this report, we have pictured young children as being developmentally and experientially immature, while also being tremendously eager to learn. Do these same

---

[2]Mark Wolery provided extensive and helpful comment on this section.

principles apply to young children with identified disabilities? What is needed so that such children's eagerness to learn is realized?

In just a generation there has been a sea change in public attitudes about the care and upbringing of children with disabilities. Thirty or 40 years ago, children with mental retardation, autism, and other serious disabilities were routinely placed in institutions with little thought given to education or intervention strategies. In a recent compendium of articles on the effectiveness of early intervention, Michael Guralnick describes the prevailing conditions in those years: "the context for families [seeking early intervention] was one in which services were poorly developed and highly fragmented, access to information was limited, qualified professionals were not always available or were difficult to locate, expectations of children with disabilities or those significantly at risk were low, and families often found themselves isolated from the general community" (Guralnick, 1997:12). In her preface to that volume, Nancy Robinson, remarking on the distance we have come, makes the trenchant observation that the text on mental retardation she and her husband completed in 1964 (Robinson and Robinson, 1965) had no index entry for intervention, to say nothing about early intervention.

Over the next three decades, however, the idea took root in public opinion and in law that people with disabilities should be equipped to participate fully in American society. The theme appears in the regulations implementing Section 504 of the Rehabilitation Act of 1973 (P.L. 93-112): Section 504 "establishes a mandate to end discrimination and to bring handicapped persons into the mainstream of American Life" (Federal Register, May 4, 1977:22676). And the Federal mandate was extended beyond employment policy to education with the passage of the Education for All Handicapped Children Act (P.L. 94-142), the predecessor to the current Individuals with Disabilities Act (IDEA). This was an expression of the civil rights concerns of the era, buttressed by the advocacy work of parents on behalf of their children. The right to early intervention services has been available to all children with disabilities (and to many who are at risk as well) since the passage of the 1986 amendments to P.L. 94-142.

The Early Intervention Program for Infants and Toddlers with

Disabilities (under Part C of IDEA), and the Preschool Grants Program (under Part B of IDEA) are together designed to provide integrated service delivery for children with disabilities from birth through age 5. The Preschool Grants Program assists States in providing special education and related services to children with disabilities ages 3-5. To receive federal funds under the program, a state must provide a free and appropriate education to all 3- through 5-year-old children with disabilities. As with school-age children, children in the preschool years must be served in the least restrictive environment possible (U.S. Department of Education, 1999). In 1997-98, 571,049 children ages 3 through 5—4.69 percent of the total population of children in that age group— were served under the Preschool Grants Program. About half of those children were served in regular classroom settings (U.S. Department of Education, 1999). Figure 4-1 in Box 4-2 displays the numbers of children in each type of setting.

The expression of a public interest in early childhood interventions is consistent with theory and research showing the importance of the first few years of life for cognitive, language, and social development in general (Kolb, 1995; Chugani et al., 1987; Ramey et al., 1992; Dunham and Dunham, 1992). There are clearly major effects of early experience on a host of developmental phenomena, though we should not lose track of the fact that development is also resilient in many key ways (Kagan, 1998). Research also establishes the specific value of interventions for infants and young children with disabilities (Guralnick, 1997; Greenspan and Wieder, 1998; Meisels et al., 1994; Shonkoff et al., 1992; Dunst et al., 1989). But as is the case with interventions for children from disadvantaged backgrounds, we know more about the overall effectiveness of early intervention than about the particular program features that generate the desired outcomes (Ramey and Ramey, 1998).

While children with disabilities are often referred to as a single entity, the type and severity of the disability can vary enormously, from children with Down syndrome to children with hearing impairments; from children with autism to children with language delays; from children with single disabilities to those with multiple disabilities. The federal requirement that each child served under IDEA have an individualized plan that specifies needs, intervention components, and anticipated developmental progress or outcomes is an effort to respond to the individual manifestations of disability. In practice, however, a wide variety of assessment instruments are often used in an inconsistent fashion, (Johnson and Beauchamp, 1987) and most curricula for young children with disabilities are eclectic rather than tailored to the individual child's assessment results (Hanson and Lynch, 1995).

In a review of research on curricula used in early childhood programs for children with disabilities, Bruder (1997) concludes: "contemporary adaptations of curricula in early childhood intervention seem to be influenced by a number of complex factors. Rather than subscribe to a particular theoretical perspective, it appears that curriculum development in early childhood intervention is dependent on factors such as an individual interpretation of child and family needs (see Sands et al., 1995), the availability of curriculum models and materials that fit these perceived needs (Odom et al., 1994), and professional training and orientation (McWilliam and Bailey, 1994)." Even for more narrowly defined disabilities such as Down syndrome, "second generation" questions regarding the effects of curricula, aptitude-treatment interaction, and parent involvement have not been answered (Spiker and Hopmann, 1997). In a review of 56 studies of children with communication disorders, McLean and Cripe conclude that early intervention is both effective and more efficient than intervention at later ages, but regarding intervention strategy they conclude "the interventionist must still rely on informed clinical judgment to determine specifically which treatment objectives, settings, and procedures are most appropriate for any one child" (McLean and Cripe, 1997:418).

Research syntheses and meta-analyses of interventions for *school-aged* children with learning disabilities suggest that the principles for effective teaching are not different in kind from those for typically developing children, although deliberateness of the intervention and attention to task difficulty must be emphasized (Vaughn et al., 2000). While second generation research may do much to improve our understanding of early intervention programs for children with disabilities, existing research, program and clinical experience, and guidelines for practice lead to a similar conclusion as that for interventions with school-aged stu-

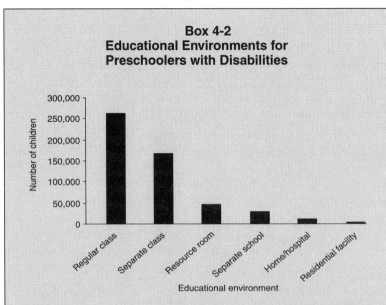

Box 4-2
Educational Environments for
Preschoolers with Disabilities

FIGURE 4-1 Number of children with disabilities ages 3 through 5 served in different educational environments 1996-1997. SOURCE: U.S. Department of Education (1999:Fig. 11-7).

Regular class includes children who receive services in programs designed primarily for nondisabled children, provided the children with disabilities are in a separate room for less than 21 percent of the time receiving services. This may include, but is not limited to, Head Start centers, public or private preschool and child care facilities, preschool classes offered to an age-eligible population by the public school system, kindergarten classes, and classes using co-teaching models (special education and general education staff coordinating activities in a general education setting).

Resource room includes children who receive services in programs designed primarily for nondisabled children, provided the children with disabilities are in a separate program for 21 to 60 percent of the time receiving services. This includes, but is not limited to, Head Start centers, public or private preschools or child care facilities, preschool classes offered to an age-eligible population by the public school system, and kindergarten classes.

Separate class includes children who receive services in a separate program for 61 to 100 percent of the time receiving services. It does not include children who received education programs in public or private separate day or residential facilities.

Separate school (public and private) includes children who are served in publicly or privately operated programs, set up primarily to serve children with disabilities, that are NOT housed in a facility with programs for children without disabilities. Children must receive special education and related services in the public separate day school for greater than 50 percent of the time.

Residential facility (public and private) includes children who are served in publicly or privately operated programs in which children receive care for 24 hours a day. This could include placement in public nursing care facilities or public or private residential schools.

Homebound/hospital includes children who are served in either a home or hospital setting, including those receiving special education or related services in the home and provided by a professional or paraprofessional who visits the home on a regular basis (e.g., a child development worker or speech services provided in the child's home). It also includes children 3-5 years old receiving special education and related services in a hospital setting on an inpatient or outpatient basis. However, children receiving services in a group program that is housed at a hospital should be reported in the separate school category. For children served in both a home/hospital setting and in a school/community setting, report the child in the placement that comprises the larger percentage of time receiving services.

NOTE: These categories will change for the 1998-1999 data on educational environments, which will be reported in the 23rd *Annual Report to Congress*.

SOURCE: U.S. Department of Education (1999:Table II-1).

dents. The principles guiding high-quality early childhood programs for typically developing children are relevant and necessary for programs for children who have disabilities. Teachers' practices need to be intentional, systematic, and individualized for all children. It is especially important to recognize this for children with disabilities, who in some cases require significantly more intensive and different practices than are used with children who do not have disabilities. Just as with other children, the skills taught to a child with disabilities will vary depending on the child's development (e.g., learning to manipulate a toy as compared to playing with it in a symbolic manner.).

Similarities in the guidelines for developmentally appropriate practice (DAP) for preschool age children generally and guidelines for children with disabilities suggested by the Division for Early Childhood (DEC) of the Council for Exceptional Children have been noted (Fox et al., 1994), including the importance of attending to the child's individual development, the integration of curriculum and assessment, the importance of child-initiated activities, the importance of active engagement with the environment, an emphasis on social interaction, and attention to cultural diversity. For some children who have disabilities, precise, consistent, and frequent use of special intervention strategies may be required to ensure efficient learning (Holcombe et al., 1994), and programmed generalization of skill acquisition may be necessary (Bailey and Wolery, 1992).

Four program features common to quality programs are particularly emphasized when children have disabilities:

1. Emphasis on Communication

Language development should be a key feature of all early childhood programs both because the preschool years hold enormous potential for language development and because language, cognitive development, and social development are integrated in complex ways and are critical for survival in society. The U.S. Department of Education no longer collects data by disability category for children under 6 years of age. In 1987, however, they reported that 60 percent to 70 percent of the special education population ages 3-5 had speech or language disorders (U.S. Department of Education, 1987), though some more recent estimates are considerably lower (McLean and Cripe, 1997:350). By ages 3 through 5, children with language delays talk approximately half as much as their peers (Warren et al., 1984). The DEC recommends that language interventions be considered for all children with special needs to help improve overall development (DEC Task Force on Recommended Practices, 1993). In addition, attention to language/communication is important because nearly every disability has a negative impact on the development of language and communication skills.

A large body of research suggests the efficacy of language intervention for a broad spectrum of communication disorders in young children (McLean and Snyder-McLean, 1987; McLean and Cripe, 1997), though no single intervention can be identified as best. Since the 1980s, language interventions have emphasized "naturalistic" approaches (McLean and Cripe,1997), in which language learning is incorporated throughout the day's activities rather than concentrated in a single block of time, and makes use of the child's focus and interests. *Incidental* or *milieu teaching* combine more highly structured, didactic interventions with more naturalistic features; they use the child's focus, but actively target specific language skills. Opportunities for the child to use the targeted language skill are created (waiting for the child to put a request into words, for example) and the adult responds to the child's communication with requests and prompts for further language use as well as responding to the intent of the child's request. (For additional discussion of naturalistic interventions, including *mand-model* and *milieu teaching*, see Chapter 5.)

Yoder, Kaiser, and Alpert (1991) compared the effectiveness of a milieu language program with a more didactic approach and found that the former was more successful in increasing language development, but the results suggest an aptitude by treatment interaction: children who benefited most from milieu teaching were those who scored lower before the intervention (had less intelligible speech and more limited vocabulary). Conversely, those who benefited more from the didactic approach scored higher during pretreatment.

2. Emphasis on Social and Emotional Skills

Young children with disabilities often manifest difficulties in establishing relationships with their peers and developing friendships (Guralnick, 1990). They engage less in social interaction than children of the same developmental level without disabilities (Odom et al., 1990). Gresham (1982) suggests that over time, poor development of social skills and a lack of support for social development can cause emotional responses in children that are as limiting as the primary disability.

Numerous educational and therapeutic techniques have been demonstrated to promote young children's peer interactions, including modeling and observational learning, coaching, prompting, rehearsal, direct teaching of social strategies, and reinforcement procedures (Guralnick and Neville, 1997). Some interventions intentionally involve children without disabilities as models and as initiators or responders to the social behavior of children with disabilities. Further, a central feature of many of these interventions is that the child with disabilities has competent peers with whom to interact. Greenspan and Wieder (1998) suggest the importance of interaction with peers without disabilities who can reach out and involve more withdrawn students in communication and play, and provide feedback when a student who has a disability does communicate.

There has been increased attention to the environmental and social context characteristics that encourage peer interaction, including the number and familiarity of the children in a social setting (with small familiar groups encouraging interaction), the types of toys available (those that can be used by more than one child at a time, or those that encourage pretend play among children), and the physical arrangement of the classroom (to encourage interaction) (McEvoy et al., 1992; Odom and Brown, 1993; Sainato and Carta, 1992; Bailey and Wolery, 1992; Quilitch and Risley, 1973).

While increased attention has been focused in the last two decades on the importance of social interaction and the development of social skills for children with disabilities, the social interaction skills that the techniques above support for the most part have not generalized to other contexts over time (Guralnick, 1994). Guralnick and Neville (1997) suggest that factors that contribute to the lack of transfer include constraints associated with the child's developmental characteristics, reputational factors, the existence of social status hierarchies that resist change, family-child interaction patterns, and restricted peer networks for children with disabilities.

3. Attention to Individual Differences

A theme that pervades this report is the importance of an adult who recognizes and responds to the child's individual characteristics and developmental level in promoting learning. For children with disabilities, this feature of early childhood programs is particularly challenging and requires specialized knowledge. The capacity for self-regulation and attention is nascent in all children in the preschool years; for many children with disabilities, that capacity is a far greater challenge. Some children, for example, those with certain kinds of cerebral palsy or autism, may have heightened sensitivity to their environment, including the degree to which it is loud, bright, active, crowded, or visually stimulating. Others may not be very aware of changes in their environment, even salient changes. For teachers to plan meaningful programs, they must understand (a) children's sensitivity to environmental stimuli, (b) the degree to which they are readily engaged by the environment in adaptive ways, and (c) the behaviors they use to express their attention, interests, and intentions (Greenspan and Wieder, 1998).

Circle time for example, a common feature of early childhood programs, can be particularly challenging to children with delayed development of regulatory capacities. On the basis of long clinical experience, Greenspan and Wieder argue that while a child needs to learn to attend in preparation for later schooling, "every task has its developmental sequence. A child cannot relate to a group of six until he's learned to relate one-on-one, and then to a group of three. To ask him to do so is like asking him to read without first teaching him the letters." (p. 405). As Chapter 2 suggests, challenges are key to learning and development, but adults must be sensitive and responsive to children's behavior while promoting those challenges for children (Dunst et al., 1987; Kaiser et al., 1992).

4. Emphasis on Parent Participation

Parent participation is, as we suggested at the outset of this chapter, a common feature of quality early childhood programs. Parent engagement is considered particularly important by many who work with and study children with developmental delays (Greenspan and Wieder, 1998; Girolametto, 1988; Camarata, 1993; Girolametto et al., 1994). Since many children who have disabilities experience delayed development of language and social skills, parent participation in early childhood interventions can extend and reinforce the child's progress in these areas. Several studies suggest the importance of interventions that are spread throughout the day (Bricker and Cripe, 1992; McWilliam, 1996; Eiserman et al., 1992) and are contextually relevant (Drasgow et al., 1996). Parents are well situated to extend classroom interventions beyond the confines of the school day.

Dunst (1985) suggests a central challenge for parents and caregivers of children with disabilities is one of readability: any factor that distorts a child's emotional and communicative signals will make it more difficult for those involved with the child to interpret and respond. Irrespective of the category of disability, these children are characterized as less predictable in their interactive behavior, and less likely to take the initiative during social interaction with their caregivers (Field, 1980). Descriptions of caregivers' interactions with young children with disabilities indicate that they tend to provide more stimulation, be more directive, and take more dominant roles than do those with children without disabilities (McCollum and Hemmeter, 1997). Deliberate efforts to draw the parent or caregiver's attention to strategies that will improve the child's ability to engage and communicate may therefore be particularly important when the child is disabled. The goal, as Dunst (1985) explains, is not for parents to engage in isolated training sessions, but to have the parents' usual interaction patterns with their children be growth promoting.

Several studies suggest the potential of parent involvement. Camarata (1993) found that speech production improved in children with language delays when mothers supplied accurate models of words and sentences in natural conversation and interactions. Girolametto (1988) found that when parents of children with developmental delays participated in intervention programs, they were more responsive to their children, and to the child's conversational leads. The children were able to initiate on more topics, were better able to take turns, and had a more diverse vocabulary. Eiserman, Weber, and McCoun (1992) found that training in therapeutic techniques for parents of children with speech disorders effectively increased children's personal and social skills, their adaptive behavior, and their speech.

While some research suggests parent involvement and training can enhance and extend the benefits of early intervention programs, both the quantity and the quality of research in this regard is limited. Moreover, some research on early intervention for disadvantaged children suggests that parent involvement and training is not an adequate substitute for direct intervention (Ramey and Ramey, 1998). In a review of studies involving young children with communication disorders, McLean and Cripe (1997) argue that parent-implemented intervention may be differentially effective in different treatment situations. As a cautionary note, they point to an intervention that was effective in treating phonology disorders when implemented by clinicians, but not by parents. As in many areas of early intervention research, existing research suggests a potential, but a second generation of studies that differentiate characteristics of parents, children, and parent training and involvement will be needed for a fuller understanding of the features of effective interventions to enhance the effectiveness of parent involvement (McCollum and Hemmeter, 1997). It is important to note that professionals' involvement with families must be more than just assisting families in teaching their children or promoting their development. There is an informative literature that shows other kinds of family support that are critical to good child outcomes and are unrelated to the issue of parents as teachers (Dunst et al., 1994, 1997).

Effects of Inclusion

Research on the effectiveness of early intervention for young children with disabilities has, for the most part, taken place in programs in which all of the participants have identified disabilities (Casto and Mastropieri, 1986; Shonkoff and Hauser-Cram, 1987). More recently, model programs that are inclusive have been developed and evaluated. Two points emerge from the research comparing integrated and segregated programs: (a) children with disabilities make similar levels of developmental progress in both types of programs, and (b) children in integrated programs tend to have more advanced social and behavioral skills than their counterparts (Buysse and Bailey, 1993; Lamorey and Bricker, 1993). But like all research on model programs, positive outcomes may not be generalizable to community-based programs of lower quality. Not surprisingly, Kontos et al. (1998) found a relationship between quality of inclusive programs and outcomes for children with disabilities. However, since many community-based programs are not of high quality, the effect of inclusion more generally cannot be assumed; much depends on the quality both of the inclusive program and of the segregated program to which it is being compared. In particular, the benefits of inclusion will depend on the extent to which the teacher has support from specialists (e.g., early intervention specialists, special educators, therapists). What occurs within programs is what results in outcomes.

In a naturally occurring experiment in London, 36 children with Down syndrome were studied, half of whom attended general nursery or primary schools, and half of whom attended segregated special schools (Casey et al., 1988). Results suggested that at baseline the two groups were comparable on most measures (the special schools group was slightly older than the mainstream group, and girls had higher expressive language scores than boys). Improvements in both math and reading scores over a 2-year period were greater for the mainstreamed children than for the segregated children. The research, however, has the limitations associated with non-random assignment (characteristics of the districts in which the children lived, the parents who chose to live in those districts, or the characteristics of other children in the classroom) were not controlled for. In another evaluation of children with Down syndrome, researchers found that the amount of time spent in integrated settings was not a strong predictor of developmental progress (Fewell and Oelwein, 1990, 1991).

The research on inclusion has not been refined enough to suggest for which children (by type or severity of disability) it is beneficial in which types of inclusive programs. However, the importance of settings that will develop the capacity of children with disabilities to communicate and engage socially suggests a potential benefit of interacting with typically developing peers. Greenspan and Wieder argue:

"The greatest problem with class makeup is that students are often grouped with peers who have similar special needs, so, for example, it is common to have eight noncommunicative, withdrawn, and intermittently aimless children in one class. Naturally, there will be little interaction among them, so if one spurts ahead in gestural communication, he will receive little feedback from his peers. With lack of feedback, the students' precarious new ability may be jeopardized. Without being immersed in a communicative world with children who reach out, interact, engage in pretend play, and speak, the child will not have adequate opportunities to learn his critical early lessons—to relate, communicate, and think" (1998:406).

But whether the potential opportunity created by an inclusive setting is realized will depend on the training the teacher gets, how much in-class help is made available, how much contact the teacher has with specialists who can give the appropriate help, how many children the teacher has in class, the materials available, and, of course, the effort of the teacher to support inclusion.

Young children with disabilities can be included in social interactions by their classmates. In a study of mixed-age inclusive classrooms, the frequency of contact (primarily parallel play) that children with mild to severe disabilities had with their classmates during free play periods did not differ from the amount of contact that typically developing children had with their classmates (Okagaki et al., 1998). According to parents' and teachers' reports, a majority of children with disabilities who attended inclusive preschool programs had at least one mutual friend (Buysse, 1993).

Young children with mild and moderate disabilities engage in more social interaction in inclusive settings than in noninclusive settings (Erwin, 1993; Guralnick et al., 1996; Hauser-Cram et al., 1993; Lamorey and Bricker, 1993). Children with severe disabilities also engage in frequent interactions with typically developing children in inclusive settings (Hanline, 1993). However, it is not clear that children with severe disabilities interact more frequently with other children in inclusive, compared with noninclusive, settings (Hundert et al., 1998).

Young children with disabilities are more likely to experience rejection by peers than are children without disabilities (Guralnick and Nelville, 1997). In particular, children with developmental delays are less likely to have a mutual friend than are children with mild disabilities (Guralnick et al., 1995). However, even though children with disabilities are rated as being less well liked than their counterparts without disabilities, they still engage in frequent social contact with their classmates in inclusive settings (Guralnick et al., 1996; Hanline, 1993; Okagaki et al., 1998). There is some evidence that attending mixed-age inclusive classrooms facilitates the social interactions of young children with disabilities. Children with disabilities in mixed-age groups are more engaged in conversations than are children with disabilities in same-age groups (Roberts et al., 1994). Participation in mixed-age inclusive classrooms also enhances the play of young children with disabilities (Blasco et al., 1993). The critical point is that if social interaction, peer-to-peer conversations, social play, and the other positive outcomes that are more likely in inclusive settings are desired, then interventions are necessary at the level of the individual child to prevent peer rejection (Wolery and Wilbert, 1994).

Recently, some attention has been directed toward the effects of inclusion on typically developing young children. Contact between typically developing children and children with disabilities in inclusive classrooms increases children's knowledge of disabilities. Normally developing preschool children in inclusive classes are sensitive to the limitations associated with physical disabilities. However, they seem to be less certain about sensory disabilities (Diamond and Hestenes, 1994; Diamond et al., 1997; Okagaki et al., 1998).

Young children who have regular contact with children with disabilities are more accepting of them. Participation in an inclusive classroom promotes young children's appreciation for diversity and enhances the development of their prosocial skills

(Buysse, 1993; Favazza and Odom, 1996; Diamond et al., 1997; Hanline, 1993; Peck et al., 1992). Typically developing children in inclusive classrooms give higher social acceptance to ratings of hypothetical children with disabilities than do children in noninclusive classrooms (Diamond et al., 1997; Okagaki et al., 1998). In a case study of an inclusive, 8-week summer program with three preschool children with severe disabilities and three typically developing young children, Hanline (1993) found no evidence of social rejection of children with severe disabilities by their peers. In fact, typically developing children tended to be more persistent in obtaining a response from a child with a disability than from another peer.

SUMMARY

Even across the disparate approaches used in program models, some common processes and content are evident. Many of the programs consciously exposed children to classroom processes that differed from their interactions at home, but were similar to those that they would experience in formal school: whole class, small group, and individual interactions with teachers. Early childhood teachers used a discourse pattern, at least some of the time, which is typical of schooling: the initiation-reply-evaluation sequence. The preschool children also learned strategies for remembering, such as rehearsal and categorization, since this is a by-product of schooling in our culture.

The lack of familiarity with school challenges many children as they move from the home environment into school settings. The routine activities of school are different from those in most homes and are likely to differ even more in some minority cultures, placing a double burden of learning on those children when they enter early childhood settings and schools (Nelson, 1986). Early childhood programs can serve as a bridge for children between home and school by providing exposure to the varied interaction styles (large group, small group, one-on-one learning) that the child will encounter in school.

Even though the programs studied applied different and in some cases novel theories of development, the content relied on by most teachers was drawn from that traditional in kindergarten and nursery school. Consistent across every program is a strong focus on language. The teachers, most often, provided a model of standard English, and the programs were strongly oriented toward getting children to talk and be understood, to understand others' speech, and to experiment with symbolic concepts through speech and books. The classroom materials and teacher-planned activities and discussions involved typical concepts such as shapes, colors, sizes, numbers, animals, transportation, prepositions, seasons, holidays, etc. The fact that the activities, processes, and content emphasized in the approaches are similar suggests that the broad parameters of early childhood education are a matter of general agreement.

A review of several strands of research on program quality suggests that teachers who have higher levels of education and specialized training, are attentive to individual children, have fewer children in their care, and use strategies associated with developmentally appropriate practice generally are more competent at enhancing children's learning and growth. This analysis of the longitudinal studies of experimental preschools and newer studies of the effects of quality in early childhood education and care suggests that the benefits of early childhood programs are related to the interrelated factors of program structure (class size, the ratio of children to teachers, and service intensity); processes that help teachers respond to individual children (highly qualified teachers using reflective teaching practice and close relationships with parents); and curricula that serve as a bridge between home and school.

Promoting the development and addressing the needs of children with disabilities is not something a teacher can do alone. It requires an intervention team, including, for example, speech/ language pathologists, occupational therapists, physical therapists, social workers, or psychologists, which in turn requires careful attention to how the members of the intervention team work with the teacher and how they carry out their part of the intervention. McWilliam (1996) offers a useful discussion of these issues.

Many of the curriculum practices used in the programs found to have lasting benefits for children can be seen as strategies that increased the ability of teachers to recognize and take advantage of each child's level of development. Teachers are more likely to gain the specialized knowledge they need to tailor their teaching when they work with relatively few children for a long period of time and when they have a chance to reflect on their teaching practices. Such teachers are more able to understand the children's individual interests, and they can create activities and interactions to meet them.

Children who do well in school tend to have parents who have close relationships with teachers and caregivers, reinforcing the traditional belief in the importance of such partnerships. The teacher who has extensive contact with the child's family can better understand the child as an individual and have an appreciation for the contexts in which the child functions, the parents' aims and hopes for the child, and the values of the child's culture. When parents and teachers are teamed in such a collaboration, the adults can do the work to build consistency in the world of the child, rather than leaving it up to the child to integrate disparate contexts.

Program quality has been found to be associated with children's developmental outcome. The prevalence of quality factors—teacher-child ratio and class size, program intensity and coherence, responses to parents, staff qualifications, teachers as reflective practitioners, and teacher preparation—in the experimental preschools contrasts with their absence in many of today's typical community programs for low-income children. We cannot identify the ideal levels of each quality factor based on current research, particularly as these will vary with the characteristics of the children and goals of the programs. However, it can be safely concluded that most early education and care programs in the United States do not approach ideal levels of quality and that programs designed to reduce the gap between rich and poor in early childhood educational opportunity are far from optimal. If early intervention is to live up to the promise of the longitudinal results, then Head Start, Title I, child care, and other programs should approximate the standard of quality suggested by the research reviewed here.

Curriculum and Pedagogy: The What and the How of Early Childhood Education

IN THIS CHAPTER WE TAKE A FOCUSED LOOK at curriculum and pedagogy. In an important sense, pedagogy is the overarching concept; it refers broadly to the deliberate process of cultivating development within a given culture and society. From this point of view, pedagogy has three basic components: (1) curriculum, or the content of what is being taught; (2) methodology, or the way in which teaching is done; and (3) techniques for socializing children in the repertoire of cognitive and affective skills required for successful functioning in society that education is designed to promote.

Curriculum, or the content of teaching, may be designed to encourage learning processes (memory, attention, observation) and cognitive skills (reasoning, comparing and contrasting, classification), as well as the acquisition of specific information, such as the names of the letters of the alphabet (Wiggins and McTighe, 1998). The teaching strategies or methods used in implementing the curriculum are the arranged interactions of people and materials planned and used by teachers. They include the teacher role, teaching styles, and instructional techniques (Siraj-Blatchford, 1998). The third aspect of pedagogy, which might be thought of as cognitive socialization, refers to the role that teachers in early childhood settings play, through their expectations, their teaching strategies, their curricular emphases, in promoting the repertoire of cognitive and affective characteristics and skills that the young child needs to move down the path from natal culture to school culture to the culture of the larger society.

CURRICULUM GOALS

This intellectual framing of the idea of pedagogy supposes a coherence and deliberateness that is often absent in practice. Indeed, a review of the literature on early childhood curriculum suggests some reluctance to spell out even a limited set of specific goals. The three well-known programs briefly mentioned below are ones that have clearly articulated goals.

The Montessori approach (Montessori, 1964) promotes children's active, independent observation and exploration of concrete materials to develop concepts/skills. Through this activity children develop a clear image of what they were trying to accomplish, thus developing self-discipline, self-reliance, and intrinsic motivation. J. McV. Hunt, in his introduction to the above referenced volume, describes the teacher's role in this method, giving clarity to the pedagogical goals: "If a teacher can discern what a child is trying to do in his informational interaction with the environment, and if the teacher can have on hand materials to that intention, if he can impose a relevant challenge with which the child can cope, supply a relevant model for imitation, or pose a relevant question that the child can answer, that teacher can call forth the kind of accommodative change that constitutes psychological development or growth" (p. xxxiv).

High/Scope is one of the most widely adopted preschool curriculum models to have emerged during the early days of Project Head Start (Hohmann and Weikart, 1995). The curriculum offers children active engagement in planning their learning, as well as opportunity to enhance language and develop concepts through experiencing and representing different aspects of classification, seriation, number, spatial relations, and time.

Core Knowledge Foundation (2000) advocates a curriculum designed to immerse preschoolers in a clearly sequential set of experiences that will ensure their "cultural literacy." At the preschool level of core knowledge, children follow a curriculum that addresses five dimensions of readiness: (1) physical well-being and motor development, movement, and coordination; (2) language development, oral language, nursery rhymes, poems, finger plays and songs, storybook reading and storytelling, emerging literacy skills in reading and writing; (3) social and emotional development, autonomy, and social skills; (4) approaches to learning, work habits; and (5) knowledge acquisition and cognitive development, mathematical reasoning and number sense, orientation in time and space, scientific reasoning and the physical world, music, visual arts.

Although the various advocates of curriculum models or approaches may differ in emphasis on particular goals associated with their own orientations, all would agree that the early childhood educator must be concerned with supporting children's physical, social, emotional, and cognitive growth.

Efforts to compare curriculum effectiveness do not identify one curriculum as clearly superior to others. This is not surprising if one considers the evidence pointed to in previous chapters regarding the importance to learning of the adult-child relationship, temperament, social class, and cultural traditions. The effect of the individual teacher may overwhelm the effect of the curriculum. Moreover, the fidelity of implementation may vary from teacher to teacher and program to program. And because learning takes place on so many dimensions simultaneously, a particular curriculum might do better than others on one dimension and worse on another.

We do know, however, that having a planned curriculum in a preschool program is better than having none (see Chapter 4). And there is a research base on learning that can inform the development and evaluation of curriculum components. While no single program can be claimed superior, quality programs will be those that incorporate knowledge regarding what children are capable of learning, and how they learn effectively.

A recent report of the National Research Council suggests three principles of learning that have a solid foundation in research and are directly applicable to classroom teaching (National Research Council, 1999b). Furthermore, there is evidence to suggest that these principles are applicable in the preschool years as well as in later years (National Research Council, 1999a):

1. Children develop ideas and concepts at very young ages that help them make sense of their worlds. Learning is not the transfer of new information into an empty receptacle; it is the building of new understandings by the child on the foundation of existing understandings. Learning will be most effective when the child's preconceptions are engaged. Curricula can be evaluated on the extent to which they draw out and build on children's existing ideas.

2. Developing expertise requires both a foundation of factual knowledge and skills *and* a conceptual understanding that allows facts to become "usable" knowledge. In the preschool years, key concepts can be quite basic and therefore easily overlooked. In mathematics, for example, children need to develop more than verbal counting skills and number recognition. They need to grasp "quantity." Similarly, emergent literacy requires not just that children recognize letters, but that they grasp the concept of "representation" involved in written words and illustrations. Because the preschool years are a time when children are rapidly developing skills and acquiring new knowledge, the importance of concepts can be overlooked. Curricula can be judged on the extent to which they promote learning of concepts as well as information and skills.

3. Children can be taught to monitor their thinking in the form of learning strategies. These "metacognitive skills" are used by some children spontaneously. But efforts to help all children learn more deliberately can be incorporated into curricula.

These three principles are woven into the discussion below of children's learning in early literacy, math, and science. Preschool programs often provide learning experiences in a great many areas beyond these three, including music, social studies, arts and crafts, and physical education (for coverage of the research in these areas see Spodek, 1993). The development of social competence is also a central feature of many preschool programs, and research suggests its importance to later school success (Katz and McClellan, 1997; Ladd, 1990). We emphasize that our focus on the more academic subjects does not imply that these are of greater or singular importance. Rather, we focus on these areas because a dynamic research literature provides insight into learning in the preschool years, with implications for the development of preschool curricula.

CURRICULUM CONTENT

Emergent Literacy

There are few more attractive cultural icons in late 20th century America than the image of a parent sharing a picture book with a child. Shared reading embraces goals of educational advancement, cultural uplift, and literate discourse. It is, to use a phrase of Jerome Kagan (1994), "a pleasing idea."

This pleasing idea is the foundation of "emergent literacy," a term that denotes the idea that the acquisition of literacy is best conceptualized as a developmental continuum with its origins early in the life of a child, rather than an all-or-none phenomenon that begins when children start school. This departs from other perspectives on reading acquisition in suggesting that there is no clear demarcation between reading and prereading.

Current inquiry into emergent literacy represents a broad field with multiple perspectives and research methodologies. The study of emergent literacy includes the skills, knowledge, and attitudes that are presumed to be developmental precursors to conventional forms of reading and writing (Sulzby, 1989; Sulzby and Teale, 1991; Teale and Sulzby, 1986) and the environments that support these developments (e.g., shared book reading; Lonigan, 1994; Whitehurst et al., 1988). In addition, the term refers to a point of view about the importance of social interactions in literacy-rich environments for prereaders (Fitzgerald et al., 1992) and to advocacy for related social and educational policies (Bush, 1990; Copperman, 1986).

Components of Emergent Literacy

Grant Wiggins and Jay McTighe (1998) suggest that the components of an emergent literacy curriculum can be stratified in a manner that distinguishes between "enduring understandings" that are critical to development at a particular preschool age, features that are "important to know and do," but are somewhat less

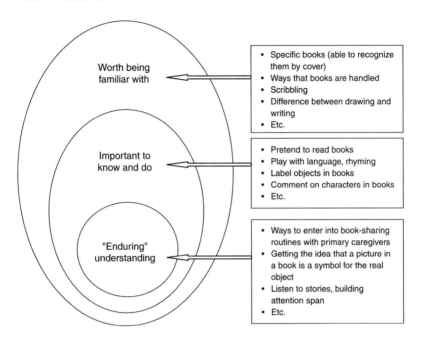

FIGURE 5-1 Possible emergent literacy examples of curriculum priorities, ages 2-3.

central, and those that are "worth being familiar with" but are less critical still.   Figures 5-1 and 5-2 provide an illustration for emergent literacy at ages 2-3 and 3-4.

The importance of development in multiple domains can be seen clearly: at age 2-3, the cognitive concept of an illustration in a book serving as a symbol for the real object is an "enduring understanding." A grasp of representation is central to cognitive development at this age; it is a key concept that allows other information to become usable or meaningful. But also of enduring importance is the ability to have a relationship with a caregiver that allows for book-sharing (a social-emotional task) and the ability to attend during the story (a task of physical regulation). An environment that is well endowed with books, providing opportunities for children to pretend to read ("important to know and do") and to learn to identify and handle books ("worth being familiar with") is certainly very positive. But pretending to read presupposes a grasp of the idea of a book, just as treating a book

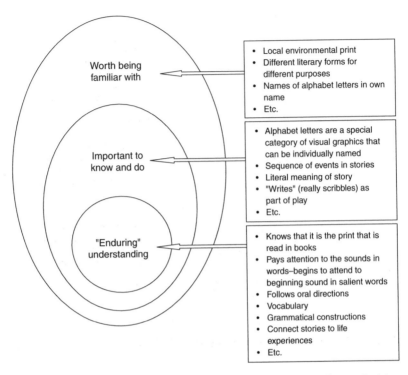

FIGURE 5-2 Possible emergent literacy examples of curriculum priorities, ages 3-4.

with respect will come more easily in the context of a child-caregiver relationship characterized by shared understandings—thus the distinction between enduring understandings and those that are important or worthwhile.

The principles of learning outlined earlier suggest that the understanding of concepts must go hand in hand with the acquisition of skill and knowledge to develop competence. The skill and knowledge base of emergent literacy includes the domains of language (e.g., vocabulary), conventions of print (e.g., knowing that writing goes from left to right across a page), beginning forms of printing (e.g., writing one's name), knowledge of graphemes (e.g., naming letters of the alphabet), grapheme-phoneme correspondence (e.g., that the letter b makes the sound /b/), and phonological awareness (e.g., that the word bat begins with the sound /b/) (Whitehurst and Lonigan, 1998).

A substantial body of research suggests that individual differences in emergent literacy are positively correlated with later differences in reading achievement. Within the language domain, for example, a longitudinal relation between the extent of oral language and later reading proficiency has been demonstrated with three broadly defined types of children: typically developing, reading delayed, and language delayed (e.g., Bishop and Adams, 1990; Butler et al., 1985; Pikulski and Tobin, 1989; Scarborough, 1989; Share et al., 1984). This relationship is much stronger for reading comprehension (reading for meaning) than for reading accuracy (sounding out individual words), and much stronger for older children than for children who are just beginning to read (Gillon and Dodd, 1994; Share and Silva, 1987; Vellutino et al., 1991; Whitehurst and Lonigan, 1998).

Another domain in which there is substantial evidence of developmental continuity is phonological awareness. Individual differences in phonological sensitivity are related to the rate of acquisition of reading skills (Bradley and Bryant, 1983, 1985; Mann and Liberman, 1984; Share et al., 1984; Stanovich et al., 1984; Wagner and Torgesen, 1987). Children who are better at detecting syllables, rhymes, or phonemes are quicker to learn to read (i.e., decode words), and this relation is present even after variability in reading skill due to intelligence, receptive vocabulary, memory skills, and social class is removed statistically (Bryant et al., 1990; MacLean et al., 1987; Wagner et al., 1994).

Literacy Environments

Understanding the source of differences among children in emergent literacy skills is critical to the development of interventions to enhance emergent literacy. Most relevant research has focused on differences in home environments. This research is relevant to preschool pedagogy in pointing the way towards interaction patterns that are likely to be as important in organized preschool settings as in the home. Significant correlations exist between the home literacy environment and preschool children's language abilities (e.g., Beals et al., 1994; Crain-Thoreson and Dale, 1992; Mason, 1980; Mason and Dunning, 1986; Rowe, 1991; Snow et al., 1991; Wells et al., 1984; Wells, 1985; see also recent review by Bus et al., 1995). It has also been suggested that the home literacy environment is associated with the development of other components of emergent literacy (e.g., Anderson and Stokes, 1984; Purcell-Gates, 1996; Purcell-Gates and Dahl, 1991; Teale, 1986); however, there has been less quantitative work that has focused on these components.

Language Outcomes

The protoypical and iconic aspect of home literacy, shared book reading, provides an extremely rich source of information and opportunity for children to learn language in a developmentally sensitive context (e.g., DeLoache and DeMendoza, 1987; Ninio, 1980; Pellegrini et al., 1985; Sénéchal et al., 1995; Wheeler, 1983). For instance, Wells (1985) found that approximately 5 percent of the daily speech of 24-month-old children occurred in the context of story time. Ninio and Bruner (1978) reported that the most frequent context for maternal labeling of objects was during shared reading. Shared reading and print exposure foster vocabulary development in preschool children (e.g., Cornell et al., 1988; Elley, 1989; Jenkins et al., 1984; Sénéchal and Cornell, 1993; Sénéchal et al., 1996; Sénéchal et al., 1995). Print exposure also has substantial effects on the development of reading skills at older ages, when children are already reading (e.g., Allen et al., 1992; Anderson and Freebody, 1981; Cunningham and Stanovich, 1991; Echols et al., 1996; Nagy et al., 1987).

Sénéchal et al. (1996) reported that other aspects of the home literacy environment (e.g., number of books in the home, library visits, parents' own print exposure) were related to children's vocabulary skills; however, only the frequency of library visits was related to children's vocabulary after controlling for the effects of children's print exposure. Payne et al. (1994) found that adult literacy activities (e.g., the amount of time a parent spends reading for pleasure) were not significantly related to children's language, which was best predicted by activities that directly involved the child (i.e., frequency of shared reading, number of children's books in the home, frequency of library visits with child). Other aspects of adult-child verbal interactions have also been implicated in the acquisition of some emergent literacy skills. For example, Dickinson and Tabors (1991; see also Beals et al., 1994) reported that features of conversations among parents and children during meals and other conversational interactions (e.g., the proportion of narrative and explanatory talk) contributed to the development of language skills valued in the classroom.

Book and Print Awareness. A child's sensitivity to print is a major first step toward reading. Young children can begin to understand that print is everywhere in the world around them, and that reading and writing are ways for them to get ideas, information, and knowledge. Children quickly settle into book-sharing routines with primary caregivers. Toddlers start recognizing favorite books by their cover, pretend to read books, and understand that books are handled in certain ways. As they reach their fourth and fifth years, children increasingly come to understand that it is the print that is read in stories, and that this print contains alphabet letters that are a special category of visual items, different even from numbers. They begin to recognize that print in English has a number of features, such as starting at the top of the page (top to bottom) and on the left side of the page (left to right). They recognize print in their home, neighborhood, and other local environments (Box 5-1). Efforts to engage children in early literacy activities cultivate that emerging awareness.

Functions of Print. Children need to understand that print is meaningful in their daily lives and has many functions. For example, young children can learn that print provides information—such as directions to a friend's house, how to bake a cake. They can learn that print helps solve problems, like written instructions for assembling a toy. Through exposure to a wide array of books, children learn that print can entertain, amuse, and even comfort. Through experiences with "writing," children learn to distinguish between drawing and writing. Their scribbling becomes more purposeful, and as older toddlers they make some scribbles that, to their total joy, look somewhat like English writing. In the preschool years they can be encouraged to write (scribble) messages as part of playful activity (Boxes 5-2, 5-3).

BOX 5-1
Little Books

Even simple emergent literacy interventions can be effective if they are sufficiently intensive. McCormick and Mason (1986) conducted two quasi-experimental studies evaluating the efficacy of providing their "Little Books" to prereaders from low- and middle-income families. Little Books are small, easy-to-read books that contain simple words, simple illustrations, and repetitive text. Intervention group children in the first study were given a Little Book to keep, their parents were provided additional Little Books and a printed guideline for their use, and more Little Books were mailed to the child's home during the summer and fall. The intervention group of the second study received only the first packet of Little Books. Emergent literacy skills were assessed at the beginning and end of the following school year. In the first study, the intervention group scored higher than the control group on several composite measures, including word knowledge, spelling knowledge, and number of words read from the Little Books. In the second study, the intervention group read more words from the Little Books but did not differ on any other measure.

BOX 5-2
Literacy Enhanced Sociodramatic Play

Every preschool classroom should have special materials and play areas geared toward developing children in particular domains while appealing to their interests. Such play centers might include an art center, a nature center, a puppet center, and "real world" play areas, such as a store or a restaurant.

These areas should be stocked with writing supplies and printed materials that can be incorporated into play. For example, in the block area, maps and labeled photos of buildings and construction sites might be provided. In the toy area, use some originally labeled toy containers for storage. In a woodworking area, add tool catalogs, home repair magazines, and picture reference books about building. In the house area, include food packaging, menus, appliance instructions, plane tickets, travel brochures, and computer keyboards. In the outdoor area, provide colored chalk, gardening books, and bird and tree guides.

BOX 5-3
Literacy as a Source of Enjoyment

Children need to feel positive about reading and literacy experiences. They often make displays of reading or writing attempts, calling attention to themselves: "Look at my story." Such displays provide opportunities for positive reinforcement.

Children need access to a variety of paper, writing utensils, and materials for bookmaking—glue, tape, stapler, and book covers. A well-equipped art area should offer paper in several sizes and colors, paints, markers, crayons, and colored pencils. You may also wish to set up a separate writing or office area that includes blank books, paper, envelopes, mailing labels, stickers, and stamps. Don't discourage scribbling and pretend writing, but do provide support and encouragement for writing letters. As you do so, expect, gradually, that more letters will be recognizable. As the children learn to form letters and develop phonological awareness, expect, too, that invented spellings will appear. It may take a few years before many conventional spellings come. Some, such as the child's own name and special phrases such as "I love you," may appear early and be memorized, but a true appreciation of conventional spelling comes later.

Source: National Research Council (1999c).

Knowledge of Narrative. Once children reach school age, stories will become a central part of their reading classes, so it is helpful for young children to become comfortable with narrative and its elements, such as characters, dialogue, and "what happens next." Young children are sensitive to sequence in language, such as following directions, and to sequences of events in stories.

Letter and Early Word Recognition. Preschool-age children can begin to recognize some printed alphabet letters and words, such as their own names. Many children learn the names of the letters first by singing the alphabet song or reciting them to pushes on the swing. At 3 and 4 they begin to attach the names of letters to their shapes. With help, they may soon begin to attend to beginning letters and sounds in words that they are familiar with in printed form. Children should have easy access to letters in many forms: alphabet blocks, letter cards, and board games, ABCs on wall charts at the child's eye height.

Listening Comprehension. As children move from toddlerhood to school age, they should increasingly be able to grasp the meaning of language they hear spoken in everyday conversation, as well as in narrative forms, such as books. They show this understanding through their questions and comments in a conversation or about a book. When read a story, they should freely relate information and events in the book to real-life experiences. As they get older, they should become comfortable with following who said or did what in a story.

Nonlanguage Outcomes

Compared with research examining the relation between home literacy environments and children's oral language skills, there has been relatively little quantitative research concerning home literacy environments and other emergent literacy skills. Both Wells (1985) and Crain-Thoreson and Dale (1992) found that the frequency of shared reading was related to concepts of print measures. Purcell-Gates (1996), in a study of 24 4- to 6-year-old children from low-income families, reported that families in which there were more higher-level literacy events occurring in the home (i.e., reading and writing texts at the level of connected discourse) had children with a higher level of knowledge about the uses and functions of written language, more knowledge of the written language register, and more conventional concepts about print. Mason (1992) reported that shared reading and children's reading and writing at home were associated with children's abilities to label environmental print. Print motivation may also be the product of early experiences with shared reading (e.g., Lomax, 1977; Lonigan, 1994).

Existing studies do not support a direct link between shared reading and growth in phonological skills (e.g., Lonigan et al., 1996; Raz and Bryant, 1990; Whitehurst, 1996). For example, Lonigan et al. found that growth in preschool phonological sensitivity was related to parental involvement in literacy activities in the home, but growth in phonological sensitivity was not associated with shared reading frequency. Recently, Sénéchal et al. (1998) reported that kindergarten and first grade children's written language knowledge (i.e., print concepts, letter knowledge, invented spelling, word identification) was associated with parental attempts to teach their children about print but not with exposure to storybooks. In contrast, children's oral language skills were associated with storybook exposure but not with parents' attempts to teach print.

Literacy Environments in Child Care Programs

Neuman (1996) studied the literacy environment in child care programs. Child care providers were targeted because of their role in providing care for infants, toddlers, and preschoolers; in many situations, the literacy needs of these children are not the caretakers' primary concern.

Caretakers were given access to books and training on techniques for (a) book selection for children at different ages, (b) reading aloud, and (c) extending the impact of books. The program was evaluated with a random sample of 400 3- and 4-year-olds who received the intervention, as well as 100 children in a comparison group. Results showed that literacy interaction increased in the intervention classrooms; literacy interactions averaged 5 per hour before the intervention and increased to 10 per hour after the intervention. Before the intervention, classrooms had few book centers for children; after the intervention, 93 percent of the classrooms had such centers. Children with caretakers who received the intervention performed significantly better on concepts of print (Clay, 1979), narrative competence (Purcell-Gates and Dahl, 1991), concepts of writing (Purcell-Gates, 1996), and letter names (Clay, 1979) than did the children in the comparison group. At follow-up in kindergarten, the children were examined on concepts of print (Clay, 1979), receptive vocabulary (Dunn and Dunn, 1981), concepts of writing (Purcell-Gates, 1996), letter names (Clay, 1979), and two phonemic awareness measures based on children's rhyming and alliteration capacity (MacLean et al., 1987). Of these measures, children in the intervention group performed significantly better on letter names, phonemic awareness, and concepts of writing.

Dialogic Reading

Whitehurst and colleagues have demonstrated that a program of shared reading, called dialogic reading, can produce substantial changes in preschool children's language skills. Dialogic reading involves several changes in the way adults typically read books to children. Central to these changes is a shift in roles. During typical shared reading, the adult reads and the child listens, but in dialogic reading the child learns to become the storyteller. The adult assumes the role of an active listener, asking questions, adding information, and prompting the child to increase the sophistication of descriptions of the material in the picture book. A child's responses to the book are encouraged through praise and repetition, and more sophisticated responses are encouraged by expansions of the child's utterances and by more challenging questions from the adult reading partner. For 2- and 3-year-olds, questions from adults focus on individual pages in a book, asking the child to describe objects, actions, and events on the page (e.g., "What is this? What color is the duck? What is the duck doing?"). For 4- and 5-year-olds, the questions increasingly focus on the narrative as a whole or on relations between the book and the child's life (e.g., "Have you ever seen a duck swimming? What did it look like?"). See Box 5-4 for a fuller description of this procedure.

Dialogic reading has been shown to produce larger effects on the language skills of children from middle- to upper-income families than a similar amount of typical picture book reading (Arnold et al., 1994; Whitehurst et al., 1988). Studies conducted with children from low-income families attending child care demonstrate that both child care teachers and parents using a six-week small-group center-based or home dialogic reading intervention can produce substantial positive changes in the development of children's language as measured by standardized and naturalistic measures (Lonigan and Whitehurst, 1998; Valdez-Menchaca and Whitehurst, 1992; Whitehurst et al., 1994a) that are maintained six months following the intervention (Whitehurst et al., 1994a).

Whitehurst evaluated the combination of dialogic reading and a center-based phonological sensitivity training program. It was adapted from Byrne and Fielding-Barnsley's (1991) *sound foundations* program with a group of 280 children who attended eight different Head Start centers as 4-year-olds (Whitehurst et al., 1994b, 1998). Children in control classrooms received the regular Head Start curriculum, and children in the intervention condition were involved in small-group dialogic reading several times each week in intervention classrooms over the course of the school year. These same children brought home the book that was being used in the classroom each week for use with their primary caregivers.

Children were pretested on entry into Head Start, posttested on exit from Head Start, and followed up at the end of kindergarten, the end of first grade, and the end of second grade. During Head Start and kindergarten, children were tested in five areas of emergent literacy skills: memory (naming letters, identifying sounds and letters, blending C-V-C words), linguistic awareness

---

BOX 5-4
Dialogic Reading

The fundamental reading technique in dialogic reading is the PEER sequence. This is a short interaction between a child and the adult. The adult prompts the child to say something about the book, evaluates the child's response, expands the child's response by rephrasing and adding information to it, and repeats the prompt at some later point to make sure that the child has learned from the expansion.

Here is an example of a PEER sequence: The teacher is sitting with a group of four children. They are reading the picture book, *Dibble and Dabble*. In the book, two ducks, Dibble and Dabble, see what appears to be a furry snake. They alert their friends, vole, frog, fish, kingfisher, and heron. Everyone becomes frightened as they imagine that the horrible snake is chasing them. They meet a boy, Pete, who calms them down. He takes them to see the furry snake. As the furry snake begins to move behind the reeds, a cat appears. It turns out that the furry snake was only the cat's tail.

At the page in the story in which the furry thing is shown stick-

Box continued on next page

BOX 5-4 Continued

ing out of the reeds, the teacher asks, "What's this?" That is the prompt. Prompts are often questions, but can be statements or requests such as "Tell me about this page." When one of the children responds to the teacher's prompt by saying "grass," the teacher follows by saying "You can say grass. It's kind of a grass." That is the evaluation. An evaluation involves both the teacher's judgment about the child's performance and feedback to the child. In this case, she is acknowledging that the children are on the right track in saying "grass" but also gently telling them that a better word is available with the phrase "It's kind of a grass." She immediately gives the children the information they need to improve their response. She says "It's called reeds"; that is the expansion. An expansion is a form of feedback. It takes what the child has said and demonstrates how the answer could be improved. Even correct answers can be expanded by modeling for children how to make their answers longer or better. The teacher pauses and lets the children repeat what they have heard; that is the repetition. At this time, one of the children says, "weeds." The teacher provides another evaluation and repetition sequence by saying, "Not weed, reed." She pauses and gives them another chance to repeat, which they do.

Except for the first reading of a book to children, PEER sequences should occur on nearly every page. For many books, the adult should do less and less reading of the written words in the book each time the book is shared with the child and leave more to the child.

Prompts are not always necessary. If a child says something spontaneous about a book, then the adult can follow with an evaluation, expansion, and repetition. This is just a PEER sequence without the initial prompt. The child begins it instead of the adult.

There are five types of prompts that are used in dialogic reading to begin PEER sequences. You can remember these prompts with the word CROWD:

C stands for completion prompts. The adult leaves a blank at the end of a sentence for the child to fill in. These are typically used in books with rhymes or books with repetitive phases. Completion prompts provide children with information about the structure of language that is critical to later reading. An example of a completion prompt is: "I think I'd be a glossy cat. A little plump but not too
_____."

Recall prompts are questions about what happened in a book that a child has already read. Recall prompts work for nearly everything except alphabet books. They help children in understanding story plot and in describing sequences of events. They can be used not only at the end of a book, but also at the beginning if a child has been read that book before. An example of a recall prompt is: "Remember when we read *Dibble and Dabble* yesterday. Who were Dibble and Dabble?"

Open-ended prompts focus on the pictures in books. They work best for books that have rich, detailed illustrations. Open-ended prompts help children increase their expressive fluency and attend to detail. They are open-ended because there is no single correct response and many things that a child might say in response to the prompt. An example of an open-ended prompt is: "I read that page. Now it's your turn to read this page. What is happening on this page?"

Wh- prompts include what, where, when, and why. Like open-ended prompts, Wh- prompts focus on the pictures in books. Their primary function is to teach children new vocabulary. An example of a Wh- prompt is: The teacher points to the reeds that are illustrated in *Dibble and Dabble* and says, "What's this?"

Distancing prompts ask children to relate the pictures or words in the book they are reading to experiences outside the book. Distancing prompts help children form a bridge between books and the real world, as well as helping with verbal fluency, conversational abilities, and narrative skills. An example of a distancing prompt is: The teacher is reading the picture book, *Rotten Ralph.* She says, "I don't think Ralph likes the cake. What's your favorite dessert? Are there any desserts that you don't like?"

Dialogic reading techniques should be used while reading a book with a small group of children for repeated readings, spread out over several days. Procedures should differ when reading the book the first time versus after children have mastered the book. The first reading of a book should consist much more of straight reading than prompting so that children can be exposed to the story that the book conveys. Children should be oriented to the book the first time with a few comments about the cover and the title. Subsequent readings should introduce prompts and increasingly turn the task of talking about the book to the children. After children have a lot of experience with a book, they can be given classroom activities that incorporate it. For instance, they can dramatize the book.

Dialogic reading is just children and adults having a conversation about a book. Children will enjoy dialogic reading more than traditional reading as long as the adult mixes up prompts with straight reading, varies questions and focus from reading to reading, and follows the child's interest. Children shouldn't be pushed with more prompts than they can handle happily. Keep it fun.

(identifying same/different words, segmenting sentences, segmenting compound words, segmenting words, rhyming), print concepts (holding a book/turning pages, identifying people engaged in reading, differentiating print from pictures and letters from numerals, identifying functions of print, identifying components of written communication), writing (demonstrating left/ right progression, printing first name, drawing a person); and language (matching pictures to words, describing pictures with words). For the first and second grade assessments, children were tested on decoding (pronouncing nonsense words) and comprehension (matching pictures to printed words). Results showed significant overall effects of the intervention at Head Start posttest and kindergarten follow-up. At posttest, the largest effects were in the domains of memory, print concepts, and writing. At kindergarten follow-up, the largest effects were in the domains of language, memory, linguistic awareness, and writing. Effects of this emergent literacy intervention did not generalize to reading at the end of second grade: differences between children in the intervention condition and those in the control condition did not approach statistical significance. As other studies have suggested (Campbell and Ramey, 1995; Ramey and Ramey, 1998; and Reynolds, 1999), in order for benefits to persist, support for student achievement must continue.

Mathematics and Science

Findings from research support moves to develop suitable learning opportunities for preschool children in mathematics and science, opportunities that embed language learning, strengthen conceptual knowledge, and develop metacognitive skills. Preschool children can develop skills in observing, predicting, and measuring, while learning to lengthen their attention span and regulate their thinking.

Numerical Thinking

The fundamentals of numerical thinking are present very early in life; even babies possess an informal mathematics (Canfield and Smith, 1996; Saxe, 1991; Starkey, 1992; Wynn, 1996).

These fundamental abilities are implicit and sketchy. For example, they can see that there is more *here* than *there* or that *this* has the same amount as *that*. They realize that adding makes more and taking away makes less. Although crude and effective only with very small numbers of objects, their judgments seem to be genuinely quantitative. Much of this is manifest before the onset of language.

The social environment provides young children in virtually all cultures with rich counting systems that can serve as a basic tool for mathematical thinking (Lave, 1988; Rogoff, 1990). Children are active in making good use of this environment. They learn the counting words. But more important, children's counting usually employs mathematical principles of one-to-one correspondence, order, and cardinality in fairly short order (Gelman and Gallistel, 1978). To a large extent, early counting is an abstract, principled activity.

Before entering school, many (but not all) children spontaneously develop operational definitions of addition and subtraction (Griffin and Case, 1998). Addition is combining sets and then counting the elements to get a sum; subtraction is taking away a subset from a larger set and then counting the elements to get a remainder. Over the course of the preschool years, children refine these strategies, making them more efficient and extending their use from concrete objects to imaginary ones. Young children's reasoning about these operations has some basic limitations, but it reflects the beginnings of what could be a sound understanding of basic mathematical ideas (Griffin and Case, 1998).

Children's early, informal conceptions in mathematics can serve as a useful foundation for formal instruction. Mathematics educators need to appreciate young children's informal mathematics on entry into school—their versions of counting, adding and subtracting, and understanding.

That appreciation is a starting point: preschool programs can play an important role in consolidating children's informal understandings by providing opportunities to use and extend mathematical concepts and skills. Moreover, while most children have a well-developed intuitive understanding of number in the preschool years (Hiebert, 1986; Case 1985; Siegler and Robinson,

1982), some children do not. In tests of conceptual knowledge administered to groups of kindergarten children in low-income, inner-city communities, a significant number had not acquired the knowledge typical of their middle-income peers (Griffin et al., 1994, 1995; Griffin and Case., 1996, 1998; Case et al., 1999).

Based on a series of studies done in the 1980s, Case and Sandieson (1987) argue that 4-year-olds generally differ predictably from 6-year-olds in their conceptual understanding of quantity. A typical 4-year-old can solve a problem that requires a distinction between objects that are bipolar: large vs. small, heavy vs. light, etc., and can solve problems where their only task is to count small arrays of objects. But unlike the typical 6-year-old, they have not combined these two understandings into a "central conceptual structure" in which quantity is represented with two poles (e.g., heavy and light) with a continuum of values in between.

The conceptual structure that 6-year-olds generally have in place allows them to successfully master a first grade mathematics curriculum. Students who have difficulty with that curriculum (a disproportionate number of whom come from low-income families) appear not to have that structure in place (Griffin et al., 1994, 1995). The structure requires that the very young child who understands only the distinction between two poles (i.e., a little and a lot) must learn:

1. to verbally count from 1 to 10 forward and backward;
2. to understand the one-to-one correspondence with which the sequence of numbers is mapped onto objects;
3. to understand the cardinal value of each number (i.e., that 3 represents a set whose size is indicated by the number);
4. to understand the rule that relates the adjacent values (that 4 is a set like 3 but with one more added, or that 3 is a set like 4 but with one taken away).

When all four understandings are mastered and integrated, the child is able to solve problems as if he or she is using a mental number line.

The **Rightstart** curriculum (now incorporated into a more extensive preK-2 curriculum called Number Worlds) was designed

---

Box 5-5
Rightstart™ The Number Line Game

The **Rightstart** Curriculum is a series of 30 games designed to put in place a conceptual structure required to use a "mental number line." Each game allows for multiple levels of understanding so children with different knowledge and learning rates learn something from each activity. Each game is designed to be affectively as well as cognitively engaging, and each involves physical, social, and verbal interaction.

The Number Line Game is a board game played in small groups, and each child is assigned a color-coded number line. After a roll of the die, the player computes the quantity, then asks a banker for that many counting chips. She places the chips in sequence on the number line while counting aloud. She then moves her playing piece along the chips (counting again), and rests the piece on the last chip. When children are comfortable with this level of play (i.e., when they can count reliably, quantify sets, match sets to numbers), they are asked to make judgments about who is closest to the goal, and how they know. Chance cards are introduced that require that their position on the number line be incremented or decremented by 1.

The 29 other games are distinct from the number line game, but they too provide opportunities for children to consolidate the same knowledge structure. More than 50% of the games are cooperative rather than competitive. Opportunities or requirements to explain a quantitative assessment are built into many of the games, and are scripted into the teacher's manual in the form of questions to be asked as the students play.

---

to explicitly put this central conceptual structure into place. It consists of a series of 30 games that can be played at a variety of levels depending on the understanding of the children playing (See Box 5-5). The activities are sequenced so that the child masters each one in the order (1 through 4 above) that they are normally acquired.

The curriculum was tested in multiple sites in Canada, California, and Massachusetts, with multiple sized groups of kindergarten children from inner-city schools with large minority populations. The Rightstart children were compared to matched control groups of children who were given an equal amount of attention with a more traditional math program designed to provide a level of affective engagement that was commensurate with the Rightstart program, or to a control group that was given a language program designed with similar criteria in mind. The programs extended over a 3- to 4-month period. In a variety of tests including number knowledge and knowledge transfer, the Rightstart group significantly outperformed the control group. While almost all children in the sample failed the number knowledge test before the training, 4 or 5 months later the vast majority of children who received the training passed, while only a minority of the children in the control groups passed.

In follow-up tests at the end of first grade, many of the control children did acquire the number knowledge to pass level 1 of the test that the Rightstart children had acquired earlier. But the two groups differed in other important respects. Some children in the Rightstart group were able to solve problems at level 2, whereas none of the control children could do so. Moreover, the majority of the Rightstart group passed an oral arithmetic test and a word problem test, whereas a large portion of the control group failed. Teachers also rated the Rightstart children higher, particularly on the items: "demonstrates number sense," "understands the meaning of numbers," and "understands the use of numbers" (Griffin et al., 1996).

Big Math for Little Kids™

Another preschool mathematics curriculum that incorporates the principles of learning discussed above is *Big Math for Little Kids*™. In the words of its developers, it is a challenging mathematics curriculum with the following characteristics:

• It exploits and builds on the informal mathematics that all children construct in everyday life. Informal mathematics is a solid foundation on which at least some formal mathematics can be built (Baroody, 1987; Ginsburg, 1989; Resnick, 1989).
• It presents the study of mathematics both as a separate subject and as an integrated part of other preschool activities. Sometimes, the curriculum presents math activities like counting or

studying shapes. Sometimes, it blends the mathematics into such activities as stories, songs, block building, and the like.

• It helps children to explore mathematical ideas in depth. The goal is to explore key mathematical ideas over a lengthy period of time through extended activities.

• It engages the child in thinking like a mathematician— making interesting conjectures, engaging in problem solving, looking for patterns.

• It aims at taking young children to advanced levels and to investigate complex ideas. For example, instead of limiting the study of shapes to the standard circle, square, and triangle, the program introduces symmetries. Instead of teaching counting to 20 or 30, the program helps children to count into the hundreds. Why? Because they want to and are capable of it. Moreover, mastering challenging tasks fosters feelings of confidence and competence (Stipek, 1997).

• It encourages the rudiments of a reflective, metacognitive approach to early mathematics: self-awareness, verbalization and communication, checking and monitoring one's work, generalization, seeing relations and appreciating abstractions. This is consonant with children's spontaneous efforts and with the Vygotskian approach of helping the child to develop "scientific" concepts (Vygotsky, 1986).

• It prepares children for the formal symbolism of mathematics by establishing clear links between informal mathematics and some basic formalisms. The program does not have a heavy emphasis on symbolism, but does introduce it where it can be made meaningful.

• It employs large-group activity, small groups, and individual exploration. Young children need to learn how to behave and learn in large groups. They profit from the greater degree of teacher attention possible in small groups. And they need time for individual learning and exploration.

The goals of the program are to foster young children's enthusiastic and joyful mathematics learning and to help them prepare for later learning in school. Although the curriculum was designed primarily for 4- and 5-year-old children, it appears to be useful for 3-year-olds as well (Ginsburg et al., 1999). The curriculum is organized into six major strands or basic ideas:

Number. This strand covers such topics as counting (into the hundreds), enumerating objects, and the meaning of number (cardinality).

Shape. These activities focus on identifying and constructing various shapes in both two and three dimensions and exploring their properties, including symmetry.

Putting together and taking apart. This set of activities focuses mainly on adding and subtracting, and also deals with the relations between sets and subsets.

Spatial relations. This strand covers relations like in front of, behind, and left-right, as well as maps—all of which are important for navigating in the world.

Measurement. The exact quantification of physical attributes (like length, weight, and temperature) as well as time and money are explored in this strand.

Patterns and predictions. These activities introduce the child to patterns involving shapes, numbers, and sounds and encourage detection and use of patterns for the purpose of prediction.

The strands are covered in two ways—one involves systematically organized activities and the other daily "pastimes." In working with organized activities, the teacher introduces the six strands, in the sequence described above, over the course of a year. Of course, the level at which teachers cover the material will differ according to the age and ability of the children. Nevertheless, in all cases, the teacher employs activities designed to be continued over a fairly lengthy period of time in order to introduce children in a systematic way to the various "big ideas" or strands.

The developers believe that one distinctive feature of Big Math for Little Kids™ is that the activities are arranged systematically, lead to deep exploration of complex topics, and are pursued intensively throughout the year. The program does not involve discrete bits and pieces: it is a coherent system. And besides being conceptually rich, the activities are a great deal of fun (Box 5-6). The children enjoy the activities and get engrossed in them.

BOX 5-6
Bag It

Bag It is a deceptively simple activity which the teacher begins by presenting children with a collection of plastic ziplock baggies on which are written the numerals 0, 1, 2, 3. The teacher shows how to read the numerals written on each bag and explains that a special number of things should be placed in each. She then presents them with a collection of small objects— buttons, toy cars, miniature people, or similar objects available in the room. The first task is to place in each bag the appropriate number of objects. To do this, each child has to read the numeral on the bag, count out or otherwise determine the corresponding number of objects, carefully place them in the bag, and zip it up. After this has been done, the teacher shows them some "counting bins," boxes on which are written the numerals 0, 1, 2, 3. The job now is to place the plastic bag in the correct bin. This requires reading and matching the numeral on each. This basic task can of course be extended to larger numbers. After a while, children become quite proud of their ability to count out 20 or even 100 objects in the bag.

In fact, when working on the activities, the children often display a very lengthy attention span.

Research shows that young children are capable of and often interested in a variety of mathematical activities. Some of these activities are surprisingly complex and challenging, like constructing symmetries in three dimensions or trying to count beyond 100. In effect, through their often joyful choices, the children are telling us that engagement in challenging mathematics is within their developmental range. Young children do not have to be protected from the study of mathematics or made ready for learning (Greenes, 1999).

Scientific Reasoning

Infants, toddlers, and preschool children have considerable implicit knowledge about topics that are found in science books. Infants, for example, can form general categories that differ as to whether photographs or toys depict animals or various inanimate categories (Mandler and McDonough, 1998). Indeed, they can make inferences about them (e.g., of references for above: Baillargeon, 1994; Leslie, 1994; Spelke and Van de Walle, 1995).

Toddlers who move on their own are surprisingly sensitive to the characteristics of surfaces. For example, they adjust their gaits when moving up as opposed to down inclined surfaces; they inspect unfamiliar surfaces like ice, waterbeds, nets, etc., and then adjust their ways of moving. Sensing that a surface is not sturdy, they get down and crawl (Gibson, 1969). These capacities of obsrvation and prediction are the foundation of scientific inquiry.

Toddlers and very young children experiment with tools and work to learn about objects in the world. For example, Ann Brown has shown that 2-year-old children learn quickly about the kinds of objects they can use to retrieve something that is out of reach (Gelman and Brown, 1986). Karmiloff-Smith and Inhelder's (1974) classic experiment in which children are given blocks to stack, some of which are weighted (reported in Chapter 2), is but one of many that reveal how young children persist at a task, trying out different hypotheses, until they reach a solution.

By age 3, children have learned a surprising amount about the differences between animate and inanimate objects. Indeed, evidence is accumulating that they also know that machines constitute a category separate and different from either animals or inanimate objects (Gelman, 1998; Spelke et al., 1983; Keil, 1989, 1994; Wellman and Gelman, 1992). They already know enough to classify and make inferences about photographs of unfamiliar objects. For example, when asked whether an echidna (an "animal" from Australia that looks a lot like a cactus) can move itself up and down a hill, they give the correct affirmative answer. They also provide reasonable explanations, saying, for example, it must have feet, even if these are not visible in the photograph (Massey and Gelman, 1988).

A wide range of studies converge in concluding that preschool children are eager to learn a great deal about the animal world and to work at learning about the differences between the insides and outsides of objects, the different ways things move and change over time, and a variety of cause-and-effect relationships. They are also able to benefit from language and environments that provide opportunities to use methods of science, including data collection, predicting, recording, and talking about findings (Gelman, 1998).

Especially noteworthy is the young child's propensity to experiment with solutions and to invent solutions to simple arithmetic tasks. These interests of young children can be used as a bridge from entertainment to ongoing efforts of the staff to encourage learning about relevant language, methods, and tools of scientific and mathematical work (which is also fun). This can lead to building a knowledge base that is likely to stand young children in good stead as they move on to other experiences, both in and out of school, about the scientific and technical aspects of the world they will grow up in.

ScienceStart!™

One of the major developmental tasks of childhood is to learn about the surrounding world. Research shows that young children actively process their experiences to form mental representations of "the way things are." Important in themselves, these mental representations (often referred to as scripts or generalized event representations) also form a crucial foundation for the development of a variety of competencies, including language, social interaction, understanding of social roles, classification, and planning (French, 1985; Nelson, 1981; Nelson and Gruendel, 1981).

Young children are cognitively prepared and eager to learn about the surrounding world. Their commonly observed approach to learning—active, experiential, open-ended exploration—makes science an ideal domain for early childhood education. In ScienceStart!™, coherently sequenced science activities become the hub of an integrated curriculum with the following characteristics:

• It focuses on aspects of the everyday world that are familiar, meaningful, and apparent to young children. In general, the program addresses science topics and concepts that the child can experience in the immediate environment. This limitation excludes some popular topics with no contemporary referents (e.g.,

---

BOX 5-7
ScienceStart!™ Air

Air is a subunit of a unit on Properties of Matter (dealing with solids, liquids, gas, and change). During Phase I, Exploration, children explore a variety of features of air, including using straws, hand-held fans, and hair dryers to blow an assortment of objects. During Phase 2, Asking Questions, the teacher guides the students in organizing their explorations and observations into a set of questions. During Phase 3, Follow the Questions, the class carries out a series of activities that address the questions they have developed. During Phase 4, Culmination, children might make and fly kites, use innertubes while going swimming, or invite family members for a Wind Party featuring a dramatic enactment of a book about wind, a garden containing windsocks and pinwheels made in the classroom, and refreshments containing air (e.g., whipped cream and meringues).

---

dinosaurs), no local referents (e.g., oceans for children who live inland), and mechanisms that are highly abstract and largely invisible (e.g., magnets). See Box 5-7 for an example from a unit on Properties of Matter. (In describing ScienceStart!™, the committee does not intend to suggest that young children are incapable of learning about these more abstract topics when presented in ways that engage their imaginations. Indeed, research reviewed in Chapter 2 suggests the contrary.)

• It is coherent. Science activities are coherently organized, with each day's activities building on those of the previous day and providing a foundation for those of the next day. Activities are organized into units (e.g., Measurement and Mapping; Color, Light, and Shadow) that are investigated for four or five weeks and that are sequenced so that increasingly complex skills and concepts are developed and reinforced over time. This approach contrasts with what occurs in many early childhood classrooms, where topics change on a daily or weekly basis (e.g., Valentines, dinosaurs, and presidents' birthdays might be covered during February) or activities are organized around arbitrary themes (e.g., the color red).

• It is integrated. Activities in all areas of the classroom are linked to the daily science investigation. Books relevant to the topic are read aloud during large group time. Activity centers contain props that allow alternative ways of approaching the topic (e.g., during a unit on machines, the dramatic play area might become a car repair shop or the block area might be supplemented with pulleys and ramps). Activities include topic-appropriate extensions into mathematics and social studies and are also regularly extended into outdoor play and art and expression.

• It is open-ended. Children enter preschool with myriad patterns of interests and abilities. To accommodate this diversity, activities in the early childhood classroom must be sufficiently rich and open-ended to permit children to find their own level of participation and developmental challenge. For example, when children mix drops of colored water, some may focus on creating a variety of shades of orange while others practice the small motor skills needed to operate an eyedropper.

• It explicitly models and teaches a scientific approach to problem solving. Individual activities follow a cycle of "Reflect and Ask, Plan and Predict, Act and Observe, Report and Reflect." Early in the year, teachers assume most of the responsibility for articulating and following this cycle; over the course of the year, children gradually take increasing responsibility for doing so. This approach to problem solving extends beyond science into social disputes and carrying out complex, multiphase projects.

• It is language-rich. Language development is a primary developmental task of early childhood and language skill is a potent predictor of learning to read and subsequent academic success. The activities therefore emphasize relevant receptive and expressive language and introduce key vocabulary.

• It uses science activities to involve parents in recognizing and fostering their children's intellectual development.

The primary goal of ScienceStart!™ is to engage children's curiosity and enthusiasm for learning about the surrounding world. At the same time, ScienceStart!™ also seeks to support the growth and development of essential cognitive foundations for academic success (French and Song, 1998), including:

- vocabulary, receptive and expressive language skills, and guidelines for appropriate discourse,
- different forms of self-regulation (including attention management, appropriate participation in large and small groups, and persistence),
- skills in identifying and solving problems, and
- a rich knowledge base that can support comprehension and higher-order intellectual skills, such as inference and prediction.

ScienceStart!™ was developed in the context of a Head Start program serving low-income children, but it is sufficiently rich, open-ended, and developmentally appropriate that it can be used successfully with all preschool-age children. Children who are in a ScienceStart!™ classroom for more than the typical one year continue to develop and extend the essential cognitive foundations; they provide leadership in exploration of the science investigations and further enrich their own knowledge base about the topics covered.

ScienceStart!™ fits easily into the typical early childhood classroom. There are periods for large group activities, choice time in activity centers, and outdoor or large motor play. Teachers have a great deal of flexibility and autonomy in terms of which activities they select for investigation within a given topic area. However, an underlying structure supports the coherence and integration of the curriculum. Daily "leading activities" are organized into units (e.g., Properties of Matter; Simple Machines) and units are composed of phases (Exploration, Asking Questions, Following the Questions, Culminating Project).

Each day, the science-based leading activity serves as a core around which other classroom activities (including vocabulary, expressive and receptive language opportunities, read aloud books, mathematics, social studies, arts and expression, and center-based and outdoor play) are organized. The leading activity is presented during large group time following a simple cycle of scientific reasoning (Reflect and Ask; Plan and Predict; Act and Observe; Report and Reflect) and is subsequently available for individual or small group exploration. Every two weeks, an open-ended science activity related to the unit being covered in the classroom (a Science ZipKit™) is sent home for the child to complete with parents or other family members. Three times a year, classrooms join together in a science celebration in which parents and children work together on science activities.

ScienceStart!™ is both within the developmental range of preschool children and focused on areas critical to readiness and school success. The essential cognitive foundations that form the goals of the curriculum are based on (1) what is known about the ordinary course of development during the preschool years, (2) skills commonly identified as problematic during the early school years, and (3) competencies that are believed to emerge in environmental situations to which children may have differential levels of access depending on family background.

In Head Start classrooms in which ScienceStart!™ has been used, children acquire substantial portions of the knowledge base to which they are exposed during the class investigations of the everyday environment; they show a significant increase on standardized measures, such as the Peabody Picture Vocabulary Test; their participation and language use show a marked increase; and an increase in engagement and group participation is matched by a decrease in disruptive, off-task behavior. Children appear to love the program, learn a great deal about the surrounding world, and develop essential cognitive foundations for later academic success.

Katz (1995) has suggested that all curricula at every level of education address, explicitly or implicitly, the acquisition and strengthening of four dimensions of growth: knowledge, skills, dispositions, and feelings. While young children can be instructed by adults to acquire much knowledge and many skills, dispositions and feelings are not likely to be learned from direct instruction, but by the application of particular pedagogical approaches and the nature of teacher/caregiver-child interaction. Much of the discussion above on curriculum content, particularly as it is described through exemplary programs, implies a pedagogical approach. We now turn more explicitly to research on issues of pedagogy.

PEDAGOGY/TEACHING STRATEGIES

The spectrum of education programs provided for preschool children reflects diverse philosophical beliefs and related approaches to pedagogy. They range from those in which children engage primarily in play or self-initiated activities, to those in which children sit in chairs and passively receive direct instruction. In practice, most programs combine elements of both direct instruction and free play.

Constructivists, for example, take a position between the extremes. They suggest that development results from a complex interaction between children and their environments (Dewey, 1976; Piaget, 1970). Education is child-centered, but the adult takes responsibility for placing the child in environmental circumstances that will provoke active construction of new understandings. The ideal form of education, in this view, involves neither instruction nor laissez-faire free play, but rather the adult's assumption of the responsibility to provide environmental food for thought—that is, circumstances appropriate to the child's current cognitive state that facilitate his or her natural propensity to develop and learn (Copple et al., 1979; Hohmann et al., 1979). These and other programs based on constructivist theory place a strong emphasis on children's construction of ideas and ways of thinking through social interaction.

Sociocultural theory places primacy on cognitive activity occurring through social interaction with more knowledgeable peers and adults who provide support as a child explores new understandings, knowledge and skills, a disposition toward learning, and insight about himself or herself as a learner (Dewey, 1976; Vygotsky, 1978, 1986). Pedagogy is not ultimately about free play, instruction, or placing the child in carefully chosen stimulating environments; the critical factor is a high degree of direct adult engagement and guidance in the process of construction (Bodrova and Leong, 1996). Vygotsky (1978) and Rogoff (1990) provide a description of this learning process. Its central feature requires addressing children within their zone of proximal development, the zone within which a child can actively participate in learning under the guidance of more knowledgeable peers or adults, who structure the learning so as to guide the child through tasks that are just beyond current capability. See Box 5-8 for an example of a program based on this theory.

BOX 5-8
Tools of the Mind

A series of early childhood programs based on sociocultural theory was developed by Bodrova and Leong (1996). They have engaged in long-term intervention studies using programs they have developed for teaching writing and reading as two major intervention efforts. In *Tools of the Mind* (1996), they describe their procedures for instruction in great detail built on the Vygotskian notion of the zone of proximal development (p. 3). These programs are unusual in that they have a well-established theoretical base from which all measures and teaching strategies are derived.

In addition to developing an emergent writing program, these investigators have also developed the Early Literacy Advisor (2000), which is an "advisor to teachers helping them make informed decisions about the pace and direction of classroom practices for those areas of literacy development that can be impacted by instruction." A battery of assessments has been developed and validated. Reports from teachers using the approach indicated satisfaction with its use and the help it provides in developing classroom instruction. (For more information on the Early Literacy Advisor, see Bodrova, et al., 1999.)

Play as a Teaching Strategy

The propensity to play is inherent in children (Franklin, 1999) and has been a focus for most of the major theorists and practitioners in education and developmental psychology. The interest in play is shared by ethnologists who have recognized the role of play in the development of animal species that have long childhoods, complex social organizations, and high-level skill requirements. Piaget and Vygotsky, both of whom have strongly influenced the field of early education, explicitly link symbolic play with language and literacy (Pellegrini et al., 1991) and with developing skill in representation and transformation (Schwartzman, 1978).

Different types of play are more prevalent at different ages, although all forms continue throughout the early childhood period. Infant play involves interaction with caregivers (peek-a-boo) and motor actions (dropping spoons from the high chair), and toddlers engage in locomotive and manipulative play (pull/push toys, construction toys). Infants and young children will engage in "functional play," which involves performing physical actions repetitively and simply for the sake of being active (Fein, 1981). Beginning at around age 4, children engage in "constructive play" by manipulating objects to build or make things. Gradually pretend play (taking on different characters) and language play (nonsense words) are added, with social dramatic play (collaborative social activities) and games (rule play) usually occurring in 4- and 5-year-olds. Young children are highly motivated to play, and play offers the opportunity for self-expression, social collaboration through speech and shared ideas, emotional and social understanding, and self-regulation.

Teachers have long been encouraged to use playful activities as a method to stimulate learning (Pestalozzi, 1905; Froebel, 1886; White, 1905; Dewey, 1976), and in preschools "free play" activities (child-directed interactions with materials and other children) are a large component of the daily program. Most early childhood programs structure children's play (and presumably their learning) by the provision of materials (blocks, dress-up clothes, games, toys), space (housekeeping corners, tables, building areas), and time to use them. While choice and self-directed play are highly valued in preschool programs, teachers are often directly involved and encouraged to intervene more directly in children's play by providing field trips and relevant props, for example, grocery stores, libraries, and by becoming involved in the play themselves by suggesting new activities, vocabulary, and rules (Dyson, 1993; Morrow, 1990; Neuman and Roskos, 1993).

Play as a pedagogical tool has not been extensively researched (Howes and Smith, 1995). There are two likely reasons for this: first, play often has been viewed as noneducational and not related to intentional teaching (Hall, 1991). Second, play is difficult to define (Fein, 1977); thus, much of the research is labeled for attributes of the playing process, such as social interaction, symbolic representation (literacy), role rehearsals, fantasy, enactments, and motor/perceptual coordination, rather than under the generic term "play." It is assumed that underlying children's involvement in these activities is an intrinsic motivation to derive personal pleasure and satisfaction from their chosen activities—to play. Howes and Smith (1995) found play and positive social interactions with teachers predicted more complex cognitive activities in child care centers. When adults, either mothers or teachers, play with children, the children manifest more complex combinations of pretend and are able to demonstrate distancing and decontextualization more readily (O'Reilly and Bornstein, 1993; Howes and Matheson, 1992). However, Kontos (1999) reported that the Head Start teachers she studied, although actively engaged in enhancing and managing children's play—particularly around play with objects—did not in that context provide much rich and stimulating conversation. Below we present additional studies addressing the pedagogical aspects of play, focusing on cognitive and language activity, children's development of self-regulation, and the development of social competence.

Cognitive and Language Activity in Play

Constructing narratives makes cognitive demands for recalling and sequencing information, linking references to prior utterances rather than to tangible objects, and so disembedding language from the here and now (Blank, 1982). Umiker-Sebeok (1979) recorded in three classrooms the intraconversational narratives of 62 3-, 4-, and 5-year-old children during preschool free play. The 3-year-olds initiated narratives to start a conversation: a child would suddenly launch into a story about an event or person at school and, if there was no response, he or she would simply walk away as though no answer had been expected. The 4-year-olds stated the who, when, and where in 64 percent of their narratives, and they reported events that occurred outside school. The 4-year-olds also got a response 56 percent of the time. All the narratives of the 5-year-olds contained information about the who, where, and when of the story, and a third contained one or more comments that elaborated on a current or preceding topic.

Children adapt their speech style to the listeners they are addressing and the roles they are playing. Anderson (1986) asked

24 children ages 3 to 7 to speak for puppets in a doctor's office, a school setting, and a family setting. When role-playing fathers in the family setting, the children used a direct, forceful speech style. Mothers were role-played as more polite and more talkative, using more endearments such as "honey." Unlike the fathers, the mothers that the children role-played qualified or explained almost everything they said. The children shifted into baby talk when role-playing the family child (see also Dunn and Kendrick, 1982; Sachs and Devin, 1976; Wilkinson et al., 1982; Tomasello and Mannle, 1985; Vandell and Wilson, 1987). Children exhibit rudimentary metalinguistic abilities for thinking about language, analyzing it, and playing with it.

Play fosters the use of symbols and symbolic representations (Piaget, 1962; Sigel, 1993). Young children's recall with toys is better after participating in play. In an experimental study of 4- and 5-year-olds' recall memory, children were asked to either "play" with a set of toys or to "remember" the toys (Newman, 1990). In the "remember" session, the children tended to study the toys, rehearsing, sorting, etc., and their language focused on naming the toys. In the "play" session, the children tended to play with the toys both functionally and representationally, and their language focused on elaboration about the toys (e.g., "I'm squeezing the lemon") (Newman, 1990:249). The children had better recall in the "play" condition.[1]

Self-Regulation and Play

Elena Bodrova and Deborah Leong (Bodrova, 1997; Bodrova and Leong, 1996, 1998a, 1998b) describe the work of Vygotsky (1977) and his colleague Elkonin (1978) on play and set this work within a U.S. context. In this framework, play is defined as containing three elements: an imaginary situation, defined roles, and implicit rules. Play is described as necessary for the preschool child in that it provides them with the social and self-regulatory

---

[1]This study also included a similar contrast using pictures instead of toys, and no significant differences in recall were found between the "remember" and "play" conditions. Overall recall with toys was significantly higher than with pictures.

skills needed for learning complex information. In addition to the cognitive features mentioned in the previous section, Bodrova and Leong emphasize that play provides an arena for using language or symbols to practice self-regulation and is therefore central in the young child's mental development. In play, children act according to a set of rules and roles that inhibit and restrain their behavior as they dramatize a scenario. Vygotsky proposes that in this type of play, young children are able to function within their zone of proximal development as the roles and rules of the scenario support activity that they often could not do without support. "In play it is as though he were a head taller than himself . . . as though the child were trying to jump above the head of his normal behavior" (Vygotsky, 1978:74).

Play can provide an important opportunity for children to practice self-regulation in a variety of dimensions. It often takes place with other children and involves the teacher's provisions of an appropriate physical context and time for play. It can involve group or individual intervention to support rule-governed play and to help children plan for play (Bodrova, 1997; Bodrova and Leong, 1996, 1998a, 1998b).

It is important to mention that solitary play may also function as practice for self-regulatory behavior if the play contains all of the features of the above-mentioned group play (imaginary situation, roles, implicit rules). In this context, with support for the child's working within their zone of proximal development, the child is participating in what Vygotsky (1977) terms "director's play."

Social Competence and Play

In the early, preverbal years, pretend play appears to serve the primary function of communicating intent and ideas to others (Howes and Matheson, 1992). Beginning at around age 3, social integration becomes an important function or goal of pretend play (Gottman, 1983). Indeed, social competence is one of the primary skills that children develop and practice through engagement in pretend play.

Early childhood programs are often considered contexts for the development of social competence with peers. Certainly one

of the tasks for children in these programs is to construct relationships and positive interactions with peers. These social interactions and relationships become the basis of peer group social
structure (Corsaro, 1988; Howes, 1988; Howes and Matheson,
1992). Through these early developmental experiences, children
internalize representations of social relationships and social networks, which influence their individual orientations to the social
world as older children and adolescents (Howes and Smith, 1995).
The developmental advance in social competence with peers that
children experience from ages 3 to 8 involves the construction of
more and more complex forms of social pretend play.

Scaffolding as a Teaching Strategy

The support provided to a child to go just beyond current
capability into "the zone of proximal development" (Vygotsky,
1962) is referred to as *scaffolding:* an image that suggests a support to help one work where one could not reach if unsupported.
The adult provides just enough but not too much support, matching the amount of support to the skill level the child displays,
providing more support if the child falters and decreasing support just enough to challenge the child to move ahead.

Ideally, teachers structure content learning so that experiences
are within the children's current range of competence yet challenging to further development. The teacher must then embed
newly established skills into still newer routines (Snow, 1986;
Wood, 1998). In language learning, a primary occasion for teachers to deliberately use scaffolding is during book reading, since
books incorporate vocabulary, rhymes, sentence structures, and
narratives into stories that engage children's attention and provide a context for conversation (National Research Council, 1998).
Correlational studies have shown that parents' scaffolding behaviors facilitate language learning (Ellis and Wells, 1980) when children are 1-2 years old, in the early stages of acquiring vocabulary
and syntax.

Scaffolding can be used to extend a student's competence in
all areas. Student observations about the world (the flower in
that window is growing faster than the one in this window) can
be used as opportunities to think about scientific explanations,

about hypotheses and experimentation. Similarly, student interests that involve quantity can be used as opportunities to extend understanding.[2]

Math Talk While Mixing Flour and Water

5-year-old:	I want to make an experiment with flour and paste.
Teacher:	Why? What's your prediction?
5-year-old:	The flour will make it thicker and drier and it'll be play dough for me to play with.
Teacher:	Well, how much flour would you need for this experiment?
5-year-old:	I need one cup of flour.
Teacher:	And how much paste?
5-year-old:	Two cups.
Teacher:	How much paste do you have now? (She gets a one-cup measuring cup and fills it halfway).
5-year-old:	One-half a cup.
Teacher:	Let's see. You want 2 cups of paste and 1 cup of flour. That's twice as much paste as flour. But we only have one-half a cup of paste. So how much flour should we use?
5-year-old:	One-half of a one-half a cup.
Teacher:	Okay, a quarter of a cup it is.

Peers as Scaffolders

Peers are important to learning that involves such activities as projects, block building, cooperative learning, and any activity that requires the joint involvement of children. Children's performance on a number of cognitive tasks has been found to improve as a result of social interaction with more advanced peers (Murray, 1982; Perret-Clermont et al., 1991; Roazzi and Bryant, 1998).

---

[2]Excerpted from a transcript of circle time conversations recorded as part of a collaborative study between the Child Care Service Centers of the University of California, Los Angeles, and Rochel Gelman's Laboratory.

Roazzi and Bryant (1998) examined children's performance on a simple, inferential task (about numbers) and found that children who had interacted with more competent peers improved in task performance when posttested 3 days after the interaction and then again 3 weeks later. They also found that children who interacted with peers at their same level of competence did not improve in performance.

Children need to be competent in their social interactions with peers in order to engage in such activities. Social competence is defined as the ability to engage the interest of the partner, to attend to the social communication of the partner, to work collaboratively with the partner to construct complex and interesting play sequences, to sustain interaction, and to resolve conflict. There is a literature that identifies individual variations in children's ability to engage in socially competent behaviors with peers. The largest component of this literature is based on sociometric status within peer groups. In essence, children who receive higher sociometric ratings and more sociometric nominations are those children whom classmates perceive as easy to get along with. There also is a large literature that finds strong relations between sociometric ratings and children's observed behaviors. So there is good agreement between behaviors that adults consider socially competent and children's perceptions of who they prefer as friends and work associates.

Scaffolding as a teaching technique need not imply a particular pedagogical approach; indeed, it can encompass multiple approaches. Teachers might simply invite children to engage in a learning activity when they have an initial high level of competence (Wood et al., 1978) and might provide direct instruction when a child is less competent in regard to the new learning. The teaching method employed may change as a child learns a particular skill or concept. Below we elaborate on two types of teaching behavior, child-initiated instruction and teacher-initiated, direct instruction. Most examples of research selected to explain these approaches focus on language development; however, the teaching strategies presented are applicable to other content areas, such as social skills development, emergent reading and writing, and mathematics and science.

Child-Initiated Instruction

In the area of language learning, White (1978) observed that language learning was facilitated in brief episodes precipitated by the child rather than arranged by the adult. When a child initiated interaction, the adult first tried to identify what the child wanted. "Once the interest of the child was accurately identified, the adult had what would seem to be the ideal teaching situation—a motivated student and knowledge of exactly what it was the student was focusing on. The adult then responded with what was needed and generally used some words at or above the child's apparent level of understanding. Once the child showed a lessened interest in the interchange, he was released, allowed to then return to whatever it was he was doing or wanted to do. The entire episode rarely took more than 20 or 30 seconds, although at times there were much longer interchanges" (White, 1978:156).

Hart and Risley (1995) found that although a group of 15 4-year-old children from a poverty community learned to name colors accurately in a group teaching situation, color names were rarely used (an average of less than once per hour in the group) in spontaneous speech. The teachers began requiring that children ask for the materials available during free play. When a child initiated a request for material, the teachers used incidental teaching procedures. The teacher focused on the child's topic when a child initiated, "I want paint," for example, and asked for an elaboration, "What color of paint?" With some children, teachers modeled appropriate answers, as, "Red paint?" or "I have red paint and blue paint. What color do you want?" If necessary, teachers instructed the child, to "Say red paint." When the child answered, the teacher confirmed by repeating what the child said and provided what the child requested. Children's use of color-noun combinations increased to an average of 15 per hour in the group during free play. When children were no longer required to ask for materials during free play, color names decreased to an average of 8 per hour in the group. Empirical evidence supports the efficacy of these teaching practices (Hepting and Goldstein, 1996; Kaiser et al., 1992) on learning-specific, readily measured aspects of language (such as, adjective-noun combinations, use of prepositions, action-object constructions). However, there is limited evidence of effects on language performance outside intervention contexts or on overall language development.

Teacher-Initiated Direct Instruction

Direct instruction refers to the teaching strategy commonly used to facilitate learning academic content. Learning objectives are explicitly stated, materials are carefully sequenced to promote errorless learning, and teachers' activities are specifically focused on ensuring that every child masters the content (Bereiter, 1972). Cole and Dale (1986) compared direct instruction in language to child-initiated language-teaching, as described above. Each program was presented 2 hours a day, 5 days a week for 32 weeks to two groups of 22 children with language delays ages 38 to 69 months in each group. Significant gains on posttests were found for both groups of children. The authors concluded that there was "little difference between the effectiveness of a direct instruction program and an interactive program in facilitating language development in language-delayed children" (Cole and Dale, 1986:213). They note, however, that like Weikart's (1972) comparisons, each program was well staffed with enthusiastic teachers highly trained in the respective methodologies.

Because quality preschool programs address cognitive, social, emotional, and physical development, and because young children vary considerably in each of these domains, teaching strategies need to be adapted to meet the specific needs and prior knowledge and understanding of individuals and groups of children. In effective instruction, multiple teaching strategies are used flexibly, the teacher understanding the effective use of these strategies based on curriculum goals. Direct instruction allows for the efficiency of simultaneous attention to a group of children, indirect instruction (taking advantage of moments of opportunity) makes use of the child's focus of attention, and opportunities for children to learn on their own (self-directed learning) allow for children to work at their individual developmental level. The committee believes that children's enthusiasm for learning should be encouraged and maintained by integrating their self-directed interests and a teacher-directed curriculum.

Using Computers to Support Curriculum and Pedagogy

Computers are increasingly a part of preschoolers' lives. Toward the end of the 1980s, only a fourth of licensed preschools had computers. The vast majority now have one or more computers. Unfortunately, computer access is not equitable across society. Children attending poor and high-minority schools have less access to most types of technology (Coley et al., 1997).

Younger and older preschoolers do not differ substantially in the way they use computers (Beeson and Williams, 1985; Essa, 1987), although 3-year-olds take longer to acclimate to the keyboard than 5-year-olds (Sivin et al., 1985). Those that are most interested in using computers do exhibit higher levels of cognitive maturity (e.g., vocabulary development, more organized and abstract forms of free play). They do not differ from less interested peers in creativity, estimates of social maturity, or social-cognitive ability (Hoover and Austin, 1986; Johnson, 1985).

Some research suggests 3 years of age as an appropriate time for introducing a child to discovery-oriented software. However, even younger children might be introduced to simple software, possibly for developing positive attitudes. The key is appropriately designed software (Shade and Watson, 1987). With the increasing availability of hardware and software adaptations, children with physical and emotional disabilities also can use the computer. Besides enhancing their mobility and sense of control, computers can help improve their self-esteem.

Research has moved beyond the simple question of whether computers can help young children learn. What we need to understand is how best to aid learning, what types of learning we should facilitate, and how to serve the needs of diverse populations. This does not mean every use of technology is appropriate or beneficial. The design of the software and curriculum and the social setting are critical (Clements and Nastasi, 1993).

Social Interaction

An early concern, that computers will isolate children, was dismissed by research. In contrast, computers serve as *catalysts* for social interaction. In one study, children spent nine times as much time talking to peers while on the computer than while doing puzzles (Muller and Perlmutter, 1985). It does appear that the kind of software children use affects social interactions. For example, open-ended programs foster collaboration. Drill-and-practice software, in contrast, can encourage turn-taking but also competition. Similarly, games with aggressive content can engender aggressive behavior (Clements and Nastasi, 1992).

As they interact at the computers, children seek help from each other and seem to prefer help from peers rather than the teacher (King and Alloway, 1992; Nastasi and Clements, 1993). Preschoolers may find it difficult to take the perspective of their partner and also may have trouble balancing the cognitive demands of simultaneously solving problems and managing the social relation (Perlmutter et al., 1986). Such developmental limitations do not necessarily have to preclude collaborative work for the very young. Less demanding tasks are appropriate for collaboration. Also, teachers can provide the additional support and help that they may need (Clements, 1991).

The physical environment also affects children's interactions (Davidson and Wright, 1994). Placing two seats in front of the computer and one at the side for the teacher can encourage positive social interaction. Placing computers close to each other can facilitate the sharing of ideas among children. Centrally located computers invite other children to pause and participate in the computer activity. Such an arrangement also helps keep teacher participation at an optimum level. They are nearby to provide supervision and assistance as needed, but are not constantly so close as to inhibit the children (Clements, 1991).

Computers can also contribute to the social interaction of young children with disabilities who are often unable to participate in play experiences with their peers due to physical, communicative, or other impairments. Toddlers and preschoolers with developmental disabilities who use computers exhibit more communication and social pretend play than comparison groups who do not use computers (Howard et al., 1996).

Teaching and Learning

The computer offers unique opportunities for learning. Even the simplest software, drill and practice, can provide immediate feedback, management of levels of difficulty (although this is often neglected in commercial software), and motivation. Such software helps children gain lower-level knowledge and skills.

Drill has not been as effective in improving the conceptual skills of children (Clements and Nastasi, 1993). To develop concepts and higher-order thinking skills, discovery-based software that encourages and allows ample room for free exploration is more valuable. Such software is also more consonant with widely accepted principles of early childhood education (Clements, 1993).

A long-standing concern is that software would replace other early childhood activities. Research indicates that substituting computer experience for hands-on activity is not desirable, but combining them is beneficial. Computer activities yield the best results when coupled with suitable off-computer activities. For example, children who were exposed to developmental software alone showed gains in intelligence, nonverbal skills, long-term memory, and manual dexterity. Those who also worked with supplemental activities, in comparison, gained in all of these areas and improved their scores in verbal, problem-solving, and conceptual skills (Haugland, 1992). These children spent the least amount of time on the computer. The control group that used drill-and-practice software spent three times as much time on the computer but showed less than half of the gains that the on- and off-computer group did using developmental software (Haugland, 1992). Other similar research shows that computers make a substantial, unique contribution to learning, and that this contribution is greatest when computer and noncomputer activities are combined (Clements and Nastasi, 1992).

Computers also benefit teachers. For example, observing the child at the computer provides teachers with a unique "window into a child's thinking process" (Weir et al., 1981). Research has also warned us not to curtail observations after a few months. Sometimes beneficial effects appear only after a year; ongoing observations also help to chart children's growth (Cochran-Smith et al., 1988).

Similarly, differences in children's approaches to learning are more readily visible at the computer when children have the freedom to follow diverse paths towards the goal (Wright, 1994). This is particularly valuable with children with disabilities, as the computer seems to reveal their hidden strengths.

Gender difference also can be observed and should be monitored so that equity is maintained. Some studies find that preschool boys may choose the computer more often than girls (Beeson and Williams, 1985; Escobedo and Evans, 1997). However, many studies report that girls and boys do not differ in the amount or type of their computer use (Clements and Nastasi, 1992). Considering the traditional heavy dominance of computer use by males, these researchers recommend that the early years are the ideal time to introduce students to computers. All teachers should ensure that boys do not dominate computer use.

In summary, teachers should seek to fully integrate developmentally appropriate, bias-free software matched to educational goals. Multimedia capabilities should be used when they serve educational purposes. Features such as animation, music, surprise elements, and especially consistent interaction get and hold children's interest (Escobedo and Evans, 1997). They can also aid learning *if* designed to be consistent with, and supporting, the pedagogical goals.

Curriculum and Computers

Effectively integrating technology into the curriculum demands effort, time, and commitment. Much preschool software has been found effective in the language arts area. It includes drill-and-practice software (Clements, 1987; Clements and Nastasi, 1992) and word processing programs with speech (Borgh and Dickson, 1986; Moxley et al., 1997). Talking word processors allowed 4-year-olds to take control of and experiment with language. For example, two young girls were examining a picture-word card with a colored triangle. They were unsure what the word ("triangle") was and, after a brief discussion, walked over to the word processor, typed it in, and satisfied their curiosity. A girl who knew she confused "b" and "d" experimented with the talking word processor on her own (she typed: dead dird dlue, and then bead, bird, and blue). A week later, she always chose the correct letter (Clements, 1994).

Language interventions with special populations have shown

positive results. Severely handicapped children who were trained on communication skills using a computer increased their receptive and expressive language more than those with regular classroom training (Schery and O'Connor, 1992). Most were incapable of using the computer intervention without supervision and support from a trainer, but they were able to sustain interest and respond to the format over 10 weeks.

In mathematics, the computer can provide practice on arithmetic processes and foster deeper conceptual thinking. Drill-and-practice software can help young children develop competence in counting and sorting (Clements and Nastasi, 1993; Elliott and Hall, 1997).

Enhancement of these environments through self-regulatory instruction results in significantly increased achievement. Such metacognitively oriented instruction includes the strategies of goal identification, active monitoring, modeling, questioning, reflecting, peer tutoring, discussion, and reasoning (Elliott and Hall, 1997). Other approaches are also useful, especially for higher-level concepts and problem solving. Using programs that allow the creation of pictures with geometric shapes, children have demonstrated growing knowledge and competence in working with concepts such as symmetry, patterns, and spatial order (Wright, 1994; Tan, 1985).

The "Building Blocks" project (Clements and Sarama, 1998) shows that software design based on current theory and research can help children use and develop processes, such as composing and decomposing shapes and numbers, in sophisticated ways. The basic educational approach is finding the mathematics in, and developing mathematics from, children's activity to help them extend and mathematize their everyday activities.

Computers help even young children think about thinking, as early proponents suggested (Papert, 1980). In one study, preschoolers who used computers scored higher on measures of metacognition (Fletcher-Flinn and Suddendorf, 1996). They were more able to keep in mind a number of different mental states simultaneously and had more sophisticated theories of mind than those who did not use computers.

In summary, across several subject matter areas, computers can positively affect how children learn and think, as well as their metacognitive skills. When selecting and using software, teachers should remember that while drill-and-practice software can increase basic skills and knowledge, other approaches prove more valuable in developing higher-level concepts and thinking skills.

SUMMARY

What should children learn in preschool? Our first answer—one with which few would disagree—is that preschool programs need to address social, emotional, and physical development as well as cognitive development. Given the committee's mandate, however, we have focused on the latter. Much of the research base on young children's learning investigates cognitive development in language and literacy, mathematics, and science. Because these appear to be "privileged domains" in which children have a natural proclivity to learn, experiment, and explore, they allow for nurturing and extending the boundaries of learning in which children are already actively engaged. Developing and extending children's interests is particularly important during the preschool years, when attention and self-regulation are nascent abilities.

What should be taught in a preschool curriculum? Few would disagree that a heavy emphasis should be placed on language and literacy. While we do not advocate an extension downward of the elementary school literacy curriculum, much can be done to develop emergent literacy skills that will better prepare children for elementary school, promoting an interest in, and enthusiasm for, language in oral and written form. While no single curriculum is identified as best, an extensive body of research suggests the types of activities that promote emergent literacy skills, from story reading and dialogic reading to providing materials for scribbling and "writing" in pretend play, and from participating in classroom conversation to identifying letters and words.

In mathematics and science, research suggests that children are capable of thinking that is more complex and abstract than was once believed. Curricula that work with children's emergent understandings, providing the concepts, knowledge, and opportunities to extend those understandings, have been used effectively in the preschool years. When these activities operate in the child's zone of proximal development, where the learning is within reach, but takes the child just beyond his or her existing ability, these curricula have been reported to be both enjoyable and educational.

As with learning throughout life, learning in the preschool years will be most effective if it engages and builds on children's existing understandings. In the early years, there is already substantial variation among children in their knowledge, skills, and thinking. It is therefore important that teachers attend to the developmental level of the child in whatever domain the curriculum is addressing.

The body of research suggesting that competence requires both factual knowledge and a grasp of key concepts applies in the preschool years as well. Key concepts involved in early literacy (representation), math (mental number line), and science (causation) are acquired by many, but not all, young children (see Chapter 3). If all children are to enter the school years with an adequate foundation for learning, it is particularly important that preschool curricula develop those core concepts.

Finally, the metacognitive skills that allow students to learn more deliberately and have been shown to raise achievement in all three academic areas can be introduced in preschool curricula as well. "Theories of mind" research suggests that children begin to consider what it means to learn and how to go about the task already at an early age (see Chapter 2). Curricula that encourage children to reflect, predict, question, and hypothesize set them on course for effective, engaged learning.

How should teaching be done in preschool? Research suggests that many teaching strategies can work. Both direct instruction and child-initiated instruction, teaching through play, teaching through structured activity, and engagement with older peers and with computers are effective pedagogical devices. The panoply of strategies can be used as a toolkit, with each tool serving different ends, but none being most effective for all purposes. Since preschool programs serve so many ends simultaneously— including the development of self-regulation, attention, social competence, and motor skills as well as development in language, literacy, numeracy, and science—multiple pedagogical approaches should be expected. Children are less likely to develop social competence during direct instruction than during play, but direct instruction may be efficient at building a knowledge base. Organized storytelling may help develop attention span as well as vocabulary, but vocabulary is made active when children engage—as in child-initiated instruction or in interaction with older peers.

While understanding of teaching and learning in the preschool years has broadened considerably, increasing knowledge suggests just how challenging is the task of the preschool teacher. There are no magic bullets, no right curriculum or best pedagogy. We know that children can learn a great deal in the care of an adult who is tuned into the child's current level of development and his or her developmental challenges. We know that when carefully supported or scaffolded, children can be happily engaged in relatively complex thinking and problem solving. Sensitivity to individual children's current competence may be one reason for the links between developmental outcomes, positive caregiver behaviors, and formal professional education that is observed in empirical research. In the next two chapters, we turn to the tasks of assessing young children's development and of professional development that prepares those who take on the multifaceted, complex job of preschool teacher.

Assessment in
Early Childhood Education

THE USE OF TESTS AND ASSESSMENTS[1] as instruments of education policy and practice is growing. Throughout the school years, tests are used to make decisions about tracking, promotion or retention, placement, and graduation. Many teachers use tests or assessments to identify learning differences among students or to inform instructional planning. Widespread public concern to raise education standards has led states increasingly to use large-scale achievement tests as instruments of accountability (National Research Council, 1999a). Given their prevalence in the education system as a whole, it is not entirely surprising that the use of tests

---

[1]Although the terms are not mutually exclusive, the word "test" tends to be used to refer to standardized instruments, formally administered, and designed to minimize all differences in the conditions of testing presented to test takers. There are both individually administered and group-administered standardized tests. The group-administered multiple-choice format is what people often have in mind when the term is used. Assessments embrace a wide array of formats (observations, performance measures, portfolios, essays). The term "assessment" is often used to communicate the intention to build a richer picture of the ways in which people think, learn, and work. They frequently are conducted over a longer period of time than group tests permit. Standardized tests focus on individual differences, answering the question "How does this individual compare with all others in the reference population?" Assessments reflect the interest of modern cognitive theory in the processes of learning and knowing in a given individual.

233

and assessments is increasingly common in preschool settings as well.

In the current early childhood education milieu, there are four primary reasons for assessment (Shepard et al., 1998):

- Assessment to support learning,
- Assessment for identification of special needs,
- Assessment for program evaluation and monitoring trends, and
- Assessment for school accountability.

Assessment to support learning, the first and most important of these purposes, refers to the use of assessments to provide teachers with information that can serve as a basis for pedagogical and curriculum decisions. Information presented in earlier chapters— about early learning, about the episodic course of development in any given child and the enormous variability among young children in background and preparation for school, about the centrality of adult responsiveness to healthy cognitive and emotional development—leads to the conclusion that what preschool teachers do to promote learning needs to be based on *what each child brings to the interaction*. Assessment broadly conceived is a set of tools for finding this out. The second reason for assessing young children is to diagnose suspected mental, physical, or emotional difficulties that may require special services. The final two purposes can be combined under the rubric of assessment to make policy decisions.

Each of these purposes represents an important opportunity for test or assessment data to inform judgment—if the tests or assessments are used carefully and well. No single type of assessment can serve all of these purposes; the intended purpose will determine what sort of assessment is most appropriate. There is much to be learned from the experience in other educational settings about the uses, misuses, and unintended consequences of testing (e.g., Haertel, 1989; Gifford, 1993; National Research Council, 1982a; U.S. Congress Office of Technology Assessment, 1992; Shepard, 1991). And there is much to remember about the developmental status of young children, including the nascent state of their attention and self-regulation abilities, that makes assessment even more challenging than in other populations. The psychometric models on which testing has traditionally been based make standardized tests particularly vulnerable to misinterpretation (Shepard et al., 1998).

Experts agree on a number of guiding principles that apply to any setting in which tests or assessments are used in decision processes (see, for example, American Education Research Association, American Psychological Association, National Council on Measurement in Education, *Standards for Educational and Psychological Testing*, 1999; Shepard et al., 1998; National Research Council, 1999a). Perhaps the most important of these is that no single procedure should be the sole basis for decisions, or, put positively, important educational decisions should be grounded in multiple sources of information. These might include individual assessments of various sorts, standardized tests, observation, investigation of social and cultural background, and interviews. A corollary of this statement is that no test score should be looked on as infallible or immutable.

A second point of consensus is the requirement of measurement validity. Whether test or assessment, formal or informal, criterion- or norm-referenced, the measures being used need to have a reasonable level of accuracy. This means that school officials and teachers must inform themselves. They need to understand the strengths and weaknesses of various assessment approaches for the purposes they have in mind. They need to know what the research says about the specific instruments they intend to use. They need to develop sophistication in the interpretation of the information gleaned from tests and assessments.

A third important principle is borrowed from the Hippocratic oath to first do no harm. When test or assessment information is used for placement, school readiness, or other high-stakes decisions, it behooves educators to pay attention to the consequences and to make sure that they are educationally beneficial.

ISSUES IN STANDARDIZED ASSESSMENT OF YOUNG CHILDREN

Beyond these principles that apply generally to educational testing and assessment, there are important considerations that become particularly salient in the assessment of young children. The evolution of views on the optimum conditions for assessment provides a good example. The traditional psychometric concerns with standardization have in the past been applied to assessments of young children. Individual or group tests were administered under controlled circumstances in highly structured environments that were as similar to one another as possible. But dissatisfaction among many early childhood professionals concerning the conventional model of norm-referenced assessment has in recent years brought a shift in emphasis toward conducting assessments in settings that are comfortable, familiar, nonthreatening, and of interest to the child (see Meisels and Provence, 1989; Greenspan and Wieder, 1998). There is evidence that such settings better enable young children to show what they know, what they can do, and what they are experiencing (Meisels, 1996b).

Many of the reasons that can be advanced to support this approach to assessment environments (among them the motivation to design assessments that have greater ecological validity) could also pertain to assessment of older children and adults. But there are also developmental and cultural characteristics of young children that can be attended to more effectively in more flexible settings than is possible in most standardized testing environments (Bracken, 1987). Examiner-examinee rapport, for example, is much trickier with very young children simply because of their very limited experience; race, gender, culture—even size—can significantly influence the child's ability to focus and attend. The motivation, state of arousal, and disposition of the very young child are likely to be much more variable than is the case for older test takers, who have more developed self-regulation abilities. The very young are by definition less familiar with the whole notion of and materials used for assessment, so that creating a more flexible and responsive environment that promotes the physical and emotional comfort of the child is likely to produce a more accurate picture of the child's knowledge, skills, achievement, or personality (Meisels, 1994).

Developmental Considerations

Young children have, in varying degrees, developmental limitations on several important (and often unrecognized) dimensions that can affect assessment. We have made reference above to the nascent state of the ability to focus and attend in children of the ages of concern in this report. Likewise, the capacity to be purposeful and intentional, although undergoing rapid development, is certainly less than fully formed. In assessment situations, therefore, young children often have difficulty attending to verbal instructions, situational clues, or other instructions and stimuli. They may have difficulty understanding the demand characteristics of the measurement situation, and they may not be able to control their behavior sufficiently to meet these demands (Gelman and Gallistel, 1978).

Obviously, there are also implications for assessment of the emergent state of young children's verbal abilities. Depending on the child's functional capacity to use ideas and to communicate thoughts and feelings, for example, examiners may need to make inferences based on the child's overt motor behaviors or parent report, rather than direct response. Observational modes of assessment and interviews lend themselves to this situation. And although tests or assessments that require examiners to elicit responses can be useful, for example, to assess the child's grasp of key concepts about written language, math, and science, a different view is provided when the assessment casts the child as the initiator. Elicited language in particular may be qualitatively different from language that is used functionally in everyday contexts, and thus not representative of the child's functioning.

Cultural Considerations

In an important sense, education can be viewed as the journey from natal culture to school culture to the culture of the larger society. Education inevitably involves cognitive socialization, that is, learning the repertoires of cognitive skills that are required for successful functioning in the dominant culture. A modern industrial society like the United States that is technologically advanced, as Ogbu (1994) puts it, will possess a repertoire of cognitive skills appropriate for advanced technological culture. Technological intelligence is appropriate to and a prerequisite for functioning competently in that culture.

In a highly heterogeneous society such as ours, child care centers and preschools are in a position to play an extremely important role in helping youngsters get off to a good start on that journey. But that requires teachers to be sensitive to the influences of culture both in choosing pedagogical strategies and in the use and interpretation of assessments. There are any number of obvious pitfalls that teachers are well aware of, for example, the use of English-language assessments that depend on verbal interactions with children who are growing up surrounded by a different home language. But valid assessment requires being aware of much more subtle factors as well. For example, there are great cultural variations in the ways in which adults and children communicate (National Research Council, 1999b:96-101). Ethnographic research has shown striking differences in how adults and children interact verbally. Many American Indian and African American subcultures do not cultivate the role of information giver that characterizes American middle-class children; the young are expected to learn through quietly observing adults (Heath, 1983). In some communities, children are seldom direct conversational partners with adults; children eavesdrop on adults, while older children take on the task of directly teaching social and intellectual skills (Ward, 1971). Children from these cultural backgrounds are not nearly as likely to show their actual verbal ability in assessment situations based on the elicited response model as those for whom question and answer is a familiar ritual. Culture also plays a role in determining which cues are most salient to children (Rogoff, 1990).

One of the greatest dangers in assessing young children is to associate developmental status with the norms of the dominant middle-class culture. This will lead to misunderstanding of children's functional abilities and misjudging pedagogical strategies. To draw again on Heath's ethnographic studies (1981, 1983), white, middle-class mothers begin questioning games from earliest infancy—"Where is Teddy Bear? Ah, there he is." Children exposed to these "known-answer" rituals are more likely than others to be comfortable with the question-and-answer dialogues typically encountered in preschool and school settings. Chapter 5 emphasized the importance of having a toolkit of teaching strategies, with each tool serving different ends and none being most effective for all purposes. The same can be said of assessment.

Sensitivity to the child's current competence means taking the child's home culture into account in assessment.

Assessing Children with Disabilities

One of the most difficult issues in early childhood assessment has to do with children who appear to need special assistance as a result of cognitive, emotional, visual, auditory, or motor impairments. On one hand, research has demonstrated that early intervention can often reduce or prevent later problems in school (National Research Council, 1998; Meisels and Margolis, 1988). But there is also a long and unhappy history with the unsophisticated use of IQ and achievement tests.

In a study of several hundred psychologists who work with young children, Bagnato and Neisworth (1994) found that only 4 percent of their respondents supported the use of norm-referenced, standardized intelligence tests for young children with developmental problems. Most respondents to their survey emphasized the importance of flexibility in the choice of assessment methods, the potential for modification of the instruments, and the need for a multidimensional, team-based assessment approach.

Potential problems with the use of norm-referenced tests are numerous. Some pertain to the technical adequacy of the instruments, and others derive from the way they are used (National Research Council, 1982b; Fuchs et al., 1987; Barnett and MacMann, 1992; National Research Council, 1997). In the first category are inadequate or unknown psychometric properties, including the common absence of children with disabilities in the samples used to develop test norms. Some children will require accommodations, but determining what accommodations are appropriate for whom and under what circumstances is difficult. The lack of knowledge about the functional characteristics of disability makes it difficult to determine whether or not the disability is related to the construct being measured, which in turn makes the interpretation of test results difficult. But even when tests are carefully developed, the test content may be inappropriate for certain subgroups of the population or biased against economically disadvantaged children. And finally, as is true of any assessment, whether norm-referenced or not, the assessment may be irrelevant to the intervention process.

In addition to recognizing these challenges and problems, it is important to consider the assessment approach chosen in light of the purpose one has in mind. There are attributes of standardized, norm-referenced instruments that may make them well suited to certain high-stakes decisions, such as school accountability (although the issue of age appropriateness still obtains in preschool settings), but they should not be the cornerstone of an assessment system for working with individual children to help them develop new intellectual capacities, in which careful observation of the child in context is essential (Greenspan and Wieder, 1998). As Meltzer and Reid (1994) point out, standardized tests emphasize the end product of learning, ignoring the processes and strategies children use for problem solving. They fail to distinguish between a child's current level of performance and his or her ability to learn and acquire new skills and information. And they tend to ignore the role of motivation, personality, social factors, and cultural issues. As a consequence, the use of norm-referenced instruments has often led to misclassification and incorrect special education placements.

Perhaps the most important thing to remember about assessment of young children—whether the children are disabled, high risk, or developing typically—is that their development is episodic and uneven, with great variability within and among children. Intelligence, however one defines it, is not a stable construct in young children (e.g., Cronbach, 1990; Anatasi, 1988). This is manifest in the lack of agreement across measures and in the unreliability of assessment instruments. Standardized, norm-referenced tests are particularly vulnerable to misinterpretation because they imply a degree of certainty that assessments of young children simply cannot provide.

All of these cautionary statements about developmental and cultural issues and the potential shortcomings and misuses of standardized tests do not alter the fact that assessment is a key ingredient in the teaching and learning process. Assessment, whether of the informal variety that nearly all teachers engage in on a spontaneous basis, or of a more formal kind, can help to guide instruction and is an integral part of learning.

ASSESSMENT FOR PEDAGOGICAL AND INSTRUCTIONAL PLANNING

We know from research that learning is a process of building new understandings on the foundation of existing understandings. Learning will be most effective, therefore, when the child's preconceptions are engaged. This has direct implications for teaching and for the development of curricula. It is essential for teachers to ascertain the nature of thinking and the extent of learning for each child in order to make good decisions about what concepts, materials, and learning experiences will support the child's further growth. Perhaps the most significant change to take place in early childhood assessment in recent years concerns the linking of assessment and instruction. In their report to the National Education Goals Panel, Shepard and colleagues (1998) put it succinctly: "Assessing and teaching are inseparable processes."

The idea behind the fusion of assessment and instruction is relatively simple and rests on three fundamental assumptions (Meisels and Atkins-Burnett, 2000). The first is that assessment is a dynamic enterprise that calls on information from multiple sources collected over numerous time points, reflecting a wide range of child experiences and caregiver interpretations. The second assumption is that the formal act of assessment is only the first step in the process of acquiring information about the child and the family. Through intervention—by putting into practice the ideas or hypotheses raised by the initial assessment procedures—more information will be acquired that can serve the dual purpose of refining the assessment and enhancing the intervention. Third, assessment is of limited value in the absence of instruction or intervention. The meaning of an assessment is closely tied to its utility—to its contributions to decision making about practice or intervention or its confirmation of a child's continuing progress.

Nearly all early childhood educators rely on some form of informal monitoring of child learning in order to design programs and plan curricula—that is, in order to engage in pedagogy. However, relatively few early childhood teachers systematically observe, record, evaluate, and document children's learning—although the need for systematic documentation is rapidly being imposed from many directions, including the new Head Start child performance standards.

Teachers can learn to observe and document children's skills, knowledge, and accomplishments as they participate in classroom activities and routines, interact with peers, and work with educational materials. Curriculum-embedded forms of assessment, for example, are contextualized methods that allow children opportunities to demonstrate their knowledge or skills through active engagement in classroom activities. Teachers who practice curriculum-embedded assessment rely on checklists, portfolios, and other collections of children's work to document learning and to monitor instruction (Meisels, 1996a, 1987; Wiggins, 1998).

Assessment of Competencies in Young Children

Research on cognition shows that young children's knowledge is more complex than expected. We are a long way from being able to integrate knowledge of developing competence and assessment methodology and practice. At present, a National Research Council Committee on the Foundations of Assessment, chaired by Robert Glaser and James Pellegrino, is attempting to rethink and enrich methods of assessment in light of advances in the science of human cognition, development, and learning. The goals they hold out for a new science of assessment are maximizing student competence, making students' reasoning processes more transparent, and creating a system where curriculum, instruction, and assessment are integrated in a mutually supportive fashion.

As learning scientists, measurement experts, and practitioners gradually create a new science and practice of assessment, there are several useful assessment methods that can be used to help to dig beneath the surface of overt behavior to get at thought processes. Chapter 5 described the use of specially designed tasks that can help uncover a child's grasp of important concepts, for example, the idea of "quantity" that is fundamental to understanding mathematics or the idea of "representation" that underlies words and illustrations that is the foundation of literacy. We look below in detail at two approaches to uncovering such information: clinical interview methods (Ginsburg, 1997), and dynamic assessment (Bodrova and Leong, 1996; Burns, 1996; Burns et al., 1992; Day et al., 1997; Lidz and Pena, 1996), which often employs combinations of special tasks, observation, and clinical interviews. The discussion of assessing competence then moves on to performance assessment which, in contrast, focuses on concrete, observable behavior.

Clinical Interview

Piaget developed the "clinical interview" method, which is a most informative—and difficult—technique by which to assess children's thinking. While the technique is most commonly used by trained therapists to assess children with learning problems and other disabilities, the clinical interview also lends itself to use by the teacher when the knowledge she wants to gain about a child is not evident in his or her performance.

The goal of the clinical interview is to identify the child's underlying processes of thought. Its essence is its flexible, responsive, and open-ended nature. In the clinical interview, the interviewer asks the child to reflect on and articulate thinking processes. Although at the outset the interviewer has available several tasks likely to be appropriate for the topic at hand, initial questions are intentionally quite general, allowing the child's response to influence the direction and content of the interview. The interview is a highly theory-bound activity that employs nonspecific questions such as "How did you do it?" "What did you say to yourself?" and "How would you explain it to a friend?" so as to encourage rich verbalization and to avoid biasing the response. As the interview evolves, tasks and questions are determined in part by the child's responses. Tasks are varied and modified, becoming more specific in order to focus on particular aspects of thinking, and more difficult in order to test the limits of understanding. In the clinical interview, the examiner's behavior is to some degree contingent on the child's; in standardized testing, the child's behavior is always contingent on the examiner's questions.

The clinical interview permits the interviewer to formulate, test, and revise hypotheses about the child's thinking. The interview combines several methods: observation, test, experimentation, and "think aloud." The interviewer observes the child's behavior and listens to the child's verbalizations; presents "test items"—problems of various sorts, often involving concrete objects; experiments with different questions or tasks to test hypotheses; and asks the child to think aloud, to verbalize thought processes as explicitly as possible.

An interview is time-consuming and demanding, requiring 20 minutes to an hour of concentrated effort. A good interviewer must have command of the relevant content being assessed and must be familiar with typical thinking—that is, with normative behavior—at the child's level. Because it is a highly interactive technique, the interviewer must be able to generate useful hypotheses concerning the child's thinking on the spot, must have the ability to devise methods for testing these hypotheses as the interview proceeds, and must be sensitive to the nuances of the child's affect and motivation so as to establish rapport and motivation.

Many would agree that the interview method is powerful. But can it be used effectively by ordinary teachers? Or more precisely, can teachers who put the effort into learning the method make practical use of it in the hurly-burly of the everyday classroom? Several different approaches to adapting the interview method for classroom use have been suggested.

The National Council of Teachers of Mathematics (NCTM), for example, has been advocating the use of "authentic" assessment in classrooms, including the conduct of informal interviews. The NCTM journals frequently describe interview methods for teachers and give examples of their use. An article by Jencks (1989) described a procedure for interviewing students every five to six weeks at the beginning of a new topic of study. Another study reported research involving administration of 10- to 15-minute interviews by a mathematics specialist, who was then able to uncover difficulties hidden by correct responses on tests and to provide diagnostic information helpful to the teacher and the students' parents (Dionne and Fitzback-Labrecque, 1989). Others have described how interview activities can be integrated into, and can indeed transform, classroom instruction (Ginsburg et al.,

1993; Moon and Schulman, 1995). The experience with classroom use of interview methods is limited and the opportunities for adequate teacher training even more so. Yet there is much to recommend the approach to the research, practitioner, and professional development communities.

For one category of children, namely children with disabilities, the clinical interview is a critically important approach to assessment and will usually need to involve a trained therapist working with teachers. Most children with disabilities have problems in more than one area, which makes it very easy to make incorrect assumptions about the child's capabilities. Many children diagnosed with cognitive deficits, for example, also have problems with sensory processing and motor planning. It is essential to understand the unique profile of a child with special needs, to observe how that child interacts with family, teachers, and caregivers, in order to create the optimal intervention program tailored to the child's specific needs (Greenspan and Wieder, 1998:22-23).

Assessment in the Vygotskian Mode

One essential aspect of assessment to support learning is to provide information concerning children's ability to profit from teaching. The teacher is not interested in what the child knows or has mastered at any given point in time for its own sake, but as a clue to what concepts, knowledge, and opportunities can be provided in order to extend the child's emergent understandings. The goal is to understand a child's zone of proximal development—that area where learning is within reach but takes the child just beyond his or her existing ability (see Chapters 2 and 5). From this perspective, the role of assessment is to provide insight into the kind of educational experiences that will be most effective in helping particular children learn (Bodrova and Leong, 1996; Burns, 1996; Burns et al., 1992; Cronbach, 1990; Day et al., 1997; Ginsburg et al., 1999; Lidz and Pena, 1996)

In recent years, the concepts of two major theorists, Lev Vygotsky and Reuven Feuerstein, have stimulated and legitimated efforts to develop assessment techniques designed to promote children's learning potential. Vygotsky's theory describes the human being as goal directed, an active seeker of information. Children come to formal education with a range of prior skills, understandings, knowledge, beliefs, and concepts built on experience which help the child navigate the surrounding world. These prior conceptions influence what the child notices about the environment and how they interpret it (National Research Council, 1999b, 1999c). The role of assessment, from this point of view, is to draw out and make explicit the child's prior conceptions or skills so that the teacher knows how and where to intervene to help the child advance. What the child is capable of at the present time becomes the pedagogical bridge to what a child can do, given assistance.

This pedagogical framework encourages the fusion of instruction and assessment. Consider the example of an assessment of children's equilibrium. Bodrova and Leong (1996) describe Teresa and Linda as they walk a balance beam: ". . . neither Teresa nor Linda can walk across a balance beam. Both of them stand on the end and stare down the beam. The teacher holds out her hand to assist each girl's performance. Although each is given the same teacher support, Teresa can only stand on the balance beam holding the teacher's hand tightly while Linda walks across the beam easily. Independent performance is misleading in this example. When we see how the two girls respond to assistance, we can tell that they are at very different levels." If the question motivating assessment were "Can this child walk the balance beam?" (or, Can this child add and subtract?), then the test would have stopped with each child's standing immobilized at the end of the balance beam and the simple answer for both would be "No." But because the emphasis is on understanding each child's current level of functioning (each child's zone of proximal development) as a guide for instruction, the more flexible and interactive assessment provided teachers with important information about what each particular child would need.

Similarly, Feuerstein (1979), much of whose work centered around the assessment of disadvantaged children's mental abilities, proposed a system of "dynamic assessment," in which the examiner engages in assisted instruction as a method for measuring the child's learning potential. Dynamic assessment techniques have also been designed to measure one or more skills accurately and meaningfully over time. Teachers can then use repeated measurement on those behaviors to (a) model growth, (b) describe student difficulties, and (c) identify and plan programs for children who warrant intervention early in their lives. The disadvantage of this method is that the long-term indicators are only as good as the initial measurement—if an inaccurate measurement is used, the models developed will be inaccurate.

Dynamic Indicators of Basic Early Literacy Skills (DIBELS; Good and Kaminski, 1996; Kaminski and Good, 1998) is an example of a dynamic indicator. DIBELS focuses on story retelling, picture description, picture naming, letter naming, letter sounds, rhyming fluency, blending fluency, phonemic segmentation fluency, and onset recognition fluency tasks—the behaviors thought to represent the "critical" prereading skills needed for entering and succeeding in first grade. Important progress toward the development of a system to model growth, describe student difficulties, and identify and plan programs for children who warrant intervention early in their lives has been made; DIBELS's phonemic segmentation fluency measure demonstrates strong traditional reliability and validity and suggests promise in terms of its capacity to model student literacy growth. Additional research on DIBELS and other alternative systems to monitor children's development is needed to define their relative strengths and weaknesses.

Performance Assessment

Performance assessment takes a somewhat different approach to the assessment of competence. It is best understood in the context of learning about children's knowledge, skills, and accomplishments through observing, recording, and evaluating their performance or work. Many feel that performance assessments lessen the likelihood of invidious comparisons between children, since each is evaluated according to how his or her specific levels of performance conform to the aims of the curriculum, rather than on how closely the performance conforms to the average performance of a normative group. In addition, they are not typically designed to sort and categorize children.

Some performance assessments can be described as "authentic assessment" when they avoid "on-demand" tasks and focus instead on the assessment of concrete, observable behaviors on real (or realistic) tasks that are part of children's ordinary classroom experiences. To the epistemological question "What is knowing?" performance assessment answers that the evidence of knowing is in the doing (see Meisels et al., 1995a). Hence, authentic performance assessments thrive on context and on the evidence acquired from natural settings.

With this focus on the evidence of knowing as represented in concrete behaviors or products, competence is not assessed on the basis of a single performance. Performance assessments require multiple sources of information and multiple observations of the same or related phenomena before conclusions can be drawn. They rely on extensive sampling of behavior in order to derive meaningful conclusions about individual children. A variety of documentation methods (e.g., a portfolio, a set of systematic checklists) can be brought into the assessment system. Over time and in the context of numerous performances, teachers observe "the *patterns* of success and failure and the reasons behind them" (Wiggins, 1998:705). These patterns constitute the evidence on which the assessment is based.

A significant virtue of performance assessments is that they permit children to demonstrate different approaches to performance. Different children may have highly comparable skills, but they may demonstrate these skills in very different ways. (Examples of performance assessment are presented in Box 6-1). Many also believe that a classroom emphasis on hands-on performance can enhance children's motivation and offer a more informative way of engaging families in their children's intervention progress.

There are several characteristics common to performance assessment that make the technique particularly attractive to many who work in the early childhood field (see Calfee, 1992; Herman et al., 1992; Shepard, 1991; Wiggins, 1998). They can encourage systematic processes of:

  • documenting children's daily activities to show their initiative and creativity,

• providing an integrated means for evaluating the quality of children's performance and behavior,
• reflecting on an individualized approach to pedagogy,
• evaluating those elements of learning and development that most conventional assessments do not capture very well,
• utilizing the information acquired in the teaching process to further elaborate the evaluative picture of the child that is emerging from the assessment, and
• shifting the teacher's attention and activity away from the typical content of test taking and onto the learning of the child and the environment in which instruction is taking place.

Traditional norm-referenced ability and achievement tests provide a summative statement about the test taker. An important point to be made about all three of the approaches to the assessment of competence discussed here, including performance assessment, is that they are formative: they provide information that can be used both to change the process of intervention and to keep track of children's progress and accomplishments. Information about the child and the setting that is gathered on a structured but continuing basis is then used to inform the intervention-instructional process. Because the emphasis is on continuous assessment, they can be used to monitor a child's progress frequently, rather than summarizing that progress on annual or semiannual occasions. But performance assessments, like all of the assessments, will only be as strong as the theory on which they are based. Assessment involves theorizing—having informed ideas about the processes of learning and developing hypotheses about a child's strengths and deficits on the basis of assessment information.

Instructional Assessment and Pedagogy

When pedagogy is defined as it has been in this volume—as an interactional construct that reflects a joint focus on the child's status and the characteristics of the educational setting—two conditions are critical for the assessment of learning (see Meisels, 1999, for an elaboration of these ideas). First, there must be sus-

---

BOX 6-1
Approaches to Performance Assessment

Work Sampling System

Widely used throughout the nation since 1991, the Work Sampling System (Meisels, 1987; Meisels et al., 1994) is a performance assessment designed for children from preschool through grade 5. This approach relies on developmental guidelines and checklists, portfolios, and summary reports. It is based on using teachers' perceptions of their students in actual classroom situations while simultaneously informing, expanding, and structuring those perceptions. It involves students and parents in the learning and assessment process, instead of relying on measures that are external to the community, classroom, and family context, and it makes possible a systematic documentation of what children are learning and how teachers are teaching.

The Work Sampling System draws attention to what the child brings to the learning situation and what the learning situation brings to the child. As active constructors of knowledge, children should be expected to analyze, synthesize, evaluate, and interpret facts and ideas. This approach to performance assessment allows teachers the opportunity to learn about these processes by documenting children's interactions with materials, adults, and peers in the classroom environment and using this documentation to evaluate children's achievements and plan future educational interventions. Evidence of the reliability and validity of the Work Sampling System with kindergarten children is available (Meisels et al., 1995b; Meisels et al., 1998).

Child Observation Record

Developed by High/Scope, this assessment provides a means of systematically observing children's activities in the ongoing con-

---

tained opportunities for the interactions between teacher and child to occur, and, second, these interactions must occur over time, rather than on a single occasion. This view does not hold that one can round up all of the kindergarten children in a community on a given day and test them to determine what they know and can do. Rather, it suggests that learning can be assessed only over time and in context.

Several methods exist today that can provide the type of as-text of their classroom experiences, including prolonged activity and across time periods (High/Scope Research Foundation, 1992). The focus of the observations is on "important developmental experiences that should happen in all developmentally appropriate early childhood programs" and on "existing strengths and weaknesses rather than skills that have not yet emerged." Six broad areas are assessed: initiative, social relations, creative representation, music and movement, language and literacy, and logic and mathematics. The system is comprehensive, providing behaviors to observe, a systematic way to collect anecdotal remarks, and a means to draw conclusions about the children's performance in order to plan instruction.

Project Construct

"Project Construct is a process-oriented curriculum and assessment framework for working with children ages three through seven" (Missouri Department of Elementary and Secondary Education, 1992:3). It is based on constructivist theory and includes curriculum and assessment guidelines organized into four interrelated domains: sociomoral, cognitive, representational, and physical development. The project design provides a variety of resources for educators and parents, including curriculum materials, assessment instruments, and training and professional development opportunities. The Project Construct Assessment System is an integrated set of evaluation tools aligned with the Project Construct curriculum goals for children. Two components make up the assessment system—the Formative Assessment Program and the Inventory. Both parts utilize multiple sources of information that are primarily collected by teachers over extended periods of time.

sessment that occurs over time and in interaction. They contain not only a joint focus on the child's status and the characteristics of the child's educational setting, but they also encourage individual planning, programming, and evaluation. The Work Sampling System, designed for preschool-grade 5 (Meisels et al., 1994; Meisels, 1996b), is one example of an assessment system designed to achieve these goals.

The three types of instructional assessment described above

are not adopted easily or without expense. They require extensive professional development for teachers; changes in orientation regarding testing, grading, and student classification by educational policy makers; and alteration in expectations by parents and the community. Such changes entail financial burdens, centralized coordination and program evaluation, and long-term commitment from teachers, parents, and the community—all of which are potential obstacles to implementation.

The path to progress has been demarked in the most recent call to the field from the Goal 1 Technical Planning Group of the National Education Goals Panel: "The Technical Planning Group, while understanding the complexity of the technical challenges associated with defining and assessing early development and learning . . . is convinced that new assessments are doomed to repeat past problems unless such efforts are permeated by a conceptual orientation that accommodates cultural and contextual variability in *what* is being measured and in *how* measurements are constructed. Within the broad parameters of standardization, then, flexibility and inventiveness must be brought to bear on the content and the process of assessment" (Kagan et al., 1995:42).

ASSESSMENT FOR SELECTION AND DIAGNOSIS

Two important functions served by testing are selection and diagnosis. Selection or "readiness" assessments are intended to determine a child's preparedness to profit from a particular curriculum. Diagnostic testing is used to determine the type and extent of a special need or disability. A third type of assessment, developmental screening, is a relatively brief testing instrument typically used to determine whether further diagnostic testing is indicated. Each type of assessment is quite distinct from the others.

Developmental Screening

Developmental screening is a brief procedure designed to identify children at high risk for school failure. These are norm-referenced standardized tests that typically evaluate a broad range of abilities, including intellectual, emotional, social, and motor abilities. Developmental screening is typically performed individually on large numbers of children, requiring very little time per child. There are several instruments that have been developed with attention to *Standards for Educational and Psychological Testing* (APA, AERA, NCME, 1986) (AERA, APA, NCME 2000) and have high reliability and predictive validity (Meisels, 1987, 1988; Nuttall et al., 1999). When appropriate instruments are used, developmental screening is an extremely valuable source of information. They should be considered as the first step in an evaluation and intervention process that can help prevent the emergence of more serious problems in children before they have had an opportunity to affect the course of development (Meisels and Atkins-Burnett, 1994).

Diagnostic Assessment

Diagnostic assessment is intended to determine conclusively whether a child has special needs, ascertain the nature and character of the child's problems, and suggest the cause of the problems, if possible. According to federal law, diagnostic assessments administered by schools must be conducted in a team setting that utilizes multiple sources of data and is part of a system of special education services. Such an assessment provides the data that are used to create individualized family service plans (IFSPs) and individual educational plans (IEPs) (Bailey and Wolery, 1992).

In the past, the most common tools used for diagnostic purposes were intelligence tests, which focused primarily on the child in isolation. Today, assessments are considered incomplete unless they view the child in relation to three domains. The first is the child's biology. The second is the child's interactive patterns with parents, teachers, siblings, and others. And the third is comprised of the patterns of the family, the culture, and the larger environment (Greenspan and Wieder, 1998; Greenspan, 1992). Unless the child is examined within these contexts, inferences about his or her developmental status will be incomplete and generalizations about developmental trajectories may be seriously flawed.

Greenspan and Wieder (1998) posit six fundamental development skills that lay the foundation for all learning and underlie all advanced thinking, problem solving, and coping (pp. 3-4):

1. The dual ability to take an interest in the sights, sounds, and sensations of the world and to calm oneself down.
2. The ability to engage in relationships with other people.
3. The ability to engage in two-way communications.
4. The ability to create complex gestures, to string together a series of actions into an elaborate and deliberate problem-solving sequence.
5. The ability to create ideas.
6. The ability to build bridges between ideas to make them reality-based and logical.

These "functional emotional skills" provide the theoretical framework for assessing the child's developmental progress over time and guide the course of interventions.

Greenspan draws heavily on the clinical interview procedures described earlier as a means of getting underneath the disability categories that so influence our expectations of children (autism, attention deficit disorder, mental retardation, pervasive developmental disorder) to the "functional emotional skills" of the individual child. He argues compellingly from his work with infants and young children that the differences among children who bear the same label are greater than their similarities and that, with careful assessment, it is possible to tailor a treatment approach that helps the individual child climb the developmental ladder.

Whatever combination of assessments is used for the purposes of diagnosing disabilities and learning problems, it is important that any cognitive, behavioral, or sensory measures used meet high standards of validity and reliability. The very real challenges of interpreting the performance of children with special needs on standardized instruments also means that it should be in the hands of trained professionals.

Readiness Testing

Readiness tests indicate a child's relative preparedness to participate in a particular classroom, rather than addressing general developmental status. The most commonly used readiness tests include items that assess children's perceptual skills (matching one shape from an array of other shapes), knowledge of alphabet letters, awareness of the use of prepositions (on, under, behind), colors, and sometimes receptive vocabulary. Note that the emphasis is very different from Greenspan's functional emotional skills listed above.

Early learning readiness measures are widely used—many would say misused—to determine whether children are ready for kindergarten. For example, many programs designed to prepare poor and immigrant children for kindergarten or first grade use readiness tests during the last year of preschool, typically at 5 years of age, to make promotion recommendations.

It is interesting to note that what readiness tests measure is not well aligned with what teachers think is important. Teachers' views of readiness were surveyed by the U.S. Department of Education's Kindergarten Teacher Survey on Student Readiness (National Center for Education Statistics, 1999). As shown in Figure 6-1, over 75 percent of the teachers surveyed considered it very important or essential that children be physically healthy, rested, nourished, enthusiastic and curious in approaching new activities, and able to communicate needs, wants, and thoughts verbally in their primary language. In contrast, 25 percent or fewer of the teachers considered the following items very important or essential: counts to 20, has good problem-solving skills, can use a pencil or paintbrush, and knows letters of the alphabet. In short, teachers' opinions about readiness seem to reflect the importance of receptivity to learning, rather than the particular skills that a child may or may not have acquired before coming to school.

While it is easy to endorse what the survey indicates that teachers think, it is also important to recognize that these characteristics fall far short of what the cognitive and developmental research shows that young children are capable of. This misalignment between current goals and future possibilities will eventually find a measure of resolution as advanced learning principles are incorporated into learning and instruction in preschool and child care settings and as more and more children have the advantage of such instruction.

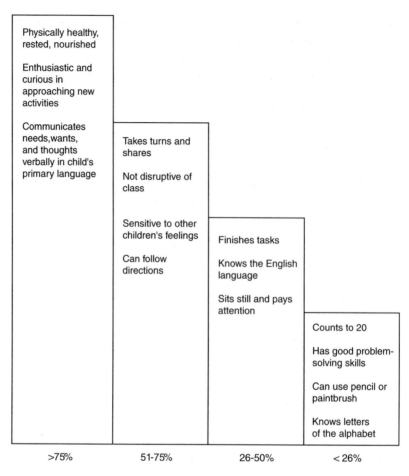

FIGURE 6-1 Percentage of public school kindergarten teachers indicating whether various factors for kindergarten readiness were very important or essential. SOURCE: National Center for Educational Statistics (1999).

In the meantime, schools and programs need to think carefully about the use of readiness tests. Readiness is a very complex construct, including intellectual and social abilities, and its assessment will be affected greatly by young children's episodic and unstable growth patterns and by variations in how children live and are raised. Some children may do very poorly on readiness tests at the outset of school simply because they were not exposed to or taught the items that are on tests. Once enrolled in kindergarten, these same children may thrive. This is a particular concern for children from minority and disadvantaged backgrounds. And since schools and programs differ, the fundamental requirement in every evaluation of a child's school readiness should be that the assessment is grounded in direct relevance to the criterion, namely, functioning in that school or program.

These considerations have led many to conclude that readiness tests are not suited for use in child placement and promotion decisions, although they may have value for purposes of instructional planning (Meisels, 1987, 1989a, 1989b; Stallman and Pearson, 1990).

ASSESSMENT FOR POLICY DECISIONS

Tests and assessment results are increasingly used as a basis for important policy decisions in education. Large-scale testing programs generate data that inform about which schools or programs should be funded, which should be closed, who should be rewarded, what types of programs should be developed, and who should be informed that improvement is required if further assistance is to be forthcoming. Public reporting of assessment data by district or by school has become commonplace, as has the use of these data for rewards and potential sanctions. These types of decisions are known as high-stakes decisions (see Madaus, 1988; National Research Council, 1997).

High-stakes testing also refers to the use of assessment data to make decisions about individual students or teachers. The use of readiness tests to make decisions about enrolling a child in kindergarten provides one illustration. Other uses include retention, promotion, tracking, placement in special education, and selection into advanced programs (Madaus, 1988; Meisels, 1989a, 1989b; National Research Council, 1999a).

High-stakes testing is closely tied to the notion of accountability, so that poor scores on such examinations will result in negative sanctions of one sort or another. It is widely believed that tangible rewards or punishments will provide strong incentives for schools, teachers, and children to improve their performance.

The use of assessment to support policy decisions is much

more prevalent in the public school system than in preschool settings. However, most early childhood programs for poor children and children with disabilities are supported with public monies, and agencies typically seek to evaluate the effectiveness of their programs in order to justify the spending of taxpayers' dollars. The evaluation studies of Head Start and other such programs are of this genre. As more and more young children are cared for and educated outside the home, the pressure for accountability is likely to increase—not just to satisfy a demand for reporting on public expenditures but as an expression of society's interest in protecting its youngest and most vulnerable members.

Such uses of assessment data for purposes external to the classroom, rather than improve educational practice directly, place a particularly heavy burden both on the assessment instruments and on the responsible adults. The data must be collected in a standardized way that permits comparisons across schools. This means, for example, that teachers should not give help during the assessment unless it is part of the standard administration to do so (Shepard et al., 1998). Note how different the protocols for appropriate test use are for this sort of testing than for assessment designed to support pedagogy and instruction.

Although there are many attempts under way to rethink testing and assessment to combine some of the statistical power and generalizability of standardized tests with the richer portrait of individual learning and development that characterizes many alternative assessments, we are a long way from achieving that goal. Some researchers are proposing that the aggregate of classroom-based assessment be used for accountability reporting (Bridgeman et al., 1995). If the use of external standardized tests increases in the preschool environment for reasons of public policy, it is essential that they meet the highest standards of reliability and validity.

Above all, any tests used for policy purposes must not be mistaken for statements about the learning trajectory of the individual child or allowed to diminish the importance of the kinds of assessments that will support learning. Likewise, standards for child performance such as those articulated by Head Start should absolutely not have any consequences associated with them for the individual child (AERA, APA, NCME, 2000; Shepard et al., 1998).

SUMMARY

What are the roles of assessment in preschool? We have described three broad categories that constitute the major purposes of assessment in early childhood settings—assessment to inform instruction, assessment for diagnostic and selection purposes, and assessment for accountability and program evaluation. Just as there are different purposes for assessment, there are many different types of assessments, from the clinical interview to the statewide assessment used for school accountability. No single assessment will satisfy all educational needs or solve all educational problems.

Assessments must be used carefully and appropriately if they are to resolve, and not create, educational problems. This means using each assessment in the way in which it was designed and intended. To use assessment as a blunt instrument, in which one type of assessment is expected to perform the functions of others, squanders resources and places children at risk for school difficulties. The Committee on School Health and the Committee on Early Childhood of the American Academy of Pediatrics (1995) made clear the dangers inherent in the inappropriate use of tests and assessments (p. 437):

> When instruments and procedures designed for screening are used for diagnostic purposes, or when tests are administered by individuals who have a limited perspective on the variations of normal development, or when staff with little formal training in test administration perform the screening, children can be wrongly identified and their education jeopardized.

We have written at length about the need for a fusion of assessment and instruction in early childhood settings. Assessment has an important role to play in revealing a child's prior knowledge, development of concepts, and ways of interacting with and understanding the world so that teachers can choose a pedagogical approach and curricular materials that will support the child's further learning and development. We have described a number of promising approaches to assessment to support learning—the clinical interview, dynamic assessment, performance assessment.

The fact is, however, that most early childhood educators are not trained in traditional testing and measurement, to say nothing of the newer kinds of assessment. Moreover, assessment in early childhood tends to be considered external and irrelevant to the teaching and learning process, rather than something that can complement educational programs and, indeed, is essential to making the program work for each child. If we are to use the important findings about human learning from the cognitive, neurological, and developmental sciences to improve early childhood pedagogy and instruction, it is important that early childhood educators and caregivers be trained to use assessments for purposes that will advance teaching and learning (Arter, 1999; Brookhart, 1999; Jones and Chittenden, 1995; Meisels, 1999; Sheingold et al., 1995; Stiggins, 1991, 1999).

Finally, we have emphasized the importance of using assessments and tests particularly carefully with young children. The first five years of human life are a time of incredible growth and learning. The rapid growth of the brain in the early years provides an opportunity for the environment to play an enormous role in development. But the course of development in young children is uneven and episodic, with great spurts in learning in one and lags in another. As a consequence, assessment results can easily be misinterpreted. Standardized tests are particularly vulnerable to misuse with this population, but any assessment procedures must be used intelligently and with care. The developmental characteristics of young children make it even more important that teachers and caregivers be trained to think about and use assessment well.

7

The Preparation of Early Childhood Professionals

THE HISTORY OF THE PREPARATION of teachers is as diverse as other aspects of early childhood programs. In the United States, there have been no state or national standards or certification processes for teachers of young children. Indeed, before 1965, few states included qualifications for teachers in their licensing standards. College-educated teachers attended liberal arts colleges or were enrolled in departments of home economics (Bowman, 1990) and had little course work in curriculum or pedagogy. More often, mothers with varying education drifted into the field, capitalizing on their past experience as mothers and caregivers.

While more attention has been paid to the skills and knowledge necessary for early childhood teachers in recent years, the field is still characterized by teachers with a minimum of training. There is a serious mismatch between the preparation (and the compensation) of the average early childhood professional and the growing expectations of parents and policy makers—expectations that this report will dramatically reinforce. Teachers of young children are being asked to promote high levels of achievement among *all* children, respond sensitively and appropriately to a wide array of diverse student needs, implement complex pedagogy, have a deep understanding of subject-matter disciplines, engage in serious reflection about their practices, and work collaboratively with colleagues and families.

Over the past century, learning goals for children have

changed, and instructional strategies have often failed to keep pace. A National Research Council study on developments in the science of learning (National Research Council, 1999) notes that "functional literacy," which at the turn of the century referred to decoding simple or easily interpreted text, now is a measure of reading for information and analyzing and interpreting complex ideas. The new emphasis has vastly increased both the range and depth of knowledge expected of even young children, placing pressure on teachers and parents to pay more attention both to children's capacity to learn new information and to the conditions under which they learn.

The knowledge and skills of teachers are among the most important factors in determining how much a young child learns. Studies in Texas, Alabama, and New York of K-12 teachers concluded that "teachers' qualifications (based on measures of knowledge, education, and experience) account for a larger share of the variance in students' achievement than any other single factor" (Darling-Hammond et al., 1999:228). What early childhood teachers know and are able to do is one of the major influences on the learning and development of young children. Clearly, the preparation and ongoing professional development of teachers in early childhood education and care is fundamental to the vision expressed in this report.

In this chapter, we discuss professional development and its relationship to program quality, the preparation of early childhood teachers, the variety of teacher education experiences and requirements, and research related to in-service education. Much of the literature reviewed here draws from the body of research on teacher development more generally. While the content of teacher knowledge and the nature of the responsiveness of teachers to their students distinguishes the preparation required of preschool teachers, in many respects their professional development is similar to that of teachers of older children. The principles of learning discussed in Chapter 5 (engaging and building on existing understandings, providing a deep foundation of factual knowledge within a conceptual framework, and stressing metacognition) must be effectively understood and deployed by all teachers, and the efforts to teach teachers at all levels must also incorporate those principles.

PROFESSIONAL DEVELOPMENT

The professional development of teachers has been shown to be related to quality of early childhood programs (Howes et al., 1992; Kontos et al., 1997), and program quality predicts developmental outcomes for children (see Chapter 5; Kontos et al., 1997; Vandell and Corasaniti, 1990). Formal professional education has consistently been linked to positive caregiver behaviors (Bollin and Whitehead, 1990; Espinosa, 1980; Fischer, 1989; Howes, 1997; Darling-Hammond, 1998). Studies have generally found the strongest relationship between the number of years of education and the appropriateness of a teacher's classroom behavior (Arnett, 1989; Berk, 1985; Clarke-Stewart and Gruber, 1984; Howes, 1997; Kontos et al., 1997; Ruopp et al., 1979). There is also research support for the proposition that education focused specifically on child development and early childhood education improves the performance of child care providers (Epstein, 1999; Ruopp et al., 1979; Kontos et al., 1997). The authors of *Who Cares for America's Children* (National Research Council, 1990), concluded that, although both overall education and caregiver training specific to child development are related to positive outcomes for children, "the two existing national studies point to caregiver training as the more important factor" (p. 91).

The Florida Child Care Improvement Study (Howes et al., 1995) found that an increase in required professional preparation and in-service education for child care workers in Florida resulted in improved overall quality as measured by the Early Childhood Environmental Rating Scale (ECERS) as well as increases in teacher sensitivity and responsiveness (with accompanying decreases in teacher harshness and detachment). Classroom ratings of global quality and of teacher effectiveness (i.e., sensitivity, responsiveness, positive initiations, decrease in negative management, promotion of positive peer interaction) were most likely to improve when the teacher had at least a child development associate credential (or equivalent); the highest scores were obtained by teachers with a B.A. and advanced education.

Cassidy et al. (1995) studied the effects of college course work on caregiver beliefs and practices. They found that, after enrolling in an associate degree program in early childhood education or child development and completing 12-20 credit hours of community college course work, participants demonstrated significantly more developmentally appropriate beliefs and practices, as measured by the ECERS and the Teacher Beliefs Scale (TBS), than a comparison group that did not attend the college classes. The TBS assesses teachers' beliefs about the importance of certain classroom practices, such as working silently, preparing written materials, and having time for free play. It was constructed and validated as an assessment of the extent to which the teachers' beliefs about teaching are congruent with the principles of developmentally appropriate practice (Charlesworth et al., 1993b). Cassidy and her colleagues emphasized, however, that although they found improvements in practices and beliefs after the college course work, the majority of the courses completed by the participants (87 percent) focused on child development or early childhood methods content, thus explaining the correlation of years of education with course content.

The pattern of evidence in these studies, together with the evidence on early learning and the centrality of the responsive adult presented in earlier chapters, points out the need for major investments in teacher preparation and professional development to support new capacities in teachers of early childhood education. But in fact, early childhood centers spend considerably less than do elementary schools on the professional development of their teachers: elementary schools devote 3.6 percent of teachers' work time to professional development, child care centers 1.3 percent, and Head Start 3.04 percent (Center for Early Childhood Leadership, 1999).

Teachers' Thinking and Beliefs

Research on teaching effectiveness has shown that teachers have implicit beliefs about subject matter, their students, and their roles and responsibilities that significantly influence how they behave in the classroom (Ball and Cohen, 1996). Classrooms are complex environments with many overlapping interactions going on between adults, children, materials, and conceptual tasks. Teachers respond to this complexity by referring to their own store of beliefs, experiences, and priorities, establishing a teaching stance that gets the job done.

A number of studies have documented the importance of teachers' unwillingness to accept research on teaching unless the information fits with their already formed beliefs; even then, they are more apt to adapt than to adopt new ideas (Kennedy, 1997). Teachers' belief systems have been shown to be related to whether or not they successfully adopt new educational practices (Hollingsworth, 1989; Richardson et al., 1991). When a proposed educational practice is inconsistent with a teacher's stated belief, the teacher has more difficulty adopting the proposed innovation. These finding are, of course, completely consistent with the learning research presented in Chapter 2 and described more fully in *How People Learn: Mind, Brain, Experience, School* (National Research Council, 1999). Just as it is necessary to work with children's preconceptions in order to guide them to more advanced understanding, so adults' prior conceptions need to be consciously engaged if they are to continue learning and improving in their occupations.

Views about teaching and learning are particularly deeply entrenched, and are developed, as Lortie (1975) describes it, during the apprenticeship of observation that occurs during the many years each of us spends in the classroom being a student. These early experiences as a student exercise a powerful influence on teachers' beliefs about what it takes to be an effective teacher, how students learn best, and how students should behave (Clark, 1988; Nespor, 1987; Wilson, 1990). These basic beliefs, shaped by early experiences of being a *student*, have also been shown to be unrealistic, overly optimistic, and centered on teaching as a process of transmitting knowledge and of dispensing information (Brookhart and Freeman, 1992) that is at odds with contemporary research on cognition and learning. If early childhood educators are to develop a professional orientation based on knowledge, reflection, and analysis, it is critical that pre-service and in-service education directly address these memories of early experience and the resulting resistance to change (Lortie, 1975; Buchmann and Schwille, 1983).

In addition to the early experiences of the classroom that we all share, there are some broadly-held cultural attitudes that have an impact on the assumptions that shape the behavior of teachers. For example, one of the most powerful and pervasive attitudes in the United States has to do with the notion of intelligence or IQ. Americans tend to approach learning through the lens of intelligence and thus see school performance as a reflection of native ability. In Japan, by way of contrast, the emphasis is on effort. There is strong evidence of the efficacy of effort and practice in the cognitive science literature (National Research Council, 1999, Chapter 2), but all too often the idea that intelligence is determinative is reflected in education policy and practice.

Teachers' beliefs are also influenced by views of learning that derive from research, often as it is relayed in the popular press or school texts. Whether consciously or not, some teachers espouse what might be called the *romantic* view, which stresses the natural unfolding of development in the child. Others embrace the *didactic* view, an adult-centered approach in which the child is provided a well-structured sequence of lessons that transmit what the adult determines the child needs to know. Those who are versed in the more recent research may adopt a *constructivist* theory of learning, which emphasizes children's strong propensity to gather information and construct ideas about how the world works as they engage the surrounding environment, or the related *sociocultural* approach, which proposes that children learn to construct ideas and ways of thinking primarily through social interactions with more knowledgeable peers and adults.

Although a specific theoretical perspective is seldom seen in pure form in practice, teachers often explain the rationale for their teaching style in terms of one or another of these developmental perspectives (Bereiter et al., 1970; Genishi, 1992). Some educators have emphasized the need for teachers to develop a single, coherent theoretical framework as opposed to an eclectic approach (Marcon, 1999); however, others have argued that a unifying theory of education that sums up all the phenomena of education is not likely to exist (Malaguzzi, 1993).

Research on the relationship between teachers' stated beliefs and their observed teaching practices has been inconsistent and tied to some extent to the type of beliefs expressed. Early childhood teachers who accept behaviorist principles of development tend to employ teaching practices that are consistent with this belief, whereas teachers who express views based on the principles of developmentally appropriate practices (Bredekamp,

1986, 1995) display much more variability in their practices (Charlesworth et al., 1993a; Isenberg, 1990). Delclos et al. (1993) found that teachers' theoretical orientation (DISTAR [Direct Instruction System for Teaching and Remediation] versus cognitively oriented) was influential in their interpretation of assessment reports on preschool children.

The biggest danger posed by a superficial understanding of learning research is that these theories of learning can easily be misunderstood to dictate particular methods of teaching. As the reading wars demonstrate, there is a strong propensity, when it comes to educating our children, for theory to change into ideology (National Research Council, 1998), a state that is antithetical to the kind of reflective practice that this report is intended to encourage. It is important that the education of teachers help them to develop the ability to reflect on their beliefs, and to cultivate the metacognitive capacities that will help them tailor their teaching strategies and approaches to the needs of their students.

Effective Teaching Strategies

The relationship between the goals of education and effective instructional strategy has received recent attention from the Committee on Developments in the Science of Learning of the National Research Council (National Research Council, 1999). While much of the committee's focus is on teaching older children, there are some relevant findings for teachers of preschool children as well. The committee stresses the importance of teaching for understanding, a strategy that requires teachers to familiarize themselves with what children have already learned in order to build on or correct prior knowledge. They also note the importance of knowing children's personal and cultural background in order to accurately assess their learning and developmental accomplishments. The committee draws attention to the importance of teacher knowledge in framing lessons that are meaningful to children. They admonish against creating a false dichotomy between learning rote information and skills and learning to understand and think. Both types of learning are important and ideally occur together.

A number of different approaches have been used to study

teaching effectiveness. One group of studies has investigated the characteristics of effective early childhood teachers (Bloom, 1985; Katz, 1999). Bloom, for instance, studied the qualities most often associated with the first teachers of talented adults. During the early stages in the acquisition of high-level skills, he suggests that the teacher qualities to be desired are more social than cognitive or technical. He found the first teachers in his study liked children, made learning pleasant and rewarding for the children by using play activities, and set high standards for their students using positive reinforcement. In addition, the teachers' relationships with the children's families were friendly, and they enlisted parental cooperation to monitor children's performance at home (p. 514).

Manaf (1994) identified teacher characteristics that appear to be related to teacher effectiveness, including warmth, enthusiasm, clarity, variety, individualization, feedback, and cognitive demand of tasks. There is no evidence, however, that these variables are valid across age groups or cultures. Cruickshank and Sheffield (1996), in a review of teacher effectiveness studies, identified a cluster of teacher behaviors that were associated with student learning: "clarity, variability, enthusiasm, task-oriented or business-like behavior and student opportunity to learn the criterion material" (p. 53). He then goes on to caution that while some of the teacher behaviors are effective regardless of the grade and ages being taught, others must be tailored to specific ages and grades.

Clark's (1988) list of desirable teacher attributes includes such characteristics as the ability to plan and reflect, to tolerate ambiguity and uncertainty, to think for themselves; making and correcting inferences about pupil performance; and using appropriate teaching techniques. He notes that it is only if things are not working that teachers are willing to examine their practice and accept new interpretations, new priorities, and new routines. "The teacher encounters a host of interrelated and competing decision situations both while planning and during teaching. There are no perfect or optimal solutions to these decisions. A gain for one student or in one subject matter may mean a foregone opportunity for others. Conflicting goals combined with endemic uncertainty about how to achieve designed outcomes can lead to knots in teachers' thinking" (Clark, 1988).

In the field of early childhood education and care, the teacher characteristics identified as critical to teaching effectiveness have seldom been based on empirical studies of teachers (Saracho and Spodek, 1993; Spodek, 1996). Until the recent flurry of research focused on studying the implementation of developmentally appropriate practices, most recommendations about desirable teacher characteristics had grown from assumptions about what young children need. In 1949, Almy and Snyder suggested that teachers of early childhood education and care should have physical stamina, world mindedness, an understanding of human development, a respect for personality, and a scientific spirit. This list was updated by Whitebook and Almy (1986) to include patience, warmth, and ingenuity.

More recent empirical studies have found certain teacher behaviors to be associated with higher program quality and improved developmental outcomes for young children: indirect guidance, encouragement, responsive verbal interaction, sensitivity to children's cues, and promotion of positive, prosocial behaviors (Berk, 1985; Howes, 1993, 1997; Whitebook et al., 1989).

Teacher Efficacy

Tschannen-Moran et al. (1998), in a summary of the research on teacher efficacy for teachers in second through twelfth grades, defined it as teachers' belief in both their general and personal ability to affect the learning outcomes of students. They contend that these beliefs are constructed from teachers' personal experience of teaching, their expectations or ideals about teaching, their inner state, their knowledge of subject matter, and the reinforcement they receive for their behavior from others. Teachers' belief about their efficacy influences other behaviors, such as willingness to work and openness to new ideas, and affects not only school achievement but also social and emotional growth. Tschannen-Moran et al. (1998) also point out a body of research noting that efficacy is not a stable characteristic but responds to a host of context-specific factors in the school and in the population served. Given these findings, it is important to better understand the nature of efficacy for teachers of young children in early care and education settings.

TEACHER EDUCATION

Early childhood teacher education is a patchwork of pre-service and in-service education opportunities and credentials, characterized by varied state and local requirements across types of programs, auspices, and roles. Many states permit child care providers and preschool teachers to begin to teach without any professional preparation; others have preservice requirements that range from a week of orientation to four years of college. In-service education is equally diverse, encompassing a variety of educational opportunities designed to hone professional skills or update professional knowledge, but it is most often character-ized by poorly designed and uncoordinated workshops and conferences.

Preservice Education

Given the strong relationship between years of education and teaching effectiveness, consideration of professional (i.e., focused on early childhood content) education as distinct from years of schooling is important. Most early efforts to improve the quality of preschool education have stressed professional rather than advanced education. Some studies have shown "compelling evi-dence" (Ashton, 1996) of the superiority of teachers with profes-sional education course work in promoting the higher achieve-ment of school-age children. Graduates of teacher education programs drop out of teaching less frequently than teachers with-out such experience, suggesting that preservice professional edu-cation affects a teacher's decision to continue teaching.

Although research focused on early childhood teacher educa-tion is sparse (Bredekamp, 1996; Ott et al., 1990), it is reasonable to draw implications from related research about how teachers of young children should be prepared. In the recent *Yearbook of the National Society for the Study of Education* devoted to teacher edu-cation (1999), Griffin argues that "teacher education is best ac-complished when it is context-sensitive (rather than exclusively or mainly abstract and unconnected to real-life teaching and learning situations), ongoing (rather than sporadic and discon-nected in its components), cumulative in its intentions (rather than having a set of features that do not lead to and build upon one another), reflective (rather than prescriptive and promoted as a set of truths), and knowledge-based (rather than rooted solely in conventional wisdom and untested proposals)" (p. 16). In addition, some studies on early childhood preparation have found that teachers who chose a major related to child development were more likely to be positive and nurturing in their interactions (Layzer et al., 1993). Snider and Fu (1990) found that for early childhood education teachers, carefully supervised student teaching, in addition to course work in the following five areas, was related to the use of appropriate teaching practices: "planning, implementing, and evaluating developmentally appropriate content; creating, selecting, and evaluating materials; creating learning environments; curriculum models; and observing and recording behaviors" (p. 75).

In a recent commissioned paper for the National Institute on Early Childhood Development and Education, Isenberg (1999) argues that "Early childhood educators need to have a strong, high quality liberal arts background in order to be able to conceptualize learning experiences so that diverse learners find them meaningful" (p.14). Early childhood professional preparation programs should have a strong grounding in the liberal arts and include professional course work in the areas of child development, curriculum, assessment, diversity, inclusion, and family relations as recommended by the National Association for the Education of Young Children (1996). Isenberg then goes on to make seven recommendations about the content and structure of early childhood preparation programs, which include "that each state develop its own free-standing early childhood teacher license that includes a minimum of a baccalaureate degree. Such a change would recognize the specialized knowledge needed to work with children across the full spectrum from birth through age eight and better prepare early childhood educators for the variety of roles and settings that exist in both public and nonpublic settings" (p. 50).

The committee concludes, on the basis of evidence from the research on program quality combined with the research on teacher education, that a college degree with specialized education in child development and the education of young children ought to be required for teachers of young children. The relative importance of preservice education to eventual teaching effectiveness has been questioned by several researchers who studied high-quality, intensive in-service models (Epstein, 1993; Layzer et al., 1993). However, the weight of the evidence and analysis of the tasks that early childhood teachers are expected to perform in quality early child care programs indicate otherwise. Moreover, research on the relative importance of preservice education for early childhood teachers has failed to take into account the bias that results if, as seems likely, the most talented teachers with college degrees choose higher-paying elementary teaching over preschool jobs.

In-Service Education

Many teachers feel that well-designed in-service programs greatly influence their ability to learn and implement improved teaching practices (Katz, 1999). The amount, scope, and quality of staff development offered to early childhood educators vary greatly from program to program and in their effectiveness. While there is some research suggesting that well-designed and implemented in-service education programs can lead to better results than preservice degrees (Epstein, 1993; Layzer et al., 1993), there is still enormous variability in the content, approach, duration, and impact of in-service programs. Epstein (1993), in an evaluation of a High/Scope trainer of trainers project, demonstrated that a well-designed, intensive, and theoretically coherent in-service program can significantly improve early childhood teachers' practices and developmental outcomes for children. In a later study (1999), Epstein further examined the differences in teacher qualifications, in-service training, program quality, and children's development in Head Start, public school, and private nonprofit preschool classrooms. In this study, she found that in Head Start only, in-service training was significantly related to program quality, whereas in the public school programs only, the amount of formal education was significantly correlated with program quality. This finding can be partially explained by the fact that the Head Start teachers received both more and higher-quality in-service training than teachers in the other two settings. Although the Head Start teachers were less likely to hold bachelor's or master's degrees than public school teachers (Epstein, 1999), they were more likely to have a degree in early childhood education with specific course work in child development (Head Start Bureau, 1997).

The literature documenting the effects of in-service education on caregiver quality is mixed. On one hand, some research suggests that educating family child care providers can positively affect the global quality of care they provide (Howes et al., 1987). On the other hand, after reviewing the results of studies focused on family child care provider education, Kontos et al. (1992) concluded that evidence of positive change in caregiver knowledge, attitudes, and behavior would be weak if not nonexistent since most of the scant research that exists on family child care provider education has serious methodological limitations. The studies are typically quasi-experimental or correlational designs with no control group. The most frequently documented result is caregiver self-reported level of satisfaction, which is overwhelmingly positive.

Some of these methodological challenges are illustrated in the more recent work. Espinosa et al. (1999), for example, grappled with the difficulties of studying the effectiveness of an education program focused on child care providers in very small, low-income rural communities. In this study, 114 child care providers participated in a year-long education program that was individualized according to each caregiver's needs and abilities and included both group workshops and on-site follow-through with specially designed materials. Quality was assessed with the ECERS and caregiver-child interactions were rated using the Caregiver Interaction Scale (CIS) (Arnett, 1989). Because it was not feasible to have a control group in such small communities, the analyses focused on pre-and post-training assessments. While recognizing that this design would not support strong causal inferences, the authors concluded that, in contrast to traditional classroom-based education programs, the individualized, comprehensive approach implemented . . . *"was related to* (emphasis added) meaningful and sustained improvements in both teaching beliefs and observed practices" (p. 28). Because of high attrition in the subject population over time, the long-term effects, while positive, are less clear.

In a study of urban providers in three states, Kontos and colleagues (1997) looked at the effectiveness of the Family to Family training program. This study involved a group of providers, some of whom had had earlier training, and a comparison group of licensed providers. Outcome variables included overall quality and observational measures of provider behaviors. The effects of the intervention were at best modest; two of three sites showed small positive changes on the measure of overall quality, with no observable effects on provider behaviors, leading the authors to question the efficacy of training in workshop settings. Both of these studies support the conclusion that for in-service training to be effective, it must extend beyond a simple workshop format.

The school improvement and teacher education literature has revealed the difficulty in changing teacher beliefs and practices through in-service education (Fullan and Stiegelbauer, 1991). It has been repeatedly demonstrated that in-service programs must go beyond the fragmented classroom-based approach in order to effect changes in practice. Bruce Joyce (1986) developed a "coaching" metaphor to illustrate the desirable trainer-trainee relationship. Galinsky and her colleagues (1994) have pointed out that although individualized, site-based coaching experiences are highly desirable aspects of provider education, they are rarely incorporated into early childhood education and care programs. Several researchers have concluded that successful in-service education must reflect the following characteristics: (1) opportunities to apply knowledge, (2) a continuous program of study, not one-shot workshops, (3) individualized delivery, (4) expert mentoring provided on-site, and (5) immediate feedback (Epstein, 1993; Klein and Sheehan, 1987; Venn and Wolery, 1992). For family child care providers, joining a professional network and thus decreasing feelings of isolation may be beneficial to caregivers (National Research Council, 1990), and frequent supervision can lead to improved interactions with children (Corsini and Caruso, 1989).

In addition, it has been pointed out that education content and delivery must be uniquely suited to the audience (Kontos et al., 1992). A "one size fits all" approach cannot be equally effective for a diverse group of participants. The education must be tailored to the needs, experience, prior education, and abilities of the participants. Epstein (1993) found that exemplary, in-house trainers, who emphasized active participation and sharing experiences, showed the highest levels of developmentally appropriate adult-child interactions and the most positive developmental outcomes.

Whitebook and her colleagues have argued that mentoring programs can effectively contribute to meeting the need for a skilled and stable child care workforce (Whitebook et al., 1994). In mentoring programs, the "older, more experienced person who is committed to helping a younger, less experienced person become prepared for all aspects of life" (Odell, 1990) is the avenue through which novices learn the knowledge, skills, and attitudes of their profession. These relationships have been found to be complex, highly personal, and potentially powerful influences for both the mentor and the apprentice (Hawkey, 1997).

A recent review of innovative approaches to improving child care in rural areas (Macro International, 1994) recommended several specific strategies. These researchers surveyed and visited four states—Kentucky, Montana, North Carolina, and Oregon—to identify promising practices in the use of the Child Care Development Block Grant to improve rural child care quality and availability. They recommended providing financial incentives to encourage provider participation, involving local community organizations to build trust, and supporting resource and referral agencies.

Clearly, all in-service education is not equally advantageous. Effective in-service education must be intensive, continuous, and individualized. Most child care education efforts have not included all of these recommended components. This may explain why their impact on practices and beliefs has been modest and equivocal in many studies.

SUMMARY

The demands to teach effectively a more diverse range of children to higher levels of performance are new to most early childhood education and care teachers. The knowledge and skills of teachers are among the most important factors in determining how much a young child learns.

The professional development of teachers has been shown to be related to quality of early childhood programs, and program quality predicts developmental outcomes for children. Studies have generally found the strongest relationship between the number of years of education and the appropriateness of a teacher's classroom behavior. One study (the Florida Child Care Improvement Study; Howes et al., 1995) found that classroom ratings of global quality and teacher effectiveness (i.e., sensitivity, responsiveness, positive initiations, decrease in negative management, promotion of positive peer interaction) were most likely to improve when the teacher had at least a child development associate credential (or equivalent); the highest scores were obtained by teachers with a B.A. and advanced education.[1]

Early childhood teacher education is a patchwork of preservice and in-service education opportunities and credentials, characterized by varied state and local requirements across types of programs, auspices, and roles. Although research focused on early childhood teacher education is sparse, it is reasonable to draw implications from related research about how teachers of young children should be prepared. The committee concludes, on the basis of evidence from the research on program quality combined with the research on teacher education, that a college degree with specialized education in child development and the education of young children ought to be required for teachers of young children. In addition, all early childhood teachers should have some course work focused on creating inclusive classrooms for children with special needs and children who are culturally and linguistically diverse.

Although there is some evidence that well-designed and implemented in-service education programs can lead to improved program quality, it has been repeatedly documented that the amount, scope, and quality of professional development provided to early childhood teachers is inconsistent, fragmented, and often chaotic. Effective in-service education must be intensive and continuous, with opportunities to apply knowledge and receive individualized feedback and mentoring in order to support improved teaching practices and positive outcomes for children.

---

[1] In a very important step forward, the recent congressional reauthorization of Head Start set performance standards for programs that include a requirement for B.A.-qualified classroom staff.

Program and Practice Standards

S THE UPBRINGING OF AMERICA'S CHILDREN, and therefore the transmission of its culture, relies more and more on out-of-home providers of early education and care, there is a growing public interest in ensuring that this happens well and safely. In this vein, this report recommends the adoption of program standards and professional requirements. Still, it is important to note at the outset that establishing standards of quality for early education in a country as large, diverse, and rapidly changing as the United States is challenging. There is the danger that attempts to set common standards, or even to formulate what children need, may reflect the preferences of a particular group rather than the American population as a whole.

At their best, the promise of standards is that they provide a floor for program quality; they ensure that what we know children are capable of mastering in the early years they indeed have the opportunity to master in all state-approved programs. At their worst, standards put a ceiling on quality; they become an end rather than a departure point for the design and aspirations embodied in a program. Standards that are too low encourage mediocrity. Standards that are too high can be stressful and demoralizing. Standards that are too specific can undermine creativity and diversity; standards that are too broad can encourage compliance with the letter, but not the spirit of accountability.

Any effort to use standards to ensure quality must therefore be a dynamic one that involves continual evaluation, and that allows for revision when the outcomes are counterproductive.

PROGRAM STANDARDS

The more we emphasize instructional assessment, the more necessary it becomes to confront the issue of the standards against which children's learning should be assessed. Standards consist of the values, expectations, and outcomes of education. Various national curricular organizations (e.g., the National Council of Teachers of Mathematics, the American Association for the Advancement of Science, the National Council for Teachers of English, the International Reading Association) and nearly all states have proposed standards of achievement. However, very few of the content area standards apply meaningfully to very young children. Instructional or performance assessments that relate to children ages 2 to 5 articulate standards that are consistent with developmentally appropriate practice, child development research, and Head Start performance standards, but specific standards of learning for the early childhood years are not well developed in all curriculum areas. Table 8-1 presents the standards for mathematics developed by the National Council of Teachers of Mathematics and those for reading and writing developed by the National Association for the Education of Young Children (NAEYC) and the International Reading Association.

It is important to deal with the issue of standards in early childhood, because standards provide a baseline of expectations to which pedagogy and assessment can be aimed. Standards also help us understand and define the goals of early childhood pedagogy.

Currently, more than 30 states sponsor some type of prekindergarten program for at least some of the children in their boundaries (only Georgia has a universal pre-K program). Most of these states have published standards for what should be taught and what should be learned. Table 8-2 summarizes these standards as of 1996.

A national survey of state-funded preschool initiatives was conducted in 1997-1998 (Ripple et al., 1999). Data collected for

TABLE 8-1 Examples of Children's Development in Early Reading and Writing and in Mathematics

Continuum of Children's Development in Early Reading and Writing[a]

Goals for preschool: Children explore their environment and build the foundations for learning to read and write.

Children can:
enjoy listening to and discussing storybooks;
understand that print carries a message;
engage in reading and writing attempts;
identify labels and signs in their environment;
participate in rhyming games;
identify some letters and make some letter-sound matches;
use known letters or approximations of letters to represent written language
    (especially meaningful words like their name and phrases such as "I love you")

Standards for Children: Grades PreK-2[b]

Standards: Grades (PreK-2 Selected items): Understand numbers, ways of representing numbers, relationships among numbers, and number systems

Students should:
count fluently with understanding and recognize "how many" in small sets of
    objects;
understand the cardinal and ordinal meaning of numbers in quantifying, measuring,
    and identifying the order of objects;
connect number words, the quantities they represent, numerals, and written words
    and represent numerical situations with each of these;
develop an understanding of the relative magnitude of numbers and make
    connections between the size of cardinal numbers and the counting sequence;
use computational tools and strategies fluently and estimate appropriately;
develop and use strategies and algorithms to solve number problems;
understand various types of patterns and functional relationships;
sort and classify objects by different properties;
order objects by size or other numerical property (seriation);
identify, analyze, and extend patterns and recognize the same pattern in different
    manifestations;
use mathematical models and analyze change in both real and abstract contexts;
make comparisons and describe change qualitatively (e.g., taller than)

[a]This list is intended to be illustrative, not exhaustive. Children at any grade level will function at a variety of phases along the reading/writing continuum.
[b]Only a few of the items listed in this section in order to give a sense of the standards for the younger children.

SOURCES: For reading and writing, information from Newman et al. (1999); for mathematics, information from National Council of Teachers of Mathematics 2000).

TABLE 8-2 Summary of State Content Standards for Teaching Children in Prekindergarten Programs

State	Program Name	Standards	Motor	Health, Safety, and Nutrition
AR	Arkansas Better Chance	NAEYC guidelines used as basis for state child care accreditation, and program appropriateness	Indoor, outdoor play that encourages development of habits; gross and fine motor skills	Encourage good health and safety
AZ	At-Risk Preschool Program	State guidelines for comprehensive early childhood programs	Opportunity to acquire and refine fundamental movements	Encourage appreciation for health and safety
CA	State preschool	State Preschool Program Quality Requirements	Facilitate physical and motor competence	Provide a developmentally appropriate nutrition component and a healthy environment that refers children to appropriate agencies based on their health needs

Cognitive (General)	Numeracy	Language	Social-Emotional	Aesthetics
Support cognitive development	Not specified	Promote language development by means of reading materials	Foster communication skills, social skills, positive self-esteem, and an appreciation for cultural diversity	Creative expression, art, music, dramatic play
Learning, using strategies such as experimentation, thinking games, play, self-directed learning, investigation; children encouraged to explore, question, participate in group discussions, give responses	Encourage math vocabulary, concepts, and math-directed activities	Library (reading-listening); reading/writing, curriculum materials multilingual as appropriate; day structured to facilitate child-to-child talk	Encourage growth of social skills, communication, self-confidence, independence, respect, manners; appreciation for cultural diversity and current events	Become competent artistically and musically; encourage child-initiated play
Developmentally appropriate activities that facilitate a child's cognitive development	—	—	Foster social and emotional development	—

Table continued on next page

TABLE 8-2 *Continued*

State	Program Name	Standards	Motor	Health, Safety, and Nutrition
CO	Colorado Preschool Program	Standards based on NAEYC, cross-referenced to Head Start and state licensing	—	Nutrition and health services by local decision
DE	Early Childhood Assistance Program	Head Start	—	—
FL	Pre-K Early Intervention Program	NAEYC encouraged but not required	Developmentally appropriate practices (DAP)	DAP
GA	Georgia Prekindergarten Program		Move with balance and coordination; indoor/outdoor activity; facilitate development of large and small muscle skills	Make health referrals; provide breakfast, snack, and lunch
IA	Child Development Coordinating Council	NAEYC, Head Start	—	—

Cognitive (General)	Numeracy	Language	Social-Emotional	Aesthetics
—	—	—	—	—
—	—	—	—	—
DAP	DAP	DAP	Enhance emotional maturity and social confidence	DAP
Encourage exploration, observation, and communication of knowledge	Activities dealing with counting concepts and resorting objects; shape and size comparison	Recognition of pictures words, ABCs, and stories; understand and tell stories; understand that writing is communication	Encourage cooperative play and work; positive interaction with other children, self-help skills; pride; care and self-control	Express ideas and thoughts in creative ways, including crafts, drawing, and music
—	—	—	—	—

Table continued on next page

TABLE 8-2 *Continued*

State	Program Name	Standards	Motor	Health, Safety, and Nutrition
KY	State Preschool Program	State regulations reflect NAEYC, Head Start standards	Indoor/outdoor activities; play areas with safe and appropriate equipment	Assist understanding of nutrition
LA	Preschool Block Grant	Local school district policies	Indoor/outdoor play	

Cognitive (General)	Numeracy	Language	Social-Emotional	Aesthetics
Encourage exploration; concrete experiential learning; integrate skills across content areas (integrative learning)	Materials for math and problem solving	Language experience approach (language understanding and use among children and adults, language arts, library area)	Assist development of interpersonal skills, self-management and independence; positive self-esteem, self-regulation of behavior; multicultural curriculum	Space and material for dramatic play, art, block building, cooking, house-keeping; opportunities for self-expression
Activities including active exploration; problem solving; experimentation with hands-on, real-life materials; integrated learning through all developmental areas; learning through themes		Language stimulation through varied opportunities of self-expression	Child-initiated play, child-to-child and child-to-adult; positive guidance and encouraging of expected behavior	Development of creativity and imagination

Table continued on next page

TABLE 8-2 *Continued*

State	Program Name	Standards	Motor	Health, Safety, and Nutrition
MA	Community Partnerships for Children	NAEYC and state-established Early Childhood Standards	Indoor/outdoor play; enhance physical development and skills by use of developmentally appropriate equipment, materials, and activities	Routine tasks (eating, toileting, and dressing) incorporated into the program to further children's learning; access to a health care consultant; enhance health and safety of children; meal times as social learning experiences; nutritious food
MD	Extended Elementary Education Program (EEEP)	Standards for Implementing Quality Pre-K Programs (similar to NAEYC)	—	—
ME		Family Focused Standards for Early Intervention (in keeping with serving the child and family as outlined in the state created Individualized Family Service Plan (IFSP))	Indoor/outdoor environment provide basic health activities management should be	Snack provided; required school nurse, needs. Behavior age appropriate, environment should be safe and minimize the risk of transmission of communicable disease

Cognitive (General)	Numeracy	Language	Social-Emotional	Aesthetics
Encourage children to think, reason, and question and opportunities to make comparisons, analyze, observe, plan, and discuss experiences, observations, and feelings; science activities in work areas	Provide an area to accommodate and encourage math	Encourage language development (in children's native language and English)	Foster a positive self-concept, respect cultural and economic diversity, develop social skills; ability to have child-initiated play and teacher-initiated play; smooth transitions between activities; encouraged good manners	Encourage creative expression and appreciation for the arts by means of dramatic play, art, and music
—	—	—	—	—
Age-appropriate	—	—	Encourage self-esteem, behavior management	—

Table continued on next page

TABLE 8-2 *Continued*

State	Program Name	Standards	Motor	Health, Safety, and Nutrition
MI	Michigan School Readiness Program	Standards of Quality and Curriculum Guidelines	Encourage indoor/outdoor play; small and large muscle development; body awareness	Safe and secure facility; nutritious snack available during each school day; program structured to ensure that children's biological needs are met
MN	Learning Readiness	Follow NAEYC guidelines but not part of requirements	Develop appropriate physical skills	Meet children's daily nutritional needs
NE	Early Childhood Projects	NAEYC	—	—
NJ	Early Childhood Program Aid	Localities Determine their own standards within general state guidelines	DAP	Provide supplementary health, nutrition and social services
NY	New York State Prekinder-garten Program	DAP outlined in state regulations	—	—

Cognitive (General)	Numeracy	Language	Social-Emotional	Aesthetics
Encourage exploration, spontaneous learning experiences, creative problem-solving skills, decision-making skills utilizing different methods and techniques, asking questions	—	Each child's primary language valued and used for communication; auditory discrimination; listening and speaking skills	Receive positive attention, constructive discipline, respect; encourage child-to-child interaction, interpersonal relation; build esteem, autonomy, respect for others, multicultural awareness	Development of imagination, appreciation of art, music, poetry, prose, and wonders of the natural world; dramatic play
Help develop cognitive skills	—	—	Help develop appropriate social skills and emotional well-being	—
—	—	—	—	—
DAP	DAP	DAP	DAP	DAP
—	—	—	—	—

Table continued on next page

TABLE 8-2 *Continued*

State	Program Name	Standards	Motor	Health, Safety, and Nutrition
OH	Head Start, Public School Preschool	Head Start	—	—
OK	Early Childhood Four-Year-old Program	State standards and individual programs coordinators given Department of Education model for early childhood education: "Four-Year-Old Developmental Learning Skills"	Provide a playground area that is accessible and safe	Environment must have restroom facilities that accommodate the children, be safe, and accessible; snack provided
OR	Oregon Head Start Prekindergarten	Head Start	—	—
SC	Early Childhood Program	State appropriate standards and adequate physical facilities provided	One nutritional supplement (snack) provided daily; program complies with appropriate state board of education requirements	Provide a developmental educational program in classroom setting

Cognitive (General)	Numeracy	Language	Social-Emotional	Aesthetics
—	—	—	—	—
Curriculum appropriate for children's developmental level	DAP	DAP	—	—
—	—	—	—	
—	—	Instructional models reflect a comprehensive study of current test data, instructional trends and research, and school and community demographics	—	—

Table continued on next page

TABLE 8-2 *Continued*

State	Program Name	Standards	Motor	Health, Safety, and Nutrition
TX	Public school prekindergarten	DAP guidelines	—	—
VA	Virginia Preschool	—	—	—
VT	Early Education Initiative	Core Standards for Center-Based Programs in Vermont	Indoor/outdoor physical development; strengthening large and small muscles; encouraging eye-hand coordination; body awareness, rhythm, and movement; age appropriate equipment	Encourage good nutritional, health, and safety practices; provide a safe, clean, and healthy learning environment; provide a meal/snack at least every three hours

Cognitive (General)	Numeracy	Language	Social-Emotional	Aesthetics
Integrated developmental approach, with opportunities to think, reason, solve problems, and make decisions; information linked to meaningful, relevant, concrete experiences	Promotes understanding and application of skills	—	Encourage teamwork, collaboration, self-help, and personal management skills	—
—	—	—	—	—
Encourage problem solving, experimentation, mastery through learning by doing; science	Provide opportunities in numerical concepts	Language arts, language, and literacy activities encouraging children's emerging interest in writing	Enhance children's social skills, positive self-concepts; provide opportunities for success (i.e., praise effort, allowing children to be independent); cultural diversity	Creative expression and appreciation; opportunities in art, music, dance, dramatic play, doing artwork to explore rather than for product

Table continued on next page

TABLE 8-2 *Continued*

State	Program Name	Standards	Motor	Health, Safety, and Nutrition
WA	Early Childhood Education and Assistance Program	State Program Performance Standards	Appropriate environment for physical growth	—

NOTE: States not listed did not have programs as of 1996.

this endeavor were based on information from fiscal year 1996 that was provided by contacts from each of the 50 states and the District of Columbia. From this information, Ripple and colleagues identified 31 states with preschool education programs that met their criteria for inclusion in the study.[1] It should be noted that the preschool education standards differ from, and in most case are more stringent than, state licensing standards for child care programs serving children ages 2 to 5.

In order to summarize these state-funded programs in terms of the standards that they adopted to guide program implementation and practices, we identified seven domains that were addressed by most of the guidelines. As shown in Table 8-2, each of

[1]In order to be considered as a state-funded preschool initiative, programs had to provide classroom-based education services directly to preschool-age children, had to be mounted and implemented by the state, did not exclusively serve children with disabilities, and were universal or targeted children from low-income families. Title I programs, or those funded solely by localities or school districts, were not included.

Cognitive (General)	Numeracy	Language	Social-Emotional	Aesthetics
Consistent with sound child development practices; minimum of 10 hrs/wk of child participation in center activities; foster intellectual growth; expose children to new ideas concepts and experiences	—	Language skills curriculum by local decision	Meet unique local community needs; cultural and ethnic pride; appropriate environment for emotional and social growth	—

the 31 states' standards varied across these domains: (1) motor development, (2) health, safety, and nutrition, (3) general cognitive development, (4) numeracy, (5) language, (6) social-emotional, and (7) aesthetics.

Generally speaking, state preschool programs followed one of three overarching frameworks for their guidelines. One group of three states (Delaware, Ohio, and Oregon) reported that they adopted Head Start standards and require that all state-funded preschool programs adhere to those guidelines. A second group of states (Massachusetts[2] and Nebraska) adopted National Association for the Education of Young Children guidelines.

The third group, consisting of the remaining 26 state-funded preschool education programs, developed and implemented their own standards. Although many of these individualized standards are based on Head Start or NAEYC guidelines (in some cases these guidelines are recommended but not required), each

---

[2]In Massachusetts, all programs must be NAEYC accredited. In addition, programs located in public schools must meet state standards.

state developed its own unique approach to establishing program requirements. General observations based on data provided by these 26 states are provided below.[3]

Structural Components

Preschool program standards typically guide both structural and program components or activities. Structural specifications include materials available in the classroom, the site and layout of work and play areas, safety demands that ensure appropriate classroom and playground equipment, health and nutrition, class size, teacher-child ratios, and teacher qualifications.

With regard to classroom materials, standards require reading materials to promote language development (Arkansas) and "real-life materials" to provide hands-on experimentation (Louisiana). Classroom layout is addressed in required space for dramatic play, art, and block building (Kentucky) and areas to accommodate and encourage mathematics skills (Massachusetts). In general, state standards regarding structural aspects of programming addressed both materials and classroom environment.

In terms of health, nutrition, and safety standards, guidelines ranged from basic (e.g., Oklahoma programs must provide bathroom facilities) to more detailed descriptions (e.g., Massachusetts and Vermont). Preschool education program regulations for class size and teacher-child ratios were comparable from state to state and are related to the ages of the children in the program. The majority of programs limited class size to 15 to 20 students and permitted a teacher-child ratio of no more than 1:10. Standards addressing teacher qualifications varied widely: many states required a bachelor's degree in early childhood or elementary education, whereas other states recommended a designated number of documented hours or years of experience in the child care field

---

[3]Incomplete information exists for the following states: Colorado, District of Columbia, Illinois, Iowa, Maryland, New York, Pennsylvania, Texas, Virginia, West Virginia, and Wisconsin. In 1998, legislation was passed in New York mandating the implementation of a universal state-funded preschool program (subsequently defunded).

along with a teaching certificate. Overall, state standards in this domain were more stringent than those for Head Start, for which a child development associate (CDA) degree is currently sufficient. Certification issues are discussed in more detail below.

Program Components

Standards related to program components determine what goes on in the classroom. These may include guidelines for curriculum content, daily activities, and peer or teacher-child interactions. Standards may be very specific (e.g., in specifying the activities children should participate in, such as those activities that develop numeracy and shape recognition, aid in the development of gross and fine motor skills, and encourage vocabulary development), such as those developed in Arizona, Georgia, and Michigan. In contrast, some standards were less specific and established a general approach to teaching (e.g., recommending developmentally appropriate practices), as in California, New Jersey, and Maine. As shown in Table 8.2, standards for program process tended to consist of creating opportunities for learning. Language that builds on terms such as "encourage," "facilitate," and "promote" is typical, as is appropriate to preschool settings. Program standards also addressed the domain of socioemotional development. Most state program standards mentioned aspects of developmentally appropriate practices, such as positive self-esteem, social skills, emotional well-being, and behavioral self-regulation.

Summary of State Standards

State standards are generally very vague in their reflection of current understanding of children's thinking and learning. They were generally strong on requiring adequate teacher training. However, one aspect of program implementation and administration is a potential cause for concern: in some states—notably Louisiana and New Jersey—legislation guiding the program gives full control of program details to local areas. Whereas this level of devolution from central to local control could be seen as a positive move, because it allows individual sites to tailor the program to local needs, it also makes it virtually impossible to determine the nature of the program as a whole.

STANDARDS OF PRACTICE

Over the past 20 years, there have been a number of attempts to improve the quality of programs for children by setting standards for practice. Some efforts have focused on centers and homes as the point of entry and created accreditation systems, while others have stressed certificates or credentials for individuals. Approaches also differ in whether systems are mandatory, as are state licensing, public school teacher certification, and Head Start performance standards, or voluntary, as are certification by the National Board for Professional Teacher Standards and center accreditation by the National Association for the Education of Young Children.

Teacher Certification

As a general rule, most early childhood educators have neither certification nor standard preservice preparation. Public schools and Head Start are the only two systems that require certification: public schools usually require a certificate before beginning to teach, and Head Start requires that a percentage of the teachers in a program have a credential. Both systems serve children at risk of school failure because of poverty, home language other than English, and developmental disabilities. Currently 17 states require preschool teaching certification for early childhood teachers in the public schools (Knitzer and Page, 1996). In special education, teachers often first have a B.A. and a regular early childhood education teaching credential and then specialized education in early childhood special education. Because of the legal and regulatory requirements that children be placed in the least restrictive environment which serves their educational needs, most young children with disabilities will be included in regular early childhood programs. According to National Council for the Accreditation of Teacher Education guidelines, all teacher credentialing programs must integrate the special education content throughout all teacher education courses; however, most regular early childhood education programs do not adequately prepare teacher candidates to work with children with special needs.

Standardized tests sharply limit the number of students who complete the requirements for teacher certification. As a result, racial and cultural imbalance between the population of children in public schools and their teachers affects early childhood programs (Meek, 1998). Fields reported in the *Chronicle of Higher Education* that in 19 states in which test failures were reported by race, 38,000 blacks, Hispanics, Asians, American Indians, and other minorities did not pass the state exam (Fields, 1988). The high failure rate of these potential teachers is presumably explained by the poor quality of their general education, as well as by the teacher preparation program. Many critics of competency examinations claim that the minorities who fail them are the same ones who do poorly on other standardized tests because of their linguistic and cultural differences. The disproportionate failure rate of blacks, Hispanics, and American Indians is also reported by the National Board for Professional Teaching Standards. While test makers assert that the tests correct for cultural bias, the failure rate of minorities nevertheless reinforces the imbalance between students of color and their teachers (Fields, 1988).

In 1972, Head Start established the child development associate program nationwide, in order to meet the needs for skilled early childhood teachers (Hinitz, 1998). The CDA identifies six competencies indicating basic skills that a teacher must master to teach young children: (1) establishes safe and healthy environment, (2) advances physical and intellectual competence, (3) builds positive self-concept and individual strength, (4) promotes positive functioning of children in groups, (5) brings about optimal coordination of home and center childrearing practices and expectations, and (6) carries out supplementary responsibilities related to programs. Kontos, et al. (1997) found that teachers with a CDA credential or its equivalent were warmer and more sensitive and had higher-quality classrooms than teachers with less education.

Candidates for the CDA demonstrate their competence through the preparation of portfolios and are assessed by parents, a trainer/supervisor, and an independent observer. The

CDA credential is awarded to teachers who are judged competent. In the early years, few teachers applied for or received the credential because early childhood programs seldom gave additional compensation to teachers with a certificate. However, the program has gradually expanded; since 1990, as a part of the efforts of the Council for Early Childhood Professional Recognition, it has experienced considerable growth. Its value to the quality of children's programs has been increasingly recognized (Kontos et al., 1997), and it is now required by Head Start. Currently the council provides an assessment and credentialing process for teachers in three settings—center-based, family child care, and home visitor—with endorsements for working with infants or toddlers, preschool, and bilingual children.

Education for the CDA is provided by qualified trainers; in 1996, all but four states had colleges and universities that provide CDA education (postsecondary education institutions offering CDA training), and many schools give 12 hours of college credit to students who complete a CDA in nonacademic systems.

Professional Standards

Professional communities have also influenced education through the development of standards of good practice. In response to the school reform movement of the 1980s, the National Board for Professional Teaching Standards was established in 1987. Probably the best known standards were published by the National Association for the Education of Young Children under the title, *Developmentally Appropriate Practice* (DAP).

National Board for Professional Teaching Standards

The primary mission of the National Board for Professional Teaching Standards is to establish high, rigorous standards and develop a voluntary accreditation system to recognize exemplary teachers. Committees of teachers and experts in a variety of grade levels and disciplinary fields were given the tasks of defining specific standards, and the national board developed an assessment and certification system. Standards committees were guided by five core propositions in defining what teachers should know and be able to do: (1) teachers are committed to students and their learning; (2) teachers should know the subjects they teach and how to teach students; (3) teachers are responsible for managing and monitoring student learning; (4) teachers think systematically about their practice and learn from experience; and (5) teachers are members of learning communities.

Among the first set of standards developed were those for early childhood generalists, teachers working with children ages 3 to 8. Eight standards, equally important, define excellent early childhood teaching: (1) understand young children, (2) promote child development and learning, (3) knowledge of integrated curriculum, (4) multiple teaching strategies for meaningful learning, (5) assessment, (6) reflective practice, (7) family partnerships, and (8) professional partnerships.

Each standard contains more specific required knowledge or skills, but they do not mandate a particular philosophical or theoretical bias. Unlike best practice documents, no research rationale is provided for the standards; rather, they represent the professional judgment of teachers and other experts about what excellent teachers know and can do. Teams of professional assessors, arriving at consensus judgments, decide if certification candidates' work meets these standards.

Developmentally Appropriate Practice

The document *Developmentally Appropriate Practice* was first approved by the Board of National Association for the Education of Young Children in 1987 and was disseminated broadly. To convey the implications of developmental principles in determining practices, examples of good and bad practice were given, with the rationale for why they were so judged. This format led to considerable misunderstanding, with many practitioners viewing DAP as a set of good practices instead of principles of practice. In 1996, the NAEYC board charged a new committee to review the principles and make clearer the relationship of the practices to developmental principles.

The current version of developmentally appropriate practices (Bredekamp and Copple, 1997) was approved by the board of NAEYC in 1997 and focuses on three developmental principles as relevant to early childhood professional practice: children's ages, their individual differences, and their home language and culture. The revised version of DAP continues to reflect a constructivist orientation and directs teachers' (and parents') attention to children's need to make meaning from their experiences. It wisely cautions against either/or approaches that pit child-initiated against teacher-directed curricula. As Chapter 5 of this report emphasizes, research suggests that many teaching strategies can work, and no teaching strategy is sufficient for all purposes. The key is for a teacher to be attuned to the child's current level of development and developmental challenges, and to select from a toolkit of possible pedagogical approaches one that complements the learning opportunity in question.

The principles of developmentally appropriate practice have been widely accepted and endorsed by other professional groups and incorporated into teacher education programs through the National Council for the Accreditation of Teacher Education (NCATE). Colleges and universities offering teacher certification in early childhood and seeking NCATE approval are expected to explain in their applications how their program meets these standards. A number of states have incorporated the NCATE standards into their state accreditation process, further expanding the acceptance of DAP as the underlying structure for early childhood teachers.

The heavy emphasis in DAP on play and self-selected activities for children and the teacher as an observer has led to criticisms of it as a model for practice. Objections include that teachers misinterpret it to mean that children learn by themselves; that it lacks subject-matter substance; that it fails to provide the information children need, particularly low-income and minority children; and that it does not take advantage of new information regarding young children's intellectual potential.

As educators become conversant with the new research on learning, they will be better equipped to understand the implications of constructivist learning theory for teaching in a way that guides and supports learning. Two useful sources of guidance for early childhood educators who want to enrich their DAP-oriented classrooms are the joint NAEYC-IRA (International Reading Association) statement clarifying the expectations for literacy and language stimulation and a book by Neuman and Copple (2000), published by IRA.

Regulation of Early Childhood Education and Care

Often neglected, the regulation of child care and early education facilities is a critical part of quality programs. Facility regulations are important because there is a clearly documented and unequivocal relationship between regulation and quality. States with more demanding licensing requirements have fewer poor-quality centers that put children at risk of harm and do little to enhance their development (Kagan and Newton, 1989; Cost, Quality and Child Outcomes Study Team, 1995).

When facility regulations are more stringent, children show more advanced cognitive, social, and language development and have more secure attachments to teachers and fewer behavioral problems (Galinsky et al., 1995; Howes et al., 1995; Kontos, 1992; Kontos et al., 1995).

Although regulation is designed to safeguard children from harm and to provide parents with basic rights and consumer protections, the reality is that states vary significantly in their degree of regulation and in the stringency of enforcement (Azer et al., 1996). The situation is complex because, in a given state, regulatory authority is often delegated to one or more agencies, sometimes without the involved agencies realizing that regulatory responsibility is spread. Regulations may be contradictory and, in some cases, domains may be totally neglected (U.S. Advisory Commission on Intergovernmental Relations, 1994). The result is that often programs must figure out and bear the burden and cost of multiple regulatory entities, each of which is imperfect.

Many states have attempted to raise standards for teachers through their licensing requirements. All states have mandatory licensing regulations based on minimum standards for the care and education of young children and include requirements for the facility as well as for staff-child ratios and teacher education. The licensing standards vary enormously from state to state (see Table 8-3 for a recent review of child care licensing).

Variations in requirements usually involve the number of hours of operation and size of the center, and they differ for cen-

TABLE 8-3 Child Care Licensing, State Requirement

Requirement or Guideline[a]	Percentage of States with Requirement or Meeting Guideline
Require Preservice for Teachers[b]	
CDA	23
BA	2
Require Preservice for Program Directors[b]	
CDA	45
BA	4
Specified Group Sizes for 2- and 3-year-olds	
≤12%	18
≤18%	44[c]
≤24%	60[c]
Staff/Child Ratios for 2- and 3-year-olds[d]	15
Staff/Child Ratios for 3- and 5-year-olds[d]	3.8

NOTE: CDA, Child Development Associate; BA, Bachelor of Arts.

[a]Data from The Children's Foundation (1999).
[b]Azer and Hanrahan (1998).
[c]Scores cumulative.
[d]Data from Standards set forth in American Public Health Association and American Academy of Pediatrics Collaborative Project (1992).

ter-based staff and family child care providers. Some states exempt large numbers of family child care homes, church-sponsored programs, part-day programs, and school-sponsored programs from all licensing requirements. Indeed, it has been estimated that nationwide, more than 40 percent of all children in early childhood education and care attend programs that are legally exempt from state regulation (Adams, 1990). As an example, in 38 states, many family child care homes are not subject to facility licensing requirements.

Efforts to advance a more stringent and effective regulatory system at the federal level have taken place over time, but with little success (Garwood et al., 1989). Resistance to the development of regulations reflects not only a difficulty in building a national consensus around the content of the recommendations, but also the fear that more stringent requirements could result in higher parent fees, the need for additional government investment, and the reduced availability of care (Gormley, 1992, 1995).

Findings, Conclusions, and Recommendations

T HE RESEARCH ON EARLY CHILDHOOD learning and program effectiveness reviewed in this report provides some very powerful findings:

• *Young children are capable of understanding and actively
building knowledge,* and they are highly inclined to do so. While
there are developmental constraints on children's competence,
those constraints serve as a ceiling below which there is enormous room for variation in growth, skill acquisition, and understanding.

• *Development is dependent on and responsive to experience,*
allowing children to grow far more quickly in domains in which a
rich experiential base and guided exposure to complex thinking
are available than in those where they receive no such support.
Environment—including cultural context—exerts a large influence on both cognitive and emotional development. Genetic en-
dowment is far more responsive to experience than was once
thought. Rapid growth of the brain in the early years provides an
opportunity for the environment to influence the physiology of
development.

• *Education and care in the early years are two sides of the
same coin.* Research suggests that secure attachment improves

306

both social competence and the ability to exploit learning opportunities.

Furthermore, research on early childhood curricula and pedagogy has implications for how early childhood programs can effectively promote development:

- *Cognitive, social-emotional (mental health), and physical development are complementary, mutually supportive areas of growth all requiring active attention in the preschool years.* Social skills and physical dexterity influence cognitive development, just as cognition plays a role in children's social understanding and motor competence. All are therefore related to early learning and later academic achievement and are necessary domains of early childhood pedagogy.
- *Responsive interpersonal relationships with teachers nurture young children's dispositions to learn and their emerging abilities.* Social competence and school achievement are influenced by the quality of early teacher-child relationships, and by teachers' attentiveness to how the child approaches learning.
- *While no single curriculum or pedagogical approach can be identified as best, children who attend well-planned, high-quality early childhood programs in which curriculum aims are specified and integrated across domains tend to learn more and are better prepared to master the complex demands of formal schooling.* Particular findings of relevance in this regard include the following:

1. Children who have a broad base of experience in domain-specific knowledge (for example, in mathematics or an area of science) move more rapidly in acquiring more complex skills
2. More extensive language development—such as a rich vocabulary and listening comprehension—is related to early literacy learning.
3. Children are better prepared for school when early childhood programs expose them to a variety of classroom structures, thought processes, and discourse patterns. This does not mean adopting the methods and curriculum of the elementary school; rather it is a matter of providing children with a mix of whole

class, small group, and individual interactions with teachers, the experience of different kinds of discourse patterns, and such mental strategies as categorizing, memorizing, reasoning, and metacognition.

• *While the committee does not endorse any particular curriculum, the cognitive science literature suggests principles of learning that should be incorporated into any curriculum:*

1. Teaching and learning will be most effective if they engage and build on children's existing understandings.
2. Key concepts involved in each domain of preschool learning (e.g., representational systems in early literacy, the concept of quantity in mathematics, causation in the physical world) must go hand in hand with information and skill acquisition (e.g., identifying numbers and letters and acquiring information about the natural world).
3. Metacognitive skill development allows children to solve problems more effectively. Curricula that encourage children to reflect, predict, question, and hypothesize (examples: How many will there be after two numbers are added? What happens next in the story? Will it sink or float?) set them on course for effective, engaged learning.

• *Young children who are living in circumstances that place them at greater risk of school failure—including poverty, low level of maternal education, maternal depression, and other factors that can limit their access to opportunities and resources that enhance learning and development—are much more likely to succeed in school if they attend well-planned, high-quality early childhood programs.* Many children, especially those in low-income households, are served in child care programs of such low quality that learning and development are not enhanced and may even be jeopardized.

The importance of teacher responsiveness to children's differences, knowledge of children's learning processes and capabilities, and the multiple developmental goals that a quality preschool program must address simultaneously all point to the centrality of teacher education and preparation.

• *The professional development of teachers is related to the quality of early childhood programs, and program quality predicts developmental outcomes for children.* Formal early childhood education and training has been linked consistently to positive caregiver behaviors. The strongest relationship is found between the number of years of education and training and the appropriateness of a teacher's classroom behavior.

• *Programs found to be highly effective in the United States and exemplary programs abroad actively engage teachers and provide high-quality supervision.* Teachers are trained and encouraged to reflect on their practice and on the responsiveness of their children to classroom activities, and to revise and plan their teaching accordingly.

• *Both class size and adult-child ratios are correlated with greater program effects.* Low ratios of children to adults are associated with more extensive teacher-child interaction, more individualization, and less restrictive and controlling teacher behavior. Smaller group size has been associated with more child initiations, more opportunities for teachers to work on extending language, mediating children's social interactions, and encouraging and supporting exploration and problem solving.

CONCLUSIONS AND RECOMMENDATIONS

What is now known about the potential of the early years, and of the promise of high-quality preschool programs to help realize that potential for all children, stands in stark contrast to practice in many—perhaps most—early childhood settings. How can we bring what we know to bear on what we do?

A committee of the National Research Council recently addressed that question with regard to K-12 education (National Research Council, 1999). While the focus of this report differs from theirs, the conceptual framework for using research knowledge to influence educational practice applies. In this model, the impact of research knowledge on classroom practice—the ultimate goal—is mediated through four arenas, as depicted in Fig-

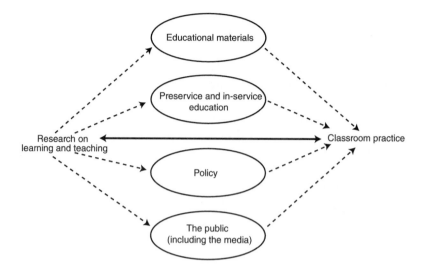

FIGURE 9-1 Arenas through which research knowledge influences class-room practice.

ure 9-1. When teachers are directly engaged in using research-based programs or curricula, the effect can be direct. This is the case in some model programs. But if research knowledge is to be used systematically in early childhood education and care programs, preservice and in-service education that effectively transmits that knowledge to those who staff the programs will be required.

While we have argued that the teacher is central, effective teachers work with curricula and teaching materials. In Chapter 5 we refer to exemplary curricula that incorporate research knowledge. Changing practice requires that teachers know about, and have access to, a store of teaching materials.

Quality preschool programs can be encouraged or thwarted by public policy. Regulations and standards can incorporate research knowledge to put a floor under program quality. Public funding and the rules that shape its availability can encourage quality above that floor, and can ensure accessibility to those most in need. And finally, program administrators and teachers, as well as policy makers, are ultimately accountable to parents and to the public. Parents' expectations of, and support for, preschool programs, as well as their participation in activities that support early development, can contribute to program success.

The chance of effectively changing early childhood education will increase if the four arenas that influence practice are ad- dressed simultaneously and in a mutually supportive fashion. The committee's recommendations address each of these four arenas of influence.

Professional Development

At the heart of the effort to promote quality preschool, from the committee's perspective, is a substantial investment in the education and training of preschool teachers.

Recommendation 1: Each group of children in an early childhood education and care program should be assigned a teacher who has a bachelor's degree with specialized education related to early childhood (e.g., developmental psychology, early childhood education, early childhood special education). Achieving this goal will require a significant public investment in the professional development of current and new teachers.

Sadly, there is a great disjunction between what is optimal pedagogically for children's learning and development and the level of preparation that currently typifies early childhood educators. Progress toward a high-quality teaching force will require substantial public and private support and incentive systems, including innovative educational programs, scholarship and loan programs, and compensation commensurate with the expectations of college graduates.

Recommendation 2: Education programs for teachers should provide them with a stronger and more specific foundational knowledge of the development of children's social and affective behavior, thinking, and language.

Few programs currently do. This foundation should be linked to teachers' knowledge of mathematics, science, linguistics, literature, etc., as well as to instructional practices for young children.

Recommendation 3: Teacher education programs should require mastery of information on the pedagogy of teaching preschool-aged children, including:

• Knowledge of teaching and learning and child development and how to integrate them into practice.
• Information about how to provide rich conceptual experiences that promote growth in specific content areas, as well as particular areas of development, such as language (vocabulary) and cognition (reasoning).
• Knowledge of effective teaching strategies, including organizing the environment and routines so as to promote activities that build social-emotional relationships in the classroom.
• Knowledge of subject-matter content appropriate for preschool children and knowledge of professional standards in specific content areas.
• Knowledge of assessment procedures (observation/performance records, work sampling, interview methods) that can be used to inform instruction.
• Knowledge of the variability among children, in terms of teaching methods and strategies that may be required, including teaching children who do not speak English, children from various economic and regional contexts, and children with identified disabilities.
• Ability to work with teams of professionals.
• Appreciation of the parents' role and knowledge of methods of collaboration with parents and families.
• Appreciation of the need for appropriate strategies for accountability.

Recommendation 4: A critical component of preservice preparation should be a supervised, relevant student teaching or internship experience in which new teachers receive ongoing guidance and feedback from a qualified supervisor.

There are a number of models (e.g., National Council for Accreditation of Teacher Education) that suggest the value of this sort of supervised student teaching experience. A principal goal of this experience should be to develop the student teacher's ability to integrate and apply the knowledge base in practice. Collaborative support by the teacher preparation institution and the field placement is essential. Supervision of this experience should be shared by a master teacher and a regular or clinical university faculty member.

Recommendation 5: **All early childhood education and child care programs should have access to a qualified supervisor of early childhood education.**

Teachers should be provided with opportunities to reflect on practice with qualified supervisors. This supervisor should be both an expert teacher of young children and an expert teacher mentor. Such supervisors are needed to provide in-service collaborative experiences, in-service materials (including interactive videodisc materials), and professional development opportunities directed toward improvement of early childhood pedagogy.

Recommendation 6: **Federal and state departments of education, human services, and other agencies interested in young children and their families should initiate programs of research and development aimed at learning more about effective preparation of early childhood teachers.**

Of particular concern are strategies directed toward bringing experienced early childhood educators, such as child care providers and prekindergarten and Head Start teachers, into compliance with standards for higher education and certification. Such programs should ensure that the field takes full advantage of the knowledge and expertise of existing staff and builds on diversity and strong community bonds represented in the current early childhood care and education work force. At the same time, it should assure that the fields of study described above are mastered by those in the existing workforce. These programs should include development of materials for early childhood professional education. Material development should entail cycles of field testing and revision to assure effectiveness.

Recommendation 7: **The committee recommends the development of demonstration schools for professional development.**

Many people, including professional educators of older children, do not know what an early childhood program should look like, what should be taught, or the kind of pedagogical strategies that are most effective. Demonstration schools would provide contextual understanding of these issues.

The Department of Education should collaborate with universities in developing the demonstration schools and in using them as sites for ongoing research:

• on the efficacy of various models, including pairing demonstration schools in partnership with community programs, and pairing researchers and in-service teachers with exemplary community-based programs;
• to identify conditions under which the gains of mentoring, placement of pre-service teachers in demonstration schools, and supervised student teaching can be sustained once teachers move into community-based programs.

Educational Materials

Good teachers must be equipped with good curricula. The content of early childhood curricula should be organized systematically into a coherent program with overarching objectives integrated across content and developmental areas. They should include multiple activities, such as systematic exploration and representation, planning and problem solving, creative expression, oral expression, and the ability and willingness to listen to and incorporate information presented by a teacher, sociodramatic and exercise play, and arts activities.

Important curriculum areas are often omitted from early education programs, although there is research to support their inclusion (provided they are addressed in an appropriate manner). Methods of scientific investigation, number concepts, phonological awareness, cultural knowledge, languages, and computer technology all fall into this category.

Because children differ in so many respects, teaching strategies used with any curriculum, from the committee's perspective, need to be flexibly adapted to meet the specific needs and prior knowledge and understanding of individual children. Embedded in the curriculum should be opportunities to assess children's prior understanding and mastery of the skills and knowledge being taught.

Teachers will also need to provide different levels of instruction in activities and use a range of techniques, including direct instruction, scaffolding, indirect instruction (taking advantage of moments of opportunity), and opportunities for children to learn on their own (self-directed learning). The committee believes it is particularly important to maintain children's enthusiasm for learning by integrating their self-directed interests with the teacher-directed curriculum.

Recommendation 8: The committee recommends that the U.S. Department of Education, the U.S. Department of Health and Human Services, and their equivalents at the state level fund efforts to develop, design, field test, and evaluate curricula that incorporate what is known about learning and thinking in the early years, with companion assessment tools and teacher guides.

Each curriculum should emphasize what is known from research about children's thinking and learning in the area it addresses. Activities should be included that enable children with different learning styles and strengths to learn.

Each curriculum should include a companion guide for teachers that explains the teaching goals, alerts the teacher to common misconceptions, and suggests ways in which the curriculum can be used flexibly for students at different developmental levels. In the teacher's guide, the description of methods of assessment should be linked to instructional planning so that the information acquired in the process of assessment can be used as a basis for making pedagogical decisions at the level of both the group and the individual child.

Recommendation 9: The committee recommends that the U.S. Department of Education and the U.S. Department of Health and Human Services support the use of effective technology, including videodiscs for preschool teachers and Internet communication groups.

The process of early childhood education is one in which interaction between the adult/teacher and the child/student is the most critical feature. Opportunities to see curriculum and pedagogy in action are likely to promote understanding of complexity and nuance not easily communicated in the written word. Internet communication groups could provide information on curricula, results of field tests, and opportunities for teachers using a common curriculum to discuss experiences, query each other, and share ideas.

Policy

States can play a significant role in promoting program quality with respect to both teacher preparation and curriculum and pedagogy.

Recommendation 10: All states should develop program standards for early childhood programs and monitor their implementation. These standards should recognize the variability in the development of young children and adapt kindergarten and primary programs, as well as preschool programs, to this diversity. This means, for instance, that kindergartens must be readied for children. In some schools, this will require smaller class sizes and professional development for teachers and administrators regarding appropriate teaching practice, so that teachers can meet the needs of individual children, rather than teaching to the "average" child. The standards should outline essential components and should include, but not be limited to, the following categories:

- School-home relationships;
- Class size and teacher-student ratios;
- Specification of pedagogical goals, content, and methods;
- Assessment for instructional improvement;
- Educational requirements for early childhood educators; and
- Monitoring quality/external accountability.

Recommendation 11: Because research has identified content that is appropriate and important for inclusion in early childhood programs, *content* standards should be developed

and evaluated regularly to ascertain whether they adhere to current scientific understanding of children's learning.

The content standards should ensure that children have access to rich and varied opportunities to learn in areas that are now omitted from many curricula—such as phonological awareness, number concepts, methods of scientific investigation, cultural knowledge, and language.

Recommendation 12: A single career ladder for early childhood teachers, with differentiated pay levels, should be specified by each state.

This career ladder should include, at a minimum, teaching assistants (with child development associate certification), teachers (with bachelor's degrees), and supervisors.

Recommendation 13: The committee recommends that the federal government fund well-planned, high-quality center-based preschool programs for all children at high risk of school failure.

Such programs can prevent school failure and significantly enhance learning and development in ways that benefit the entire society.

The Public

Policies that support the provision of quality preschool on a broad scale are unlikely without widespread public support. To engender that support, it is important for the public to understand both the potential of the preschool years, and the quality of programming required to realize that potential.

Recommendation 14: Organizations and government bodies concerned with the education of young children should actively promote public understanding of early childhood education and care.

Beliefs that are at odds with scientific understanding—that maturation automatically accounts for learning, for example, or that children can learn concrete skills only through drill and practice—must be challenged. Systematic and widespread public education should be undertaken to increase public awareness of the importance of providing stimulating educational experiences in the lives of all young children. The message that the quality of children's relationships with adult teachers and child care providers is critical in preparation for elementary school should be featured prominently in communication efforts. Parents and other caregivers, as well as the public, should be the targets of such efforts.

Recommendation 15: Early childhood programs and centers should build alliances with parents to cultivate complementary and mutually reinforcing environments for young children at home and at the center.

FUTURE RESEARCH NEEDS

Research on early learning, child development, and education can and has influenced the development of early childhood curriculum and pedagogy. But the influences are mutual. By evaluating outcomes of early childhood programs we have come to understand more about children's development and capacities. The committee believes that continued research efforts along both these lines can expand understanding of early childhood education and care, and the ability to influence them for the better.

Research on Early Childhood Learning and Development

Although it is apparent that early experiences affect later ones, there are a number of important developmental questions to be studied regarding how, when, and which early experiences support development and learning.

Recommendation 16: The committee recommends a broad empirical research program to better understand:

- The range of inputs that can contribute to supporting environments that nurture young children's eagerness to learn;
- Development of children's capacities in the variety of cog-

nitive and socioemotional areas of importance in the preschool years, and the contexts that enhance that development;

• The components of adult-child relationships that enhance the child's development during the preschool years, and experiences affecting that development for good or for ill;

• Variation in brain development, and its implications for sensory processing, attention, and regulation;

• The implications of developmental disabilities for learning and development and effective approaches for working with children who have disabilities;

• With regard to children whose home language is not English, the age and level of native language mastery that is desirable before a second language is introduced and the trajectory of second language development.

Research on Programs and Curricula

Recommendation 17: The next generation of research must examine more rigorously the characteristics of programs that produce beneficial outcomes for all children. In addition, research is needed on how programs can provide more helpful structures, curricula, and methods for children at high risk of educational difficulties, including children from low-income homes and communities, children whose home language is not English, and children with developmental and learning disabilities.

Much of the program research has focused on economically disadvantaged children because they were the targets of early childhood intervention efforts. But as child care becomes more widespread, it becomes more important to understand the components of early childhood education that have developmental benefits for all children.

With respect to disadvantaged children, we know that quality intervention programs are effective, but better understanding the features that make them effective will facilitate replication on a large scale. The Abecedarian program, for example, shows many developmental gains for the children who participate. But in addition to the educational activities, there is a health and nutrition component. And child care workers are paid at a level comparable to local public school teachers, with a consequent low turnover rate in staff. Whether the program effect is caused by the education component, the health component, or stability of caregiver, or some necessary combination of the three, is not possible to assess. Research on programs for this population should pay careful attention to home-school partnerships and their effect, since this is an aspect of the programs that research suggests is important.

Research on programs for any population of children should examine such program variations as age groupings, adult-child ratios, curricula, class size, looping, and program duration. These questions can best be answered through random assignment, longitudinal studies. Such studies raise concerns because some children receive better services than others, and because they are expensive. However, random assignment between programs that have very similar quality features, but vary on a single dimension (a math curriculum, for example, or class size) would seem less controversial. The cost of conducting such research must, of course, be weighed against the benefits. Given the dramatic expansion in the hours that children spend in out-of-home care in the preschool years, new knowledge can have a very high payoff.

Research is also needed on the interplay between an individual child's characteristics, the immediate contexts of the home and classroom, and the larger contexts of the formal school environment in developing and assessing curricula. An important line of research is emerging in this area and needs continued support.

Recommendation 18: A broad program of research and development should be undertaken to advance the state of the art of assessment in three areas: (1) classroom-based assessment to support learning (including studies of the impact of methods of instructional assessment on pedagogical technique and children's learning), (2) assessment for diagnostic purposes, and (3) assessment of program quality for accountability and other reasons of public policy.

All assessments, and particularly assessments for accountability, must be used carefully and appropriately if they are to resolve, and not create, educational problems. Assessment of young children poses greater challenges than people generally realize. The first five years of life are a time of incredible growth and learning, but the course of development is uneven and sporadic. The status of a child's development as of any given day can change very rapidly. Consequently, assessment results—in particular, standardized test scores that reflect a given point in time—can easily misrepresent children's learning.

Assessment itself is in a state of flux. There is widespread dissatisfaction with traditional norm-referenced standardized tests, which are based on early 20th century psychological theory. There are a number of promising new approaches to assessment, among them variations on the clinical interview and performance assessment, but the field must be described as emergent. Much more research and development are needed for a productive fusion of assessment and instruction to occur and if the potential benefits of assessment for accountability are to be fully realized.

Research on Ways to Create Universal High Quality

The growing consensus regarding the importance of early education stands in stark contrast to the disparate system of care and education available to children in the United States in the preschool years. America's programs for preschoolers vary widely in quality, content, organization, sponsorship, source of funding, relationship to the public schools, and government regulation.

As the nation moves toward voluntary universal early childhood programs, parents, and public officials face important policy choices, choices that should be informed by careful research.

Recommendation 19: Research to fully develop and evaluate alternatives for organizing, regulating, supporting, and financing early childhood programs should be conducted to provide an empirical base for the decisions being made.

• Compare the effects of program variations on short-term and long-term outcomes, including studies of inclusion of children with disabilities and auspices of program regulation.

• Examine preschool administration at local, county, and state levels to assess the relative quality of the administrative and support systems now in place.

• Consider quality, infrastructure, and cost-effectiveness.

• Review the evidence that should inform state standards and licensing, including limits on group size and square footage requirements.

• Develop instruments and strategies to monitor the achievement of young children that meet state and national accountability requirements, respect young children's unique learning and developmental needs, and do not interfere with teachers' instructional decision making.

CONCLUSION

At a time when the importance of education to individual fulfillment and economic success has focused attention on the need to better prepare children for academic achievement, the research literature suggests ways to make gains toward that end. Parents are relying on child care and preschool programs in ever larger numbers. We know that the quality of the programs in which they leave their children matters. If there is a single critical component to quality, it rests in the relationship between the child and the teacher/caregiver, and in the ability of the adult to be responsive to the child. But responsiveness extends in many directions: to the child's cognitive, social, emotional, and physical characteristics and development.

Much research still needs to be done. But from the committee's perspective, the case for a substantial investment in a high-quality system of child care and preschool on the basis of what is already known is persuasive. Moreover, the considerable lead by other developed countries in the provision of quality preschool programs suggests that it can, indeed, be done on a large scale.

Appendix:
Scientific Evidence

THE SCIENTIFIC METHODS

ETHODS USED BY SOCIAL SCIENTISTS to gain knowledge are very
diverse. Especially in the field of education, a field that calls
on several social sciences in order to constitute its knowledge
base, a variety of methods are relevant and useful. Each method
has its strengths and is best suited to a particular set of questions,
and less well suited to a different set of questions. Despite the
relative merits of all social science methods, their application in
the service of research requires that several basic standards
be met if the answers they yield are to be considered valid and
valuable.

This note on evidence makes explicit those standards of the
scientific communities to which we are accountable in conducting research on young children, and to which we have held researchers accountable in conducting our review. We identify and
briefly describe those standards, highlighting areas in which the
consensus is not as strong, as well as areas in which important
advances have been made in recent decades.

Empiricism: Theory Building

Scientists pose hypotheses based on their observations in the
world and in the laboratory. In order to test their hypotheses and

refine theories, they design research studies that entail the collection of data in some form. Those data are then analyzed, results or findings are arrived at, and interpretations of those results are made. These interpretations then can be used to frame future research and guide policy making and program design and implementation.

Replicability and Falsifiability

All theories must be falsifiable. In other words, any theory derived from a study must be sufficiently elaborated so that other scientists can replicate the study and collect additional empirical data to either corroborate or contradict the original theory. It is this willingness to abandon or modify a theory in the face of new evidence that is one of the most central defining features of the scientific method.

The extent to which one particular theory can be viewed as uniquely supported by a particular study depends on the extent to which alternative explanations have been ruled out. A particular research result is never equally relevant to all competing theoretical explanations. A given experiment may be a very strong test of one or two alternative theories but a weak test of others.

Validity and Generalizability

Validity is defined as the extent to which the instrument is actually measuring what the researcher intends it to measure. External validity concerns the generalizability of the conclusions to the larger population and setting of interest. Internal and external validity are often traded off across different methodologies. The alleged trade-off between internal and external validity presents some interesting questions. In what sense can a biased estimate (one that is inaccurate for the whole population) be said to be generalizable? What we mean is that we are willing to risk a small amount of bias for a large increase in confidence that the estimate generalizes to a much larger set of children and programs. Willingness to take that risk requires some confidence that the size of the bias introduced by lack of experimental control is small relative to the bias introduced by applying an unbiased estimate obtained from a narrow set of children and programs to a broader set of programs and children.

Convergence

Scientists and those who apply scientific knowledge must often make a judgment about where the preponderance of evidence points. When this is the case, the principle of converging evidence is an important tool, both for evaluating the state of the research evidence and also for deciding how future research should be designed.

Research is highly convergent when a series of studies consistently supports a given theory while collectively eliminating the most important competing explanations. Although no single study can rule out all alternative explanations, taken collectively, a series of partially diagnostic studies can lead to a strong conclusion if the data converge. This aspect of the convergence principle implies that we should expect to see many different methods employed in all areas of educational research. A relative balance among the methodologies used to arrive at a given conclusion is desirable because the various classes of research techniques have different strengths and weaknesses. The results from many different types of investigation are usually weighed to derive a general conclusion, and the basis for the conclusion rests on the convergence observed from the variety of methods used. This is particularly true in the domains of classroom and curriculum research.

Types and Uses of Empirical Methods

There are several ways to categorize the empirical methods used in research on early childhood development and education. They may be classified according to:

- the **purpose** of the study (e.g., evaluation of a program, open-ended inquiry for hypothesis or theory building, hypothesis testing, comparison of groups or of individuals),
- the **design** aspects of the study (e.g., the number of times

data are collected: longitudinal, cross-sectional; the type of data that are collected: quantifiable, qualitative), and

- the **data analysis** aspects and the unit of analysis used when the data are analyzed (e.g., univariate, bivariate, and multivariate analyses, qualitative analyses).

Across these groups of studies, methodological rigor can be defined and ensured through attention to the standards outlined above (replicability, generalizability, convergence).

Purposes of Research

Open-ended Inquiry: Qualitative, Ethnographic Research

In order to record and collect data in a naturalistic setting, social scientists conduct various types of ethnographic or qualitative research. These include case studies of individual learners or teachers, classroom ethnographic observations, open-ended and introspective interviews, and combinations of these methods. Qualitative research is most useful for in-depth descriptions of complex processes, such as teaching and learning. It may be important, for example, to assess the beliefs and attitudes of the adults involved in an intervention in order to evaluate the role of those adults in the implementation of a particular educational intervention.

The strengths of qualitative inquiry include a focus on depth, attention to the meaning of phenomena to the people being studied, and a quality of openness that enables new questions and perspectives to be uncovered throughout the research process. In most cases, however, qualitative studies sacrifice breadth for depth, and it is difficult to judge if the results are applicable or generalizable to a different population.

Identifying Causal Relationships: Experimental and Quasi-Experimental Design

If the purpose of the research is to identify cause-and-effect relationships between variables, then experimental and quasi-experimental studies are useful. An experimental study is one in which the researchers randomly select a control group and a treatment group, administer an intervention (such as an educational program) to the treatment group, and then compare the results by measuring before-and-after treatment variables on both the control and treatment groups. A true experiment is one in which all extraneous variables are controlled and only the single variable of interest is allowed to vary, so that the effect of that variable on the outcome variable can be clearly measured. This pure experimental design is the strongest inferential tool for statistical analysis.

In social science research, and especially in the education field, is often difficult and even unethical to ensure that the control group remains a true control throughout the duration of the intervention. There are several reasons why this may be the case and which therefore justify quasi-experimental or other types of research. First, there are logistical difficulties associated with carrying out classroom and curriculum research that may preclude true experimental designs. For example, members of control groups may engage in an alternative program, not that of the treatment group, but which will have some effect on those members. In some cases, ensuring a true control group would be unethical, as it would require withholding treatment from children even though the purpose of the research may be to gain knowledge that will help those same children in the future. Also, variables such as birth order, sex, and age cannot be manipulated, and therefore the relationships among these can only be correlational. By collecting observational and interview data from all participants, and by using statistical control mechanisms to neutralize the effects of the alternative programs on the control group members, researchers can overcome these limitations.

Researchers can also plan the study so as to minimize such problems. For example, the research plan may require providing a treatment that is of much higher quality and intensity than ordinary child care or even public preschool education and Head Start where these are provided. When service availability varies geographically, study locations might be chosen based on the lack of close substitutes for the treatment.

In any case, it is vital that researchers document all of the potentially significant educational activities that both the treatment and the control groups experience. The Abecedarian study provides a good example of a successful experiment in which much of the control group attended other early childhood programs. In this study, the difference in quality and intensity was so large that program effects were apparent. Moreover, an estimate of the diminishment of group differences due to control group experiences was produced. However, it may well be that the critical public policy issue is what is the effect of a program without taking into account the child care and preschool education experiences of the control group. If the research is to investigate the impact of providing a particular program, as it is currently implemented, given what is already available, then what the control group receives is irrelevant (assuming appropriate sampling procedures), and experimental studies produce good answers. Thus, whether a true experiment is useful depends on (a) the expected difference between the treatment and what occurs naturally and (b) the precise question being asked.

Quasi-experimental studies often suffer some of the same problems in assessing treatment effects as experimental studies. An example of this is when a comparison group is not examined carefully enough to determine interventions that they have received. Some correlational studies of Head Start and other preschool programs have failed to take into account the attendance of children in child care centers, despite the fact that these may not be particularly different from the "treatment" in terms of the child's educational experiences and given the fact that children tend to spend longer hours in child care.

Evidence can be combined across studies looking at different parts of causal chains that might not be completely encompassed by very many studies. For example, studies that link smoking and cancer need not follow subjects all the way to premature death, when there are many studies linking the kinds of cancer caused by smoking to premature death.

Identifying Relationships and Patterns: Correlational Studies

Although experimental studies represent a most powerful design for drawing causal inferences, their limitations must be recognized. A not uncommon misconception is that correlational (i.e., nonexperimental) studies cannot contribute to knowledge. This is false for a number of reasons.

First, many scientific hypotheses are stated in terms of correlation or lack of correlation, so that such studies are directly relevant to these hypotheses. Second, although correlation does not imply causation, causation *does* imply correlation. That is, although a correlational study cannot definitively prove a causal hypothesis, it may rule one out. Third, correlational studies are more useful than they once were due to more recently developed correlational designs. For example, the technique of partial correlation, widely used in studies cited in this report, makes possible a test of whether a particular third variable is accounting for a relationship.

RESEARCH IN EARLY CHILDHOOD EDUCATION

Researchers in early childhood education study a vast number of questions. For example: What are the processes through which knowledge is transmitted to young children? What are the effects of educational experiences and of different types of programs on young children? How do factors such as gender, social class, culture, and ethnicity affect the development and education of young children? Given this wide scope of investigation and the inherent complexity of studying young children's development, the design of precise and accurate measurements is a challenging task. Below we elaborate on a number of questions that should be addressed both in designing research studies and in evaluating the quality of research results.

Precision of the Questions Being Asked in the Research

Did the researcher have a defined purpose for comparing results? Are the questions being asked too broad in nature and are inappropriate measures used? Are we clearly specifying the multiple variables that might underlie the expected change? Are we defining relevant dimensions that may or may not be factors within the child? How do measurement indexes relate to the goals of programs?

The Variability of Young Children's Performance

Variability in any sample of living organisms should initially be examined in terms of the phenomenon or phenomena under study before attributing variability to measurement error (Farran, 2000). The consequence of ignoring within-group variability or of neglecting the potential significance of outliers in an aggregated data base is a missed opportunity. By focusing so narrowly on the "normal," a great deal of potentially useful information is overlooked, and understanding of the phenomena under study is thereby greatly handicapped. Within-group variability is not necessarily a random, inconsequential event. An inadequate understanding of the sources of variation should not automatically lead to an interpretation of random error. The argument for randomization is based on the assumption that randomness ensures that the phenomenon under study has an equal chance of being distributed in the entire population. The samples employed in many studies are too small, however, to uphold the validity of this assumption.

Use of Common Measures Versus
Trying Innovative Measures

Using measures that are commonly used by others in similar studies allows communication and comparison among different research groups and studies. A persistent use of measures known to have serious limitations, however, may allow these measures to gain acceptance and "incremental validity" simply by the fact that everyone uses these measures to answer a particular set of research questions. In other words, measures often become institutionalized, or part of a research culture.

Designing innovative measures, however, also has potentially negative consequences. If these measures are entirely new and therefore still under question within the scientific community, it may be difficult to interpret the results that they yield to the satisfaction of all. In addition, new measures present difficulties when it comes to training those who will administer them.

We suggest that the solution to this dilemma lies in the use of multiple measures. For example, measuring verbal intelligence among young children would include administration of a commonly used measure such as the Peabody Picture Vocabulary Test in combination with conducting clinical interviews of at least a subsample of children.

Triadic Nature of Early Childhood Education

In a recent comparative study of preschool programs, it was found that children in classrooms in which teachers strongly believed in the curriculum model they were implementing did better on standardized measures of development than children whose teachers were torn between conflicting models. This finding is supported in the literature showing how belief systems create environments in which particular beliefs are resistant to change even when the data support alternative points of view. The work of Shepard and Smith from the University of Colorado is an example of such research. Evaluations of the effects of preschool education on children should therefore take account of the mode of implementation of the programs being evaluated. In other words, the unit of analysis in such assessments is not only the program, or the child, but rather a triad composed of teacher, child or group of children, and program in the context of classroom.

The factors that constrain or facilitate the interactions among these three factors include the social characteristics of the children and of the teacher and the target and/or goal of the program relative to the transactions in the classroom. The social characteristics of the child are for the most part characteristics of the household, race and/or ethnicity, income and access to other economic resources, and even the level of parental education that influences the processes that take place in the home. These factors are important for a number of reasons: first, they shape the processes that occur in the home. Second, they shape the interactions between the parents and children and their environments (including access to and choice of nonparental care and education arrangements). Finally, the social characteristics of the child shape the perceptions (or interpretations) of the experiences of the child and parents in all of their environments.

Conceptual Orientation of the Investigator

In addition to taking full account of this triad, the orientation of the investigator must also be considered when examining evaluation or other types of early education studies. Research scientists approach their studies from a particular perspective with particular assumptions and understandings that guide their investigations. In evaluating their research, we feel it is important to ask such questions as: What is the ideological or conceptual orientation of the investigator? Is he or she studying children in context, or in isolation from the natural social environment? Is the perspective dominated by a search for universals, or rather for a search for differences between groups and/or cultures? Is the researcher interested in describing a dynamic model of the processes involved, or is the research instead interested in capturing a more static picture? Is the researcher more interested in endogenous or exogenous variables? Finally, does the researcher hold an individualist orientation, focusing on the child as the center of the model, or a more interactionist perspective, in which systems including the child, his or her family, and the school interact to shape development?

References

CHAPTER 1

American Heritage Dictionary of the English Language, 3rd ed.
1992   Boston: Houghton Mifflin.

Bloom, B.
1964   *Stability and Change in Human Characteristics.* New York: Wiley.

Howes, C.
1997   Children's experiences in center-based child care as a function of teacher background and adult-child ratio. *Merrill-Palmer Quarterly* 43(3):404-425.

Kamerman, S.B.
1999   Early Childhood Education and Care (ECEC): Preschool Policies and Programs in the OECD Countries. Paper commissioned for the *Global Perspectives on Early Childhood Education Workshop* hosted by the Committee on Early Childhood Pedagogy. School of Social Work, Columbia University.

Miller, P.H.
1989   *Theories of Developmental Psychology,* 2nd ed. New York: W.H. Freeman.

National Center for Education Statistics
1998   *Digest of Education Statistics.* Washington, DC: U.S. Department of Education, Office of Educational Research and Improvement.

Pianta, R.C.
1992   Conceptual and methodological issues in research on relationships between children and nonparental adults. *New Directions for Child Development* 57:121-129.

Powell, D.R.
1997   Parents' contributions to the quality of child care arrangements. In *Ad-*

vances in Early Education and Day Care. Family Policy and Practice in Early Child Care, Vol. 9, S. Reifel, C.J. Dunst, and M. Wolery, eds. Greenwich, CT: JAI Press.

Siraj-Blatchford, I., ed.
1998 *A Curriculum Development Handbook for Early Childhood Educators.* Staffordshire, U.K: Trentham Books Limited.

U.S. Bureau of Labor Statistics
1999 Labor force participation of fathers and mothers varies with children's ages. *Monthly Labor Review* June 3. Washington, DC: U.S. Department of Labor.

U.S. Bureau of the Census
1996 *Population Projections of the United States by Age, Sex, Race, and Hispanic Origin: 1995 to 2050.* Washington, DC: U.S. Department of Commerce, Economics and Statistics Administration.

U.S. Department of the Treasury
1998 *Investing in Child Care: Challenges Facing Working Parents and the Private Sector Response.* Washington, DC: U.S. Department of the Treasury.

Watkins, C., and P. Mortimore
1999 Pedagogy: What do we know? In *Understanding Pedagogy and Its Impact on Learning*, P. Mortimore, ed. London: Paul Chapman Publishing, Inc.

Wiggins, G., and J. McTighe
1998 *Understanding by Design.* Alexandria, VA: Association for Supervision and Curriculum Development.

CHAPTER 2

Akhtar, N., F. Dunham, and P.J. Dunham
1991 Directive interactions and early vocabulary development: The role of joint attentional focus. *Journal of Child Language* 18(1):41-49.

Belsky, J., M.K. Goode, and R.K. Most
1980 Maternal stimulation and infant exploratory competence: Cross-sectional, correlational, and experimental analyses. *Child Development* 51(4):1168-1178.

Bereiter, C., and M. Scardamalia
1989 Intentional learning as a goal of instruction. Pp. 361-392 in *Knowing, Learning, and Instruction*, L.B. Resnick, ed. Hillsdale, NJ: Erlbaum.

Bierman, K.L., and J. Welsh
1997 Social relationship deficits. Pp. 328-365 in *Assessment of Childhood Disorders* (3rd edition), E. J. Mash and L.G. Terdal, ed. New York: The Guilford Press.

Birch, S.H., and G.W. Ladd
1997 The teacher-child relationship and children's early school adjustment. *Journal of School Psychology* 35(1):61-79.

Bloom, L., L. Rocissano, and L. Hood
   1976   Adult-child discourse: Developmental interaction between information processing and linguistic knowledge. *Cognitive Psychology* 8(4):521-552.
Bodrova, E.
   1997   Key concepts in Vygotsky's theory of learning and development. *Journal of Early Child Teacher Education* 18(2):16-21.
Borke, H.
   1975   Piaget's mountains revisited: Changes in the egocentric landscape. *Developmental Psychology* 11:240-443.
Bornstein, M.H., and C.S. Tamis-LeMonda
   1989   Maternal responsiveness and cognitive development in children. *New Directions for Child Development* 43:49-61.
Bowlby, J.
   1969   *Attachment. Vol. 1, Attachment and Loss.* New York: Basic Books.
Boyce, W.T., E. Frank, P.S. Jensen, R.C. Kessler, C.A. Nelson, and L. Steinberg
   1998   Social context in developmental psychopathology: Recommendations for future research from the MacArthur Network on Psycopathology and Development. *Development and Psychopathology* 10:143-164.
Brown, A.L., and J.S. DeLoache
   1978   Skills, plans, and self-regulation. Pp. 3-35 in *Children's Thinking: What Develops?* R Siegler, ed. Hillsdale, NJ: Erlbaum.
Bronfenbrenner, U., and S.J. Ceci
   1994   Nature-nuture in developmental perspective: A bioecological theory. *Psychological Review* 101:568-586.
Bruer, J.T.
   1997   Education and the brain: A bridge too far. *Educational Researcher* 26(8):4-16.
Bruner, J.S., and D.R. Olson
   1977   Symbols and texts as tools of intellect. *Interchange* 8(4):77-78.
Bush, G., J.A. Frazier, S.L. Rauch, L.J. Seidman, P.J. Whalen, B.R. Rosen, and J. Biederman
   1999   Anterior cingulate cortex dysfunction in attention deficit/hyperactivity disorder revealed by fMRI and the counting Stroop. *Biological Psychiatry* 45:1542-1552.
Bush, G., P.J. Whalen, B.R. Rosen, M.A. Jenike, S.C. McInerey, and S.L. Rauch
   1998   The counting Stroop: An interference task specialized for functional neuroimaging—validation study with functional MRI. *Human Brain Mapping* 6(4):270-282.
Cairns, R.B.
   1983   The emergence of developmental psychology. In *Handbook of Child Psychology. Vol. 1. History, Theory, and Methods,* P.H. Mussen, ed. New York: Wiley
Canfield, R.L., and E.G. Smith
   1996   Number-based expectations and sequential enumeration by 5-month-old infants. *Developmental Psychology* 32:269-279.

Carey, S.
1985   *Conceptual Change in Childhood.* Cambridge, MA: MIT Press.
Case, R.
1985   *Intellectual Development: Birth to Adulthood.* New York: Academic Press.
1991   *The Mind's Staircase: Exploring the Conceptual Underpinnings of Children's Thought and Knowledge.* Hillsdale, NJ: Lawrence Erlbaum Associates.
Casey, B.J., R. Trainor, J. Giedd, Y. Vauss, C.K. Vaituzis, S. Hamburger, P. Kozuch, and J.L. Rapoport
1997a The role of the anterior cingulate in automatic and controlled processes: A developmental neuroanatomical study. *Developmental Psychobiology* 30(1):61-69.
Casey, B.J., R.J. Trainor, J.L. Orendi, A.B. Schubert, L.E. Nystrom, J.N. Giedd, F.X. Castellanos, J.V. Haxby, D.C. Noll, J.D. Cohen, S.D. Forman, R.E. Dahl, and J.L. Rapoport
1997b A developmental functional MRI study of prefrontal activation during performance of a go no-go task. *Journal of Cognitive Neuroscience* 9:835-847.
Chase, W.G., and H.A. Simon
1973   Perception in chess. *Cognitive Psychology* 1:33-81.
Chi, M.T.H.
1978   Knowledge structures and memory development. Pp. 73-96 in *Children's Thinking: What Develops*, R. Siegler, ed. Hillsdale, NJ: Erlbaum.
Corbetta, M., F.M. Miezin, G.L. Shulman, and S.E. Petersen
1993   A PET study of visuospatial attention. *Journal of Neuroscience* 13(3):1202-1226.
Crockenberg, S., and C. Litman
1990   Autonomy as competence in 2-year-olds: Maternal correlates of child defiance, compliance, and self-assertion. *Developmental Psychology* 26(6):961-971.
DeLoache, J.S., D.J. Cassidy, and A.L. Brown
1985   Precursors of mnemonic strategies in very young children's memory. *Child Development* 56:125-137.
DeLoache, J.S., K.F. Miller, and S.L. Pierroutsakos
1998   Reasoning and problem-solving. Pp. 801-850 in *Handbook of Child Psychology*, Vol. 2, D. Kuhn and R.S. Siegler, eds. New York: Wiley.
Donaldson, M.
1978   *Children's Minds.* New York: W.W. Norton.
Drevets, W.C., and M.E. Raichle
1998   Reciprocal suppression of regional cerebral blood flow during emotional versus higher cognitive processes: Implications for interactions between emotion and cognition. *Cognition and Emotion* 12(3):353-385.
Dweck, C.S.
1989   Motivation. Pp. 87-136 in *Foundations for a Psychology of Education*, A. Lesgold and R. Glaser, eds. Hillsdale, NJ: Erlbaum.

Dweck, C., and E. Elliott
   1983   Achievement motivation. Pp. 643-691 in *Handbook of Child Psychology*, Vol. IV: *Socialization, Personality, and Social Development*, P.H. Mussen, ed. New York: Wiley.
Dweck, C., and E. Leggett
   1988   A social-cognitive approach to motivation and personality. *Psychological Review* 95:256-273.
Eimas, P.D., E.R. Siqueland, P.W. Jusczyk, and J. Vigorito
   1971   Speech perception in infants. *Science* 171:303-306.
Fischer, K.W.
   1980   A theory of cognitive development: The control and construction of hierarchies of skills. *Psychological Review* 87:477-531.
Fischer, K.W., D.H. Bullock, E.J. Rotenberg, and P. Raya
   1993   The dynamics of competence: How context contributes directly to skill. Pp. 93-117 in *Development in Context: Acting and Thinking in Specific Environments*, R. Wozniak and K.W. Fischer, eds. Hillsdale, NJ: Lawrence Erlbaum Associates.
Fischer, K.W., and C.C. Knight
   1990   Cognitive development in real children: Levels and variations. In *Styles of Learning and Thinking: Interactions in the Classroom*, B. Presseisen, ed. Washington, DC: National Educational Association.
Gelman, R.
   2000   The epigenesis of mathematical thinking. *Journal of Applied Developmental Psychology* 27-38.
Gobbo, C., and M. Chi
   1986   How knowledge is structured and used by expert and novice children. *Cognitive Development* 1(3):221-237.
Gopnik, A., and A.N. Meltzoff
   1992   Categorization and naming: Basic-level sorting in eighteen-month-olds and its relation to language. *Child Development* 63(5):1091-1103.
Goswami, U.
   1995   Transitive relational mappings in three- and four-year-olds: The analogy of Goldilocks and the three bears. *Child Development* 66(3):877-892.
Gralinski, J.H., and C.B. Kopp
   1993   Everyday rules for behavior: Mothers' requests to young children. *Developmental Psychology* 29(3):573-584.
Greenfield, P.M., and L.K. Suzuki
   1998   Culture and human development: Implications for parenting, education, pediatrics, and mental health. Pp. 1059-1109 in *Handbook of Child Psychology (5th edition): Volume 4 Child Psychology in Practice*, W. Damon, ed. New York: John Wiley and Sons, Inc.
Halford, G.S.
   1982   How do we define the limits to children's understanding? Paper presented at the 20th International Congress of Applied Psychology in Edinburgh, Scotland; July 25-31, 1982.

Halford, G.S., and E. Leitch
   1988 Processing load constraints: A structure-mapping approach. Paper pre-
         sented at the 24th International Congress of Psychology in Sydney, Aus-
         tralia.
Hartup, W.W.
   1983 The peer system. Pp. 103-196 in *Handbook of Child Psychology (4th edi-
         tion): Vol. 4 Socialization, Personality and Social Development*, E.M.
         Hetherington, vol. ed. New York: John Wiley and Sons, Inc.
Harwood, R.L.
   1992 The influence of culturally derived values on Anglo and Puerto Rican
         mothers' perceptions of attachment behavior. *Child Development* 63:822-
         839.
Hebb, D.O.
   1983 Neuropscyhology: Retrospect and prospect. *Canadian Journal of Psy-
         chology* 37(1):4-7.
Howes, C.
   1997 Children's experiences in center-based child care as a function of
         teacher background and adult-child ratio. *Merrill-Palmer Quarterly*
         43(3):404-425.
   1999 Attachment relationships in the context of multiple caregivers. In *Hand-
         book of Attachment Theory and Research*, J. Cassidy, and P.R. Shaver, eds.
         NY: Guilford Publications.
Howes, C., and E.W. Smith
   1995 Relations among child care quality, teacher behavior, children's play
         activities, emotional security, and cognitive activity in child care.
         EarlyChildhood Research Quarterly 10(4):381-404.
Howes, C., and H.A. Tonyan
   in   Peer relations. In *Child Psychology: A Handbook of Contemporary Issues*,
   press C. Tamis-LeMonda and L. Balter, eds. New York: Garland.
Howes, C., C.C. Matheson, and C.E. Hamilton
   1994 Children's relationships with peers: Differential associations with as-
         pects of the teacher-child relationship. *Child Development* 65(1):253-263.
Howes, C., C.E. Hamilton, and L.C. Phillipsen
   1998 Stability and continuity of child-caregiver and child-peer relationships.
         Child Development 69(2):418-426.
Howes, C., L. Phillipsen, and E. Peisner-Feinberg
   in   The consistency and predictability of teacher-child relationships dur-
   press ing the transition to kindergarten. *Journal of School Psychology.*
Johnson, M.
   1998 Developing an attentive brain. Pp. 427-433 in *The Attentive Brain*, R.
         Parasuraman, ed. Cambridge, MA: MIT Press.
Johnson, M.H., M.I. Posner, and M.K. Rothbart
   1991 Components of visual orienting in early infancy: Contingency learn-
         ing, anticipatory looking, and disengaging. *Journal of Cognitive Neuro-
         science* 3(4):335-344.

Karmiloff-Smith, A., and B. Inhelder
1974- If you want to get ahead, get a theory. *Cognition* 3:195-212.
1975
Kochanska, G.
1997 Mutually responsive orientation between mothers and their young children: Implications for early socialization. *Child Development* 68(1):94-112.
Kuczynski, L.
1984 Socialization goals and mother-child interaction: Strategies for long-term and short-term compliance. *Developmental Psychology* 20(6):1061-1073.
Kuhl, P.K., K.A. Williams, F. Lacerda, N. Stevens, and B. Lindblom
1992 Linguistic experience alters phonetic perception in infants by 6 months of age. *Science* 255:606-608.
Landry, S.L., K.E. Smith, C.L. Miller-Loncar, and P.R. Swank
1997 The role of child-centered perspectives in a model of parenting. *Journal of Experimental Child Psychology* 66(3):341-361.
Lantz, D.
1979 A cross-cultural comparison of communication abilities: Some effects of age, schooling, and culture. *International Journal of Psychology* 14(3):171-183.
Londerville, S., and M. Main
1981 Security of attachment, compliance, and maternal training methods in the second year of life. *Developmental Psychology* 17(3):289-299.
Lynch, M., and D. Cicchetti
1992 Maltreated children's reports of relatedness to their teachers. Pp. 81-107 in *Beyond the Parent: The Role of Other Adults in Children's Lives. New Directions for Child Development, No. 57*, R.C. Pianta et al., eds. San Francisco, CA: Jossey-Bass Inc., Publishers.
1997 Children's relationships with adults and peers: An examination of elementary and junior high school students. *Journal of School Psychology* 35(1):81-99.
Maccoby, E.E.
1984 Middle childhood in the context of family. In *Development During Middle Childhood: The Years Six to Twelve*, C.W. Collins, ed. Washington, DC: National Academy Press.
Maccoby, E.E., and J.A. Martin
1983 Socialization in the context of the family: Parent-child interaction. In *Handbook of Child Psychology. Vol. 4: Socialization, Personality, and Social Behavior*, P.H. Mussen, ed. New York: Wiley.
Matas, L., R.A. Arend, and L.A. Sroufe
1978 Continuity of adaptation in the second year: The relationship between quality of attachment and later competence. *Child Development* 49(3):547-556.

McCandliss, B.D., M.I. Posner, and T. Givon
  1997   Brain plasticity in learning visual words. *Cognitive Psychology* 33(1):8-110.
Mehler, J., G. Lambertz, P. Juszyk, and C. Amiel-Tison
  1986   Discrimination de la langue maternelle par le nouveau-né. *Comptes Rendus de l'Academie de Science* 303:637-640.
Morton, J., and M.H. Johnson
  1991   CONSPEC and CONLEARN: A two-process theory of infant face recognition. *Psychological Review* 98:164-181.
National Research Council
  1999   *How People Learn: Brain, Mind, Experience, and School*, Committee on Developments in the Science of Learning, J.D. Bransford, A.L. Brown, and R.R. Cocking, eds. Washington, DC: National Academy Press.
Neville, H.J.
  1995   Effects of experience on the development of the visual systems of the brain on the language systems of the brain. Paper presented in the series Brain Mechanisms Underlying School Subjects, Part 3. University of Oregon, Eugene.
Olson, S.L., J.E. Bates, and K. Bayles
  1984   Mother-infant interaction and the development of individual differences in children's cognitive competence. *Developmental Psychology* 20(1):166-179.
Parke, R.D., and G.W. Ladd
  1992   *Family-peer Relationships: Modes of Linkage.* Hillsdale, New Jersey: Erlbaum.
Parker, J.G., K.H. Rubin, J.M. Price, and M.E. DeRosier
  1995   Peer relationships, child development, and adjustment: A developmental psycho-pathology perspective. Pp. 96-161 in *Developmental Psychopathology: (Vol. 2) Risk, Disorder and Adaptation,* D. Cicchetti, and D. Cohen, eds. New York: John Wiley and Sons, Inc.
Parpal, M., and E.E. Maccoby
  1985   Maternal responsiveness and subsequent child compliance. *Child Development* 56(5):1326-1334.
Pascual-Leone, J.
  1988a Affirmations and negotiations, disturbances and contradictions in understanding Piaget: Is his later theory causal? *Contemporary Psychology* 33:420-421.
  1988b Organismic processes for neo-Piagetian theories: A dialectic causal account of cognitive development. In *The Neo-Piagetian Theories of Cognitive Development: Toward an Integration,* A. Demetriou, ed. Amsterdam: Elsevier.
Patterson, G.R.
  1986   Performance models for antisocial boys. *American Psychologist* 41(4):432-444.
Piaget, J.
  1967   *Six Psychological Studies.* New York: Random House.

Pianta, R.
1994 Patterns of relationships between children and kindergarten teachers. *Journal of School Psychology* 32:1-16.

Pianta, R.C., and M. Steinberg
1992 Teacher-child relationships and the process of adjusting to school. Pp. 61-80 in *Beyond the Parent: The Role of Other Adults in Children's Lives. New Directions for Child Development, No. 57,* R.C. Pianta et al., eds. San Francisco, CA: Jossey-Bass Inc.

Pierson, D., M.Bronson, E. Dromey, J. Swartz, T. Tivnan, and D. Walker
1983 The impact of early education measured by classroom observation and teacher ratings of children in kindergarten. *Evaluation Review* 7:191-216.

Posner, M.L., and M.E. Raichle
1994 *Images of Mind.* New York: Scientific American Library/Scientific American Books.

Posner, M.I., and M.E. Raichle, eds.
1998 Neuroimaging of human brain function. *Proceedings of the National Academy of Sciences of the U.S.A.* 95:763-929.

Posner, M.I., and M.K. Rothbart
1998 Summary and commentary: Developing attentional skills. Pp. 317-323 in *Cognitive Neuroscience of Attention: A Developmental Perspective,* J.E. Richards, ed. Mahwah, NJ: Lawrence Erlbaum Associates, Inc.

Power, T.G., and M.L. Chapieski
1986 Childrearing and impulse control in toddlers: A naturalistic investigation. *Developmental Psychology* 22(2):271-275.

Quartz, S., and T.J. Sejnowski
1997 The neural basis of cognitive development: A constructivist manifesto. *Behavioral and Brain Sciences* 20(4):537-596.

Raichle, M.E., J.A. Fiez, T.O. Videen, A-M.K. MacLeod, J.V. Pardo, P.T. Fox, and S.E. Rotersen
1994 Practice-related changes in human brain functional anatomy during nonmotor learning. *Cerebral Cortex* 4(1):8-26.

Rocissano, L., and Y. Yatchmink
1984 Joint attention in mother-toddler interaction: A study of individual variation. *Merrill-Palmer Quarterly* 30(1):11-31.

Rogoff, B.
1990 *Apprenticeship in Thinking: Cognitive Development in Social Context.* New York: Oxford University Press.

Rovee-Collier, C.
1989 The joy of kicking: Memories, motives, and mobiles. Pp. 151-180 in *Memory: Interdisciplinary Approaches,* P.R. Solomon, G.R. Goethals, C.M. Kelly, and B.R. Stephens, eds. New York: Springer-Verlag.

Sameroff, A.
1975 Transactional models in early social relations. *Human Development* 18(1-2):65-79.

1994   Developmental systems and family functioning. Pp. 199-214 in *Exploring Family Relationships with Other Social Contexts. Family Research Consortium: Advances in Family Research*, R.D. Parke, and S.G. Kellam, eds. Hillsdale, NJ: Lawrence Erlbaum Associates, Inc.

Schliemann, A.D., C. Araujo, M.A. Cassunde, S. Macedo, and L. Niceas
1998   Use of multiplicative commutativity by school children and street sellers. *Journal for Research in Mathematics Education* 29(4):422-435.

Scribner, S.
1984   Studying working intelligence. Pp. 9-40 in *Everyday Cognition*, B. Rogoff and J. Lave, eds. Cambridge, MA: Harvard University Press.
1985   Knowledge at work. *Anthropology & Education Quarterly* 16(3):199-206.

Schaffer, H. and C. Crook
1980   Child compliance and maternal control techniques. *Developmental Psychology* 16:54-61.

Siegler, R.S.
1988   Individual differences in strategy choices: Good students, not-so-good students, and perfectionists. *Child Development* 59:833-851.

Spelke, E.S.
1990   Principles of object perception. *Cognitive Science* 14:29-56.

Sperry, R.W., C.D. Gilbert, A. Das, M. Ito, M. Kapadia, G. Westheimer, and M.H. Johnson
2000   Part V: Development and plasticity. Pp. 209-258 in *Cognitive Neuroscience: A Reader*, M.S. Gazzaniga, ed. Malden, MA: Blackwell Publishers.

Sternberg, R.J.
1985   *Beyond IQ: A Triarchic Theory of Human Intelligence*. New York: Cambridge University Press.

Thatcher, R.W., G.R. Lyon, J. Rumsey, and N. Krasnegor, eds.
1996   *Developmental Neuroimaging: Mapping the Development of Brain and Behavior*. San Diego, CA: Academic Press, Inc.

Tomasello, M., and M.J. Farrar
1986a   Joint attention and early language. *Child Development* 57(6):1454-1463.
1986b   Object permanence and relational words: A lexical training study. *Journal of Child Language* 13(3):495-505.

Tronick, E.Z.
1989   Emotions and emotional communication in infants. *American Psychologist* 44(2):112-119.

Ungerleider, L.G., S.M. Courtney, and J.V. Haxby
1998   A neural system for human visual working memory. *Proceedings of the National Academy of Sciences of the U.S.A.* 95:883-890.

Vygotsky, L.S.
1978   *Mind in Society: The Development of the Higher Psychological Processes*. Cambridge, MA: The Harvard University Press. (Originally published 1930, New York: Oxford University Press.)

Wasik, B.H.
1997   Kindergarten predictors of elementary children's social and academic

performance. In *Influences on and Linkages Between Children's Social and Academic Performance: A Developmental Perspective*, B.H. Wasik, chair. Symposium conducted at the annual meeting for Social Research in Child Development, Washington, DC.

Wasik, B.H., J.L. Wasik, and R. Frank
1993 Sociometric characteristics of kindergarten children at risk for retention. *Journal of School Psychology* 31:241-257.

Weiss, B., K.A. Dodge, J.E. Bates, and G.S. Pettit
1992 Some consequences of early harsh discipline: Child aggression and a maladaptive social information processing style. *Child Development* 63(6):1321-1335.

Wellman, H.M., K. Ritter, and J.H. Flavell
1975 Deliberate memory behavior in the delayed reactions of very young children. *Developmental Psychology* 11:780-787.

CHAPTER 3

Ahadi, S.A., M.K. Rothbart, and R. Ye
1993 Children's temperament in the US and China: Similarities and differences. *European Journal of Personality* 7(5):359-377.

Bates, E., I. Bretherton, and L. Snyder
1988 *From First Words to Grammar: Individual Differences and Dissociable Mechanisms*. New York: Cambridge University Press.

Batshaw, M.L. ed.
1997 *Children with Disabilities* (4th ed.). Baltimore, MD: Paul H. Brookes Publishing Co.

Bruner, J.S.
1974 The organization of early skilled action. In *The Integration of a Child into a Social World*, M.P.M. Richards, ed. New York: Cambridge University Press.

Bryk, A.S., and S.W. Raudenbush
1992 *Hierarchical linear models: Applications and data analysis methods*. Newbury Park, CA: Sage Publications, Inc.

Case, R., and S. Griffin
1990 Child cognitive development: The role of central conceptual structures in the development of scientific and social thought. In *Developmental Psychology: Cognitive, Perceptual Motor and Psychological Perspectives*, C.A. Hauert, ed. North-Holland: Elsevier.

Case, R., S. Griffin, and W.M. Kelly
1999 Socioeconomic gradients in mathematical ability and their responsiveness to intervention during early childhood. Pp. 125-149 in *Developmental Health and the Wealth of Nations: Social, Biological, and Educational Dynamics*, D.P. Keating and C. Hertzman, eds. New York: Guilford Press.

Caspi, A., B. Henry, R.O. McGee, T.E. Moffitt, and P.E. Silva
 1995 Temperamental origins of child and adolescent behavior problems:
     From age three to fifteen. *Child Development* 66(1):55-68.
Chisholm, J.S.
 1981 Residence patterns and the environment of mother-infant interaction
     among the Navajo. Pp. 3-19 in *Culture and Early Interactions*, T.M. Field,
     A.M. Sostek, P. Vietze, and P.H. Leiderman, eds. Hillsdale, NJ: Erlbaum.
Choi, S., and M. Bowerman
 1991 Learning to express motion events in English and Korean: The influ-
     ence of language-specific lexicalization patterns. *Cognition.* 41(1-
     3)(Dec):83-121.
Cole, M.
 1996 *Cultural Psychology: A Once and Future Discipline.* Cambridge, MA:
     Belknap Press of Harvard University Press.
Cole, M., J. Gay, J.A. Glick, and D.W. Sharp
 1971 *The Cultural Context of Learning and Thinking: An Exploration in Experi-
     mental Anthropology.* New York: Basic Books, Inc.
Deci, E. L., and R.M Ryan
 1994 Promoting self-determined education. *Scandinavian Journal of Educa-
     tional Research* 38(1):3-14.
deTocqueville, A.
 1945 *Democracy in America.* The Henry Reeve text as revised by Francis
     Bowen; P. Bradley, ed. New York: A.A. Knopf.
Duncan, G.J., J. Brooks-Gunn, and P.K. Klebanov
 1994 Economic deprivation and early childhood development. *Child Devel-
     opment* 65(2):296-318.
Durrett, M.E., S. O'Bryant, J. Pennebaker, and W. James
 1975 Child-rearing reports of White, Black, and Mexican-American families.
     Developmental Psychology 11(6):871.
Erickson, J.J.
 1993 Multicultural education comes to Lake Wobegon. *Quarterly of the Na-
     tional Writing Project and the Center for the Study of Writing and Literacy*
     15(1)(Win):6-9.
Fajardo, B.F., and D.G. Freedman
 1981 Maternal rhythmicity in three American cultures. Pp. 133-147 in *Cul-
     ture and Early Interactions*, T.M. Field, A.M. Sostek, P. Vietze, and P.H.
     Leiderman, eds. Hillsdale, NJ: Erlbaum.
Fenson, L., P.S. Dale, J.S. Reznick, E. Bates, D.J. Thal, and S.J. Pethick
 1994 Variability in early communicative development. *Monographs of the So-
     ciety for Research in Child Development* 59(5):v-173.
Fernald, A., and H. Morikawa
 1993 Common themes and cultural variations in Japanese and American
     mothers' speech to infants. *Child Development* 64(3):637-656.
Field, T.M., and S.M. Widmayer
 1981 Mother-infant interactions among lower SES black, Cuban, Puerto

Rican and South American immigrants. Pp. 41-62 in *Culture and Early Interactions*, T.M. Field, A.M. Sostek, P. Vietze, and P.H. Leiderman, eds. Hillsdale, NJ: Erlbaum.

French, L. and M. Song
1998   Developmentally appropriate teacher-director approaches: Images from Korean kindergartens. *Journal of Curriculum Studies* 30:409-430.

Gallimore, R., J.W. Boggs, and C. Jordan
1974   *Culture, Behavior and Education: A Study of Hawaiian-Americans*. Beverly Hills, CA: Sage.

García-Coll, C., and K. Magnuson
2000   Cultural differences as sources of developmental vulnerabilities and resources. Pp. 94-114 in *Handbook of Early Childhood Intervention*, 2nd ed., J.P. Shonkoff and S.J. Meisels, eds. New York: Cambridge University Press.

Garrett, P., N. Ng'andu, and J. Ferron
1994   Poverty experiences of young children and the quality of their home environments. *Child Development* 65(2):331-345.

Gauvain, M., and B. Fagot
1995   Child temperament as a mediator of mother-toddler problem solving. *Social Development* 4(3):257-276.

Gelman, R., and C.R. Gallistel
1978   *The Child's Understanding of Number*. Cambridge, MA: Harvard University Press.

Ginsburg, H.P., Y.E. Choi, L.S. Lopez, R. Netley, and C.Y. Chi
1997   Happy birthday to you: Early mathematical thinking of Asian, South American and US children. Pp. 163-207 In *Learning and Teaching Mathematics: An International Perspective*, T. Nunes and P. Pryant, eds. East Sussex, England: Erlbaum (UK) Taylor and Francis.

Ginsburg H.P., and R.L. Russell
1981   Social class and racial influences on early mathematical thinking. *Monographs of the Society for Research in Child Development* 46(Serial, 193)(6).

Gordon, E., and W.S. Shipman
1979   Human diversity, pedagogy, and educational equity. *American Psychologist* 34(10):1030-1036.

Gottfried, A.W., ed.
1984   *Home Environment and Early Cognitive Development: Longitudinal Research*. New York: Academic Press.

Greenbaum, P.E.
1985   Nonverbal differences in communication style between American Indian and Anglo elementary classrooms. *American Educational Research Journal* 22(1):101-115.

Griffin, S.A., R. Case, and R.S. Siegler
1996   Evaluating the breadth and depth of transfer effects when central conceptual structures are taught. In *The Role of Central Conceptual Structures in the Development of Children's Thought*, R. Case and Y. Okamoto,

eds. Monographs of the Society for Research in Child Development, 60(Serial 246)(5-6).

Guerin, D.W., and A.W. Gottfried
1994 Developmental stability and change in parent reports of temperament: A ten-year longitudinal investigation from infancy through preadolescence. *Merrill Palmer Quarterly* 40(3):334-355.

Guralnick, M.J.
1990 Social competence and early intervention. *Journal of Early Intervention* 14(1):3-14.

Guralnick, M.J., and D. Paul-Brown
1986 Communicative interactions of mildly delayed and normally developing preschool children: Effects of listener's developmental level. *Journal of Speech and Hearing Research* 29(1):2-10.

Hammill, D.D., and G. McNutt
1980 Language abilities and reading: A review of the literature on their relationship. *Elementary School Journal* 95(4):367-385.

Hart, B., and T.R. Risley
1995 *Meaningful Differences in the Everyday Experience of Young American Children.* Baltimore, MD: Paul H. Brookes Publishing Co.
1999 *The Social World of Children Learning to Talk.* Baltimore, MD: Paul H. Brookes Publishing Co.

Heath, S.B.
1983 *Ways with Words: Language, Life, and Work in Communities and Classrooms.* Cambridge, U.K: Cambridge University Press.
1989 Oral and literate traditions among Black Americans living in poverty. *American Psychologist* 44:367-373.

Hemphill, L., and G.N. Siperstein
1990 Conversational competence and peer response to mildly retarded children. *Journal of Educational Psychology* 82(1):128-134.

Herink, N., and P.C. Lee
1985 Patterns of social interaction of mainstreamed preschool children: Hopeful news from the field. *Exceptional Child* 32(3):191-199.

Huntsinger, C.S., P.E. Jose, and S.L. Larson
1998 Do parent practices to encourage academic competence influence the social adjustment of young European American and Chinese American children? *Developmental Psychology* 34:747-756.

Huttenlocher, J., W. Haight, A. Bryk, M. Seltzer, and Lyons
1991 Early vocabulary growth: Relation to language input and gender. *Developmental Psychology* 27(2):236-248.

Kagan, J.
1989 Temperamental contributions to social behavior. *American Psychologist* 44(4):668-674.
1994 *Galen's Prophecy.* New York: BasicBooks.

Kagan, S.L., E. Moore, and S. Bredekamp
1995 *Reconsidering Children's Early Development and Learning: Toward Com-*

mon Views and Vocabulary. Washington DC: National Educational Goals Panel.

Kochanska, G.
1991 Patterns of inhibition to the unfamiliar in children of normal and affectively ill mothers. *Child Development* 62(2):250-263.
1995 Children's temperament, mother's discipline, and security of attachment: Multiple pathways to emerging internalization. *Child Development* 66(3):597-615.

Kochanska, G., K. Murray, T.Y. Jacques, A.L. Koenig, and K.A. Vandegeest
1996 Inhibitory control in young children and its role in emerging internalization. *Child Development* 67(2):490-507.

Krechevsky, M., and S. Seidel
1998 Minds at work: Applying multiple intelligences in the classroom. Pp. 17-42 in *Intelligence, Instruction, and Assessment: Theory into Practice*, R.J. Sternberg and W.M. Williams, eds. Mahwah, NJ: Lawrence Erlbaum Associates, Inc.

Landon, S.J., and R.K. Sommers
1979 Talkativeness and children's linguistic abilities. *Language and Speech* 22(3):269-275.

McCormick, C.E., and J.M. Mason
1986 Intervention procedures for increasing preschool children's interest in and knowledge about reading. Pp. 90-115 in *Emergent Literacy: Writing and Reading*, W.H. Teale and E. Sulzby, eds. Norwood, NJ: Ablex.

Meisels, S.J., S. Atkins-Burnett, and J. Nicholson
1996 *Assessment of Social Competence, Adaptive Behaviors, and Approaches to Learning.* Working Paper #96-18, National Center for Education Statistics. Washington, DC: U.S. Department of Education, Office of Educational Research and Improvement.

Meisels, S.J., L.W. Henderson, F. Liaw, K. Browning, and T. Ten Have
1993 New evidence for the effectiveness of the Early Screening Inventory. *Early Childhood Research Quarterly* 8:327-346.

Meisels, S.J., D.B. Marsden, M.S. Wiske, and L.W. Henderson
1997 *The Early Screening Inventory – Revised (ESI – R).* Ann Arbor, MI: Rebus, Inc.

Meisels, S.J., and J.P. Shonkoff
2000 Early childhood intervention: A continuing evolution. Pp. 3-33 in *Handbook of Early Childhood Intervention*, 2nd ed., J.P. Shonkoff and S.J. Meisels, eds. New York: Cambridge University Press.

National Center for Education Statistics (NCES)
2000 *America's Kindergartners: Findings from the Early Childhood Longitudinal Study, Kindergarten Class of 1998-99, Fall 1998.* J. West, K. Denton, and E. Germino Hausken, authors, Office of Educational Research and Improvement. Washington, DC: U.S. Department of Education.

National Research Council
1998 *Preventing Reading Difficulties in Young Children* Committee on Preven-

tion of Reading Difficulties in Young Children, C.E. Snow, M.S. Burns, and P. Griffin, eds. Washington, DC: National Academy Press.

1999 *How People Learn: Brain, Mind, Experience, and School.* Committee on Developments in the Science of Learning, J.D. Bransford, A.L. Brown, and R.R. Cocking, eds. Washington, DC: National Academy Press.

Neisser, U., G. Boodoo, T.J. Bouchard, A.W. Boykin, N. Brody, S.J. Ceci, D.F. Halpern, J.C. Loehlin, R. Perloff, R.J. Sternberg, and S. Urbina

1996 Intelligence: Knowns and unknowns. *American Psychologist* 51:77-101.

Nelson, K.

1973 Structure and strategy in learning to talk. *Monographs of the Society for Research in Child Development* 38(1-2)(Serial 149):136.

Ochs, E.

1986 From feelings to grammar: A Samoan case study. Pp. 251-272 in *Language Socialization Across Cultures: Studies in the Social and Cultural Foundations of Language,* Schieffelin, B.B. and E. Ochs, eds. New York: Cambridge University Press.

Oller, D.K., R.E. Eilers, D. Basinger, M. L. Steffens, et al.

1995 Extreme poverty and the development of precursors to the speech capacity. *First Language* 15(44, Pt 2):167-187.

Peters, A.M.

1983 *The Units of Language Acquisition.* New York: Cambridge University Press.

Plomin, R., R.N. Emde, J.M. Braungart, and J. Campos

1993 Genetic change and continuity from fourteen to twenty months: The MacArthur Longitudinal Twin Study. *Child Development* 64(5):1354-1376.

Posner, M.I., and M.K. Rothbart

1998 Summary and commentary: Developing attentional skills. Pp. 317-323 in *Cognitive Neuroscience of Attention: A Developmental Perspective,* J.E. Richards et al., eds. Mahwah, NJ: Lawrence Erlbaum Associates, Inc., Publishers.

Pye, C.

1986 One lexicon or two? An alternative interpretation of early bilingual speech. *Journal of Child Language* 13(3)(Oct):591-593

Renninger, A.

1992 *The Role of Interest in Learning and Development.* K. A. Renninger, S. Hidi, and A. Krapp, eds. Hillsdale, NJ: L. Erlbaum Associates.

Rescorla, L.

1989 The language development survey: A screening tool for delayed language in toddlers. *Journal of Speech and Hearing Disorders* 54(4):587-599.

Rice, M.L., M.A. Sell, and P.A. Hadley

1991 Social interactions of speech and language-impaired children. *Journal of Speech and Hearing Research* 34(6):1299-1307.

Richman, A.L., P.M. Miller, and M.J. Solomon

1988 The socialization of infants in suburban Boston. Pp. 65-74 in *Parental*

Behavior in Diverse Societies, R.A. LeVine, P.M. Miller, and M.M. West, eds. San Francisco, CA: Jossey-Bass.

Roe, A.M.
   1974 Educational psychology: The view from the gun deck. *Bulletin of the British Psychological Society* 28:199-200.

Rothbart, M.K., and L. Jones
   1998 Temperament, self-regulation and education. *School Psychology Review* 27:479-491.

Rothbart, M.K., S.A. Ahadi, and D.E. Evans
   2000 Temperament and personality: Origins and outcomes. *Journal of Personality & Social Psychology* 78(1)(Jan):122-135.

Sameroff, A.J.
   1989 Commentary: General systems and the regulation of development. Pp. 219-235 in *Systems and Development: The Minnesota Symposia on Child Psychology*, Vol. 22, M.R. Gunnar, E. Thelen, et al., eds. Hillsdale, NJ: Lawrence Erlbaum Associates, Inc.

Saville-Troike, M.
   1988 Private speech: Evidence for second language learning strategies during the 'silent' period. *Journal of Child Language* 15:567-590.

Saxe, G.B.
   1991 *Culture and Cognitive Development: Studies in Mathematical Understanding*. Hillsdale, NJ: Lawrence Erlbaum Associates Publishers.

Scarborough, H.S.
   1998 Early identification of children at risk for reading disabilities: Phonological awareness and some other promising predictors. Pp. 77-121 in *Specific Reading Disability: A View of the Spectrum*, B.K. Shapiro, P.J. Accardo, and A.J. Capute, eds. Timonium, MD: York Press.

Schieffelin, B.B. and A.R. Eisenberg
   1984 Cultural variations in children's conversations. Pp. 377-420 in *The Acquisition of Communicative Competence*, R.L. Schiefelbusch and J Pikar, eds. Baltimore: University Park Press.

Schieffelin, B.B., and E. Ochs
   1983 A cultural perspective on the transition from prelinguistic to linguistic communication. Pp. 115-131 in *The Transition from Prelinguistic to Linguistic Communication*, R.M. Golinkoff, ed. Hillsdale, NJ: Erlbaum.
   1986 Language socialization. *Annual Review of Anthropology* 15:163-191.

Silva, P. A.
   1980 Experiences, activities and the pre-school child: A report from the Dunedin multidisciplinary child development study. *Australian Journal of Early Childhood* 5(2):13-19.

Slobin, D.I., ed.
   1985 *The Crosslinguistic Study of Language Acquisition*, Vol. 1: *The Data*. Hillsdale, NJ: Lawrence Erlbaum Associates, Inc.
   1985 *The Crosslinguistic Study of Language Acquisition*, Vol.2: *Theoretical Issues*. Hillsdale, NJ: Lawrence Erlbaum Associates, Inc.

Small, M.
    1998 *Our Babies, Ourselves: How Biology and Culture Shape the Way We Parent.*
          New York: Anchor Books.
Smitherman, G.
    1977 *Talkin' and Testifyin': The Language of Black America.* Boston: Houghton
          Mifflin.
Stevenson, H.W., and C.L. Richman
    1976 Predictive value of teachers' ratings of young children. *Journal of Educa-
          tional Psychology* 68(5)(Oct):507-517.
Stipek, D.J., and R.H. Ryan
    1997 Economically disadvantaged preschoolers: Ready to learn but further
          to go. *Developmental Psychology* 33(4):711-723.
Swartz, J.P., and D.K. Walker
    1984 The relationship between teacher ratings of kindergarten classroom
          skills and second-grade achievement scores: An analysis of gender dif-
          ferences. *Journal of School Psychology* 22:209-217.
Tardiff, T.
    1996 Nouns are not always learned before verbs: Evidence from Mandarin
          speakers' early vocabularies. *Developmental Psychology* 32(492):504.
Tharp, R.G.
    1989 Psychocultural variables and constants: Effects on teaching and learn-
          ing in schools. *American Psychologist* 44:349-359.
Thomas, A., and S. Chess
    1984 Genesis and evolution of behavioral disorders: From infancy to early
          adult life. *American Journal of Psychiatry* 141(1):1-9.
Tomasello, M.
    1992 *First Verbs: A Case Study in Early Grammatical Development.* New York:
          Cambridge University Press.
Tramontana, M.G., S. Hooper, and S.C. Selzer
    1988 Research on preschool prediction of later academic achievement: A re-
          view. *Developmental Review* 8:89-146.
Trueba, H.T.
    1988 Culturally based explanations of minority students' academic achieve-
          ment. *Anthropology and Education Quarterly* 19:270-287.
U.S. Department of Education
    1999 *Digest of Education Statistics, 1998.* National Center for Education Sta-
          tistics, T. Snyder author. Washington, DC: Department of Education.
Vandell, D.L., and L.B. George
    1981 Social interaction in hearing and deaf preschoolers: Successes and fail-
          ures in initiations. *Child Development* 52(2):627-635.
Vogt, L.A., C. Jordan, and R.G. Tharp
    1987 Explaining school failure, producing school success: Two cases. *Anthro-
          pology and Education Quarterly* 18(4):276-286.
Ward, M.
    1971 *Them Children: A Study in Language Learning.* New York: Holt, Rinehart
          and Winston.

Weisner, T.S., R. Gallimore, and C. Jordan
  1988 Unpackaging cultural effects on classroom learning: Native Hawaiian peer assistance and child-generated activity. *Anthropology and Education Quarterly* 19(4):327-353.
Whitehurst, G.J., and J.E. Fischel
  1994 Practitioner review: Early developmental language delay: What, if anything, should the clinician do about it? *Journal of Child Psychology and Psychiatry* 35:613-648.
Zuniga, M.E.
  1992 Families with Latino roots. Pp. 151-179 in *Developing Cross-Cultural Competence: A Guide for Working with Young Children and Their Families,* E.W. Lynch and M.J. Hanson, eds. Baltimore, MD: Brookes.

CHAPTER 4

Achilles, C.M., P. Harman, and P. Egelson
  1995 Using research results on class size to improve pupil achievement outcomes. *Research in the Schools* 2(2):23-30.
Arnett, J.
  1989 Caregivers in day-care centers: Does training matter? *Journal of Applied Developmental Psychology* 10:541-552.
August, D., and K. Hakuta, eds.
  1997 *Improving Schooling for Language-Minority Children: A Research Agenda.* National Research Council and Institute of Medicine. Washington, DC: National Academy Press.
Bailey, D.B., and M. Wolery
  1992 *Teaching Infants and Preschoolers with Disabilities,* 2nd ed. Englewood Cliffs, NJ: Prentice Hall Publishers.
Baker, A.J.L., and C.S. Piotrkowski
  1995 *The Home Instruction Program for Preschool Youngsters: An Innovative Program to Prevent Academic Underachievement: Final Report.* New York: National Council of Jewish Women.
Ballou, D., and M. Podgursky
  1997 *Teacher Pay and Teacher Quality.* Kalamazoo, MI: Upjohn Institute for Employment Research.
Barnett, W.S
  1995 Long-term effects of early childhood programs on cognitive and school outcomes. *The Future of Children* 4:25-50.
  1998 Long-term effects on cognitive development and school success. Pp. 11-14 in *Early Care and Education for Children in Poverty: Promises, Programs, and Long-Term Outcomes,* W.S. Barnett and S.S. Boocock, ed. Buffalo, NY: State University of New York Press.

Barnett, W.S., and S.S. Boocock, eds.
  1998 *Early Care and Education for Children in Poverty: Promises, Programs, and Long-Term Outcomes*. Buffalo, NY: State University of New York Press.
Barnett, W.S., and K.C. Brown
  2000 *Issues in Children's Access to Dental Care Under Medicaid*. Dental Health Policy Analysis Series. Chicago: American Dental Association.
Barnett, W.S., and G. Camilli
  in   Compensatory preschool education, cognitive development, and
  press "race." In *Race and Intelligence: Separating Science from Myth*, J. Fish, ed. Mahwah, NJ: Lawrence Erlbaum Associates.
Barnett, W.S., E.C. Frede, H. Mobasher, and P. Mohr
  1987 The efficacy of public preschool programs and the relationship of program quality to efficacy. *Educational Evaluation and Policy Analysis* 10(1):37-49.
Barnett, W.S., J.E. Tarr, and E.C. Frede
  1999 *Children's Educational Needs and Community Capacity in the Abbott Districts*. New Brunswick, NJ: Center for Early Education Research, Rutgers University.
Bereiter, C.
  1986 Does direct instruction cause delinquency? *Early Childhood Research Quarterly* 1(3):289-292.
Bereiter, C., and S. Engelmann
  1966 *Teaching Disadvantaged Children in the Preschool*. Engelwood Cliffs, NJ: Prentice Hall.
Blasco, P.M., D.B. Bailey, and M.A. Burchinal
  1993 Dimensions of mastery in same-age and mixed-age integrated classrooms. *Early Childhood Research Quarterly* 8(2)(Jun):193-206.
Bloom, B.S.
  1964 *Stability and Change in Human Characteristics*. New York: Wiley.
Boehm, A.E., and B.R. Slater
  1981 *Cognitive Skills Assessment Battery*. Hagerstown, PA: Teachers College Press.
Boocock, S.S., W.S. Barnett, and E.C. Frede
  1999 *Long-Term Outcomes of Early Childhood Programs in Other Nations*. New Brunswick, NJ: Center for Early Education Research, Rutgers University.
Boutte, G.S.
  1992 The effects of home intervention on rural children's home environments, academic self-esteem, and achievement scores: A longitudinal study. Unpublished dissertation, UMI Dissertation Services.
Bowman, B.
  1997 Preschool as family support. Pp. 157-170 in *Advances in Early Education and Day Care: Family Policy and Practice on Early Child Care*, Vol. 9, S. Reifel, ed. Greenwich, CT: JAI Press, Inc.

Boyd-Zaharias, J., and H. Pate-Bain
  2000 The continuing impact of elementary small classes. Paper presented at the annual meeting of the American Educational Research Association, April 24-28, New Orleans, LA.
Bredekamp, S., and C. Copple, eds.
  1997 *Developmentally Appropriate Practice in Early Childhood Programs* (Revised ed.). Washington, DC: National Association for the Education of Young Children.
Bricker, D., and J.J.W. Cripe
  1992 *An Activity-Based Approach to Early Intervention.* Baltimore, MD: Paul Brookes.
Bruder, M.B.
  1997 The effectiveness of specific educational/developmental curricula for children with established disabilities. Pp. 523-548 in *The Effectiveness of Early Intervention,* M.J. Guralnick, ed. Baltimore, MD: Paul H. Brookes Publishing Co.
Bruner, J.
  1962 *The Process of Education.* Cambridge, MA: Harvard University Press, 1962.
  1985 Models of the learner. *Educational Researcher.* 14(6):5-8.
Brush, L., A. Gaidurgis, and C. Best
  1993 Indices of Head Start Program Quality. Report prepared for the Administration of Children, Youth, and Families, Head Start Bureau. Washington, DC: Pelavin.
Bryant, D.M., M. Burchinal, L. Lau, and J.J. Sparling
  1994 Family and classroom: Correlates of Head Start children's developmental outcomes. *Early Childhood Research Quarterly* 9:289-309.
Bryant, D.M., R.M. Clifford, and E.S. Peisner-Feinberg
  1989 *Best Practices for Beginners: Quality Programs for Kindergartners.* Chapel Hill, NC: Frank Porter Graham Child Development Center.
Bunce, B.H.
  1995 Building a language-focused curriculum. In *Building a Language-Focused Curriculum for the Preschool Classrooms: Vol. 1. A Foundation for Lifelong Communication.* Baltimore: Paul H. Brookes Publishing Co.
Burts, D.C., C.H. Hunt, R. Charlesworth, and L. Kirk
  1990 A comparison of frequencies of stress behaviors observed in kindergarten children in classrooms with developmentally appropriate versus developmentally inappropriate instructional practices. *Early Childhood Research Quarterly* 5:407-423.
Buysse, V.
  1993 Friendships of preschoolers with disabilities in community-based child care settings. *Journal of Early Intervention* 17(4):380-395.
Buysse, V., and D.B. Bailey
  1993 Behavioral and developmental outcomes in young children with disabilities in integrated and segregated settings: A review of comparative studies. *Journal of Special Education* 26(4):434-461.

Caldwell, B.M., and J.R. Richmond
  1968 The Children's Center in Syracuse, New York. Pp. 326-358 in *Early Child Care: The New Perspectives*, L.L. Dittman, ed. New York: Atherton Press.
Caldwell, B.M., and L.E. Smith
  1968 Day-care for the Very Young: Prime Opportunity for Primary Prevention. Paper presented at the American Public Health Association Meeting, Detroit, MI.
Camarata, S.
  1993 The application of naturalistic conversation training to speech production in children with speech disabilities. *Journal of Applied Behavior Analysis* 26(2):173-182.
Campbell, F.A., and C.T. Ramey
  1993 Mid-Adolescent Outcomes for High-Risk Students: An Examination of the Continuing Effects of Early Intervention. Paper presented at the biennial meeting of the Society for Research in Child Development, March 26, New Orleans.
  1994 Effects of early intervention on intellectual and academic achievement: A follow-up study of children from low-income families. *Child Development* 65: 684-698.
Campos, M.M., and F. Rosenberg
  1995 *Our Day-Care Settings Respect Children: Quality Criteria for Day Care.* ERIC Document Reproduction Service, ED 394646.
Casey, W., D. Jones, B. Kugler, and B. Watkins
  1988 Integration of Down's syndrome children in the primary school: A longitudinal study of cognitive development and academic attainments. *British Journal of Educational Psychology* 58:279-286.
Casto, G., and M. Mastropieri
  1986 The efficacy of early intervention programs: A meta-analysis. *Exceptional Children,* 52:417-424.
Cataldo, C.Z.
  1978 A follow-up study of early intervention. *Dissertation Abstracts International* 39:657A (University Microfilms No. 7813990).
Charlesworth, R., C. Hart, D. Burts, and M. DeWolf
  1993 The LSU studies: Building a research base for developmentally appropriate practice. *Advances in Early Education and Day Care* 3:3-28.
Chubrich, R.E., and M.F. Kelley
  1994 Head Start expansion in the 1990s: A critique. *Association of Childhood Education International's Focus on Early Childhood* 6:1-3.
Chugani, H.T., M.E. Phelps, and J.C. Mazziotta
  1987 Positron emission tomography study of human brain functional development. *Annals of Neurology* 22(4):487-497.
Clarke-Stewart, A., and L. Gruber
  1994 *Children at Home and in Day Care.* Hillsdale, NJ: Lawrence Erlbaurn Associates.

Cole, K., P. Dale, and P. Mills
  1991 Individual differences in language delayed children's responses to direct and interactive preschool instruction. *Topics in Early Childhood Special Education* 11(1)99-124.
Cole, K., P. Dale, P. Mills, and J. Jenkins
  1993 Interaction between early intervention curricula and student characteristics. *Exceptional Children* 60(1):17-28.
Cole, M., F. Frankel, and D. Sharp
  1971 Development of free recall learning in children. *Developmental Psychology* 4(2)(Mar):109-123.
Coleman, J.S., E. Campbell, C. Hobson, J. McPartland, A. Mood, F. Weinfeld, and R. York
  1966 *Equality of Educational Opportunity*. Washington, DC: U.S. Office of Education, National Center for Educational Statistics.
Condry, S.
  1983 History and background of preschool intervention programs and the Consortium for Longitudinal Studies. Pp. 1-31 in *As the Twig is Bent . . . Lasting Effects of Preschool Programs*, The Consortium for Longitudinal Studies, ed. Hillsdale, NJ: Lawrence Erlbaum.
Cost and Quality Team, The
  1995 *Cost, Quality, and Child Outcomes in Child-Care Centers: Executive Summary*. Denver, CO: University of Colorado.
Dale, P., and K. Cole
  1988 Comparison of academic and cognitive programs for young handicapped children. *Exceptional Children* 54:439-447.
Datta, L.
  1983 Epilogue: We never promised you a rose garden, but one may have grown anyway. Pp. 467-480 in *As the Twig is Bent . . . Lasting Effects of Preschool Programs*, The Consortium for Longitudinal Studies, ed. Hillsdale, NJ: Erlbaum.
Day, M.C., and R.K. Parker, eds.
  1977 *The Preschool in Action: Exploring Early Childhood Programs*. Boston, MA: Allyn and Bacon, Inc.
Diamond, K.E., and L.L. Hestenes
  1994 Preschool children's understanding of disability: Experiences leading to the elaboration of the concept of hearing loss. *Early Education and Development* 5(4):301-309.
Diamond, K.E., L.L. Hestenes, E.S. Carpenter, and F.K. Innes
  1997 Relationships between enrollment in an inclusive class and preschool children's ideas about people with disabilities. *Topics in Early Childhood Special Education* 17(4):520-536.
Division of Early Childhood Task Force on Recommended Practices
  1993 *DEC Recommended Practices: Indicators of Quality in Programs for Infants and Young Children with Special Needs and Their Families*. Reston, VA: Council for Exceptional Children.

Drasgow, E., J.W. Halle, M.M. Ostrosky, and H.M. Harbers
  1996 Using behavioral indication and functional communication training to establish an initial sign repertoire with a young child with severe disabilities. *Topics in Early Childhood Special Education* 16:500-521.
Dunham, P., and F. Dunham
  1992 Lexical development during middle infancy: A mutually driven infant-caregiver process. *Developmental Psychology* 28(3):414-420.
Dunn, L.
  1993 Proximal and distal features of day care quality and children's development. *Early Childhood Research Quarterly* 8(2):167-192.
Dunst, C.J.
  1985 Rethinking early intervention. *Analysis and Intervention in Developmental Disabilities* 5(1-2):165-201.
Dunst, C.J., J. Lesko, K. Holbert, L. Wilson, K. Sharpe, and R. Liles
  1987 A systematic approach to infant intervention. *Topics in Early Childhood Special Education* 7(2):1937
Dunst, C.J., S.W. Snyder, and M. Mankinen
  1989 Efficacy of early intervention. Pp. 259-294 in *Handbook of Special Education: Research and Practice—Low Incidence Conditions*, M.C. Wang, M.C. Reynolds, and G.H. Walberg, eds. New York: Pergamon Press.
Dunst, C.J., C.M. Trivette, and A.G. Deal, eds.
  1994 *Supporting and Strengthening Families: Methods, Strategies, and Practices.* Cambridge, MA: Brookline Books.
Dunst, C.J., C.M. Trivette, and W. Jodry
  1997 Influences of social support on children with disabilities and their families. In *The Effectiveness of Early Intervention*, M.J. Guralnick, ed. Baltimore, MD: Paul Brookes.
Eiserman, W., C. Weber, and M. McCoun
  1992 Two alternative program models for serving speech-disordered preschoolers: A second year follow-up. *Journal of Communication Disorders* 25:77-106.
Erwin, E.J.
  1993 Social participation of young children with visual impairment in specialized and integrated environments. *A Journal of Visual Impairments and Blindness* 87:134-142.
Favazza, P.C., and S.L. Odom
  1996 Use of the acceptance scale to measure attitudes of kindergarten-age children. *Journal of Early Intervention*, 20(3):232-248.
Federal Register
  1977 The Rules Regulating Implementing of P.L. 94-142. Washington, DC: U.S. Government Printing Office.
Fenichel, F., ed.
  1992 *Learning through Supervision and Mentorship to Support the Development of Infants, Toddlers and Their Families: A Source Book.* Washington, DC: Zero to Three/National Center for Clinical Infant Program.

Ferguson, R.F.
1998   Can schools narrow the black-white test score gap? Pp. 318-374 in *The Black-White Test Score Gap*, C. Jencks and M. Phillips, eds. Washington, DC: Brookings Institution Press.

Fewell, R.R., and P.L. Oelwein
1990   The relationship between time in integrated environments and developmental gains in young children with special needs. *Topics in Early Childhood Special Education* 10:104-116.
1991   Effective early intervention: Results from the model preschool program for children with down syndrome and other developmental delays. *Topics in Early Childhood Special Education* 11:56-68.

Field, T.
1980   Interactions of high-risk infants: Quantitative and qualitative differences. Pp. 120-143 in *Exceptional Infant: Psychosocial Risks in Infant-Environment Transactions*, S.B. Sawin, R.C. Hawkins, L.O. Walker, and J.H. Penticuff, eds. New York: Brunner/Mazel.

Finkelstein, J.M.
1983   *Kindergarten Scheduling Study: Results for Administrators, Results for Teachers, Midwestern State Survey, Midwest University Professors Study.* ERIC Document Reproduction Service, ED 248979.

Finn, J.D., S.B. Gerber, C.M. Achilles, and J. Boyd-Zaharias
1999   Short and long-term effects of small classes. Paper prepared for conference on the economics of school reform, May 23-26, SUNY, Buffalo.

Fosburg, L.B., N. Goodrich, and M. Fox
1984   *The Effects of Head Start Health Services: Report of the Head Start Health Evaluation.* Cambridge, MA: Abt Associates.

Fox, L., M.F. Hanline, C.O. Vail, and K.R. Galant
1994   Developmentally appropriate practice: Applications for young children with disabilities. *Journal of Early Intervention* 18(3):308-327.

Frede, E.C.
1998   Preschool program quality in programs for children in poverty. Pp. 77-98 in *Early Care and Education for Children in Poverty: Promises, Programs, and Long-Term Outcomes*, W.S. Barnett and S.S. Boocock, ed. Buffalo, NY: SUNY Press.

Frede, E.C., A.B. Austin, and S.K. Lindauer
1993   The relationship of specific developmentally appropriate teaching practices to children's skills in first grade. *Advances in Early Education and Child Care* 5:95-111.

Garber, H.L.
1988   *The Milwaukee Project.* Washington, DC: American Association for Mental Retardation.

Gersten, R.
1986   Response to "Consequences of three preschool curriculum models through age 15." *Early Childhood Research Quarterly* 1(3):293-301.

Girolametto, L.E.
1988   Improving the social-conversational skills of developmentally delayed

children: An intervention study. *Journal of Speech and Hearing Disorders* 53:156-167.

Girolametto, L.E., M. Verbey, and R. Tannock
1994 Improving joint engagement in parent-child interaction: An intervention study. *Journal of Early Intervention* 18(2):155-167.

Goelman, H., and A.R. Pence
1988 Children in three types of day care: Daily experiences, quality of care and developmental outcomes. *Early Child Development and Care* 33: 67-76.

Goffin, S.G.
1994 *Curriculum Models and Early Childhood Education: Appraising the Relationship.* New York: Merrill.

Gomby, D., R Culross, and R. Behrman
1999 Home visiting: Recent program evaluations—Analysis and recommendations. *Future of Children* 9(1):4-26.

Gormley, W.T., Jr.
1995 *Everybody's Children: Child Care as a Public Problem.* Washington, DC: The Brookings Institution.

Gray, S.W., B.K. Ramsey, and R.A. Klaus
1982 *From 3 to 20: The Early Training Project.* Baltimore: University Park Press.

Greenspan, S.I., and S. Wieder
1998 *The Child with Special Needs: Encouraging Intellectual and Emotional Growth.* Reading, MA: Perseus Books.

Gresham, F.M.
1982 Misguided mainstreaming: The case for social skills training with handicapped children. *Exceptional Children* 48:422-433.

Guralnick, M.J.
1990 Peer interaction and the development of handicapped children's social and communicative competence. Pp. 275-305 in *Children Helping Children,* H. Foot, M. Morgan, and R. Shute, eds. New York: John Wiley & Sons.
1994 Social competence with peers: Outcome and process in early childhood special education. Pp. 45-71 in *Year-Book in Early Childhood Education: Early Childhood Special Education,* Vol. 5, P.L. Safford, ed. New York: Teacher's College Press.
1997 Second-generation research in the field of early intervention. In *The Effectiveness of Early Intervention,* Guralnick, M.J., ed. Baltimore, MD: Paul H. Brookes Publishing Co.

Guralnick, M.J., R.T. Connor, and M.A. Hammond
1995 Parent perspectives of peer relationships and friendships in integrated and specialized programs. *American Journal on Mental Retardation* 99(5)(Mar):457-476.

Guralnick, M.J., R.T. Connor, M.A. Hammond, J.M. Gottman, and K. Kinnish
1996 The peer relations of preschool children with communication disorders. *Child Development.* 67(2)(Apr):471-489.

Guralnick, M.J., and B. Nelville
    1997 Designing early intervention programs to support children's social
          competence. Pp. 579-610 in *The Effectiveness of Early Intervention*. Balti-
          more, MD: Paul H. Brookes.
Hale, B., V. Seitz, and E. Zigler
    1990 Health services and Head Start: A forgotten formula. *Journal of Applied
          Developmental Psychology* 11:447-458.
Hanline, M.F.
    1993 Inclusion of preschoolers with profound disabilities: An analysis of
          children's interactions. *Journal of the Association for People with Severe
          Handicaps* 18(1):28-35.
Hanson, J., and E. Lynch
    1995 *Early Intervention: Implementing Child and Family Services for Infants and
          Toddlers Who Are At-Risk or Disabled.* 2nd ed. Austin, TX: PRO-ED.
Hanushek, E.A.
    1971 Teacher characteristics and gains in student achievement: Estimation
          using micro data. *American Economic Review* 60(2):280-288.
Harms, T., and R.M. Clifford
    1980 *Early Childhood Environmental Rating Scale.* New York: Teachers Col-
          lege Press.
Haskins, R.
    1989 Beyond metaphor: The efficacy of early childhood education. *Ameri-
          can Psychologist* 44(2):274-282.
Hauser-Cram, P. D.E. Pierson, D.K. Walker, and T. Tivnan
    1991 *Early Education in the Public Schools.* San Francisco: Jossey-Bass.
Hauser-Cram, P. et al.
    1993 The effects of the classroom environment on the social and mastery
          behavior of preschool children with disabilities. *Early Childhood Re-
          search Quarterly* 8(4):479-497.
Heath, S.B.
    1983 *Way with Words: Language, Life and Work in Communities and Classrooms.*
          Cambridge, MA: Cambridge University Press.
Hebb, D.O.
    1949 *Organization of Behavior.* New York: Wiley.
Herrnstein, R.J., and C. Murray
    1994 *The Bell Curve: Intelligence and Class Structure in American Life.* New
          York: Free Press.
High/Scope Educational Research Foundation
    1998 *High/Scope Program Quality Assessment—Preschool Version.* Ypsilanti, MI:
          High/Scope Press.
Holcombe, A., M. Wolery, and E. Snyder
    1994 Effects of two levels of procedural fidelity with constant time delay on
          children's learning. *Journal of Behavioral Education* 4:49-73.
Holloway, S.
    1999 Early childhood education and care (ECEC): Preschool policies and
          programs in the OECD countries. Paper presented at Global Perspec-

tives on Early Childhood Education workshop hosted by the Committee on Early Childhood Pedagogy of the National Research Council, Washington, DC.

Holloway, S.D., and M. Reichart-Erickson
1988 The relationship of daycare quality to children's free-play behavior and social problem-solving skills. *Early Childhood Research Quarterly* 3:39-54.

Honig, A.S., and J.R. Lally
1982 The Family Development Research Program: A retrospective review. *Early Childhood Development and Care* 10:41-62.

Howes, C.
1997 Children's experiences in center-based child care as a function of teacher background and adult-child ratio. *Merrill-Palmer Quarterly* 43(3):404-425.

Howes, C., and M. Olenick
1986 Child care and family influences on toddlers' compliance. *Child Development* 57:202-216.

Howes, C., and P. Stewart
1987 Child's play with adults, toys and peers: An examination of family and child care influences. *Developmental Psychology* 23:423-430.

Howes, C., D. Phillips, and M. Whitebook
1992 Thresholds of quality: Implications for the social development of children in center-based child care. *Child Development* 63:449-460.

Hundert, J., B. Mahoney, F. Mundy, and M.L. Vernon
1998 A descriptive analysis of developmental and social gains of children with severe disabilities in segregated and inclusive preschools in Southern Ontario. *Early Childhood Research Quarterly* 13(1):49-65.

Hunt, J. McV.
1961 *Intelligence and Experience.* New York: Ronald Press.
1964 The psychological basis for preschool enrichment as an antidote for cultural deprivation. *Merrill-Palmer Quarterly of Behavior and Development* 10:209-248.

Hyson, M., K. Hirsh-Pasek, and L. Rescorla
1990 The classroom practices inventory: An observation instrument based on NAEYC's guidelines for developmentally appropriate practice for 4- and 5-year-old children. *Early Childhood Research Quarterly* 5(4):475-594.

Infant Health and Development Program Consortium
1990 Enhancing the outcomes of low birth weight, premature infants: A multi-site randomized trial. *Journal of the American Medical Association* 263:3035-3042.

Jencks, C.
1972 *Inequality: A Reassessment of the Effect of Family and Schooling in America.* New York: Basic Books.

Johnson, J.E., and K. D. Beauchamp
1987   Preschool assessment measures: What are teachers using? *Journal of the Division for Early Childhood* 12(1):70-76.

Jorde-Bloom, P.
1988   *A Great Place to Work: Improving Conditions for Staff in Young Children's Programs.* Washington, DC: National Association for the Education of Young Children.

Kagan, J.
1998   *Three Seductive Ideas.* Cambridge, MA: Harvard University Press

Kagitcibasi, C.
1996   *Family and Human Development Across Cultures.* Hillsdale, NJ: Erlbaum.

Kaiser, A.P., P. Yoder, and A. Keetz
1992   Evaluating milieu therapy. Pp. 9-147 in *Cause and Effects in Communication and Language Intervention,* S.F. Warren and J. Reichle, eds. Baltimore, MD: Paul Brookes.

Kamii, C., ed.
1990   *Achievement Testing in the Early Grades: Games Grown-ups Play.* Washington, DC: National Association for the Education of Young Children.

Karnes, M.B., A.M. Schwedel, and M.B. Williams
1983   A comparison of five approaches for educating young children from low-income homes. Pp. 133-170 in *As the Twig Is Bent: Lasting Effects of Preschool Programs,* Consortium for Longitudinal Studies, ed. Hillsdale, NJ: Lawrence Erlbaum Associates.

Karnes, M., R. Zehrbach, and J. Teska
1972   An ameliorative approach in the development of curriculum. Pp. 353-381 in *The Preschool in Action: Exploring Early Childhood Programs,* R.K. Parker, ed. Boston: Allyn and Bacon.
1977   Conceptualization of GOAL (Game-Oriented Activities for Learning). Pp 255-287 in *The Preschool in Action: Exploring Early Childhood Programs,* M.D. Day and R.D. Parker, eds. Boston: Allyn and Bacon.

Kirk, S.A.
1958   *Early Education of the Mentally Retarded.* Chicago: University of Illinois Press.

Kolb, B.
1995   *Brain Plasticity and Behavior.* Mahwah, NJ: Lawrence Erlbaum.

Kontos, S.
1991   Child care quality, family background, and children's development. *Early Childhood Research Quarterly* 6:249-262.

Kontos, S., and R. Fiene
1991   *Predictors of Quality and Childrens' Development in Day Care: Licensing of Children Service Programs.* Richmond, VA: Virginia Commonwealth University, School of Social Work.

Kontos, S., C. Howes, and E. Galinsky
1997   Does training make a difference to quality in family child care. *Early Childhood Research Quarterly* 12:351-372.

Kontos, S., D. Moore, and K. Giorgetti
  1998 The ecology of inclusion. *Topics in Early Childhood Special Education* 18(1):38-48.
Krueger, A.
  1997 *Experimental Estimates of Educational Production Functions.* Princeton, NJ: Princeton University.
  1999 Experimental estimates of education production functions. *Quarterly Journal of Economics* 114(2):497-532.
Lally, J.R., and A.S. Honig
  1977 The Family Development Research Program: A program for prenatal, infant, and early childhood enrichment. Pp. 149-174 in *The Preschool in Action: Exploring Early Childhood Programs*, M.D. Day and R.K. Parker, eds. Boston: Allyn and Bacon.
Lally, J.R., P. Mangione, and A. Honig
  1987 *Long-Range Impact of an Early Intervention with Low-Income Children and Their Families.* San Francisco: Far West Laboratories.
Lamorey, S., and D.D. Bricker
  1993 Integrated programs: Effects on young children and their parents. Pp. 249-270 in *Integrating Young Children with Disabilities into Community Programs: Ecological Perspectives on Research and Implementation*, C.A. Peck, S.L. Odom, et al., eds. Baltimore, MD: Paul H. Brookes Publishing.
Layzer, J.I., B.D. Goodson, and M. Moss
  1993 *Life in Preschool—Volume One of an Observational Study of Early Childhood Programs for Disadvantaged Four-Year-Olds: Final Report.* Cambridge, MA: Abt Associates.
Lazar, I., R. Hubble, H. Murray, M. Rosche, and J. Royce
  1977 *The Persistence of Preschool Effects: A Long-Term Follow-up of Fourteen Infant and Preschool Experiments, Summary.* Washington, DC: U.S. Department of Health, Education, and Welfare, Administration for Children, Youth and Families.
Lee, V., and S. Loeb
  1995 Where do Head Start attendees end up? One reason why preschool effects fade out. *Educational Evaluation and Policy Analysis* 17(1):62-82.
Lewis, C. C.
  1996 Fostering social and intellectual development: The roots of Japan's educational success. Pp. 79-97 in *Teaching and Learning in Japan*, T.P Rohlen, G.K. LeTendre, et al., eds. New York: Cambridge University Press.
Locurto, C.
  1991 Beyond IQ in preschool programs? *Intelligence* 15:295-312.
Maccoby, E., and M. Zellner
  1970 *Experiments in Primary Education: Aspects of Project Follow-Through.* New York: Harcourt Brace.
Marcon, R.A.
  1992 Differential effects of three preschool models on inner-city 4-year-olds. *Early Childhood Research Quarterly* 7(4):517-530.

1994   *Early Learning and Early Identification Follow-up Study: Transition from the Early to the Later Grades.* A report prepared for the District of Columbia Public Schools. Washington, DC: District of Columbia Public Schools.

Mardell-Czudnowski, C.D., and D.S. Goldenberg
1984   Revision and restandardization of a preschool screening test: DIAL becomes DIAL-R. *Journal of the Division for Early Childhood* 8:149-156.

McCartney, K.
1984   The effect of a quality day-care environment upon children's language development. *Developmental Psychology* 20:244-260.

McCartney, K., S. Scarr, D. Phillips, and S. Grajek
1985   Day care as intervention: Comparison of varying quality programs. *Journal of Applied Developmental Psychology* 6:247-260.

McCollum, J.A., and M.L. Hemmeter
1997   Parent-child interaction intervention when children have disabilities. Pp. 549-576 in *The Effectiveness of Early Intervention*, M.J. Guralnick, ed. Baltimore, MD: Paul H. Brookes.

McEvoy, M.A., S.L. Odom, and S.R. McConnell
1992   Peer social competence intervention for young children with disabilities. Pp. 113-133 in *Social Competence of Young Children with Disabilities: Issues and Strategies for Intervention*, S.L. Odom, S.R. McConnell, and M.A. McEvoy, eds. Baltimore, MD: Paul H. Brookes.

McGurk, H., A. Mooney, P. Moss, and G. Poland
1995   *Staff-Child Ratios in Care and Education Services for Young Children.* London: HMSO.

McKey, R., L. Condelli, H. Ganson, et al.
1985   *The Impact of Head Start on Children, Families, and Communities. Final Report of the Head Start Evaluation, Synthesis, and Utilization Project.* Washington, DC: U.S. Department of Health and Human Services.

McLean, L.K., and J.W. Cripe
1997   The effectiveness of early intervention for children with Down syndrome. In *The Effectiveness of Early Intervention*, M.J. Guralnick, ed. Baltimore, MD: Paul H. Brookes.

McLean, M.E., and S.L. Odom
1993   Practices for young children with and without disabilities: A comparison of DEC and NAEYC identified practices. *Topics in Early Childhood Special Education* 13:274-292.

McLean, J. and L. Snyder-McLean
1987   Form and function of communicative behavior among persons with severe developmental disabilities. *Australia and New Zealand Journal of Developmental Disabilities* 13(2):83-98.

McWilliam, R.A., ed.
1996   *Rethinking Pull-Out Services in Early Intervention: A Professional Resource.* Baltimore, MD: Paul H. Brookes.

McWilliam, R.A., and D.B. Bailey, Jr.
  1994 Predictors of service-delivery models in center-based early interven-
         tion. *Exceptional Children* (61) 1:56-71
Mehan, H.
  1979 *Learning Lessons: Social Organization in the Classroom.* Cambridge, MA:
         Harvard University Press.
Meisels, S.J., M. Dichtmiller, and F.R. Liaw
  1994 A multidimensional analysis of early childhood intervention programs.
         Pp. 361-385 in *Handbook of Infant Mental Health,* C.H. Zeanah, ed. New
         York: Guilford Press.
Miller, L.B.
  1979 Development of curriculum models in Head Start. Pp. 195-220 in *Project
         Head Start: A Legacy of the War on Poverty,* E. Zigler and J. Valentine, ed.
         New York: The Free Press.
Miller, L.B., and R.P. Bizzell
  1983 The Louisville experiment: A comparison of four programs. Pp. 171-
         199 in *As the Twig is Bent: Lasting Effects of Preschool Programs,* Consor-
         tium for Longitudinal Studies, ed. Hillsdale: Lawrence Erlbaum Asso-
         ciates.
  1984 Long-term effects of four preschool programs: Ninth and tenth-grade
         results. *Child Development* 55(4):157-187.
Miller, L.B., and J.L. Dyer
  1975 Four preschool programs: Their dimensions and effects. *Monographs of
         the Society for Research in Child Development* 40 (5-6)(Serial 162).
Mills, P., P. Dale, K. Cole, and J. Jenkins
  1995 Follow-up of children from academic and cognitive preschool curricula
         at age 9. *Exceptional Children* 61(4):378-393.
Mosteller, F.
  1995 The Tennessee study of class size in the early school grades. *Future of
         Children* 5(2):113-127.
Murnane, R.J., and B. Phillips
  1981 What do effective teachers of inner-city children have in common? *So-
         cial Science Research* 10:83-100.
National Institute of Child Health and Human Development (NICHD) Early
Child Care Research Network
  1996 Characteristics of infant child care: Factors contributing to positive
         caregiving. *Early Childhood Research Quarterly* 11(3):269-306.
Neilson, L.
  1990 Research comes home. *The Reading Teacher* 44:248-250.
Neisser, U., G. Boodoo, T.J. Bouchard, A.W. Boykin, N. Brody, S.J. Ceci, D.F.
Halpern, J.C. Loehlin, R. Perloff, R.S. Sternberg, and S. Urbina
  1995 *Intelligence: Knowns and Unknowns.* Report of a task force established
         by the Board of Scientific Affairs of the American Psychological Asso-
         ciation. Washington, DC: American Psychological Association.

Nelson, K.
1986 *Event Knowledge: Structure and Function in Development.* Hillsdale, NJ: Erlbaum.

Odom, S.L., and W.H. Brown
1993 Social interaction skills interventions for young children with disabilities in integrated settings. Pp. 29-64 in C.A. Peck, S.L. Odom, and D.D. Bricker, eds. *Integrating Young Children with Disabilities into Community Programs: Ecological Perspectives on Research and Implementation.* Baltimore: Paul H. Brookes.

Odom, S.L, S.R. McConnell, and L.K. Chandler
1994 Acceptability and feasibility of classroom-based social interaction interventions for young children with disabilities. *Exceptional Children* 60(3):226-236

Odom, S.L., C. Peterson, S. McConnell, and M. Ostrosky
1990 Ecobehavioral analysis of early education/specialized classroom settings and peer social interaction. *Education and Treatment of Children* 13(4):316-331.

Okagaki, L., K.E. Diamond, S.J. Kontos, and L.L. Hestenes
1998 Correlates of young children's interactions with classmates with disabilities. *Early Childhood Research* 13(1):67-86.

Palmer, F.H.
1983 The Harlem Study: Effects by type of training, age of training, and social class. Pp. 201-236 in *As the Twig is Bent: Lasting Effects of Preschool Programs,* The Consortium for Longitudinal Studies. Hillsdale, NJ: Lawrence Erlbaum.

Palmer, F.H., and R.J. Siegel
1977 Minimal intervention at age two and three and subsequent intellective changes. Pp. 3-25 in *The Preschool in Action: Exploring Early Childhood Programs,* M.D. Day and R.K. Parker, eds. Boston: Allyn and Bacon.

Paul, B.B., and C.H. Jarvis
1992 *The Effects of Native Language Use in New York City Prekindergarten Classes.* ERIC Document Reproduction Services. ED 351874.

Peck, C.A, P. Carlson, and E. Helmstetter
1992 Parent and teacher perceptions of outcomes for typically developing children enrolled in integrated early childhood programs: A statewide survey. *Journal of Early Intervention.* 16(1)(Win):53-63.

Phillips, D., K. McCartney, and S. Scarr
1987 Child-care quality and children's social development. *Developmental Psychology* 23:537-543.

Phillips, D., S. Scarr, and K. McCartney
1986 Dimensions and effects of child care quality: The Bermuda study. In *Quality in Child Care,* D. Phillips, ed. Washington, DC: NAEYC.

Phillipsen, L., M. Burchinal, C. Howes, and D. Cryer
1997 The prediction of process quality from structural features of child care. *Early Childhood Research Quarterly* 12:281-304.

Powell, D.R.
  1991 Parents and programs: Early childhood as a pioneer in parent involvement and support. Pp. 91-109 in *The Care and Education of America's Young Children: Obstacles and Opportunities*, S.L. Kagan, ed. Ninetieth Yearbook of the National Society for the Study of Education. Chicago, IL: National Society for the Study of Education.
Quilitch, H.R., and T.R. Risley
  1973 The effects of play materials on social play. *Journal of Applied Behavior Analysis* 6(3):573-578.
Ramey, C.T., D.M. Bryant, and T.M. Suarez
  1985 Preschool compensatory education and the modifiability of intelligence: A critical review. Pp. 247-296 in *Current Topics in Human Intelligence*, D. Detterman, ed. Norwood, NJ: Ablex.
Ramey, C.T., D.M. Bryant, B.H. Wasik, J.J. Sparling, K.H. Fendt, and L.M. LaVange
  1992 The Infant Health Development Program for low birth weight, premature infants: Program elements, family participation, and child intelligence. *Pediatrics* 89:454-465
Ramey, C.T., and F.A. Campbell
  1984 Preventive education for high-risk children: Cognitive consequences of the Carolina Abecedarian Project. *American Journal of Mental Deficiency* 88(5):515-523.
Ramey, C.T., G.D. McGinness, L. Cross, A.M. Collier, and S. Barrie-Blackey
  1982 The Abecedarian approach to social competence. Cognitive and linguistic intervention for disadvantaged preschoolers. Pp. 145-174 in *The Social Life of Children in a Changing Society*, K.M. Borman, ed. Hillsdale, NJ: Erlbaum.
Ramey, C.T., and S.L. Ramey
  1998 Early educational intervention with disadvantaged children—to what effect? *Applied and Preventive Psychology* 1:131-140.
Rice, M.L.
  1991 Children with specific language impairment: Toward a model of teachability. Pp. 447-480 in *Biological and Behavioral Determinants of Language Development*, N. Krasnegor, D. Rumbaugh, R. Schiefelbusch, and M. Studdert-Kennedy, eds. Hillsdale, NJ: Lawrence Erlbaum Associates
Rice, M.L., and K.A. Wilcox
  1990 *Language Acquisition Preschool: A model preschool for language disordered and ESL children.* (Grant No. G008630279). Washington, DC: U.S. Department of Education, Office of Special Education Programs.
Rice, M.L., and K.A. Wilcox, eds.
  1995 *Building a Language-Focused Curriculum for the Preschool Classrooms: Vol. 1. A Foundation for Lifelong Communication.* Baltimore, MD: Paul H. Brookes.
Richardson, V., ed.
  1994 *Teacher Change and the Staff Development Process: A Case in Reading Instruction.* New York: Teachers College Press.

Rivlin, A.M., and P.M. Timpane, eds.
1975 *Planned Variation in Education: Should We Give Up or Try Harder?*
      Brookings Studies in Social Experimentation. Washington, DC: The
      Brookings Institution.
Roberts, J.E., M.R. Burchinal, and D.B. Bailey
1994 Communication among preschoolers with and without disabilities in
      same-age and mixed-age classes. *American Journal on Mental Retarda-
      tion* 99(3)(Nov):231-249.
Robinson, H.B., and N.M. Robinson
1965 *The Mentally Retarded Child: A Psychological Approach.* New York:
      McGraw-Hill.
Rodriguez, JL., R.M. Diaz, D. Duran, and L. Espinosa
1995 The impact of bilingual preschool education on the language develop-
      ment of Spanish-speaking children. *Early Childhood Research Quarterly*
      (10):475-490.
Roopnarine, J.L., and J.E. Lohnson, eds.
1993 *Approaches to Early Childhood Education.* New York: Macmillan.
Ruopp, R., J. Travers, F.M. Glantz, and C. Coelen
1979 Children at the center: Summary findings and their implications. In
      Final Report of the National Day Care Study: Children at the Center, Vol. 1.
      Cambridge, MA: Abt Associates.
Russell, A.
1985 *An Observational Study of the Effect of Staff-Child Ratios on Staff and Child
      Behavior in South Australian Kindergartens.* Adelaide: Fiinder Univer-
      sity.
Sands, D.J., L. Adams, and D.M. Stout.
1995 A statewide exploration of the nature and use of curriculum in special
      education. *Exceptional Children* 62(1):68-83.
Sainato, D.M., and J.J. Carta
1992 Classroom influences on the development of social competence in
      young children with disabilities. Pp.93-109 in *Social Competence of Young
      Children with Disabilities: Issues and Strategies for intervention,* S.L. Odom,
      S.R. McConnell, and M.A. McEvoy, eds. Baltimore, MD: Paul H.
      Brookes.
Scarr, S., M. Eisenberg, and K. Deater-Deckerd
1994 Measurement of quality in child care centers. *Early Childhood Research
      Quarterly* 9(2):131-152.
Schliecker, E., D.R. White, and E. Jacobs
1989 Predicting preschool language comprehension from SES, family struc-
      ture, and day care quality. Paper presented at the biennial meeting of
      the Society for Research in Child Development, Kansas City, MO.
Schweinhart, L.J., and D.P. Weikart
1993 Success by empowerment: The High/Scope Perry Preschool Study
      through age 27. *Young Children* 49:54-58.

Schlossman, S.
   1986   Family as educator, parent education, and the perennial family crisis. Pp. 31-45 in *Child Rearing in the Home and School*, R.J. Griffore and R.P. Boge, et al., eds. New York: Plenum Press.
Schweinhart, L.J., H.V. Barnes, D.P. Weikart, W.S. Barnett, and A.S. Epstein
   1993   Significant benefits: The High/Scope Perry preschool study through age 27. *Monographs of the High/Scope Educational Research Foundation*, No. 10. Ypsilanti, MI: High/Scope Educational Research Foundation.
Schweinhart, L.J., D.P. Weikart, and M.B. Larner
   1986   Consequences of three preschool curriculum models through age 15. *Early Childhood Research Quarterly* 1(1):15-45.
Seppanen, P.S., K.W. Godon, and J.L. Metzger
   1993   *Observational Study of Chapter 1: Funded Early Childhood Programs. Final Report, Volume 2*. Washington, DC: U.S. Department of Education.
Shonkoff, J.P., and P. Hauser-Cram
   1987   Early intervention for disabled infants and their families: A quantitative analysis. *Pediatrics* 80:650-658.
Shonkoff, J.P., P. Hauser-Cram, M.W. Krauss, and C.C. Upshur
   1992   Development of infants and toddlers with disabilities and their families. *Monographs of the Society for Research in Child Development* 57(Serial 230).
Shonkoff, J.P., and S.J. Meisels
   2000   *The Handbook of Early Childhood Intervention* (2nd edition). New York: Cambridge University.
Sigel, I.E., A. Secrist, and G. Forman
   1973   Psycho-educational intervention beginning at age two: Reflections and outcomes. Pp. 25-62 in *Compensatory Education for Children, Ages Two to Eight: Recent Studies of Educational Intervention*. Baltimore: Johns Hopkins University Press.
Skeels, H.M.
   1966   Adult status of children with contrasting early life experiences. *Monographs of the Society for Research in Child Development* 31(3)(Serial 105):1-65.
Skeels, H.M., and H.B. Dye
   1939   A study of the effects of differential stimulation on mentally retarded children. *Proceedings and Addresses of the American Association on Mental Deficiency* 44:114-136.
Skodak, M., and Skeels, H.M.
   1949   A final follow-up study of one hundred adopted children. *Journal of Genetic Psychology* 75:85-125.
Smith, A.B.
   1999   Quality child care and joint attention. *International Journal of Early Years Education* 7(1):85-98.
SocioTechnical Research Applications, Inc.
   1996   *Report on the ACYF Bilingual/Multicultural Survey*. Washington, DC: The Head Start Bureau.

Spiker, D., and M.R. Hopmann
  1997 Effectiveness of early intervention for children with Down syndrome.
        In *The Effectiveness of Early Intervention*, M.J. Guralnick, ed. Baltimore,
        MD: Paul Brookes Publishing Co.
Spitz, H.H.
  1986 *The Raising of Intelligence: A Selected History of Attempts to Raise Retarded
        Intelligence.* Hillsdale, NJ: Erlbaum.
Spitz, R.A.
  1945 Hospitalism: An inquiry into the genesis of psychiatric conditions of
        early childhood. *Psychoanalytic Study of the Child* 1:53-74.
Spitz, R.A., and K.M. Wolfe
  1946 The smiling response: A contribution to the ontogenesis of social rela-
        tions. *Genetic Psychology Monographs* 34:57-125.
Spodek, B.
  1991 Early-childhood curriculum and cultural knowledge. In *Issues in Early-
        Childhood Curriculum, Yearbook in Early-Childhood Education, Volume 2*, B.
        Spodek and O. Saracho, eds. New York: Teachers College Press.
St. Pierre, R.G., J.I. Layzer, and H.V. Barnes
  1998 Regenerating two-generation programs. In *Early Child Care and Educa-
        tion for Children in Poverty: Promises, Programs, and Long-Term Results*,
        W.S. Barnett and S.S. Boocock, eds. Albany, NY: State University of
        New York Press.
Sternberg, R., and D. Detterman, eds.
  1986 *What is Intelligence?* Norwood, NJ: Ablex.
Stipek, D., D. Daniels, D. Galuzzo, and S. Milburn
  1992 Characterizing early childhood education programs for poor and
        middle-class children. *Early Childhood Research Quarterly* 7:1-19.
Tabors, P.O.
  1997 *One Child, Two Languages: A Guide for Preschool Educators of Children
        Learning English as a Second Language.* Baltimore, MD: Paul H. Brookes
        Publishing Co.
Tizard, B., J. Philps, and I. Plewis
  1976 Play in preschool centers, II: Effects on play of the child's social class
        and of the educational orientation of the center. *Journal of Child Psychol-
        ogy and Psychiatry* 17:265-274.
U.S. Bureau of the Census
  1997 *Statistical Abstract of the United States* (115th ed.). Washington, DC: U.S.
        Government Printing Office.
U.S. General Accounting Office
  1995 *Early Childhood Centers: Services to Prepare Children for School Often Lim-
        ited.* GAO/HEHS-95-21. Washington, DC: General Accounting Office.
U.S. Department of Education
  1987 *Ninth Annual Report to Congress on the Implementation of the Education of
        the Handicapped Act* (prepared by the Division of Innovation and Devel-
        opment, Office of Special Education Programs). Washington, DC: U.S.
        Department of Education.

1999   *To Assure the Free Appropriate Public Education of all Children with Disabilities.* Twenty-First Annual Report to Congress on the Implementation of the Individuals with Disabilities Education Act. Jessup, MD: Education Publication Center.

Vaughn, S., R. Gersten, and D. Chard
2000   A search for the underlying message in the intervention research on learning disabilities: Findings from research syntheses. *Exceptional Children* 67(1).

Wagner, D.A.
1978   Memories of Morocco: The influence of age, schooling, and environment on memory. *Cognitive Psychology* 10:1-28.

Warren, S.F., R.J. McQuarter, and A.K. Rogers-Warren
1984   The effects of mands and models on the speech of unresponsive language-delayed preschool children. *Journal of Speech and Hearing Disorders* 49:43-52.

Wasik, B.H., C.T. Ramey, D.M. Bryant, and J.J. Sparling
1990   A longitudinal study of two early intervention strategies: Project CARE. *Child Development* 61:1682-1696.

Weikart, D.P
1972   A traditional nursery program revisited. Pp. 189-215 in *The Preschool in Action: Exploring Early Childhood Programs*, R.K. Parker, ed. Boston: Allyn and Bacon.

Weikart, D.P., A.S. Epstein, L.J. Schweinhart, and J.T. Bond
1978   *The Ypsilanti Preschool Curriculum Demonstration Project: Preschool Years and Longitudinal Results.* Ypsilanti, MI: High/Scope Press.

Weikart, D.P., C.K. Kamii, and N.L. Radin
1967   Perry Preschool Project progress report. Pp. 1-88 in *Preschool Intervention: A Preliminary Report of the Perry Preschool Project*, D.P. Weikart, ed. Ann Arbor, MI: Campus Publishing.

Wellman, B.L.
1940   Iowa studies on the effects of schooling. *Yearbook National Sociological Studies in Education* 39:377-399.

Wenglinsky, H.
1997   How money matters: The effect of school district spending on academic achievement. *Sociology of Education* 70(3):221-237.

White, K.R., and G. Casto
1985   An integrative review of early intervention efficacy studies with at-risk children: Implications for the handicapped. *Analysis and Intervention in Developmental Disabilities* 5:7-31.

White, K.R., M. Taylor, and B. Moss
1992   Does research support claims about the benefits of involving parents in early intervention programs? *Review of Education Research* 62(1)91-125.

Whitebook, M., C. Howes, and D. Phillips
1989   *Who Cares? Child Care Teachers and the Quality of Care in America—Final Report of the National Child Care Staffing Study.* Oakland, CA: Child Care Employee Project.

Whitebook, M., D. Phillips, and C. Howes
  1993 *National Child Care Staffing Study Revisited: Four Years in the Life of Center-based Child Care.* Oakland, CA: Child Care Employee Project.
Winsler, A., R.M. Diaz, L. Espinosa, and J.L. Rodriguez
  1999 When learning a second language does not mean losing the first: Bilingual language development in low-income, Spanish-speaking children attending bilingual preschool. *Child Development* 70(2)(Mar-Apr):349-362.
Wolery, M., and J.S. Wilbert, eds.
  1994 *Including Children with Special Needs in Early Childhood Programs.* Research Monograph of the National Association for the Education of Young Children 6. Washington, DC: National Association for the Education of Young Children.
Woodhead, M.
  1988 When psychology informs public policy: The case of early-childhood intervention. *American Psychologist* 43(6):443-454.
Yoder, P., A. Kaiser, and C. Alpert
  1991 An exploratory study of the iteration between language teaching methods and child characteristics. *Journal of Speech and Hearing Research* 34:155-167.
Zigler, E., and S.J. Styfco
  1994 Is the Perry preschool better than Head Start? Yes and no. *Early Childhood Research Quarterly* 6:269-287.
Zill, N., G. Resnick, R. McKey, C. Clark, D. Connell, J. Swartz, R. O'Brien, and M. D'Elio
  1998 *Head Start Program Performances Measures: Second Progress Report.* Washington, DC: Research, Demonstration and Evaluation Branch and Head Start Bureau, Administration on Children, Youth and Families, U.S. Department of Health and Human Services.

CHAPTER 5

Allen, L., J. Cipielewski, and K.E. Stanovich
  1992 Multiple indicators of children's reading habits and attitudes: Construct validity and cognitive correlates. *Journal of Educational Psychology* 84:489-503.
Anderson, A.B., and S.J. Stokes
  1984 Social and institutional influences on the development and practice of literacy. In *Awakening to Literacy,* H. Goelman, A. Oberg, and F. Smith, eds. Exeter, NH: Heinemann.
Anderson, E.S.
  1986 The acquisition of register variation by Anglo-American children. In *Language Socialization Across Cultures,* B.B. Schieffelin and E. Ochs, eds. New York, NY: Cambridge University Press.

Anderson, R.C., and P. Freebody

1981 Vocabulary knowledge. Pp. 77-117 in *Comprehension and Teaching: Research Reviews*, J. Guthrie, ed. Newark, DE: International Reading Association.

Arnold, D.H., C.J. Lonigan, G.J. Whitehurst, and J.N. Epstein

1994 Accelerating language development through picture book reading: Replication and extension to a videotape training format. *Journal of Educational Psychology* 86:235-243.

Baillargeon, R.

1994 Physical reasoning in infancy. Pp. 181-204 in *The Cognitive Neurosciences*, M.S. Gazzaniga, ed. Cambridge, MA: MIT Press.

Baroody, A.J.

1987 *Children's Mathematical Thinking. A Developmental Framework for Preschool, Primary, and Special Education Teachers.* New York: Teachers College Press.

Beals, D.E., J.M. DeTemple, and D.K. Dickinson

1994 Talking and listening that support early literacy development of children from low-income families. In *Bridges to Literacy: Children, Families, and Schools*, D.K. Dickinson, ed. Cambridge, MA: Blackwell.

Beeson, B.S., and R.A. Williams

1985 The effects of gender and age on preschool children's choice of the computer as a child-selected activity. *Journal of the American Society for Information Science* 36:339-341.

Bereiter, C.

1972 An academic preschool for disadvantaged children: Conclusions from evaluation studies. Pp. 1-21 in *Preschool Programs for the Disadvantaged: Five Experimental Approaches to Early Childhood Education*, J.S. Stanley, ed. Baltimore, MD: Johns Hopkins University Press.

Bishop, D.V.M., and C. Adams

1990 A prospective study of the relationship between specific language impairment, phonological disorders and reading retardation. *Journal of Child Psychology and Psychiatry and Allied Disciplines* 31:1027-1050.

Blank, M.

1982 Language and school failure: Some speculations about the relationship between oral and written language. Pp. 75-93 in *The Language of Children Reared in Poverty*, L. Feagans and D. Farran, eds. San Diego: Academic Press.

Bodrova, E.

1997 Key concepts of Vygotsky's theory of learning and development. *Journal of Early Childhood Teacher Education* 18:16-22.

Bodrova, E., and D.J. Leong

1996 *Tools of the Mind: The Vygotskian Approach to Early Childhood Education.* Columbus, OH: Merrill.

1998a Development of dramatic play in young children and its effects on self-regulation: The Vygotskian approach. *Journal of Early Childhood Teacher Education* 19:115-124.

1998b Adult influence on play. In *Play from Birth to Twelve and Beyond: Contexts, Perspectives, and Meanings*, D.P. Fromberg and D. Bergen, eds. New York: Garland Publishing, Inc.

Bodrova, E., D.J. Leong, and D.E. Paynter
1999 Literacy standards for preschool learners. *Educational Leadership* 57(2):42-46.

Borgh, K., and W.P. Dickson
1986 Two preschoolers sharing one microcomputer: Creating prosocial behavior with hardware and software. Pp. 37-44 in *Young Children and Microcomputers*, P.F. Campbell and G.G. Fein, eds. Reston, VA: Prentice-Hall.

Bradley, L., and P.E. Bryant
1983 Categorizing sounds and learning to read—A causal connection. *Nature* 301:419-421.
1985 *Rhyme and Reason in Reading and Spelling*. Ann Arbor, MI: University of Michigan Press.

Bryant, P.E., M. MacLean, L.L. Bradley, and J. Crossland
1990 Rhyme and alliteration, phoneme detection, and learning to read. *Developmental Psychology* 26:429-438.

Bus, A.G, M.H. IJzendoorn, and A. Pellegrini
1995 Joint book reading makes for success in learning to read: A meta-analysis on intergenerational transmission of literacy. *Review of Educational Research* 65:1-21.

Bush, B.
1990 Parenting's best-kept secret: Reading to your children. *Reader's Digest* 137:67-70.

Butler, S.R., H.W. Marsh, M.J. Sheppard, and J.L. Sheppard
1985 Seven-year longitudinal study of the early prediction of reading achievement. *Journal of Educational Psychology* 77:349-361.

Byrne, B., and R.F. Fielding-Barnsley
1991 *Sound Foundations*. Artarmon, New South Wales, Australia: Leyden Educational Publishers.

Campbell, F., and C. Ramey
1995 Cognitive and social outcomes for high-risk African-American students at middle adolescence: Positive effects of early intervention. *American Educational Research Journal* 32(4):743-772.

Canfield, R.L., and E.G. Smith
1996 Number-based expectations and sequential enumeration by 5-month-old infants. *Developmental Psychology* 32:269-279.

Case, R.
1985 *Intellectual Development: Birth to Adulthood*. New York: Academic.

Case, R., S. Griffin, and W.M. Kelly
1999 Socioeconomic gradients in mathematical ability and their responsiveness to intervention during early childhood. Pp. 125-149 in *Developmental Health and the Wealth of Nations: Social, Biological, and Educational Dynamics*, D.P. Keating and C. Hertzman, eds. New York: Guilford Press.

Case R., and R. Sandieson
    1987 General developmental constraints on the acquisition of special proce-
          dures (and vice versa). Paper presented at the annual meeting of the
          American Educational Research Association, Baltimore, April.
Clay, M.M.
    1979 *The Early Detection of Reading Difficulties, 3rd ed.* Portsmouth, NH:
          Heinemann.
Clements, D.H.
    1987 Computers and young children: A review of the research. *Young Chil-
          dren* 43(1):34-44.
    1991 Current technology and the early childhood curriculum. Pp. 106-131 in
          *Yearbook in Early Childhood Education, Volume 2: Issues in Early Childhood
          Curriculum*, B. Spodek and O.N. Saracho, eds. New York: Teachers
          College Press.
    1993 Early education principles and computer practices. In *Curriculum Plan-
          ning: A New Approach*, 6th ed., C.G. Hass and F.W. Parkay, eds. Boston:
          Allyn and Bacon.
    1994 The uniqueness of the computer as a learning tool: Insights from re-
          search and practice. Pp. 31-50 in *Young Children: Active Learners in a
          Technological Age*, J.L. Wright and D.D. Shade, eds. Washington, DC:
          National Association for the Education of Young Children.
Clements, D.H., and B.K. Nastasi
    1992 Computers and early childhood education. Pp. 187-246 in *Advances in
          School Psychology: Preschool and Early Childhood Treatment Directions*, M.
          Gettinger, S.N. Elliott, and T.R. Kratochwill, eds. Hillsdale, NJ:
          Lawrence Erlbaum Associates.
    1993 Electronic media and early childhood education. Pp. 251-275 in *Hand-
          book of Research on the Education of Young Children*, B. Spodek, ed. New
          York: Macmillan.
Clements, D.H., and J. Sarama
    1998 *Building Blocks—Foundations for Mathematical Thinking, Pre-Kindergarten
          to Grade 2: Research-Based Materials Development* [National Science Foun-
          dation, grant number ESI-9730804; see www.gse.buffalo.edu/org/
          buildingblocks/]. Buffalo, NY: State University of New York at Buf-
          falo.
Cochran-Smith, M., J. Kahn, and C.L. Paris
    1988 When word processors come into the classroom. Pp. 43-74 in *Writing
          with Computers in the Early Grades*, J.L. Hoot and S.B. Silvern, eds. New
          York: Teachers College Press.
Cole, K.N., and P.S. Dale
    1986 Direct language instruction and interactive language instruction with
          language delayed preschool children: A comparison study. *Journal of
          Speech and Hearing Research* 29(2):206-217.
Coley, R.J., J. Cradler, and P.K. Engel
    1997 *Computers and Classrooms: The Status of Technology in U.S. Schools.*
          Princeton, NJ: Educational Testing Service.

Copperman, P.
1986 *Taking Books to Heart: How to Develop a Love of Reading in Your Child.*
Reading, MA: Addison-Wesley.

Copple, C., I. Sigel, and R. Saunders
1979 *Educating the Young Thinker: Classroom Strategies for Cognitive Growth.*
New York: Van Nostrand.

Core Knowledge Foundation
2000 *Core Knowledge Preschool Sequence.* Charlottesville, VA: Core Knowledge Foundation. Available: http//www.coreknowledge.org [Septem-
ber 2000].

Cornell, E.H., M. Sénéchal, and L.S. Broda
1988 Recall of picture books by 3-year-old children: Testing and repetition
effects in joint reading activities. *Journal of Educational Psychology*
80:537-542.

Corsaro, W.A.
1988 Peer culture in the preschool. *Theory into Practice* 27(1):19-24.

Crain-Thoreson, C., and P.S. Dale
1992 Do early talkers become early readers? Linguistic precocity, preschool
language, and emergent literacy. *Developmental Psychology* 28:421-429.

Cunningham, A.E., and K.E. Stanovich
1991 Tracking the unique effects of print exposure in children: Associations
with vocabulary, general knowledge, and spelling. *Journal of Educational Psychology* 83:264-274.

Davidson, J., and J.L Wright
1994 The potential of the microcomputer in the early childhood classroom.
Pp. 77-91 in *Young Children: Active Learners in a Technological Age*, J.L.
Wright and D.D. Shade, eds. Washington, DC: National Association
for the Education of Young Children.

DeLoache, J.S., and O.A.P. DeMendoza
1987 Joint picturebook interactions of mothers and one-year-old children.
British Journal of Developmental Psychology 5:111-123.

Dewey, J.
1976 The child and the curriculum. Pp. 273-291 in *John Dewey: The Middle
Works, 1899-1924. Volume 2: 1902-1903*, J.A. Boydston, ed. Carnbon-
dale, IL: Southern Illinois University Press.

Dickinson, D.K., and P.O. Tabors
1991 Early literacy: Linkages between home, school, and literacy achievement at age five. *Journal of Research in Childhood Education* 6:30-46.

Dunn, J., and C. Kendrick
1982 The speech of two- and three-year-olds to infant siblings: "Baby talk"
and the context of communication. *Journal of Child Language* 9(3):579-
595.

Dunn, L.M., and L.M. Dunn
1981 *Peabody Picture Vocabulary Test, Revised.* Circle Pines, MN: American
Guidance Service.

Dyson, A.
  1993   From prop to mediator: The changing role of written language in
         children's symbolic repertoires. In *Language and Literacy in Early Child-
         hood Education*, B. Spodek and O. Saracho, eds. New York: Teachers
         College Press.
Early Literacy Advisor
  2000   *The Early Literacy Advisor: An Assessment System That Shapes Instruction.*
         Available: http://198.17.205.11/resources/literacy/ela/aboutela.asp
         [September 2000].
Echols, L.D., R.F. West, K.E. Stanovich, and K.S. Zehr
  1996   Using children's literacy activities to predict growth in verbal cognitive
         skills: A longitudinal investigation. *Journal of Educational Psychology*
         88:296-304.
Elkonin, D.
  1978   *Psikhologija Igry [The Psychology of Play].* Moscow: Pedagogika.
Elley, W.B.
  1989   Vocabulary acquisition from listening to stories. *Reading Research Quar-
         terly* 24:174-187.
Elliott, A., and N. Hall
  1997   The impact of self-regulatory teaching strategies on "at-risk"
         preschoolers' mathematical learning in a computer-mediated environ-
         ment. *Journal of Computing in Childhood Education* 8(2/3):187-198.
Ellis, R., and G. Wells
  1980   Enabling factors in adult-child discourse. *First Language* 1:46-62.
Escobedo, T.H., and S. Evans
  1997   A comparison of child-tested early childhood education software with
         professional ratings. Paper presented at the March 1997 meeting of the
         American Educational Research Association in Chicago.
Essa, E.L.
  1987   The effect of a computer on preschool children's activities. *Early Child-
         hood Research Quarterly* 2:377-382.
Fein, G.G.
  1977   Play and the acquisition of symbols. In *Current Topics in Early Educa-
         tion*, L. Katz, ed. Norwood, NJ: Ablex.
  1981   Pretend play in childhood: An integrative review. *Child Development*
         52(4)(Dec):1095-1118.
Fitzgerald, J., C.M. Schuele, and J.E. Roberts
  1992   Emergent literacy: What is it and what does the teacher of children
         with learning disabilities need to know about it? *Reading and Writing
         Quarterly* 8:71-85.
Fletcher-Flinn, C.M., and T. Suddendorf
  1996   Do computers affect "the mind"? *Journal of Educational Computing Re-
         search* 15(2):97-112.
Franklin, M.
  1999   *Meaning of Play in the Developmental Interaction Tradition.* Bronxville,
         NY: Sarah Lawrence College.

French, L.A.
   1985   Real-world knowledge as the basis for social and cognitive develop-
          ment. Pp. 179-209 in *Social and Developmental Perspectives on Social Cog-
          nition*, J.B. Pryor and J.D. Day, eds. New York: Springer-Verlag.
French, L.A., and M. Song
   1998   Developmentally appropriate teacher-directed approaches: Images
          from Korean kindergartens. *Journal of Curriculum Studies* 30:409-430.
Froebel, F.
   1886   *Autobiography of Froebel*. Translated by E. Michaelis and H.K. Moore.
          London: Swan Sonnenschein.
Gelman, R., and C.R. Gallistel
   1978   *The Children's Understanding of Numbers*. Cambridge: Harvard Univer-
          sity Press
Gelman, R.
   1967   Conservation acquisition: A problem of learning to attend to the rel-
          evant attributes. *Journal of Experimental Child Psychology* 7:167-187.
   1998   Domain specificity in cognitive development: Universals and
          nonuniversals. In *Advances in Psychological Science: Vol. 2. Biological and
          Cognitive Aspects*, M. Sabourin, F. Craik, and M. Robert, eds. Hove,
          U.K.: Psychology Press Ltd., Academic Press.
Gelman, R., and A.L. Brown
   1986   Changing views of cognitive competence in the young. Pp. 175-207 in
          Discoveries and Trends in Behavioral and Social Sciences, N. Smelser and D.
          Gerstein, eds. Commission on Behavioral and Social Sciences and Edu-
          cation, National Research Council. Washington, DC: National Acad-
          emy Press.
Gibson, E.J.
   1969   *Principles of Perceptual Learning and Development*. New York: Appleton-
          Century-Crofts.
Gillon, G., and B.J. Dodd
   1994   A prospective study of the relationship between phonological, seman-
          tic and syntactic skills and specific reading disability. *Reading and Writ-
          ing: An Interdisciplinary Journal* 6:321-345.
Ginsburg, H.P.
   1989   *Children's Arithmetic: How They Learn It and How You Teach It*, 2nd ed.
          Austin, TX: Pro Ed.
Ginsburg, H.P., R. Balfanz, and C. Greenes
   1999   Challenging mathematics for young children. Pp. 245-258 in *Teaching
          for Intelligence II: A Collection of Articles*, A.L. Costa, ed. Arlington
          Heights, IL: Skylight.
Gottman, J.M.
   1983   How children become friends. *Monographs of the Society for Research in
          Child Development* 48(3):1-86.
Greenes, C.
   1999   Ready to learn: Developing young children's mathematical powers. In

Mathematics in the Early Years, J. Copley, ed. Reston, VA: National Council of Teachers of Mathematics.

Griffin, S.A., and R. Case
1996 Evaluating the breadth and depth of training effects when central conceptual structures are taught. *Society for Research in Child Development Monographs* 59:90-113.
1998 Re-thinking the primary school math curriculum: An approach based on cognitive science. *Issues in Education* 4(1):1-51.

Griffin, S., R. Case, and A. Capodilupo
1995 Teaching for understanding: The importance of central conceptual structures in the elementary mathematics curriculum. Pp. 121-151 in *Teaching for Transfer: Fostering Generalization in Learning*, A. McKeough, I. Lupert, and A.Marini, eds. Hillsdale, NJ: Erlbaum.

Griffin, S.A., R. Case, and R.S. Siegler
1994 Rightstart: Providing the central conceptual prerequisites for first formal learning of arithmetic to students at-risk for school failure. Pp. 24-49 in *Classroom Lessons: Integrating Cognitive Theory and Classroom Practice*, K. McGilly, ed. Cambridge, MA: Bradford Books MIT Press.
1996 Evaluating the breadth and depth of transfer effects when central conceptual structures are taught. In *The Role of Central Conceptual Structures in the Development of Children's Thought*, R. Case and Y. Okamoto, eds. Monographs of the Society for Research in Child Development, 60(Serial 246)(5-6).

Hall, N.
1991 Play and the emergence of literacy. In *Play and Early Literacy Development*, J.F. Christie, ed. Albany, NY: State University of New York Press.

Hart, B. T.R. and Risley
1995 *Meaningful Differences in the Early Experiences of Young American Children*. Baltimore, MD: Bokkes Publishing.

Haugland, S.W.
1992 Effects of computer software on preschool children's developmental gains. *Journal of Computing in Childhood Education* 3(1):15-30.

Hepting, N.H., and H. Goldstein
1996 Requesting by preschoolers with developmental disabilities: Videotaped self-modeling and learning of new linguistic structures. *Topics in Early Childhood Special Education* 16(3):407-427.

Hiebert, J.
1986 *Conceptual and Procedural Knowledge: The Case of Mathematics*. Hilldale, NJ: Erlbaum.

Hohmann, M., B. Barnet, and D.P. Weikart
1979 *Young Children in Action: A Manual for Preschool Educators*. Ypsilanti, MI: High/Scope Press.

Hohmann, M., and D. Weikart
1995 *Educating Young Children*. Ypsilanti, MI: High/Scope Press.

Hoover, J.M., and A.M. Austin
1986 A comparison of traditional preschool and computer play from a so-

cial/cognitive perspective. Paper presented at the April 1986 meeting of the American Educational Research Association in San Francisco.

Howard, J., E. Greyrose, K. Kehr, M. Espinosa, and L. Beckwith
  1996 Teacher-facilitated microcomputer activities: Enhancing social play and affect in young children with disabilities. *Journal of Special Education Technology* 13:36-47.

Howes, C.
  1988 Relations between early child care and schooling. *Developmental Psychology* 24:53-57.

Howes, C., and C.C. Matheson
  1992 Sequences in the development of competent play with peers: Social and social pretend play. *Developmental Psychology* 28(5):961-974.

Howes, C., and E. Smith
  1995 Relations among child care quality, teacher behavior, children's play activities, emotional security, and cognitive activity in child care. *Early Childhood Research Quarterly* 10(4):381-404.

Jenkins, J.R., M.L. Stein, and K. Wysocki
  1984 Learning vocabulary through reading. *American Educational Research Journal* 21:767-787.

Johnson, J.E.
  1985 Characteristics of preschoolers interested in microcomputers. *Journal of Educational Research* 78:299-305.

Kagan, J.
  1994 Three pleasing ideas. *American Psychologist* 51:901-908.

Kaiser, A., P. Yoder, and A. Keetz
  1992 Evaluating milieu teaching. In *Communication and Language Intervention: Causes and Effects in Communication and Language Intervention.* S.F. Warren and J. Reichle, eds. Baltimore, MD: Paul H. Brookes Publishing 1:9-47.

Karmiloff-Smith, A., and B. Inhelder
  1974 If you want to get ahead, get a theory. *Cognition* 3:195-212.

Katz, L.G.
  1995 A developmental approach to the education of young children: Basic principles. *International Schools Journal* 14(2):49-60.

Katz, L.G., and D. McClellan
  1997 *Fostering Social Competence in Young Children. The Teacher's Role.* Washington, DC: National Association for the Education of Young Children.

Keil, F.
  1989 *Concepts, Word Meanings, and Cognitive Development.* Cambridge, MA: MIT Press.
  1994 The birth and nurturance of concepts by domains: The origins of concepts of living things. In *Mapping the Mind: Domain Specificity in Cognition and Culture,* A. Hirschfield and S.A. Gelman, eds. New York: Cambridge University Press.

King, J.A., and N. Alloway

  1992   Preschooler's use of microcomputers and input devices. *Journal of Educational Computing Research* 8:451-468.

Kontos, S.

  1999   Preschool teachers' talk, roles and activity settings during free play. *Early Childhood Research Quarterly* 14(3):363-382.

Ladd, G. W.

  1990   Having friends, keeping friends, making friends, and being liked by peers in the classroom: Predictors of children's early school adjustment? *Child Development* 61(4)(Aug):1081-1100.

Lave, J.

  1988   *Cognition in Practice: Mind, Mathematics, and Culture in Everyday Life.* Cambridge, MA: Cambridge University Press.

Leslie, A.M.

  1994   Pretending and believing: Issues in the theory ToMM. *Cognition* 50:211-238.

Lomax, C.M.

  1977   Interest in books and stories at nursery school. *Educational Research* 19:100-112.

Lonigan, C.J.

  1994   Reading to preschoolers exposed: Is the emperor really naked? *Developmental Review* 14:303-323.

Lonigan, C.J., S.M. Dyer, and J.L. Anthony

  1996   The influence of the home literacy environment on the development of literacy skills in children from diverse racial and economic backgrounds. Paper presented at the Annual Convention of the American Educational Research Association. New York, NY.

Lonigan, C.J., and G.J. Whitehurst

  1998   Relative efficacy of parent and teacher involvement in a shared-reading intervention for preschool children from low-income backgrounds. *Early Childhood Research Quarterly* 13(2):263-292.

MacLean, M., P. Bryant, and L. Bradley

  1987   Rhymes, nursery rhymes, and reading in early childhood. *Merrill-Palmer Quarterly* 33:255-282.

Mandler, J.M., and L. McDonough

  1998   On developing a knowledge base in infancy. *Developmental Psychology* 34(6):1274-1288.

Mann, V.A. and I.Y. Liberman

  1984   Phonological awareness and verbal short-term memory. *Journal of Learning Disabilities* 17(10):592-599.

Mason, J.M.

  1980   When children do begin to read: An exploration of four year old children's letter and word reading competencies. *Reading Research Quarterly* 15:203-227.

  1992   Reading stories to preliterate children: A proposed connection to reading. Pp. 215-243 in *Reading Acquisition*, P.B. Gough, L.C. Ehri, and R. Treiman, eds. Hillsdale, NJ: Lawrence Erlbaum Associates

Mason, J.M., and D. Dunning
1986   Toward a model relating home literacy with beginning reading. Paper presented to the American Educational Research Association, San Francisco.

Massey, C.M., and R. Gelman
1988   Preschooler's ability to decide whether a photographed unfamiliar object can move itself. *Developmental Psychology* 24(3):307-317.

McCormick, C.E., and J.M. Mason
1986   Intervention procedures for increasing preschool children's interest in and knowledge about reading. Pp. 90-115 in *Emergent Literacy: Writing and Reading*, W.H. Teale and E. Sulzby, eds. Norwood, NJ: Ablex.

Montessori, M.
1964   *The Montessori Method* (Translated into English by Anne E. George and originally published in 1912). New York: Schocken Books.

Morrow, L.
1990   Preparing the classroom environment to promote literacy during play. *Early Childhood Research Quarterly* 5:537-554.

Moxley, R.A., B. Warash, G. Coffman, K. Bronton, and K.R. Concannon
1997   Writing development using computers in a class of three-year-olds. *Journal of Computing in Childhood Education* 8(2/3):133-164.

Muller, A.A., and M. Perlmuter
1985   Preschool children's problem-solving interactions at computers and jigsaw puzzles. *Journal of Applied Developmental Psychology* 6:173-186.

Murray, F.B.
1982   Teaching through social conflict. *Contemporary Educational Psychology.* 7(3) Jul:257-271.

Nagy, W.E., R.C. Anderson, and P.A. Herman
1987   Learning word meanings from context during normal reading. *American Educational Research Journal* 24:237-270.

Nastasi, B.K., and D.H. Clements
1993   Motivational and social outcomes of cooperative education environments. *Journal of Computing in Childhood Education* 4(1):15-43.

National Research Council
1998   *Preventing Reading Difficulties in Young Children*. Committee on Prevention of Reading Difficulties in Young Children, C.E. Snow, M.S. Burns, and P. Griffin, eds. Washington, DC: National Academy Press.
1999a   *How People Learn: Brain, Mind, Experience, and School*. Committee on Developments in the Science of Learning, J.D. Bransford, A.L. Brown, and R.R. Cocking, eds. Washington, DC: National Academy Press.
1999b   *How People Learn: Bridging Research and Practice*. Committee on Learning Research and Educational Practice, M.S. Donovan, J.D. Bransford, and J.W. Pellegrino, eds. Washington, DC: National Academy Press.
1999c   *Starting Out Right: A Guide to Promoting Children's Reading Success.*

Committee on Prevention of Reading Difficulties in Young Children, M.S. Burns, P. Griffin, and C.E. Snow, eds. Washington, DC: National Academy Press.

Nelson, K.
1981 Social cognition in a script framework. Pp. 97-118 in *Social Cognitive Development: Frontiers and Possible Futures*, J.H. Flavell and L. Ross, eds. New York: Cambridge University Press.

Nelson, K., and J.M. Gruendel
1981 Generalized event representations: Basic building blocks of cognitive development. Pp. 131-158 in *Advances in Developmental Psychology*, Vol. 1, M. Lamb and A.L. Brown, eds. Hillsdale, NJ: Erlbaum.

Neuman, S.B.
1996 Evaluation of the Books Aloud Project: An Executive Summary. Report to the William Penn Foundation from BooksAloud!, Temple University, Philadelphia.

Neuman, S.B., and K. Roskos
1993 Access to print for children of poverty: Differential effects of adult mediation and literacy-enriched play settings on environmental and functional print tasks. *American Educational Research Journal* 30:95-122.

Newman, L.S.
1990 Intentional and unintentional memory in young children: Remembering vs. playing. *Journal of Experimental Child Psychology* 50:243-258.

Ninio, A.
1980 Picture book reading in mother-infant dyads belonging to two subgroups in Israel. *Child Development* 51:587-590.

Ninio, A., and J. Bruner
1978 The achievement and antecedents of labeling. *Journal of Child Language* 5:1-15.

O'Reilly, A.W., and M.H. Bornstein
1993 Caregiver-child interaction in play. *New Directions for Child Development* 59:55-66.

Papert, S.
1980 *Mindstorms: Computers, Children, and Powerful Ideas*. New York: Basic Books.

Payne, A.C., G.J. Whitehurst, and A.L. Angell
1994 The role of literacy environment in the language development of children from low-income families. *Early Childhood Research Quarterly* 9:427-440.

Pellegrini, A.D., G.H. Brody, and I. Sigel
1985 Parent's book-reading habits with their children. *Journal of Educational Psychology* 77:332-340.

Pellegrini, A.D., L. Galda, and J. Dresden
1991 A longitudinal study of the predictive relations among symbolic play, linguistic verbs, and early literacy. *Research in the Teaching of English* 25(2):219-235.

Perlmutter, M., S. Behrend, F. Kuo, and A. Muller
1986 Social influence on children's problem solving at a computer. Unpublished manuscript. Ann Arbor: University of Michigan.

Perret-Clermont, A., J. Perret, and N. Bell
1991 The social construction of meaning and cognitive activity in elementary school children. Pp. 41-62 in *Perspectives on Socially Shared Cognition*. L.B. Resnick and J.M. Levine, et al., eds. Washington, DC: American Psychological Association.

Pestalozzi, J.H.
1905 Letter on his work at Stanz, 1799. P. 360 in *Great Pedagogical Essays: Plato to Spencer*, F.V.N. Painter, ed. New York: American Book Co.

Piaget, J.
1962 *Play, Dreams, and Imitation in Childhood*. C. Gattegno and F.M. Hodgson, transls. New York: Norton. [Original work published in 1945]
1970 *The Science of Education and the Psychology of the Child*, D. Coleman, translator. New York: Orion Press.

Pikulski, J.J., and A.W. Tobin
1989 Factors associated with long-term reading achievement of early readers. In *Cognitive and Social Perspectives for Literacy Research and Instruction*, S. McCormick, J. Zutell, P. Scharer, and P. O'Keefe, eds. Chicago: National Reading Conference.

Purcell-Gates, V.
1996 Stories, coupons, and the TV Guide: Relationships between home literacy experiences and emergent literacy knowledge. *Reading Research Quarterly* 31:406-428.

Purcell-Gates, V., and K.L. Dahl
1991 Low-SES children's success and failure at early literacy learning in skills-based classrooms. *Journal of Reading Behavior* 23:1-34.

Ramey, C.T., and S.L. Ramey
1998 Early intervention and early experience. *American Psychologist* 53:109-120.

Raz, I.S., and P. Bryant
1990 Social background, phonological awareness and children's reading. *British Journal of Developmental Psychology* 8:209-225.

Resnick, L.B.
1989 Developing mathematical knowledge. *American Psychologist* 44(2):162-169.

Reynolds, A.
1999 The Added Value of Continuing Early Intervention into the Primary Grades. Presentation at the National Invitational Conference on Early Childhood Learning: Programs for a New Age. Sponsored by the Laboratory for Student Success and The National Center on Education in the Inner Cities at Temple University Center for Research in Human Development and Education.

Roazzi, A. and P. Bryant
  1998 The effects of symmetrical and asymmetrical social interaction on children's logical inferences. *British Journal of Developmental Psychology* 16(2) Jun:175-181.
Rogoff, B.
  1990 *Apprenticeship in Thinking: Cognitive Development in Social Context.* New York: Oxford University Press.
Rowe, K.J.
  1991 The influence of reading activity at home on students' attitudes towards reading, classroom attentiveness and reading achievement: An application of structural equation modelling. *British Journal of Educational Psychology* 61:19-35.
Sachs, J., and J. Devin
  1976 Young children's use of age-appropriate speech styles in social interaction and role-playing. *Journal of Child Language* 3(1):81-98.
Saxe, G.B.
  1991 *Culture and Cognitive Development: Studies in Mathematical Understanding.* Hillsdale, NJ: Lawrence Erlbaum Associates Publishers.
Scarborough, H.
  1989 Prediction of reading dysfunction from familial and individual differences. *Journal of Educational Psychology* 81:101-108.
Schery, T.K., and L.C. O'Connor
  1992 The effectiveness of school-based computer language intervention with severely handicapped children. *Language, Speech, and Hearing Services in Schools* 23:43-47.
Schwartzman, H.
  1978 *Transformations: The Anthropology of Children's Play.* New York: Plenum Press.
Sénéchal, M., and E.H. Cornell
  1993 Vocabulary acquisition through shared reading experiences. *Reading Research Quarterly* 28:360-375.
Sénéchal, M., E.H. Cornell, and L.S. Broda
  1995 Age-related differences in the organization of parent-infant interactions during picture-book reading. *Early Childhood Research Quarterly* 10:317-337.
Sénéchal, M., J. LeFevre, E. Hudson, and E.P. Lawson
  1996 Knowledge of storybooks as a predictor of young children's vocabulary. *Journal of Educational Psychology* 88:520-536.
Sénéchal, M., J. LeFevre, E.M. Thomas, and K.E. Daley
  1998 Differential effects of home literacy experiences on the development of oral and written language. *Reading Research Quarterly* 33(1):96-116.
Shade, D.D., and J.A. Watson
  1987 Microworlds, mother teaching behavior, and concept formation in the very young child. *Early Childhood Development and Care* 28:97-113.

Share, D.L., A.F. Jorm, R. MacLean, and R. Mathews
1984   Sources of individual differences in reading acquisition. *Journal of Educational Psychology* 76:1309-1324.
Share, D.L., and P. Silva
1987   Language deficits and specific reading retardation: Cause or effect? *British Journal of Disorders of Communication* 22:219-226.
Sheingold, K., and C.M. Myford
1988   Reasoning about evidence in portfolios: Cognitive foundations for valid and reliable assessment. *Educational Assessment* 5(1):5-40.
Siegler, R.S., and M. Robinson
1982   The development of numerical understandings. Pp 241-312 in *Advances in Child Development and Behavior*, H. W. Reese and L.P. Lipsitt, eds. New York: Academic Press.
Sigel, I.E.
1993   Educating the young thinker: A distancing model of preschool education. Pp. 237-252 in *Approaches to Early Childhood Education*, J.L. Roopnarine and J.E. Johnson, eds. Columbus, OH: Merrill/Macmillan.
Siraj-Blatchford, I., ed.
1998   *A Curriculum Development Handbook for Early Childhood Educators*. Staffordshire, U.K.: Trentham Books Limited.
Sivin, J.P., P.C. Lee, and A.M. Vollmer
1985   Introductory computer experiences with commercially-available software: Differences between three-year-olds and five-year-olds. Paper presented at the April 1985 meeting of the American Educational Research Association in Chicago.
Snow, C.E.
1986   Conversations with children. In *Language Acquisition*, P. Fletcher and M. Garman, eds. New York: Cambridge University Press.
Snow, C.E., W.S. Barnes, J. Chandler, L. Hemphill, and I.F. Goodman
1991   *Unfulfilled Expectations: Home and School Influences on Literacy*. Cambridge, MA: Harvard University Press.
Spelke, E.S., W.S. Born, and F. Chu
1983   Perception of moving, sounding objects by four-month-old infants. *Perception* 12(6):719-732.
Spelke, E.S., and G. Van de Walle
1995   Perceiving and reasoning about objects: Insights from infants. In *Spatial Representation*, N. Eilam, R. McCarthy, and B. Brewer, eds. Cambridge, MA: Blackwell.
Spodek, B., ed.
1993   *Handbook of Research on the Education of Young Children*. New York: MacMillan.
Stanovich, K.E, A.E. Cunningham, and B.B. Cramer
1984   Assessing phonological awareness in kindergarten children: Issues of task comparability. *Journal of Experimental Child Psychology* 38:175-190.

Starkey, P.
    1992   The early development of numerical reasoning. *Cognition* 43:93-126.
Stipek, D.
    1997   Success in school—for a head start in life. Pp. 75-92 in *Developmental
           Psychopathology: Perspectives on Adjustment, Risk, and Disorder*, S.S.
           Luthar, J.A. Burack, D. Cicchetti, and R.R. Weisz, eds. Cambridge, U.K.:
           Cambridge University Press.
Sulzby, E.
    1989   Assessment of writing and of children's language while writing. Pp.
           83-109 in *The Role of Assessment and Measurement in Early Literacy In-
           struction*, L. Morrow and J. Smith, eds. Englewood Cliffs, NJ: Prentice-
           Hall.
Sulzby, E., and W. Teale
    1991   Emergent literacy. Pp. 727-758 in *Handbook of Reading Research*, Vol. II,
           R. Barr, M. Kamil, P. Mosenthal, and P.D. Pearson, eds. New York:
           Longman.
Tan, L.E.
    1985   Computers in pre-school education. *Early Child Development and Care*
           19:319-336.
Teale, W.H.
    1986   Home background and young children's literacy development. In
           Emergent Literacy: Writing and Reading, W.H. Teale and E. Sulzby, eds.
           Norwood, NJ: Ablex.
Teale, W.H., and E. Sulzby, eds.
    1986   *Emergent Literacy: Writing and Reading*. Norwood, NJ: Ablex.
Tomasello, M., and S. Mannle
    1985   Pragmatics of sibling speech to one year olds. *Child Development*
           56(4):911-917.
Umiker-Sebeok, D.J.
    1979   Preschool children's intraconversational narratives. *Journal of Child
           Language* 6(1):91-110.
Valdez-Menchaca, M.C., and G.J. Whitehurst
    1992   Accelerating language development through picture book reading: A
           systematic extension to Mexican day-care. *Developmental Psychology*
           28:1106-1114.
Vandell, D.L., and K.S. Wilson
    1987   Infant's interactions with mother, sibling, and peer: Contrasts and rela-
           tions between interaction systems. *Child Development* 58(1):176-186.
Vellutino, F.R., D.M. Scanlon, and M.S. Tanzman
    1991   Bridging the gap between cognitive and neuropsychological con-
           ceptualizations of reading disability. *Learning and Individual Differences*
           3:181-203.
Vygotsky, L.S.
    1962   *Thought and Language*. Cambridge, MA: MIT Press.
    1977   Play and its role in the mental development of the child. Pp. 76-99 in

Soviet Developmental Psychology, M. Cole. ed. White Plains, NY: M.E. Sharpe. [Original work published in 1966]

1978 *Mind in Society: The Development of Higher Psychological Processes*. Cambridge, MA: Harvard University Press.

1986 *Thought and Language* (A. Kozulin, Trans.). Cambridge, MA: The MIT Press.

Wagner, R.K., and J.K. Torgesen

1987 The natural of phonological processing and its causal role in the acquisition of reading skills. *Psychological Bulletin* 101:192-212.

Wagner, R.K., J.K. Torgesen, and C.A. Rashotte

1994 Development of reading-related phonological processing abilities: New evidence of bidirectional causality from a latent variable longitudinal study. *Developmental Psychology* 30:73-87.

Weir, S., S.J. Russell, and J.A. Valente

1981 Logo: An approach to educating disabled children. *BYTE* 7:342-360.

Weikart, D.P

1972 A traditional nursery program revisited. Pp. 189-215 in *The Preschool in Action: Exploring Early Childhood Programs* R.K. Parker, ed. Boston: Allyn and Bacon.

Wellman, H.M. and S.A. Gelman

1992 Cognitive development: Foundational theories of core domains. *Annual Review of Psychology* 43:337-375.

Wells, G.

1985 *Language Development in the Preschool Years*. New York: Cambridge University Press.

Wells, G., S. Barnes, and J. Wells

1984 Linguistic influences on educational attainment. Final report to the Department of Education and Science.

Wheeler, M.P.

1983 Context-related age changes in mother's speech: Joint book reading. *Journal of Child Language* 10:259-263.

White, B.L.

1978 *Experience and Environment, Volume 2*. Englewood Cliffs, NJ: Prentice Hall.

White, J.

1905 *The Educational Ideas of Froebel*. London: University Tutorial Press.

Whitehurst, G.J.

1996 A structural equation model of the role of home literacy environment in the development of emergent literacy skills in children from low-income backgrounds. Paper presented at the Annual Convention of the American Educational Research Association. New York, NY.

Whitehurst, G.J., D.H. Arnold, J.N. Epstein, A.L. Angell, M. Smith, and J.E. Fischel

1994a A picture book reading intervention in daycare and home for children from low-income families. *Developmental Psychology* 30:679-689.

Whitehurst, G.J., J.N. Epstein, A.C. Angell, A.C. Payne, D.A. Crone, and J.E. Fischel
  1994b Outcomes of an emergent literacy intervention in Head Start. *Journal of Educational Psychology* 86:542-555.
Whitehurst, G.J., F. Falco, C.J. Lonigan, J.E. Fischel, B.D. DeBaryshe, M.C. Valdez-Menchaca, and M. Caulfield
  1988 Accelerating language development through picture-book reading. *Developmental Psychology* 24:552-558.
Whitehurst, G.J., and C.J. Lonigan
  1998 Child development and emergent literacy. *Child Development* 68:848-872.
Wiggins, G., and J. McTighe
  1998 *Understanding by Design*. Alexandria, VA: Association for Supervision and Curriculum Development.
Wilkinson, L.C., E. Hiebert, and K. Rembold
  1982 Parents' and peers' communication to toddlers. *Journal of Speech and Hearing Research* 24(3) Sep:383-388.
Wood, D.
  1998 *How Children Think and Learn*, Second Edition. Oxford, U.K.: Blackwell Publishers.
Wood, D.J., H.A. Wood, and D.J. Middleton
  1978 An experimental evaluation of four face-to-face teaching strategies. *International Journal of Behavioral Development* 1:131-147.
Wright, J.L.
  1994 Listen to the children: Observing young children's discoveries with the microcomputer. Pp. 3-17 in *Young Children: Active Learners in a Technological Age*, J.L. Wright and D.D. Shade, eds. Washington, DC: National Association for the Education of Young Children.
Wynn, K.
  1996 Infants' individuation and enumeration of actions. *Psychological Science* 7:164-169.

CHAPTER 6

American Educational Research Association, American Psychological Association, National Council on Measurement in Education
  1999 *Standards for Educational and Psychological Testing*. Washington, DC: American Educational Research Association.
American Psychological Association, American Educational Research Association, National Council on Measurement in Education
  1986 *Standards for Educational and Psychological Testing*. Washington, DC: American Psychological Association.
Anatasi, A.
  1988 *Psychological Testing* (6th edition). New York: Macmillan.

Arter, J.
1999   Teaching about performance and assessment. *Educational Measurement: Issues and Practice* 18(2):30-44.

Bagnato, S.J., and J.T. Neisworth
1994   A national study of the social and treatment "invalidity" of intelligence testing for early intervention. *School Psychology Quarterly* 9(2):81-102.

Bailey, D.B., Jr., and M. Wolery
1992   *Teaching Infants and Preschoolers with Disabilities* (2nd Edition). Englewood Cliffs, NJ: Prentice Hall Publishers.

Barnett, D.W., and G.M. MacMann
1992   Aptitude-achievement discrepancy scores: Accuracy in analysis misdirected. *School Psychology Review* 21(3):494-508.

Bodrova, E., and D.J. Leong
1996   *Tools of the Mind: The Vygotskian Approach to Early Childhood Education.* Columbus, OH: Merrill.

Bracken, B.A.
1987   Performance of black and white children on the Bracken Basic Concept scale. *Psychology in the Schools* 24(1):22-27.

Bridgeman, B., E. Chittenden, and F. Cline
1995   *Characteristics of a Portfolio Scale for Rating Early Literacy* (Center for Performance Assessment Report No. MS #94-08). Princeton, NJ: Educational Testing Service.

Brookhart, S.M.
1999   Teaching about communicating assessment results and grading. *Educational Measurement: Issues and Practice* 18(1):5-13.

Burns, M.S.
1996   Dynamic assessment: Easier said than done. In *Dynamic Assessment for Instruction: From Theory to Application*, M. Luther, E. Cole, and P. Gamlin, eds. North York, Ontario, Canada: Captus Press Inc.

Burns, M.S., V.R. Delclos, N.J. Vye, and K. Sloan
1992   Changes in cognitive strategies in dynamic assessment. *International Journal of Dynamic Assessment and Instruction* 2:45-54.

Calfee, R.
1992   Paper, pencil, potential, and performance. *Current Directions in Psychological Science.* 2(1):6-7.

Committee on School Health and Committee on Early Childhood, Adoption and Dependent Care
1995   The inappropriate use of school "readiness" tests. *Pediatrics.* 95(3):437-438 March.

Cronbach, L.J.
1990   *Essentials of Psychological Testing* (5th edition). New York: Harper & Row.

Day, J.D., J.L. Engelhardt, and E.E. Bolig
1997   Comparison of static and dynamic assessment procedures and their relation to independent performance. *Journal of Educational Psychology* 89(2):358-368.

Dionne, J. J., and M. Fitzback-Labrecque
    1989 The use of "mini-interviews" by "orthopédagogues": Three case stud-
          ies. Pp. 315-321 in *Proceedings of the Eleventh Annual Meeting*, C.A.
          Maher, G.A. Goldin, and R.B. Davis, eds. New Brunswick, NJ: Psychol-
          ogy of Mathematics Education.
Fuchs, L.S., D. Fuchs, M. Beneowitz, and D. Barringer
    1987 Using computers with curriculum-based monitoring: Effects on teacher
          efficiency and satisfaction. *Journal of Special Education Technology* 8(4):14-
          27.
Feuerstein, R.
    1979 *The Dynamic Assessment of Retarded Performers: The Learning Potential
          Assessment Device, Theory, Instruments, Techniques.* Baltimore, MD: Uni-
          versity Park Press.
Gelman, R., and C.R. Gallistel
    1978 *The Child's Understanding of Number.* Cambridge, MA: Harvard Uni-
          versity Press.
Gifford, B.R., ed.
    1993 *Policy Perspectives on Educational Testing.* Boston: Kluwer Academic
          Publishers.
Ginsburg, H.P.
    1997 *Entering the Child's Mind: The Clinical Interview in Psychological Research
          and Practice.* New York: Cambridge University Press.
Ginsburg, H. P., R. Balfanz, and C. Greenes
    1999 Challenging mathematics for young children. Pp. 245-258 in *Teaching
          for Intelligence II: A Collection of Articles*, A.L. Costa, ed. Arlington
          Heights, IL: Skylight.
Ginsburg, H.P., S.F. Jacobs, and L.S. Lopez
    1993 Assessing mathematical thinking and learning potential. Pp. 237-262
          in *Schools, Mathematics, and the World of Reality*, R.B. Davis and C.S.
          Maher, eds. Boston, MA: Allyn and Bacon.
Good, R. H. III, and R.A. Kaminski
    1996 Assessment for instructional decisions: Toward a proactive/preven-
          tion model of decision-making for early literacy skills. *School Psychol-
          ogy Quarterly* 11(4):326-336.
Greenspan, S.I.
    1992 *Infancy and Early Childhood: The Practice of Clinical Assessment and Inter-
          vention with Emotional and Developmental Challenges.* Madison, CT: In-
          ternational Universities Press, Inc.
    1996 Assessing the emotional and social functioning of infants and young
          children. Pp. 231-266 in *NEW Visions for Developmental Assessment of
          Infants and Young Children*, S.J. Meisels and E. Fenichel, eds. Washing-
          ton, DC: Zero to Three.
Greenspan, S.I., and S. Wieder
    1998 *The Child with Special Needs: Encouraging Intellectual and Emotional
          Growth.* Reading, MA: Perseus Books.
Kaminski, R.A., and R.H. Good III
    1998 Assessing early literacy skills in a problem-solving model: Dynamic

indicators of basic early literacy skills. Pp. 113-142 in *Advanced Applications of Curriculum-Based Measurement. The Guilford School Practitioner Series.* M.R. Shinn, ed., et al. New York: The Guilford Press.

Haertel, E.
  1989 Student achievement tests as tools of educational policy: Practices and consequences. Pp. 25-50 in *Test Policy and Test Performance: Education, Language, and Culture*, B.R. Gifford, ed.   Boston: Kluwer Academic Publishers.

Heath, S.B.
  1981 Questioning at home and school: A comprehensive study. In *Doing Ethnography: Educational Anthropology in Action*, G. Spindler, ed. New York: Holt, Rinehart, and Winston.
  1983 *Ways with Words: Language, Life, and Work in Communities and Classrooms.* Cambridge, England: Cambridge University Press.

Herman, J.L., P.R. Aschbacher, and L. Winters
  1992 *A Practical Guide to Alternative Assessment.* Alexandria, VA: Association for Supervision and Curriculum Development

High/Scope Research Foundation
  1992 *Child Observation Record.* M.I. Ypsilanti, MI: High/Scope Research Foundation.

Jencks, C.
  1989 If not tests, then what? Pp. 115-121 from conference remarks. *Test Policy and Test Performance: Education, Language, and Culture. Evaluation in Education and Human Services.* B.R. Gifford, ed. Boston, MA: Kluwer Academic Publishers.

Jones, J., and E. Chittenden
  1995 *Teachers' Perceptions of Rating an Early Literacy Portfolio* (Center for Performance Assessment Report No. MS #95-01). Princeton: Educational Testing Service.

Kagan, S.L., E. Moore, S. and Bredekamp
  1995 *Reconsidering Children's Early Development and Learning: Toward Common Views and Vocabulary.* Washington, DC: National Educational Goals Panel.

Lidz, C.S., and E.D. Pena
  1996 Dynamic assessment: The model, its relevance as a nonbiased approach, and its application to Latino American preschool children. *Language, Speech and Hearing Services in the Schools* 27(4):367-372.

Madaus, G.F.
  1988 The influence of testing on the curriculum. Pp. 83-121 in *Critical Issues in Curriculum. Eighty-Seventh Yearbook of the National Society for the Study of Education.* L.N. Tanner, ed. Chicago: University of Chicago Press.

Meisels, S.J.
  1987 Uses and abuses of developmental screening and school readiness testing. *Young Children* 42:4-6; 68-73.
  1988 Developmental screening in early childhood: The interaction of re-

search and social policy. *Annual Review of Public Health,* Vol. 9:527-550, L. Breslow, J. E. Fielding, and L. B. Lave, eds. Palo Alto, CA: Annual Reviews, Inc.

1989a Can developmental screening tests identify children who are developmentally at-risk? *Pediatrics* 83:578-585.

1989b High stakes testing in kindergarten. *Educational Leadership* 46:16-22.

1994 Designing meaningful measurements for early childhood. Pp. 202-222 in *Diversity in Early Childhood Education: A Call for More Inclusive Theory, Practice, and Policy.* New York: Teachers College Press.

1996a Performance in context: Assessing children's achievement at the outset of school. Pp. 410-431 in *The Five to Seven Year Shift: The Age of Reason and Responsibility,* A. J. Sameroff and M. M. Haith, eds. Chicago: University of Chicago Press.

1996b Charting the continuum of assessment and intervention. Pp. 27-52 in *New Visions for the Developmental Assessment of Infants and Young Children,* S. J. Meisels and E. Fenichel, eds. Washington, DC: Zero to Three: The National Center for Infants, Toddlers, and Families.

1999 Assessing readiness. Pp. 39-66 in *The Transition to Kindergarten,* R.C. Pianta and M. Cox, eds. Baltimore, MD: Paul H. Brookes.

Meisels, S.J., and S. Atkins-Burnett

1994 *Developmental Screening in Early Childhood: A Guide (4th ed.).* Washington, DC: National Association for the Education of Young Children.

2000 The elements of early childhood assessment. Pp. 231-257 in *The Handbook of Early Childhood Intervention* (2nd edition), J.P. Shonkoff, and S.J. Meisels, eds. New York: Cambridge University Press.

Meisels, S.J., A. Dorfman, and D. Steele

1995a Equity and excellence in group-administered and performance-based assessments. Pp. 196-211 in *Equity in Educational Assessment and Testing,* M.T. Nettles and A. L. Nettles, eds. Boston: Kluwer Academic Publishers.

Meisels, S.J., J.R. Jablon, D.B. Marsden, M.L. Dichtelmiller, and A.B. Dorfman

1994 *The Work Sampling System.* Ann Arbor, MI: Rebus Inc.

Meisels, S.J., F. Liaw, A. Dorfman, and R.F. Nelson

1995b The Work sampling system: reliability and validity of a performance assessment for young children. *Early Childhood Research Quarterly* 10(3)(Sep):277-296.

Meisels, S.J., and L.H. Margolis

1988 Is EPSDT effective with developmentally disabled children? *Pediatrics* 81:262-271.

Meisels, S.J., D. Bickel, J. Nicholson, Y. Xue, and S. Atkins-Burnett

in Trusting teachers' judgments: A validity study of a curriculum-embed-
press ded performance assessment in kindergarten-grade 3. *American Education Research Journal.*

Meisels, S.J., and S. Provence

1989 *Screening and Assessment; Guidelines for Identifying Young Disabled and*

Developmentally Vulnerable Children and Their Families. Washington, DC: National Center for Clinical Infant Programs.

Meltzer, L., and D.K. Reid

1994   New directions in the assessment of students with special needs: The shift toward a constructivist perspective. *Journal of Special Education* 28(3):338-355.

Missouri Department of Elementary and Secondary Education

1992   *Project Construct: A Framework for Curriculum and Assessment.* Jefferson City, MO: Missouri Department of Elementary and Secondary Education.

Mitchell, R.

1992   *Testing for Learning: How New Approaches to Evaluation Can Improve American Schools.* New York: The Free Press.

Moon, J., and Schulman, L.

1995   *Finding The Connections: Linking Assessment, Instruction, and Curriculum in Elementary Mathematics.* Portsmouth, NH: Heinemann.

National Center for Education Statistics

1999   *Digest of Education Statistics, 1998.* T. Snyder, author. Washington, DC: Department of Education.

National Research Council

1982a *Ability Testing: Uses, Consequences, and Controversies,* Volumes 1 and 2. Committee on Ability Testing, A.K. Wigdor and W.R. Garner, eds. Washington, DC: National Research Council.

1982b *Ability Testing of Handicapped People: Dilemma for Government, Science, and the Public.* Panel on Testing of Handicapped People, Committee on Ability Testing, S.W. Sherman and N.M. Robinson, eds. Washington, DC: National Academy Press.

1997   *Educating One and All: Students with Disabilities and Standards-Based Reform.* Committee on Goals 2000 and the Inclusion of Students with Disabilities, L.M. McDonnell, M.J. McLaughlin, and P. Morison, eds. Washington, DC: National Academy Press.

1998   *Preventing Reading Difficulties in Young Children.* Committee on Prevention of Reading Difficulties in Young Children, C.E. Snow, M.S. Burns, and P. Griffin, eds. Washington, DC: National Academy Press.

1999a *High Stakes Testing for Tracking, Promotion, and Graduation.* Committee on Appropriate Test Use, R.J. Heubert and R.M. Hauser, eds. Washington, DC: National Academy Press.

1999b *How People Learn: Brain, Mind, Experience, and School.* Committee on Developments in the Science of Learning, J.D. Bransford, A.L. Brown, and R.R. Cocking, eds. Washington, DC: National Academy Press.

1999c *How People Learn: Bridging Research and Practice.* Committee on Learning Research and Educational Practice, M.S. Donovan, J.D. Bransford, and J.W. Pellegrino, eds. Washington, DC: National Academy Press.

Nuttall, E.V., I. Romero, J. Kalesnik, eds.

1999   *Assessing and Screening Preschoolers: Psychological and Educational Dimensions* (2nd ed.). Boston, MA: Allyn & Bacon, Inc.

Ogbu, J.
1994 From cultural differences to differences in cultural frame of reference. In *Cross-Cultural Roots of Minority Child Development*, P.M. Greenfield and R.R. Cocking, eds. New Jersey: Lawrence Erlbaum Associates.

Rogoff, B.
1990 *Apprenticeship in Thinking: Cognitive Development in Social Context.* New York: Oxford University Press.

Sheingold, K., J.I. Heller, and S.T. Paulukonis
1995 *Actively Seeking Evidence: Teacher Change through Assessment Development* (Center for Performance Assessment Report No. MS #94-04).

Shepard, L.
1991 Negative policies for dealing with diversity: When does assessment and diagnosis turn into sorting and segregation? In *Literacy for a Diverse Society: Perspectives, Practices and Policies*, E. Hiebert, ed. New York: Teachers College Press.

Shepard, L., S.L. Kagan, and E. Wurtz, eds.
1998 *Principles and Recommendations for Early Childhood Assessments.* Washington, DC: National Education Goals Panel.

Stallman, A.C., and P.D. Pearson
1990 Formal measures of early literacy. Pps. 7-44 In *Assessment for Instruction in Early Literacy*, L.M. Morrow and J.M. Smith eds. Englewood Cliffs, NJ: Prentice-Hall.

Stiggins, R.J.
1991 Assessment literacy. *Phi Delta Kappan* 72(7):534-539.
1999 Evaluating classroom assessment training in teacher education programs. *Educational Measurement: Issues and Practice* 18(1):23-27.

U.S. Congress Office of Technology Assessment
1992 *Testing in America's Schools: Asking the Right Questions* (Report OTA-SET-519). Washington, DC: U.S. Government Printing Office.

Ward, M.
1971 *Them Children.* New York: Holt, Rinehart, and Winston.

Wiggins, G.
1998 *Educative Assessment: Designing Assessments to Inform and Improve Performance.* San Francisco: Jossey-Bass.

CHAPTER 7

Almy, M.C.
1949 Children's experiences prior to first grade and success in beginning reading. *Teachers College Contributions to Education* 954:124.

Arnett, J.
1989 Caregivers in day-care centers: Does training matter? *Journal of Applied Developmental Psychology* 10:541-552.

Ashton, P.
1996 Improving the preparation of teachers. *Educational Researcher* 25(9):21-22.

Ball, D.L., and D.K. Cohen,
1996 Reform by the book: What is—or might be—the role of curriculum materials in teacher learning and instructional reform? *Educational Researcher* 25(9)(Dec):6-8.

Bang, B.
1979 Public Day Care in Private Homes. *International Journal of Early Childhood* 11(1):124-130.

Berk, L.
1985 Relationship of caregiver training to child-oriented attitudes job satisfaction and behaviors to children. *Child Care Quarterly* 14:103-129.

Bereiter, C., C. Kamii, and L. Kohlberg
1970 Educational implications of Kohlberg's cognitive-developmental view. *Interchange* 1(1)(Apr):25-51.

Bloom, B.
1985 *Developing Talent in Young People*. New York: Ballantine.

Bollin, G.G., and L.C. Whitehead
1990 *Family Day Care Quality and Parental Satisfaction*. PA: EDRS.

Bowman, B.
1990 Recruitment and retention of teachers. In *Early Childhood Teacher Preparation*. B. Spodek and O. Saracho, eds. New York: Teachers College Press.

Bredekamp, S., ed.
1986 *Developmentally Appropriate Practice*. Washington, DC: National Association for the Education of Young Children.

Bredekamp, S.
1995 What do early childhood professionals need to know and be able to do? *Young Children* 50(2):67-69.
1996 25 years of educating young children: The High/Scope approach to preschool education. *Young Children* 51(4):57-61.

Brookhart, S.M., and D.J. Freeman
1992 Characteristics of entering teacher candidates. *Review of Educational Research* 62(1):37-60.

Buchmann, M., and J. Schwille
1983 Education: The overcoming of experience. *American Journal of Education* 92(1)(Nov):30-51.

Cassidy, D.J., M.J. Buell, S. Pugh-Hoese, and S. Russell,
1995 The effect of teacher education on child care teachers' beliefs and classroom quality: Year one of the TEACH early childhood associate degree scholarship program. *Early Childhood Research Quarterly* 10, 171-183.

Center for Early Childhood Leadership
1999 *Research Notes* (Spr-Win). Wheeling, IL: Center for Early Childhood Leadership, National-Louis University.

Charlesworth, R., C. Hart, D. Burts, and M. DeWolf
1993a The LSU studies: Building a research base for developmentally approprate practice. *Advances in Early Education and Day Care* 3:3-28.

Charlesworth, R., C. Hart, D. Burts, J. Thomasson, and P. Fleege
1993b Measuring the developmental appropriateness of kindergarten teachers' beliefs and practices. *Early Childhood Research Quarterly* 8:55-276.

Clark, C.
1988 Teacher preparation: Contributions of research on teacher thinking. *Educational Researcher* 17(2):5-12.

Clarke-Stewart, K., and C. Gruber
1984 Day care forms and features. Pp. 35-62 in *The Child and the Day Care Setting*, R.C. Ainslie, ed. New York: Preager.

Corsini, D.A., and G. Caruso
1989 High Quality Family Day Care: Financial Considerations. ERIC Document # ED320707. Available from ERIC Document Reproduction Service.

Cruikshank, D.E., and L.J. Sheffield
1996 *Teaching and Learning Elementary and Middle School Mathematics.* New York: Maxwell Macmillan International.

Darling-Hammond, L.
1998 Teachers and teaching: Testing policy hypotheses from a National Commission report. *Educational Researcher* 27(1):5-16.

Darling-Hammond, L., A.E. Wise, S.P. Klein
1999 *A License to Teach. Raising Standards for Teaching.* San Francisco, CA: Jossey-Bass, Inc.,

Delclos, V.R., M.S. Burns, and N.J. Vye
1993 A comparison of teachers' responses to dynamic and traditional assessment reports. *Journal of Psychoeducational Assessment* 11:46-55.

Epstein, A. S.
1993 *Training for Quality: Improving Early Childhood Programs through Systematic Inservice Training.* Monographs of the High/Scope Educational Foundation, No. 9. Ypsilanti, MI: High/Scope Press.
1999 Pathways to quality in Head Start, public school, and Private nonprofit early childhood programs. *Journal of Research in Childhood Education* 13(2):101-119.

Espinosa, L.M.
1980 The role of the caregiver. Pp. 45-55 in *Home Day Care: A Perspective*, J. Colbert and C. Mesnick, eds. Chicago: Roosevelt University Press.

Espinosa, L.M., M. Mathews, K. Thornburg, and J. Ispa
1999 Training and rural childcare providers: Results of project REACH. *NHSA Dialog: A Research-to-Practice Journal for the Early Intervention Field.* 2(3):361-387.

Fischer, J.
1989 Family Day Care: Factors Influencing the Quality of Caregiving Practices. Unpublished doctoral dissertation, University of Illinois, Champaign-Urbana.

Fullan, M., and S. Steigelbauer
1991 *The New Meaning of Educational Change.* New York: Teachers College Press.

Galinsky, E., C. Howes, and S. Kontos
  1994 *The Family Child Care Training Study: Highlights of Findings.* New York: Families and Work Institute.
Genishi, C., ed.
  1992 *Ways Of Assessing Children and Curriculum: Stories of Early Childhood Practice.* New York: Teachers College Press.
Griffin, G. A., ed.
  1999 *The Education of Teachers: Ninety-Eighth Yearbook of The National Society for The Study of Education.* Chicago, IL: University of Chicago Press
Hawkey, K.
  1997 Roles, responsibilities, and relationships in mentoring: A literature review and agenda for research. *Journal of Teacher Education* 48(5):325-335.
Head Start Bureau
  1997 *Head Start Statistical Fact Sheet.* Washington DC: U.S. Department of Health and Human Services Available: http.acf.dhhs.gov/programs/hsb/facsheet.htm.
Hollingsworth, S.
  1989 Prior beliefs and cognitive change in learning to teach. *American Educational Research Journal* 26(2):160-189.
Howes, C.
  1993 Early child care. Pp. 71-80 in *Approaches to Early Childhood Education,* J.L. Roopnarine, ed. New York: Macmillan.
  1997 Children's experiences in center-based child care as a function of teacher background and adult-child ratio. *Merrill-Palmer Quarterly* 43(3):404-425.
Howes, C., W. Pettygrove, and M. Whitebook
  1987 Cost and quality in child care: Reality and myth. *Child Care Exchange* (Nov):40-42.
Howes, C., D. Phillips, and M. Whitebook
  1992 Thresholds of quality: Implications for the social development of children in center-based child care. *Child Development* 63:449-460.
Howes, C., E. Smith, and E. Galinsky
  1995 *Interim Report on the Florida Quality Improvement Study.* Department of Education, University of California, Los Angeles, CA.
Isenberg, J.P.
  1990 Reviews of research. Teachers' thinking and beliefs and classroom practice. *Childhood Education* 66(5):322,324-327.
  1999 The state of the art in early childhood professional preparation. Commissioned paper for the National Institute on Early Childhood Development and Education, Washington, DC.
Joyce, B.
  1986 *Improving America's Schools.* New York: Longman.
Katz, L.G.
  1999 International perspectives on early childhood education: lessons from

my travels. *Early Childhood Research & Practice* 1(1)(Spr). Available: http://ecrp.uiuc.edu/v1n1/v1n1.html [August 2000].

Kennedy, M.
   1997   The connection between research and practice. *Educational Researcher* 26(7):4-12.

Klein, N., and R. Sheehan
   1987   Staff development: A key issue in meeting the needs of young children in day care settings. *Topics in Early Childhood Special Education* 7(7):1-12.

Kontos, S., C. Howes, and E. Galinsky
   1997   Does training make a difference to quality in family child care? *Early Childhood Research Quarterly* 351-372.

Kontos, S., S. Machida, S. Griffin, and M. Read
   1992   Training and professionalism in family day care. Pp. 188-208 in D. L. Peters and A.R. Pence, eds. *Family Day Care: Current Research for Informed Public Policy.* New York: Teachers College Press.

Layzer, J.I., B.D. Goodson, and M. Moss
   1993   *Life in Preschool—Volume One of an Observational Study of Early Childhood Programs for Disadvantaged Four-Year-Olds: Final Report.* Cambridge, MA: Abt Associates.

Lortie, D.
   1975   *Schoolteacher: A Sociological Study.* Chicago: University of Chicago Press

Macro International, Inc.
   1994   Improving child care in rural areas: Promising practices and strategies. *Research/Technical Report.* Washington DC: ACYF (143)(Dec):4-13.

Malaguzzi, L.
   1993   For an Education Based on Relationships. *Young Children* 49(1)(Nov):9-12.

Manaf, A.
   1994   The identification of a model of teaching behaviors of preschool student teachers. *Mid-Western Educational Researcher* 7(4):7-13.

Marcon, R.A.
   1999   Differential impact of preschool models on development and early learning of inner-city children: A three-cohort study. *Developmental Psychology* 35(2)(Mar):358-375.

National Association for the Education of Young Children
   1996   *Guidelines for Preparation of Early Childhood Professionals.* Washington DC: National Association for the Education of Young Children.

National Research Council
   1990   *Who Cares for America's Children?* Panel on Child Care Policy., C.D. Hayes, J.L Palmer, and M.J. Zaslow, eds. Washington, DC: National Academy Press.
   1998   *Preventing Reading Difficulties in Young Children* Committee on Prevention of Reading Difficulties in Young Children, C.E. Snow, M.S. Burns, and P. Griffin, eds.. Washington, DC: National Academy Press.

1999   *How People Learn: Brain, Mind, Experience, and School.* Committee on Developments in the Science of Learning, J.D. Bransford, A.L. Brown, and R.R. Cocking, eds. Washington, DC: National Academy Press.

Nespor, J.
1987   The role of beliefs in the practice of teaching. *Journal of Curriculum Studies* 19(4):317-328.

Odell, S.J.
1990   *Mentor Teacher Programs. What Resarch Says to the Teacher.* Washington, DC: National Education Association.

Ott, D.J., K.M. Zeichner, and G.G. Price
1990   Research horizons and the quest for a knowledge base in early childhood teacher education. Pp. 118-137 in *Early Childhood Teacher Education*, Vol. B. Spodeck and O.N. Saracho, eds. New York: Teachers College Press.

Richardson, V., P. Anderson, D. Tidwell, and C. Lloyd
1991   The relationship between teachers' beliefs and and practices in reading comprehension instruction. *American Educational Research Journal* 28:559-586.

Ruopp, R., J. Travers, F. Glantz, F., and C. Coelen
1979   Children at the center: Summary findings and their implications. Final Report of the *National Day Care Study.* Cambridge, MA: Abt. Associates.

Saracho, O.N., and B. Spodek
1993   Professionalism and the preparation of early childhood education practitioners. *Early Child Development and Care* 89:1-17.

Snider, M. H., and V.R. Fu
1990   The effects of specialized education and job experience on early childhood teachers' knowledge of developmentally appropriate practice. *Early Childhood Research Quarterly* 5(1):69-78.

Spodek, B.
1996   The professional development of early childhood teachers. *Early Child Development and Care.* 115(Jan):115-24.

Tschannen-Moran, M., A. Woolfolk, and W. Hoy
1998   Teacher efficacy: Its meaning and measure. *Review of Educational Research* 68(2):202-248.

Vandell, D.L., and M.A. Corasaniti
1990   Variations in early child care: Do they predict subsequent social, emotional, and cognitive differences? *Early Childhood Research Quarterly* 5(4)(Dec):555-572.

Venn, M. L., and M. Wolery
1992   Increasing day care staff members' interactions during caregiving routines. *Journal of Early Intervention* 16:304-319.

Whitebook, M., and M. Almy
1986   NAEYC's Commitment to Good Programs for Young Children: Then and Now. *A Developmental Crisis at 60 Young Children* 41(6)(Sep):37-40.

Whitebook, M., P. Hnatiuk, and D. Bellm
1994 *Mentoring in Early Care and Education: Refining an Emerging Career Path.* Washington, DC: National Center for the Early Childhood Work Force.

Whitebook, M., C. Howes, and D. Phillips
1989 *Who Cares? Child Care Teachers and The Quality of Care in America.* (Final report of the National Child Day Care Staffing Study). Oakland, CA: Child Care Employee Project.

Wilson, S.M.
1990 The secret garden of teacher education. *Phi Delta Kappan* 72:204-209.

CHAPTER 8

Adams, G.C.
1990 *Who Knows How Safe? The Status of State Efforts to Ensure Quality Child Care.* Washington, DC: Children's Defend Fund.

American Public Health Association and American Academy of Pediatrics Collaborative Project
1992 *Caring for Our Children—National Health and Safety Performance Standards: Guidelines for Out-of-Home Child Care Programs.* Washington, DC: American Public Health Association.

Azer, S.L., K.L. Capraro, and K. Elliott
1996 *Working Toward Making a Career of It: A Profile of State Career Development Initiatives in 1996.* Boston, MA: Wheelock College Center for Career Development in Early Care and Education.

Azer, S.L., and C. Hanrahan
1998 *Early Care and Education Career Development Initiatives in 1998.* Boston: Wheelock College Center for Career Development in Early Care and Education.

Bredekamp, S., and C. Copple, eds.
1997 *Developmentally Appropriate Practice in Early Childhood Programs* (Revised ed.). Washington, DC: National Association for the Education of Young Children.

Children's Foundation, The
1999 *The Family Child Care Licensing Study, 1999.* Washington, DC: The Children's Foundation.

Cost, Quality and Child Outcomes Study Team
1995 *Cost Quality and Outcomes in Center Based Child Care.* Final Report of the Cost, Quality and Outcome Study.

Fields, C.M.
1988 Poor test scores bar many minority students from teacher training. *Chronicle of Higher Education* 35(10):A1+32.

Galinsky, E., C. Howes, and S. Kontos
1995 *Family Child Care Training Study.* Los Angeles: Department of Education, University of California.

Garwood, S.G., D. Phillips, A. Hartmen, and E.F. Zigler
  1989 As the pendulum swings: Federal agency programs for children. *American Psychologist* 44(2)(Feb):434-440.
Gormley, W.T., Jr.
  1992 Public hearings on child care. *Young Children* 48(1):40-42.
  1995 *Everybody's Children: Child Care as a Public Problem.* Washington, DC: The Brookings Institution.
Hinitz, B.F.
  1998 Credentialing early childhood paraprofessionals in the United States: The Child Development Associate and other frameworks. *International Journal of Early Years Education* 6(1):87-104.
Howes, C., E. Smith, and E. Galinsky
  1995 *Interim Report on the Florida Quality Improvement Study.* Los Angeles: Department of Education, University of California.
Kagan, S.L., and J.W. Newton
  1989 Public policy report. For-profit and nonprofit child care: Similarities and differences. *Young Children* 45(1):4-10.
Knitzer, J., and S. Page
  1996 Young children and families: The view from the states. *Young Children* 51(4):51-55.
Kontos, S.
  1992 *Family Day Care: Out of the Shadows and into the Limelight.* Research Monograph, Vol. 5. Washington, DC: National Association for the Education of Young Children.
Kontos, S., C. Howes, and E. Galinsky
  1997 Does training make a difference to quality in family child care? *Early Childhood Research Quarterly.* 12:351-372.
Kontos, S., C. Howes, M. Shinn, and E. Galinsky
  1995 *Quality in the Family Child Care and Relative Care.* New York: Teachers College Press.
Meek, A.
  1998 America's teachers. *Educational Leadership* 55(5):12-17.
National Council of Teachers of Mathematics and Infosector Corporation
  2000 *Principles and Standards for School Mathematics.* Reston, VA: National Council of Teachers of Mathematics.
Neuman, S.B., C. Copple, and S. Bredekamp
  1999 *Learning to Read and Write: Developmentally Appropriate Practices for Young Children.* Washington, DC: National Assocation for the Education of Young Children.
Ripple, C.H., W.S. Gilliam, N. Chanana, and E. Zigler
  1999 Will fifty cooks spoil the broth? The debate over entrusting Head Start to the states. *American Psychologist* 12:351-372.
U.S. Advisory Commission on Intergovernmental Relations
  1994 *Child Care: The Need for Federal-State-Local Coordination.* Washington, DC: U.S. Advisory Commission on Intergovernmental Relations.

CHAPTER 9

National Research Council
  1999 *How People Learn: Bridging Research and Practice.* Committee on Learning Research and Educational Practice, M.S. Donovan, J.D. Bransford, and J.W. Pellegrino, eds. Washington, D.C.: National Academy Press.

Appendix

Farran, D.
  2000 Another decade of intervention for children who are low income or disabled: What do we know now? Pp. 510-548 in *Handbook of Early Childhood Intervention,* 2nd edition, J. P. Shonkoff, and S. J. Meisels, eds. New York: Cambridge University Press.

Biographical Sketches

Barbara T. Bowman (*Chair*) is a founding faculty member of the Erikson Institute for Advanced Study in Child Development in Chicago. Her specialty areas are early education, cultural diversity, and the education of at-risk children. In addition to teaching, Bowman has directed a wide range of projects, including ones for Head Start teachers, caregivers of infants at risk for morbidity or mortality, teachers on American Indian reservations, and the Child Development Associates program. Her most recent work has been with the Chicago Public Schools, where she provided in-service education for teachers in inner-city neighborhoods. Bowman has served on numerous professional boards, including the Family Resource Coalition and the National Association for the Education of Young Children, of which she was president (1980-1982). Currently she is on the boards of the Great Books Foundation and the National Board for Professional Teaching Standards. She has served on a variety of professional committees, including the Task Force on Early Childhood Education of the National Association of State Boards of Education, the Panel on Day Care Policy and the Committee on the Prevention of Reading Difficulties in Young Children for the National Research Council, the Leadership Initiative for the National Black Child Development Institute, and the Advisory Council on Early Childhood Education of the Illinois State Board of Education.

Honors include D.H.L. degrees from Bank Street College of Education in New York and Roosevelt University in Chicago. She has a B.A. from Sarah Lawrence College and an M.A. from the University of Chicago.

William Steven Barnett is a professor specializing in education economics and policy at the Rutgers Graduate School of Education and also director of the Center for Early Education at Rutgers. In addition to his academic career, he also has extensive experience working in public policy research and program evaluation. He has served on the editorial boards of *Early Education and Development* and *Early Childhood Research Quarterly* and on the National Head Start Advisory Committee. He has conducted research on the cost-effectiveness of early childhood education and intervention programs, the relationship between quality of preschools and efficacy, and the long-term effects of preschool education. He has also examined the effects of early education on the development of disadvantaged and developmentally disabled children. His publications include *Early Care and Education for Children in Poverty: Promises, Programs and Long-terms Results* (1998, with S. Boocock), and *Cost Analysis for Education Decisions: Methods and Examples* (1994). He has a Ph.D. in economics from the University of Michigan.

M. Susan Burns (*Study Director*) is currently a faculty member at the Graduate School of Education at George Mason University. She held faculty appointments at Tulane University and the University of Pittsburgh. At the National Research Council, she was study director for the Committee on Prevention of Reading Difficulties in Young Children. Her research interests include instructional practices that facilitate early cognitive development, dynamic assessment of young children, early childhood curriculum development, and parent-child interaction and emergent literacy. Applied interests include the development of intervention/prevention programs for young children at risk for academic problems or who have been identified with emotional or behavioral problems. She is a coauthor of *Bright Start: A Cognitive Curriculum for Young Children*. She has a Ph.D. in developmental psychology from George Peabody College of Vanderbilt University.

M. Suzanne Donovan (*Study Director*) is a senior program officer at the National Research Council's Commission on Behavioral and Social Sciences and Education and study director for the Committee on Minority Representation in Special Education and for How People Learn: Targeted Report for Teachers. Her interests span issues of education and public policy. She has a Ph.D. from the University of California, Berkeley, School of Public Policy and was previously on the faculty of Columbia University's School of Public and International Affairs.

Linda M. Espinosa is an associate professor at the College of Education of the University of Missouri. She has served on numerous boards and advisory committees, including the boards of Project Construct and the Far West Laboratory Bay Area Early Intervention Program, and is currently a member of the Task Force on Professional Development of the National Association of Educators of Young Children. She has been a consulting editor for *Early Childhood Research Quarterly*. In addition to her research and university teaching career, she has professional experience as a preschool teacher and administrator. She served on the National Research Council/Institute of Medicine's Roundtable on Head Start Research. Her research has focused on bilingual preschool education, Hispanic families and children, the effectiveness of family support programs and home intervention programs, and preschool education in rural areas. She teaches courses in early childhood assessment, parent-community involvement, child development and curriculum development. She has published over 20 journal articles and book chapters, and has written curriculum guidelines and training manuals for teachers in the early childhood field. She has a Ph.D. in educational design and implementation (1980) from the University of Chicago.

Rochel Gelman is professor of psychology at the University of California, Los Angeles. She conducts research on causal and quantitative reasoning, constraints on concept acquisition and conceptual change (with a focus on the language and the conceptual basis of fractions and scientific concepts), and is interested in the effects of schooling, language, and culture on these. At the National Research Council, she is a member of the Board on Behavioral, Cognitive, and Sensory Sciences and was a member of the Committee on Developments in the Science of Learning, the U.S. National Committee for the International Union of Psychological Science, and the Committee on Basic Research in the Behavioral and Social Sciences. Her publications include *The Epigenesis of Mind: Essays on Biology and Cognition* (1991, with S. Carey), and *The Child's Understanding of Number* (1978, with C.R. Gallistel). She has a Ph.D. in psychology (1967) from the University of California, Los Angeles.

Herbert P. Ginsburg is the Jacob H. Schiff Foundation professor of psychology and education at Teachers College, Columbia University, and was previously cochair of its Department of Human Development. He has taught at Cornell University, the University of Maryland, Harvard University, and the University of Rochester. He is a consulting editor for the *Journal of Mathematical Behavior*, and for the *Journal of Applied Developmental Psychology* and *Cognition and Instruction*. At the National Research Council, he was a member of the Committee on Strategic Education Research Program Feasibility and of the Committee on Child Development Research and Public Policy. His work has focused on the intellectual development and education of young children, particularly poor and minority children. He has conducted numerous studies of the development of mathematical thinking and the development of cognition in this domain, and examined the implications for instruction and assessment in early education. His publications include *Piaget's Theory of Intellectual Development* (1988), *Children's Arithmetic* (1989), *The Teacher's Guide to Flexible Interviewing in the Classroom* (1998). He has a Ph.D. in developmental psychology (1965) from University of North Carolina, Chapel Hill.

Edmund Gordon is the John M. Musser professor of psychology (emeritus) at Yale University and distinguished professor of educational psychology at the City University of New York. He was one of the founders of Head Start and was its first national director of research. At the National Research Council, he was a member of the Committee on Education Finance. He has conducted research on children living in poverty, cultural diversity and multicultural education, educational policies for socially disadvantaged children, and cognitive development and schooling. His publications include *Day Care: Scientific and Social Policy Issues* (1982, coedited with E. Zigler), *Human Diversity and Pedagogy* (1989), and *A View from the Back of the Bus: Education and Social Justice* (1993). He has three honorary doctorates from the Bank Street College of Education, Brown University, and Yeshiva University, as well as an honorary master's degree from Yale University. He has a Ph.D. in child development and guidance (1957) from Columbia University Teachers College.

Betty M. Hart is an associate scientist (emeritus) at the Institute for Life Span Studies at the University of Kansas Human Development Center. In addition to her career as a researcher and professor, she also has extensive experience as preschool teacher and director. Her research has focused on language development and language teaching, teaching practices and early intervention programs, and family-child interactions in home environments. She has also conducted research on children with Down syndrome. Her publications include *Meaningful Differences in the Everyday Experience of Young American Children* (1995, with T.R. Risley) and *The Early Years: Arrangements for Learning* (1984, with K.E. Allen). She has a Ph.D. in developmental and child psychology (1969) from the University of Kansas.

Carollee Howes is professor at the Graduate School of Education, University of California, Los Angeles, and was head of the division of educational psychology until 1996. She has been principal investigator for a number of studies of preschool children and quality in day care and is currently principal investigator for the National Center for Development and Learning in Early Childhood, funded by the U.S. Department of Education. She is also participating on the National Evaluation Consortium for Early Head Start through grants from the Mathematics Policy Institute and Early Head Start. Her research has focused on the social development of young children, especially the development of peer relationships in day care settings through interaction and play. She has also conducted research on attachment relations between children and their mothers and between children and child care providers. Her publications include *Keeping Current in Child Care Research: An Annotated Bibliography* (1986, 1988, 1990) and *The Collaborative Construction of Pretend: Social Pretend Play Functions* (1992, with O.A. Unger and C.C. Matheson). She has a Ph.D. in developmental psychology (1979) from Boston University.

Sharon Lynn Kagan is the Virginia and Leonard Marx professor of early childhood and family policy at Teachers College, Columbia University, and a senior research scientist at Yale University. She is the immediate past president of the National Association for the Education of Young Children and a Past President of Family Support America. A member of over 40 national boards or panels, she has served as chair of the National Education Goals Panel Technical Planning Group for Goal One, as a member of the Clinton Education Transition Team, and on numerous foundation and administration panels. Her research has centered on public policies affecting the lives of young children and families, including child care and preschool programs, family-school relationships, and leadership in early childhood education. Her publications include *United We Stand; Collaboration for Child Care and Early Education Services* (1991), *Reinventing Early Care and Education* (1997, with N. Cohen); *Putting Families First: America's Family Support Movement and the Challenge of Change* (1994 with B. Weissbourd), *Integrating Services for Children and Families: Understanding the Past to Shape the Future* (1993) and *Leadership in Early Care and Education* (1997, coedited with B. Bowman). She received an honorary doctorate from Wheelock College in 1992 and the distinguished alumna award from Teachers College in 1996. She has an Ed.D. (1979) from Teachers College, Columbia University.

Lilian Katz is professor of early childhood education and director of the ERIC Clearinghouse on Elementary and Early Childhood Education at the University of Illinois, Urbana-Champaign. She has taught at the University of Illinois, as well as a number of universities abroad, including institutions in West Germany, India, Canada, and the United Kingdom. She was a past president of the National Association for the Education of Young Children and serves on the editorial boards of several early childhood education journals. Her research has focused on early childhood and preschool education and has examined the quality of education for young children through investigations of teaching practices and teacher education. Her publications include *Current Topics in Early Childhood Education* (seven editions, for which she was editor-in-chief), *Building Social Competence in Children* (1995, with D. McClellan, J. Fuller, and G. Walz), and *Fostering Children's Social Competence: The Teacher's Role* (1997, with D.E. McClellan). She has a Ph.D. in school education and psychological studies (1968) from Stanford University.

Robert A. LeVine is the Roy E. Larsen professor of education and human development at the Harvard University Graduate School of Education and professor of anthropology at Harvard University. He has served on the boards of directors of the Social Science Research Council and the Spencer Foundation. At the National Research Council, he was a member of the National Advisory Panel to Head Start Transition Project. He has been examining questions at the intersection of psychology and anthropology for more than 40 years and has conducted research on parenting and early childhood in East Africa, Mexico, and Nepal. His areas of inquiry include the relationship between maternal schooling and infant mortality, the development of personality and its relation to culture, and parenting goals and strategies across cultures. His publications include *Culture, Behavior, and Personality* (1982), *Human Conditions: The Cultural Basis of Educational Development* (1986), and *Child Care and Culture: Lessons from Africa* (1994). He has a Ph.D. in social anthropology (1958) from Harvard University.

Samuel J. Meisels is a professor and research scientist at the University of Michigan School of Education. His areas of research include performance assessments in early childhood and elementary programs, the impact of standardized tests on young children, screening and assessment of young children's development, and policy issues in the implementation of early intervention programs.

He is the author of *The Work Sampling System* and the *Early Screening Inventory, Revised*. He serves on the editorial boards of

Applied Developmental Science, Early Childhood Research Quarterly, and the *Journal of Early Intervention.* The current president of the Board of ZERO TO THREE: The National Center for Infants, Toddlers, and Family, he has been an advisor to numerous groups, including the National School Readiness Task Force of the National Association of State Boards of Education, the National Education Goals Panel of the U.S. Department of Education, and the National Head Start Administration. He has an Ed.D. (1973) from Harvard University.

Lynn Okagaki is an associate professor in the Department of Child Development and Family Studies at Purdue University. She conducts research on Mexican-American and Asian-American children's school achievement, cultural influences on cognitive development, intelligence and intellectual development, and parental beliefs and family values. Her publications include *Directors of Development: Influences on the Development of Children's Thinking* (1991, coedited with R.J. Sternberg), and *Parenting: An Ecological Perspective* (1993, coedited with T. Luster). She currently serves on the editorial board of the *Journal of Applied Developmental Psychology* and is a consulting editor for the *Early Childhood Research Quarterly.* She is a member of the Advisory Board of the Center for Research on Education, Diversity and Excellence of the U.S. Department of Education. She has a Ph.D. in developmental psychology (1984) from Cornell University.

Michael I. Posner is the head of the Department of Psychology at the University of Oregon and a distinguished professor in its College of Arts and Sciences. His research has focused on the neural systems and cognitive computations that underlie selective attention in the human. He has studied the role of attention in high-level human tasks, such as visual search, reading, and number processing, and is currently examining the development of attention networks in infants and young children and how these influence learning, emotion, and language acquisition. He has received numerous honors for his contributions to science, including the Dana Foundation award for pioneering research in medicine and the John T. McGovern medal of the American Association for the Advancement of Sciences. He has served as editor of the *Journal of Experimental Psychology* and has conducted reviews of the psychology departments of several universities, including Northwestern University and McGill University. He was elected to the National Academy of Sciences in 1981 and became a member of the Institute of Medicine in 1988. At the National Research Council, he has served as a member of the Committee on Human Factors, the Committee on the Enhancement of Human Performance, the Committee on Research Opportunities in the Social and Behavioral Sciences, and the Committee on Research Opportunities in Biology. His numerous publications include *Contemporary Approaches to Cognitive Psychology* (1991, co-edited with C. Dwivedi and I. Singh) and *Images of Mind* (1994, coauthored with M. Raichle), which won the William James book award of the American Psychological Association in 1996. He has a Ph.D. in psychology (1962) from the University of Michigan.

Irving E. Sigel is a distinguished research psychologist (emeritus) at the Educational Testing Service in Princeton, New Jersey. Previously, he was professor of psychology at the State University of New York at Buffalo as well as lecturer at the University of Pennsylvania Graduate School of Education. He has conducted research on children's cognitive development, children's educational experiences at school and at home, and the relationship between parenting and teaching behaviors that encourage children's autonomy and competence in problem solving. He is currently the coeditor of the *Journal of Applied Developmental Psychology* (with Rodney R. Cocking), and he is editor of the book series *Advances in Applied Developmental Psychology*. He has served on a number of editorial and advisory boards, including the Advisory Board of the Center for Cognitive Growth in Early Childhood, and he was previously president of division 7 of the Piaget Society. His numerous publications include *Parental Belief Systems: The Psychological Consequences for Children* (1992, edited with A.V. McGillicuddy-DeLisi and J. Goodnow) and *Educating the Young Thinker: Classroom Strategies for Cognitive Growth* (1979 and 1984, with C. Copple and R. Saunders). He has a Ph.D. in human development (1951) from the University of Chicago.

Marie Suizzo (*Senior Research Associate*) served as senior

research associate to the Committee on Early Childhood Pedagogy. She has served as a teacher of English to adult university
students in China, then as a teacher, social studies department
chair, and junior class moderator in a U.S. high school, and finally
as a teaching assistant in the infant room of a U.S. day care center.
For her dissertation study, she collected both quantitative and
qualitative data on French parenting and examined the relationships between parents' beliefs about infants and toddlers and
their long-term goals and values for their children. She continues
to be interested in the effects of parents' and caregivers' beliefs
and behaviors on children's early emotional and social development. She has a Ph.D. in human development and psychology
from the Harvard University Graduate School of Education.

Barbara H. Wasik is a professor at the School of Education of
the University of North Carolina, Chapel Hill, and a fellow at the
Frank Porter Graham Child Development Center. She has conducted research on home visiting and family support programs
and other early childhood intervention programs, as well as the
early predictors of school failure for at-risk children. Currently,
she is conducting a longitudinal study of family literacy programs
and has developed measures and implemented interventions on
parent problem-solving skills. She serves on numerous advisory
panels and was invited to participate in the White House Conference on Child Care in October 1997. She serves on the editorial
board of the *Journal of Educational Psychology* and was associate
editor of the *Journal of Applied Behavioral Analysis*. Her publications include *Home Visiting: Procedures for Helping Families* (1990,
with D. Bryant and C. Lyons). She has a Ph.D. in clinical psychology from Florida State University.

Grover J. Whitehurst is professor of clinical psychology and
professor of pediatrics at the State University of New York, Stony
Brook. He has served as director of the Program in Developmen-
tal Psychology and as chairman of the University Committee on
Child and Family Studies at the State University of New York,
Stony Brook, and as vice president for academic affairs at the
Merrill Palmer Institute. He has conducted research on language
acquisition and language disorders, emergent literacy, therapeu-

tic and educational uses of interactive technology, and interventions to enhance the school readiness of children from low-income families. He has been editor of the *Merrill-Palmer Quarterly of Behavior and Development, Developmental Review,* and the *Annals of Child Development,* and he has served on review teams and committees of the National Institute of Mental Health, as well as various advisory boards and review panels in the area of early childhood education. He served on the National Research Council/ Institute of Medicine's Roundtable on Head Start Research. He has a Ph.D. in child psychology from the University of Illinois.

Alexandra K. Wigdor is deputy director of the Commission on Behavioral and Social Sciences and Education (CBASSE) of the National Research Council. An NRC staff officer since 1978, Wigdor is responsible for the development of the education and behavioral science programs in CBASSE. Other recent NRC studies with which she is associated include *Improving Student Learning: A Strategic Plan for Education Research and its Utilization* (1999); *Preventing Reading Difficulties in Young Children* (1998); *How People Learn: Mind, Brain, Experience, School* (1999); *How People Learn: Bridging Research and Practice;* and *Making Money Matter: Financing America's Schools* (1999).

Index

V

Verbal interaction, 67, 190-191
Vermont Early Education Initiative, 292-293, 296
Virginia Preschool, 292-293, 296n.3
Visual word form, 57
Vygotsky, Lev, 39, 42, 43, 45, 205, 215, 219, 245-247

W

Washington (state) Early Childhood and Assistance Program, 294-295
Welfare status
  and activity levels of children, 124, 126
  and articulation difficulties of children, 124, 126
  and arts and crafts with family, 79
  and attentiveness of children, 91, 124, 126
  and books and music recordings in the home, 70-73
  and creativity of children's work/play, 87
  and eagerness to learn, 87, 91

  and prosocial behaviors of children, 89, 94-95, 98-99
  and reading proficiency of children, 68-69
  and song singing with family, 78
  and story reading and telling by family, 74-77
  and task persistence, 86, 90
West Virginia, 296n.3
Whites
  interaction styles, 115
  motor skills, 118
Whiting, John and Beatrice, 110
Whole-child approach, 9-10, 32-33, 130
Wisconsin, 146, 296n.3
Wolery, Mark, 164n.2
Words
  association, 56
  beginning and ending sounds, 65, 68-69, 141
  in context, 68-69
  recognition, 10, 68-69, 193-194
Work Sampling System, 250, 251
Writing
  competence, 195, 200
  intervention, 215
  standards, 278, 279

Z

Zone of proximal development, 10, 43, 45, 214, 215, 219, 220, 245-246